YOUNG CENTER BOOKS IN ANABAPTIST & PIETIST STUDIES

Donald B. Kraybill, *Series Editor*

Two Hutterite sisters near a pond in Alberta.

The Hutterites
in North America

Rod Janzen

Max Stanton

THE JOHNS HOPKINS UNIVERSITY PRESS
Baltimore

© 2010 The Johns Hopkins University Press
All rights reserved. Published 2010
Printed in the United States of America on acid-free paper

2 4 6 8 9 7 5 3 1

The Johns Hopkins University Press
2715 North Charles Street
Baltimore, Maryland 21218-4363
www.press.jhu.edu

Library of Congress Cataloging-in-Publication Data

Janzen, Rod A.
The Hutterites in North America / Rod Janzen and Max Stanton.
p. cm. — (Young Center books in Anabaptist and Pietist studies)
Includes bibliographical references and index.
ISBN-13: 978-0-8018-9489-3 (hardcover : alk. paper)
ISBN-10: 0-8018-9489-1 (hardcover : alk. paper)
1. Hutterite Brethren—North America. 2. North America—Church history. I. Stanton,
Max Edward, 1941– II. Title.
BX8129.H8J35 2010
289.7'3—dc22   2009033024

A catalog record for this book is available from the British Library.

Frontispiece: Courtesy of Max Stanton.

*Special discounts are available for bulk purchases of this book. For more information, please contact
Special Sales at 410-516-6936 or specialsales@press.jhu.edu.*

The Johns Hopkins University Press uses environmentally friendly book materials,
including recycled text paper that is composed of at least 30 percent post-consumer waste,
whenever possible. All of our book papers are acid-free, and our jackets and covers are
printed on paper with recycled content.

Mammon is nothing else but what is temporal; and that which is another's is that which is borrowed, with which a man plays for a while like a cat with the mouse. And afterwards he must leave it to somebody else, and in the end his folly becomes evident.

—Hutterite sermon on Acts 2

Contents

Figures, Tables, and Maps

Preface

God does not want his children here on earth to live like cattle, donkeys and oxen,
which are only out to fill their bellies for themselves, without concern for others.
—Hutterite sermon on Luke 3, circa 1650

At the Wilson Siding Hutterite Colony in southern Alberta, German teacher Henry Wurz walks quickly across the yard late on a Thursday afternoon. He has been working in the garden. Sporting a reddish beard and very dusty pants, Henry says hello and invites us into his home, one of the colony's many large single-family residences, with five or six bedrooms and a full basement. Inside the house, Henry glances at the clock, sees that it is almost time for evening church, and quickly changes into plain black dress. Henry's daughters gather in the kitchen, waiting for a sign to begin walking to the church building. The youngest girls wear head coverings and simple long dresses, but they are also barefoot. This is a very hot day.

At the church service, minister Joe Wurz greets members of the congregation. Then he names a hymn and chants the first line. In response about seventy people sing out loudly and passionately, and one can see that they are being transported into a different realm of reality. The hymn is long, with many verses and lines, and there is no holding back as males and females sing at the top of their lungs in a minor key. All of them, adults and children, sing without hymnbooks, following memorized tunes, often slurring notes, and emitting one of the most ear-shattering and otherworldly sounds that one will ever hear. The hymn is followed by a short sermon, read from a collection of sacred writings that are hundreds of years old. The meeting closes with prayer. With heads bowed, all kneel reverently on the hard linoleum floor.

This is Hutterite life on any late afternoon. From south-central South Dakota to northwestern Alberta, this is what Hutterite men and women do at the end of a day of hard physical labor. A twenty-minute church service (the *Gebet*) precedes the evening meal, giving Hutterite men and women an opportunity to reflect on their lives, to worship God, and to regroup intellectually and spiritually. The late-afternoon Gebet ensures that, whatever has happened during the day, there is always a time set aside when members of the community come together to focus on the meaning and purpose of their lives.

Today nearly five hundred Hutterite communities, or colonies, are scattered across the northern plains states of the United States and the prairie provinces of Canada. Since the sixteenth century, the Hutterites have lived communally, sharing all of their material resources and maintaining as much isolation from the rest of the world as possible. Having outlasted most other communal societies, they provide a striking social and economic contrast and alternative to the individualistic way of life that is commonplace in industrialized Western countries in the postmodern world.

Hutterites are Old Order Christians who dress simply and maintain religious and cultural traditions that are hundreds of years old. They speak a distinctive German dialect, live in isolated rural areas, and manage change with careful discernment and unapologetic discrimination. Hutterites honor the earth and interact with the natural world as careful stewards of God. Uniquely adept at interpersonal relations and conflict resolution, they use democratic procedures to make the important decisions that affect their lives.

In this book we introduce a group of Old Order Christians who exude confidence as well as humility. Hutterites refuse to be assimilated into the social mainstream of the United States and Canada, and they do not vote or serve in the military. They dress like nineteenth-century eastern European villagers and for the most part keep to themselves. Yet Hutterites are some of the most hospitable, generous people one will ever meet. They are also remarkably knowledgeable about contemporary social, economic, and political developments. The Hutterites also continue to increase in numbers, with high birth and retention rates. In the 1870s, when they arrived in the Dakota Territory, 425 Hutterites lived in three small communities. Today the Hutterite population exceeds 49,000.

Since the last major work on the Hutterites, John Hostetler's *Hutterite Society*, was published in 1974, many important changes have occurred. Our book weaves research findings of the past thirty-five years together with our own analysis of Hutterite beliefs and practices.[1] Our descriptions and assessments are based on twenty-five years of interaction with Hutterites at colonies in every state and province where they have established communities. We review all aspects of Hutterite life and view it from a variety of vantage points, discussing negative and positive developments and describing how Hutterite communities function on a daily basis. Future prospects are assessed as are areas where non-Hutterites might learn things of importance from the Christian communitarians.

Hutterites view all of life communally, not individualistically. A Hutterite character in the Frederick Manfred novel *Sons of Adam* puts it this way: "We are very much like the Dakota Sioux. It is not for nothing that we have settled in their land, land that was taken away from them by other whites. Like the Sioux, we strive not for self-expression or self-interest, but strive to understand how we are related to all beings and all things. All is one and one is all."[2] The Hutterites have created a society where all males and females, in all age groups, work together and communicate openly in a highly verbal and relational community. On the grounds of the Hutterite colony, there is little holding back, little inhibition. At a colony east of Edmonton, Alberta, three-year-old Marcus Wipf walks into a neighbor's house without knocking. When asked to sing, he quickly belts out five verses of a hymn without hesitation. He is comfortable with himself and with others, embraced and nourished by a community that provides security and gives him the freedom to express himself in a variety of ways. The day is warm, but Marcus is wearing a pair of gloves. He says he is "a cowboy."

In a Hutterite colony, people look out for each other. Care, watchfulness, and judgment are provided without hesitation or undue rumination. During an evening conversation, a Hutterite woman informs her husband that he should quit interrupting her so often when she is speaking. The man takes the criticism with a smile, points to a few of her own shortcomings, and the conversation continues. A spirit of toleration is also emblematic. A teen-age boy, noticeably absent from the evening church service, walks into the room and is quickly reprimanded for this transgression. He apologizes but immediately tells a story about a boy at a neighboring colony who fell into a creek with his clothes on. Everyone laughs. The sin has been forgiven and forgotten.

The Hutterites were not the first communal group to establish colonies in North America. The continent provided fertile ground for hundreds of communal experiments in the seventeenth, eighteenth, and nineteenth centuries. In 1663, Pieter Plockhoy, a Dutch Mennonite businessman and utopian visionary, established the first North American commune with European roots, in what is now the state of Delaware. Plockhoy's idea for a communistic "little commonwealth" was influenced by the successful experience of the European Hutterites.[3]

The following centuries saw the emergence of many religious and secular communal organizations, some short-lived and some more enduring. Included were the United Society of Shakers, the Harmony society, the Amana colonies, Jemima Wilkinson's "Jerusalem," and the perfectionistic Oneida community. All of these groups had Christian roots; they established social and economic institutions that often bore striking similarities to those formed by the Hutterites. Some of the groups hailed from Europe; others were indigenous to North America. Two of them, the German-speaking Radical Pietist Harmonists and Amana Inspirationists, provided important financial and material assistance to Hutterite immigrants in the 1870s. But with the exception of the Sabbathday Lake Shakers in Maine, none of these nineteenth-century communities continue to be organized communally in the twenty-first century. Most of them no longer exist.

❧ ❧

WRITING ABOUT HUTTERITE LIFE IS COMPLICATED. All Hutterites live communally and hold similar beliefs, but there is significant diversity in how those convictions are put into practice. Change is ongoing and Hutterite life does not operate at a standstill. Members do not sit idle and unaffected while the world passes them by. New technology, rising standards of living, and broadened professional interests result in constant reanalysis of communal understandings and social structures.

North American Hutterites cannot be painted with a single brush. It is tempting to suggest that some colonies are more representative than others, but there are four Hutterite branches, nearly five hundred communities, and many variations. Progressive and conservative renditions of what it means to be Hutterite are at times represented within the same extended family. As Hutterite German teacher Tony Waldner notes, "You can always point to a few examples to prove whatever you want to prove."[4] This is what we seek to avoid. After hearing Rod Janzen talk about Hutterite diversity at a German teachers' conference, a Hutterite from Manitoba advised, "Write your book, then run." Our hope is that when Hutterites from different branches read this work, they will respond by saying "You got close to the truth."

This book is a collaborative effort by authors from different backgrounds and academic specializations. Historian Rod Janzen, the primary writer and researcher, places analysis of Hutterite social and religious practice in historical perspective. Anthropologist Max Stanton contributes important insights on how Hutterites go about their daily lives (he notes that he once plucked ducks for a few hours then spent the next three days trying to get rid of the greasy smell). We hope that together we have provided an objective account of a distinctive people. The work combines narrative history with participant-observation anthropological assessment; it offers social-cultural analysis from a historical perspective. Both authors have an appreciation for Hutterite beliefs and practices and a commitment to telling the story as it is.

Historical and anthropological study involves creative reenactment or rendering of deeply held cultural and religious values. To make sense of what makes a people tick, one has to step into their shoes and view life from their vantage point, trying to understand their sense of right and wrong, their beliefs and practices, and doing this (as much as possible) from the perspective that they hold, not only from one's own. John Lewis Gaddis notes that when dealing with the past, historians experience things vicariously, as if being sent backward in a time machine. On return (back in the present), they work hard to regain a sense of distance and autonomy before portraying and analyzing what has happened.[5] To some extent, not always including the dimension of time, this is the approach we take in studying an alternative society like the Hutterites.

As a historian and an anthropologist, we do not assume behavioral consistency. Instead we rely on a more subjective analysis of causal relationships, what Jean Elshtain describes as "impressionistic."[6] We recognize

the importance of participant enactment, via "transcendental imagination," in order to reach what David Norton refers to as "consensusship."[7]
As Clifford Geertz explains, "Understanding the people of another culture depends upon achieving an 'actor-oriented' interpretation of beliefs
and conduct, which is to say the people's own understanding."[8]

To some extent, we take a position of suspended disbelief into the intellectual and social matrix of Hutterian life. The history or anthropology
writer needs to empathize as much as possible with the subjects' values
and emotions. And such writing requires an ecological view of reality that
recognizes that events have antecedents. People do things for their own
reasons, not always taking the most obvious, rational, or direct pathways.
Gaddis notes that historians reject "the doctrine of immaculate causation
which seems to be implied in the idea that one can identify, without reference to all that has preceded it, such a thing as an independent variable."[9]

Cross-cultural studies are complex. For example, the Hutterites exhibit
many social characteristics that are found in premodern societies throughout the world. More specifically, they have attributes that sociologists
Donald B. Kraybill and Carl Desportes Bowman ascribe to "old order" Anabaptist Christians, a group that includes the Old Order Amish, Old Order
Mennonites, and Old German Baptist Brethren.[10] "Old order" characteristics include a holistic view of life that does not recognize distinctions
between religious and secular realms of existence. Old Order Christians
separate themselves from the world-at-large, making it easier to maintain
a cultural-religious identity and simultaneously creating transformative
genetic uniqueness. Old Order Christians have a communal definition of
ethics and a deep respect for the past, for traditions handed down and
the accumulated wisdom of ancestors. They are usually skeptical of higher
education, the media, and civic nationalism.

Old Order church communities emphasize the importance of a unified fellowship. They maintain this center through disciplined adherence to community guidelines and principles as well as through liturgi-
cal standardization. All of life's decisions are influenced by the centrality
of community. As Kraybill and Bowman put it, "The community, not the
individual, is the chief agent of ethical discernment; communal wisdom
supersedes individual experience and personal opinion."[11] There is also a
hardy work ethic, a cautious approach to new ideas and practices, and the
expectation that Christians will undergo some form of suffering if they
follow the teachings of Jesus. Most Old Order groups emphasize the im-

portance of plain, uniform dress and physical appearance, with noticeable gender differentiation.

Calvin Redekop and John Hostetler write that traditional cultures are "self-energizing" and are "less responsive to the environment than is normally the case with social movements." Plain people are "not concerned or interested in changing the society or environment around them to conform to their own images."[12] Perhaps it is more accurate to say that they do not recognize generally agreed-upon standards of success, believing that the world around them will always be corrupt and sinful. One's post-earthly existence in heaven is more important.

Change is not necessarily considered evil. Hutterites have a conserving mind-set, but they also evolve. Donald Pitzer points out that American communal groups in general engage in "a developmental process" that requires innovation.[13] But change is slow and is managed in a way that does not contradict theological positions. The Hutterites do not let social, economic, and political trends control them. Decisions to move in new directions are made judiciously and communally.

Anthropologists often divide human societies into four economic and political categories: band, tribe, chiefdom, and state. We suggest a fifth category, community, to more clearly characterize groups like the Hutterites (and, for example, the Old Order Amish and Hasidic Jews) who live within the boundaries of large states yet maintain organizational, behavioral, and economic boundary definers as well as biological uniqueness. These characteristics set them apart from the societies in which they live. In this book the term *Hutterites* refers to members of four different communal branches. The German word *Leut* (people) is used to denote the primary Hutterite factions. A glossary at the end of the book provides definitions for this and some other commonly used Hutterisch and German terms.

The Hutterites are an amazing people with a distinctive belief system and way of life, who offer an innovative perspective on the problems and opportunities of the twenty-first century. Hutterite colonies present an alternative social model for dealing with fast-paced change and the constant barrage of what Saul Bellow called the "Great Noise" of modern life.

❧ ☙

THIS WORK IS BOTH A SOCIOCULTURAL and a historical analysis. After establishing a general framework in chapter 1, we provide in chapter 2 a historical overview and an analysis of Hutterite beliefs and social practices. We review Hutterite geographic and ideological origins, regional developments, internal divisions, and immigration. Chapter 3 discusses the mass migration to North America in the 1870s and the establishment of three separate communal Leut along the banks of the Missouri and James rivers in the Dakota Territory. Chapter 3 follows Hutterite history into the early twenty-first century.

In chapter 4 we introduce the four Hutterite branches, outlining general similarities and differences and giving special attention to the 1992 division in one of the three Leut. Chapter 5 reviews different aspects of contemporary Hutterite religious life, including worship practices, music, sermons (*Lehren*), the selection of ministers, spirituality, church discipline, and evangelism. Chapter 6 moves into the arena of Hutterite family life and explores the implications of communalism for individuals at different ages, highlighting the important rites of passage. Chapter 7 introduces Hutterite folk traditions and the importance of ethnicity and language. Also discussed are dress, food and drink, recreation, and health practices.

Chapter 8 is devoted to Hutterite educational practices and viewpoints, including "English" and German schools and the group's views of and approaches to higher education. Chapter 9 deals with colony organizational structures, leadership roles, work patterns, and standards of living. Significant attention is given to gender and the role of women in colony life.

Hutterite population and demographics are the topic of chapter 10. We review Hutterite birth and retention rates, colony growth and expansion, and reasons why some individuals and families leave the colony. Among those reasons are the growing attraction of evangelical Christianity and the appeal of high-paying jobs in different sectors of the American and Canadian economies. Chapter 11 discusses ways that twenty-first-century Hutterites react to and manage change, including specific responses to technology and the mass media.

Chapter 12 explores relationships between Hutterites and non-Hutterites: neighbors, businessmen, other Christian groups, and government officials. The final chapter reflects on the Hutterite future and suggests what modern societies might learn from this unique group.

Acknowledgments

Representatives from each of the Hutterite groups have responded to early drafts of the book, and we have taken their suggestions seriously. We especially acknowledge John S. Hofer, Patrick Murphy, and Tony Waldner, from the Schmiedeleut Two; Arnold Hofer, Edward Kleinsasser, Jacob Kleinsasser, Dora Maendel, Jonathan Maendel, and Kenny Wollman, from the Schmiedeleut One; Heidi Entz, Hilda Entz, Noah Entz, Joseph Hofer, Margaret Hofer, and Jacob Wipf, members of the Lehrerleut; and William Gross, Annie Walter, Esther Walter, and Paul M. Wipf, of the Dariusleut.

We also thank the Mennonite Historical Society, Goshen, Indiana, for a research grant that supported this project. The Young Center for Anabaptist and Pietist Studies, Elizabethtown, Pennsylvania, offered Rod Janzen a fellowship devoted to specific aspects of the Hutterite experience. Thanks also to Merrill Ewert, Fresno Pacific University president, for a faculty research appointment that offered time and financial resources. We also note the importance of lengthy early-1980s conversations with two Hutterite individuals: Hans Decker Jr. (1928–1990), a Schmiedeleut minister, spoke with Rod Janzen; and Dariusleut member Annie Walter spoke with Max Stanton. It was Decker and Walter who first introduced the authors to the cultural and religious importance, and the natural beauty, of Old Order communal Christianity.

Visiting Hutterite colonies requires movement between the United States and Canada. Both of us have encountered skeptical American and Canadian border agents who searched our vehicles top to bottom looking for contraband. Often those officials listened suspiciously to our reason for constant border crossings: to spend time with people who live a life that is so different. But each time, when we arrived at our destinations, hospitable colony members were ready to receive us. We owe hundreds of individual Hutterites a great debt for their hospitality, friendship, and willingness to answer questions, share insights, and provide access to valuable documents.

We also thank Deborah Janzen and Margaret Stanton, spouses of the authors, who have, themselves, visited many Hutterite colonies. They always offered important insights and perspectives, and they have assisted, in different ways, in the research and writing process. Appreciation is also extended to academic scholars who read early drafts or engaged in important conversations, or both. These include Leonard Gross, Suzanne Kobzeff, Donald B. Kraybill, Ruth Baer Lambach, Stuart McFeeters, and Timothy Miller.

We are indebted as well to the manuscript editor for the Johns Hopkins University Press, Lois Crum, who made this a much better book, and to the work of Greg Nicholl.

The Hutterites in North America

CHAPTER 1

Communal Christians in North America

*We have camped out on the James River, down among the trees
by a water mill . . . not far from a settlement of Russians.*
—Laura Ingalls Wilder, 1894

Who Are the Hutterites?

In mid-July 1894, when Laura Ingalls Wilder and her family were traveling from De Smet, South Dakota, to Mansfield, Missouri, they encountered a group of "Russians" who lived in a "commune" on the James River, near the town of Bridgewater. Wilder observed in her diary that the "Russians," who were "all dressed alike," were hospitable and brought the travelers "milk and a great pan of biscuits." She noticed that the communalists were "curious and want to examine everything, talking about it and to each other." Continuing her description, Wilder added, "The man who seems to be the head of the tribe, or commune or whatever it is, said they came here five years ago . . . They have splendid barns and great corn cribs and a windmill . . . all of them together own all the stock in common."[1]

The people Wilder encountered were probably members of a Hutterite colony; a half dozen colonies were established on the banks of the James River in the 1870s and 1880s. Many years later, novelist Frederick Manfred, in his book *Sons of Adam*, had his main character, "Red," seek refuge at the Bon Homme Colony, nearby on the Missouri River bluffs. Red ultimately left the communalists. "I don't deserve to live with these people. I've sinned against their precepts," he said before leaving. According to Manfred, for the Hutterites, "all is one and one is all."[2]

In the early twenty-first century, forty-nine thousand Hutterites reside in 483 communes, or colonies, on the isolated northern plains of the United States and in the prairie provinces of Canada. Each self-sufficient communal village contains between 75 and 150 people. Hutterites dress modestly and uniformly and they do not waste things; they are opposed to the constantly changing trends of the fashion industry. Hutterites also refuse to serve in the military and refrain from most civic and political activities.

To maintain a separate identity, Hutterites speak a unique Carinthian-Austrian dialect called Hutterisch, and they maintain many eastern European folk beliefs and practices. For centuries they have lived in isolation from the social mainstream and have retained a distinctive culture and sense of religious purpose. Since the seventeenth century, few "outsiders" have joined the Hutterites; members today continue to marry almost exclusively within the group. Yet the Hutterite Church in North America has grown rapidly over the past 125 years as 85–90 percent of the group's children have chosen to remain in the colonies.

Hutterite society has roots in the sixteenth-century Anabaptist religious movement that, in later years, produced groups such as the Old Order Amish. Like the Amish, Hutterites dress plainly and speak a German dialect. But they do not attract thousands of tourists annually, as the Amish do in places like Lancaster County, Pennsylvania, and Holmes County, Ohio. The Hutterites for the most part stay out of public view, partly because many of them reside in the little-populated midsections of the United States and Canada. In addition, the Hutterites accept modern technology, so they seem less quaint than the Amish. Few businessmen and tourist agents have figured out how to market the uniqueness of technologically proficient, yet plain, communal life, even when there are dozens of colonies near population centers like Winnipeg, Manitoba, and Calgary, Alberta. Neither have Hutterite furniture and quilts been widely marketed, even though colony craftsmen and quilters construct beautiful and functional products, using the highest quality of materials.

The Hutterites represent the Austrian wing of sixteenth-century German-speaking Anabaptism. But unlike most Anabaptists, they practiced community of goods. When Jacob Wiedemann established the first commune in 1528, the goal was to create a colony of heaven on earth, a foretaste of life beyond the grave. The Hutterites (named after the early leader Jacob Hutter) still pursue this ideal, and they are the most successful communal society in modern Western history. With the exception of gendersegregated religious orders in the Roman Catholic, Orthodox, Coptic, and other Eastern Christian traditions, no other Christian communal group has been in existence so long.

From the sixteenth through the nineteenth centuries, the Hutterites established dozens of *Brüderhofe* (communes) in Moravia, Slovakia, Transylvania, and Ukraine. Persecuted and harassed by Catholics, Protestants, and Muslims (a few members were forced to become galley slaves on Ottoman Empire ships), the Hutterites fled from place to place, seeking religious freedom wherever they could find it. At one point in the 1760s in Transylvania, membership dwindled to fewer than fifty people.

A period of relative peace began in the 1870s, when the Hutterites left eastern Europe. They immigrated to the United States and established new communities on the relatively unsettled and undulated prairies of the Dakota Territory. During World War I, Hutterites were mistreated by government organizations and by American citizens who disliked German-speaking pacifists. As a result, between 1918 and 1936, all but one colony relocated (at least temporarily) to Canada. From 1944 to 1972, the province of Alberta passed laws that restricted Hutterite land ownership and expansion there. But notwithstanding these obstacles, North American Hutterites have suffered little economically or physically in comparison to what their ancestors endured in Europe. Many Hutterites eventually returned to a more receptive South Dakota, and in Canada the courts overturned Alberta's discriminatory land laws.

North American Hutterites have been remarkably successful in withstanding assimilationist social enticements. They have maintained their identity through commitment to communal living, adherence to traditional cultural and linguistic forms, having their own (often public) schools on the colony grounds, and establishing communities in rural areas. Although they have little interest in gaining converts, the Hutterites provide a countercultural model and an alternative economic structure that is founded on communal Christian principles that make sense to them materially and theologically.

Hutterites believe that every kind of work that is done for the colony (which is also the Hutterite Church), is an important aspect of the ongoing spiritual battle between good and evil, between God and Satan. Even mundane activities play a role in this "ark-building" for preservation. The belief that whatever work a person does is an important part of building the Kingdom of God keeps commitment levels high and spirits uplifted.

Although historically Hutterites were organized as a single, unified church, there are presently four institutionally separate Hutterite groups or Leut. Hutterites use the word *Leut*, meaning "people," instead of the standard German *Leute*. All four Hutterite Leut have unbroken ties to their origins in the 1860s and 1870s, although one of the groups represents a division that occurred in 1992. In this book we emphasize religious and cultural practices that typify all four groups, but we also discuss many differences.

In North America, the Hutterites have achieved economic success and demographic vitality, growing from 425 residents in three Dakota Territory colonies in 1880 to 49,000 people during the next 125 years, a hundredfold increase. How have the Hutterites achieved this phenomenal growth while retaining theological and ecclesial practices in relatively unchanged form?

The Hutterites ascribe their success to a Christ-based communal life and an unwavering commitment to the traditions of the group's founders, leaders, sermon writers, missionaries, and chroniclers. But they are also attuned to ways that technology may benefit agricultural, industrial, and domestic operations. Hutterites are resourceful and have a strong work ethic. They believe that a firm economic base is essential for everything else they want to achieve.

The Hutterites have met the challenge of life in a modern and postmodern world creatively without changing their historic beliefs and practices. They maintain a separate collective mentality supported by a unique linguistic tradition. They are an endogamous and clannish society, with most members now carrying one of fourteen family names. Their commitment to communalism is indelibly connected to the Hutterite confession of faith (written in 1542), the evolving *Ordnungen* (church rules), the Lehren (sermons), and historic hymns (*Lieder*).

The practice of forming new colonies when a population reaches about 150 people is particularly ingenious. It reduces interpersonal tension and competition and allows most Hutterite males to hold important colony positions. It fits the "maximal community size" level found in many pre-modern villages.[3] The theologically based communal economic structure, combined with a simple way of life, allows the Hutterites to compete in a capitalistic market, often to the dismay of neighboring farmers who believe that communalism is a social and economic system that should not work.

Like the Old Order Amish, the Hutterites convince high percentages of their young men and women to stay true to the faith. During their teens and early twenties, hundreds of Hutterite "runaways" (*Weggeluffene*) test the waters on the "outside" for a few months, or even for years. Many Amish youth have a similar experience before they join the church. But most Hutterite runaways return to the spiritual and economic security of the colony; they join the church, marry, and carry on the traditions.

Hutterite Diversity

Hutterite colonies are not all the same; each community has its own unique character. For example, at the conservative Miller Colony in northwestern Montana, the economy is based on agriculture. Hutterite men spend most of their time working in the fields or with the livestock. A few are carpenters, plumbers, and electricians. From an early age, every young man learns skills that are helpful in farming operations. Young women learn to sew and prepare food. Many become babysitters before they reach the age of ten.

The Miller Colony maintains as much social isolation as possible. Boys and girls attend school to learn to read, write, do basic mathematical computations, and understand a little bit about the world around them, but the colony opposes higher education and most young people do not complete high school. Miller uses computers for some farm operations, but they are gradually being phased out; the colony has never allowed Internet access. The five cell phones that the community owns are used only for business and in emergencies.

At Miller, German is the only language used in church services. Expressing deep humility, ministers read the ancient sermons without expression. The colony is opposed to musical instruments, radios, and photographs, and colony women wear full head coverings. Family residences are functional and immaculate but also very simple, with bare walls and minimal furniture. In general, there is limited interest in aesthetic expression that does not have a specific practical purpose.

Things are very different at the liberal Baker Colony in southern Manitoba. Here most colony members, even some women, work in machine shops producing ventilating systems, heat exchangers, and picnic tables. The community has a large garden but almost no farming operations, so Baker young people do not grow up with the usual agricultural skills. At Baker, most boys and girls finish high school and a few have earned university degrees.

Baker Colony factory operations are computerized and members have access to the Internet. If a non-German-speaker comes to church, the services are conducted in English. Baker also has a choir, and interested young people take piano lessons. The community also supports a variety of mission projects, including some that involve non-Hutterite organizations. Significant emphasis is placed on aesthetic expression, and some members have exhibited their paintings in nearby Portage la Prairie and in Winnipeg. At Baker, recreational opportunities abound. Members have designed a cross-country ski course in the virgin woods near the Assiniboine River, and there is a large gymnasium with a volleyball court.

Although there are significant differences between them, the Miller and Baker colonies both call themselves Hutterite. Any study of contemporary Hutterite life is thus complicated by Leut and colony diversity as well as the change that is always in the air. It is not only Hutterites who see difference and modification; they are impossible for anyone to miss. Why at one colony do residents, including ministers, sing songs accompanied by guitars and handheld drums, while at another, the use of musical instruments is grounds for church discipline? Why are Bible study groups accepted in one colony and anathema in another?

One reason for this variegation is that Hutterites have been divided into three endogamous groups since the 1870s: the Schmiedeleut, named after nineteenth-century leader Michael Waldner, a *Schmied* (blacksmith); the Dariusleut, after minister Darius Walter; and the Lehrerleut, after Jacob Wipf, a *Lehrer* (teacher). This is not the way things were historically. In eastern Europe the Hutterites were united as a single church. As Jacob Hutter wrote in one of his epistles, "He led us together to serve Him in unity and to show that God himself is one and undivided."[4] They retained

Riverside Colony in Alberta. Courtesy of Max Stanton.

unity whether the total membership was forty thousand (in the late six-teenth century) or forty-nine people (at its lowest point in 1757). Even during years when full community of goods was abandoned (between 1690 and 1757 and from 1821 to 1859), the Hutterite Church itself was united.

The change occurred in the 1850s and 1860s, when communal life was resurrected by three small Hutterite groups, each of which grew into a separate faction. By the 1870s, there were in fact four Hutterite Leut, three communal and one noncommunal. The noncommunal group was the largest, representing two-thirds of the Hutterite community. This compli-cated four-part Hutterite division existed in an 1870s population of only 1,250 people, a development that was unexpected and disruptive and be-came institutionalized in the Dakota Territory.

In North America in the late nineteenth century, the biggest social and ideological gap was between the three communal colonies and the noncommunal Hutterites. The noncommunal group was called the Prairi-eleut, or "Prairie People," since most of the members homesteaded on flat prairie land, while the communalists built their colonies along the banks of the James and Missouri rivers. The communitarians believed that the Prairieleut had turned their backs on the group's central teaching: com-munity of goods. But all the groups called themselves Hutterites.

In the 1870s and 1880s, there were serious attempts to unite the three communal groups or Leut, but even here there was no success, owing to personality conflicts between the leaders (and between their followers, too). There was considerable interaction, however, between individual members of the different Leut, since friends and relatives crossed group boundaries. Dozens of people married across Leut lines and even married members of the noncommunal Prairieleut. During the period 1874–1900, as many as two hundred people moved back and forth between communal and noncommunal living arrangements. Dozens of others crossed the com-munal Leut lines. These were difficult times, and difficult decisions had to be made. Many Hutterite men and women had a hard time deciding which direction to take.

By the early 1900s, however, the colony-prairie crossover rhythm ceased, and cross-Leut relationships also decreased. Surprisingly, the three communal groups became endogamous as each Leut mother colony branched off to form new communities and discontinued most social relationships with other Leut members. By the 1940s, all of the Prairieleut congregations, furthermore, had joined Mennonite denominations and given up most of the Hutterite religious and cultural traditions.[5]

In 1992 an additional splintering took place when the fifteen-thousand-member Schmiedeleut group divided. Details of the fissure are discussed in chapter 4. Throughout this book we employ the terms *Schmiedeleut One* and *Schmiedeleut Two* to refer to the more liberal (Group One) and more conservative (Group Two) Schmiedeleut wings.

One hundred years of Leut ethnic exclusivity in North America have created considerable diversity between the branches. But there are also differences between colonies within the same Leut, including variance in dress, behavior, and colony appearance. Within the same Leut, members at one colony openly use digital cameras, whereas at another, cameras and photographs are nowhere in sight. In some colonies, new homes have high ceilings and front porches with carefully landscaped grounds. At others, older remodeled apartments stand next to open areas of bare dirt. One new colony consists entirely, if temporarily, of a line of mobile homes. In some colonies higher education is actively promoted; in others it is feared and proscribed. The Hutterite Ordnungen (community rules and guidelines) are not cut in stone. They change regularly via collective discernment; in addition, they are not applied consistently from colony to colony.

Hutterite diversity is unsettling for historians and social scientists. A Hutterite minister once confronted John Hostetler after Hostetler criticized Hutterites for some of the changes that he saw occurring with regard to language, musical instruments, higher education, and dress. The minister told Hostetler: "You want us all to look the same and to stay that way. You don't want us to change because that makes it harder for you to write about us."[6]

The Hutterite Way of Life

Notwithstanding church divisions and varying social practices, Hutterites adhere to ideological and ecclesial traditions that have changed little over time. General rules and principles are set forth in the church's constitutional documents and in the Ordnungen. These precepts are grounded in a literal interpretation of the Bible, elucidated in the Hutterite sermons (the Lehren), which are the only sermons read at colony church services.

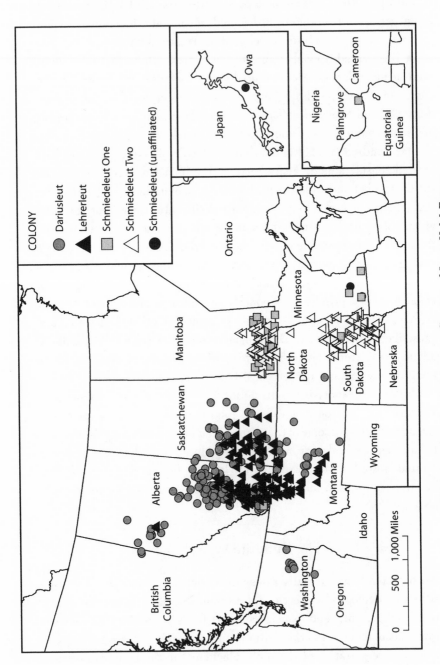

COLONY

● Dariusleut

▲ Lehrerleut

■ Schmiedeleut One

△ Schmiedeleut Two

● Schmiedeleut (unaffiliated)

Hutterite colony locations in 2009. Courtesy of Stuart K. McFeeters.

None of these basic elements fluctuate very much from Leut to Leut or from colony to colony.

All Hutterites adhere to early leader Peter Riedemann's *An Account of Our Religion, Doctrine, and Faith*, a confession of faith written between 1540 and 1542.[7] When Hutterites join the church, they agree to abide by this confession and to help their brothers and sisters do the same. Hutterites also sing from three historic hymnals and preserve a centuries-old worship service structure.

Hutterites believe that all Christians should live communally, in full economic as well as spiritual equality. They base this position on their reading of Acts 2 and other New Testament passages. Hutterites also believe that God has called them to live separately from the world, because of its evil influences. Plain dress symbolizes this separation, and pacifist precepts keep members from involvement in civic institutions that rely on force.

In general, Hutterites interact with non-Hutterites only minimally, for example, to support agricultural operations and other businesses or in times of emergency. Most Hutterites quit evangelizing in the eighteenth century, turning inward as they continued to model an alternative Christian society that they believe will be fully realized in heaven. Hutterites do not push their beliefs on anyone. But when neighbors need help, the Hutterites are there to offer their services, often before being asked.

The Hutterites are some of the most accommodating people one will ever meet. Members of the group exhibit a self-confidence that is striking, and people of all ages mingle and converse with one another effortlessly. Privacy on a Hutterite colony is virtually nonexistent; people are used to being together. There is a foundational, almost intuitive understanding of conflict management strategies and a commitment to the words of the semisacred sermons.

All of these characteristics define a communal Christian faith and social structure that has been passed down successfully and creatively from generation to generation for hundreds of years. It is an intriguing way of life that offers a conspicuous differentiation and alternative to modern Western social and economic paradigms built on the foundation of individualistic capitalism. In chapter 2 we look at Hutterite origins in central Europe and the unfolding of the Hutterites' particular understanding of Christian beliefs and practices.

Origins and History

If the whole world were like us, then would all war and injustice,
come to an end.
—Jacob Hutter, 1535

Christian Communists

The Hutterites are the only continuously existing communal group with roots in sixteenth-century Anabaptism. The Anabaptists, who emerged in various parts of western Europe in the 1520s and 1530s, did not all hold the same beliefs and practices. But they vehemently disagreed with some of the most fundamental positions held by the Roman Catholic Church and state church Protestantism.

The name Anabaptist ("rebaptizer" in Greek) was assigned by opponents to signify the group's opposition to infant baptism. In the sixteenth century, in all Christian jurisdictions, baptism was the point of entry into civil society, and baptizing babies was a legal requirement. But the revolutionary Anabaptists did not recognize the validity of child baptism nor the joining together of church and state. They "rebaptized" adherents upon their public confession of faith, and, internally, they instituted "believer's" baptism, letting their children decide when and whether they wanted to join the church.

Like Protestant churches, most Anabaptists reduced the sacraments from seven to two (baptism and the Lord's Supper) and refused to recognize the ecclesiastical and hierarchical authority of the pope, bishops, priests, and other Roman Catholic leaders. But they also refused to recognize the authority of the Protestant state churches. Following Martin Luther, Anabaptists believed in the concept of *sola scriptura*, accepting the Bible as the ultimate source for life. But they followed the teachings of Jesus more literally than Luther did and taught the separation of church and state, pacifism, and strict church discipline. Luther disagreed with these positions and asked the state (as did Roman Catholic leaders) to use force to ensure that Anabaptist beliefs did not spread. Since Anabaptists believed in a persecuted and suffering church, they were not surprised by what they encountered.

Although Anabaptists were at odds with the Roman Catholic Church on the sacraments, church governance, and many other issues, they agreed that faith in God was meaningless if not expressed through human works. Disagreeing with Luther, they taught that faith alone (*sola fide*) was not sufficient to make one a Christian. One had to follow the teachings of Jesus in order to establish the Kingdom of God (in imperfect form) on earth. Table 2.1 traces the Hutterian Christian ecclesial lineage in Europe and North America.

In the sixteenth century, Anabaptists were religious outlaws who found few places where government officials and local citizens allowed them to live in peace. Throughout Switzerland, Germany, Austria, and the Low Countries (today Belgium and the Netherlands), thousands of Anabaptists were martyred and many recanted, rejoining the state churches. Anabaptism was a diverse movement with regional and ideological differences. But all agreed that the Christian life was a visible expression of devotion, not just a private encounter with God. For some, like the Hutterites, community of goods was the fullest expression of this commitment.

In the 1520s, communal Anabaptists became the dominant non-Catholic religious faction in the Tirolean region of Austria. They agreed with what became mainstream Anabaptism on most theological issues but differed in their belief that all Christians should live communally. This was the position of an array of small Anabaptist groups in the 1520s and 1530s, but none survived as organized church societies.[1]

Communal Christianity is based on a literal interpretation of the New Testament. It relies on accounts of early church life in the book of Acts, especially the close proximity in the scriptural narrative between commu-

Table 2.1. Hutterites in Europe and North America

Early church
Roman Catholics (29)
Protestants (1517)
  Anabaptists (1525)
    Hutterites (1528)
      Habaner (1767)
      Prairieleut (1874)
      Dariusleut (1874)
      Schmiedeleut (1874)
        Schmiedeleut One (1992)
        Schmiedeleut Two (1992)
      Lehrerleut (1877)

nal organizational development and the Pentecost appearance of the Holy Spirit. Early Hutterites determined on this basis that God wanted all of his followers to live without private property, thus foreshadowing Karl Marx's maxim "From each according to his ability, to each according to his need."[2]

Hutterites refer to Acts 2:44–45: "And all who shared the faith owned everything in common; they sold their goods and possessions and distributed the proceeds among themselves according to what each one needed."[3] Acts 4:32 reads similarly: "The whole group of believers was united, heart and soul; no one claimed private ownership of any possessions, as everything they owned was held in common." The example of Jesus is also mentioned. According to one Hutterite sermon, "Jesus Christ, as soon as he began his teaching, was in community with his disciples."[4] Also cited is Jesus's instruction to the "rich young ruler" in Matthew 19:21, "Go and sell your possessions and give the money to the poor," as well as a reference in John 12 to the sharing of possessions between Jesus, his disciples, and the entourage of women who accompanied them. In Luke 14:33, Jesus states, "So in the same way, none of you can be my disciple without giving up all that he owns." In the Hutterite view, Jesus lived communally ("only Judas had the money bag")[5] and he expects all Christians to do the same.

Most Hutterites believe that the Apostle Paul as well, along with first-century missionaries and church leaders, had little or no private property. They refer to 2 Corinthians 8:7–15, where Paul stresses the importance of economic equality, that no person should have material abundance while another suffers. The sixteenth-century Hutterite leader Peter Walpot wrote that there were fully functioning first-century Christian communes in Antioch and Macedonia and in other places.[6] Hutterites admit that not all apostolic Christians practiced community of goods, but since Jesus, his disciples, and the very earliest Christians did so, this is considered the divine model. The communal way of life was established on the Day of Pentecost and was inspired by the Holy Spirit.[7] What happened in later years was misguided and irrelevant.

The communal Christian tradition is well known in the Roman Catholic Church and is exemplified in the way most clerics continue to live. Catholics believe that persons called to leadership positions bear special spiritual responsibilities that can easily be corrupted by material possessions. Commitment to the church thus replaces worldly interests and even most private property. Catholics also associate communal life with celibacy and describe it metaphorically as "marriage" to the church. The introduction of monasticism in the early medieval period took the call to communal ministry a step further as many religious orders equated Christian communism with complete commitment to God. Forms of communalism are found in most Catholic religious orders and among the general society of priests and nuns. In the early 2000s, Sister Regina Siegfried served as president of the Communal Studies Association.[8]

For Hutterites, life in heaven is the ultimate goal of all human beings, and the Hutterites believe the supernatural realm will be structured communally: they do not expect to find private property there. Therefore, as Hutterite minister Hans Decker put it, "there should be none either among God's people here on earth."[9] Looking backward and forward, the Hutterites believe they are resurrecting God's original vision for humanity, the equalitarian paradise intended for Adam and Eve in Eden and the way of life that will find fulfillment in heaven.

In the Garden of Eden as pictured in Genesis, all of creation was available to Adam and Eve, and the two were originally uninterested in personal possessions. In the Hutterite interpretation, it was when Eve, guided by Satan, corrupted Adam, that the "fall" introduced individualism and the end of community of goods. Hutterite colony life is thus viewed not only as a transitional form of existence but as a foretaste of heaven and a model of both Eden and the afterlife utopia. Moving back beyond Eden, the Hutterites find evidence for their position in the Trinity itself: in the words of one Hutterite sermon, "God the Father, the Son and the Holy Spirit have had community with one another from the very beginning."[10]

Hutterites teach the concept of *Gelassenheit*, literally surrender to God, self-abandonment, and yieldedness. To express Gelassenheit a Christian must turn his or her individual will over to God but also, simultaneously, yield to members of the church. For Hutterites, Gelassenheit means the surrender of all material goods, since the religious and the secular are intertwined. One cannot be truly committed to God without being united with other Christians in *Gütergemeinschaft* (full community).[11] This conviction does not mean that a personal relationship with God is not important; it is essential. But Hutterites view it communally: one belief does not cancel out the other because the individual and the community constitute a single socioreligious entity.

Gelassenheit governs a Hutterite's entire life. It is the central guiding philosophy of the society and affects everything that is thought and done. There is, as Hutterite Tony Waldner puts it, a "daily battle against selfishness and jealousy."[12] Gelassenheit also means freedom from personal possessions, so that it becomes easier to focus on God and other members of the church. Communal Hutterians believe that most Christians have taken the less difficult and wider path of noncommunal individualism. The Acts 2 Hutterite sermon explains: "Even so the great majority of today's Christians of this world can't adapt themselves, to live communally . . . For when one drives all the pigs from the meadow together and tries to feed them all out of one trough, we soon hear a lot of grunting and squealing and biting one another, getting into the trough with their feet, making much noise so that others dare not come near. Therefore it's not possible for the godless people to live together and share in common."[13]

Sixteenth-century Hutterites followed the teachings of Jesus in the Sermon on the Mount. They turned the other cheek and refused to retaliate. They did not swear oaths or take people to court. They believed that the church should function in separation from the world, much like a Benedictine monastic order (although they disdained the latter). The Hutterites were also active evangelists. Missionaries traveled throughout central Europe proclaiming the communal gospel, and as a result, many were jailed, tortured, and killed, martyrs for this radical understanding of the Christian faith.

Believing in strict adherence to biblical principles, Hutterites practiced church discipline and established in their communities a rigorous system of Ordnungen, which were codes of rules and regulations that governed all aspects of life and ensured a unified perspective. As an economic system, Christian communism was attractive to many of the peasants who supported social revolution in sixteenth-century central Europe; Friedrich Engels thus came to view Anabaptists as proto-Communists. Later Hutterite leader Andreas Ehrenpreis clarified the Hutterite position: "Christ wants us to love the poor. Christian community is the best way to put this into practice."[14]

Wars, Persecution, and the Golden Years

Hutterites have roots in the congregations started by George Blaurock, a Swiss Anabaptist leader who evangelized in the Hapsburg Empire in 1525 and 1526. Most of these churches were not communal, and there were differing opinions on theological issues. But all of the groups were committed to reading the Bible in the vernacular and opposed to the interpretations of Catholic and Protestant theologians. A Hutterite sermon observes, "Those [i.e., Catholics and Protestants] who thought they could lap up the Bible by a spoonful, who thought they knew it inside out," were completely mistaken.[15] But the latter had the sword on their side and were prepared to use it against heretics.

The early Hutterite story is told and documented in the *Chronicle of the Hutterian Brethren*, an invaluable and unique internal history that member Caspar Braitmichael began writing in the 1560s and which was updated regularly in the years that followed.[16] Preserving the memory of important events solidified the society's identity and provided emotional support during times of persecution and hardship, and of course this historical work provides historians with important information about the Hutterites over time.

The Chronicle includes a year-by-year account, with letters from missionaries, theological commentary, and original source materials. Now published in two large German and English volumes, it carries Hutterite history through 1873, with first- and secondhand descriptions. Persecu-

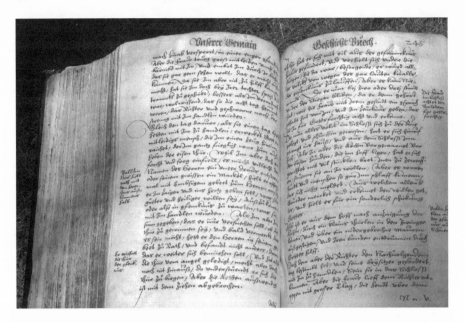

An original copy of the Hutterite Chronicle. Courtesy of Tony Waldner. Photograph by Lawrence Anderson.

tion and the struggle to live communally kept Hutterite membership small throughout much of its history, but those who held fast could always look to the Chronicle for stories of dedication and commitment.

Hutterites also composed hundreds of spiritual hymns. Wolf Sailer's sixteenth-century compositions are particularly important. They include songs of worship, praise, and ethical entreaty but also horrifying stories about Hutterite children taken away from their parents, rape, robbery, plundering, beatings, and hiding out in the mountains and forests of Austria.

Because of intense persecution in the 1520s and 1530s, most of the Austrian Anabaptists fled to Moravia and Slovakia. There they were welcomed by members of the (Catholic) nobility, who saw that expert farmers could improve the land and make agriculture more profitable. Noblemen also welcomed Hutterite educators, physicians, and craftsmen. For a time the nobility overlooked the Hutterites' proscribed theological positions.

It was in Austerlitz, Moravia, in 1528 that Anabaptist leaders Jacob Wiedemann and Philip Jager first inaugurated community of goods with a group of two hundred followers. In the mid-1530s, some members of that assembly, joined by immigrants from Austria and southern Germany, were organized into a separate church by the Tirolean hat maker Jacob Hutter.[17] Formerly a Peasant's Revolt sympathizer, Hutter was confirmed as the preeminent Anabaptist leader in Moravia after an encounter with God that was accompanied by signs and omens. Hutter described the incident this way: "On Friday, we saw three suns in the sky for a good long time, about an hour, as well as two rainbows. These had their arches turned toward each other, almost touching in the middle, and their ends pointed away from each other. Thus I, Jacob, saw with my own eyes, and many brothers and sisters saw it with me. After a while, the two suns and rainbows disappeared, and only the one sun remained. Even though the other two suns were not as bright as the one, they were clearly visible."[18] For Hutter, what he saw meant that his church group (the "sun" that remained) was the one chosen by God, not the other two Moravian Anabaptist communities. Their light was flickering.

Hutter came to believe that God called all Christians to live communally, and he excommunicated members of the two competing Anabaptist groups. The notion of the Hutterites as the "one true church" is found in many period documents. Hutterites continue to believe that they are practicing the most ideal form of Christianity.[19]

Jacob Hutter was once described as a man who wore "a short yellow leather kilt, brown pants, a black overcoat and a small black cap."[20] He believed that the End Times were near and that an egalitarian Christian order, signaling life beyond the grave, must be established immediately. But Hutter's life was short. He was executed in Innsbruck, Austria, on February 25, 1536, after returning to his homeland to help persecuted followers find hidden escape routes to Moravia. According to the Chronicle, after Hutter's arrest, "they put him in ice-cold water and then took him into a warm room and had him beaten with rods. They lacerated his body, poured brandy into the wounds, and set it on fire . . . Putting a tuft of feathers on his head, they led him into the house of their idols and in every way made a laughingstock of him."[21] Hutter was burned at the stake. But what became the largest communal Anabaptist group carried his name forward.

Peter Riedemann was another important early Hutterite leader. A cobbler by trade, Riedemann served as a missionary to various parts of Europe in the 1530s and 1540s. While imprisoned in Hesse in the early 1540s, Riedemann wrote his *Account of our Religion, Doctrine, and Faith*, which became the two-hundred-page Hutterite confession of faith.[22] He also composed forty-six hymns that took their place in the largest Hutterite hymn collection, titled *Die Lieder der Hutterischen Brüder*. In 1542, Riedemann and Leonard Lanzenstiel were selected as Hutterite coelders.[23]

In his *Account*, Riedemann notes the contention of other Christians that during apostolic times, community of goods was practiced in Jerusalem and "nowhere else."[24] Riedemann disagreed but wrote that even if this were true, it did not mean that communal Christianity was not God's preferred way. If community of goods was not found in the Epistles, this was only "because the opportunity, way and timing was wrong."[25] Later Hutterite leaders believed that apostolic-era communalism was widespread.

In any case, the early Hutterites were some of the most active and successful missionaries in the entire Anabaptist movement. Evangelists were sent to various parts of Europe, including Bavaria, Prussia, and the Rhineland, as well as to Switzerland, Italy, and even Denmark and Sweden. Upon their confession of faith, converts were sent eastward, to the place of refuge God had prepared in Moravia and Slovakia. A 1586 Chronicle entry indicates that "several hundred people from Switzerland joined the community."[26] If a transformed spouse had to leave her husband to accept the new faith (or vice versa), this was accepted, since one's eternal state of existence was at risk. More commonly, the converted spouse stayed in the relationship as long as the nonmember agreed not to disrupt her newfound faith. It is noteworthy that Hutterites were not successful in converting many Moravian or Slovakian peasants. Instead, their (usually) Catholic neighbors often expressed "hostility" toward them.[27]

Hutterites in Moravia and Slovakia often compared themselves to the Jewish people in ancient Israel. They saw themselves as a specially chosen ethnic group living in a blessed place, a new "promised land," in what Leonard Gross calls "a Christian version of the Old Testament people of God." Eastern Europe was a communal Christian refuge and, as James Stayer notes, "a prefiguration of the Kingdom that he [Christ] would perfect when he returned."[28]

In the 1560s and 1570s, the Hutterites prospered in a "Golden Years" period and grew to as many as 40,000 people. At this time there were at least seventy different communities, with an average of 500 men, women,

and children living in each one.[29] The Hutterite political and cultural center at Neumühl (Moravia), the seat of the Hutterite *Vorsteher* (elder) and
the place where church conferences were held, had as many as 1,000 residents. Neumühl was also where the Chronicle was written and the internal rules (Ordnungen) determined.

Much of the mission-minded intensity of the early Hutterites was
based on eschatological concerns and motivations. Members were certain that they were living in the End Times and wanted to convert as
many people as possible. But even as evangelists were sent out across the
continent, attention was also given to internal organization and governance.[30] Extremely important was the leadership of Peter Walpot, who
served as elder from 1565 to 1578.[31] Leonard Gross suggests that while
Jacob Hutter played the role of Hutterite "prophet" and Peter Riedemann
"synthesis[ed]" beliefs and practices, Peter Walpot provided "organizational genius."[32] It was Walpot who wrote the 376-page *Great Article Book*
(1567) that includes detailed commentary on Hutterite beliefs and practices. Other important sixteenth-century Hutterite leaders were Ulrich
Stadler, Hans Schmid, and Klaus Felbinger.

Hutterite missionaries were called apostles, and some of them wrote
Sendboten (epistles) that were read and revered in home communities. The
epistles, which include testimonies and admonitions, served to strengthen
the faith of those who stayed behind. They show God providing comfort
and support to his apostles in the midst of uncomfortable and dangerous
situations.[33]

During the Golden Years, the Hutterites were ethnically diverse and
represented a variety of social classes. Their communities comprised urban
professionals (including surgeons and teachers), ex-clergymen, craftsmen
of all kinds, and hundreds of peasant farmers. The Hutterites established
many industries, including cutlery, shoemaking, weaving, milling, sewing, brass work, rope making, bookbinding, and medicine distilling. There
were coppersmiths, wagon makers, clockmakers, blacksmiths, and tanners.
John Hostetler wrote that this type of large-scale industry was "practically
unknown before the Industrial Revolution."[34]

To ensure quality, specific standards and regulations were developed
for every craft.[35] Ordnungen covered the work of seamstresses, undertak-
ers, teachers, and all other professions, combining spiritual and secular
instruction. The "Code of the Teamsters," for example, gave both qual-

ity-control specifications and admonition on the importance of attending church. The Ordnungen also included guidelines for social interaction. For example, members were instructed that "in the barns, on the streets, and everywhere, they shall be properly quiet and not joking or acting silly."[36] In Moravia and Slovakia, the Hutterites established an elaborate apprenticeship system and became models of economic success. The community's physicians were consulted by members of the local nobility, and the latter sent their sons and daughters to Hutterite schools.

During the Golden Years, the Hutterites did not live in complete social and ideological isolation. There were important theological debates with Polish Unitarians, Czech Brethren, Swiss Brethren, and Mennonites. In these discussions Hutterites refused to relinquish their commitment to communal life, which was often a primary point of contention. The Hutterites also developed an educational system that included the first European "kindergarten," or what is more accurately described as a "preschool."

The primary goal of Hutterite education was to ensure literacy for religious and secular purposes. Peter Walpot's *Schulordnung* (School discipline), written in 1578, enunciated progressive teaching methods and influenced the sixteenth-century Moravian educational reformer Jan Comenius. "Let each schoolmaster deal with children by day and night as though they were his own," wrote Walpot, who implored that teachers "not always go to the rod" when discipline was required. Walpot also suggested that teachers model good behavior and "not accustom themselves to drinking wine and to show themselves intemperate."[37] For the use of theologians and others, the Hutterites also developed an extensive reference library, which included the works of Martin Luther, Caspar Schwenkfeld, Menno Simons, and Sebastian Franck. There was also a large collection of medical books.[38]

The Hutterites were recognized in eastern Europe for the production of fine pottery fashioned in late Italian Renaissance faience or majolica style and often decorated with Bible quotations. Some members came from the Faenze and Vicenza regions of northern Italy (near Venice), and many were proficient in the pottery craft.[39]

Golden Years economic and demographic prosperity was not without its social problems, however, and some of the problems carried theological implications. Because individualistic attitudes and practices proliferated

A seventeenth-century Habaner pottery replica from Slovakia. Courtesy of Rod Janzen.

in those good times, many members were accused of holding back money from the community treasury. Others missed church services or fell asleep during services. Astrid von Schlachta notes that as a result, from 1593 to 1605, Hutterite leaders had to undertake a renewed and "vigorous defense" of community of goods.[40]

The Hutterite Diaspora

Periods of intense persecution followed the Golden Years period. Especially devastating was the Thirty Years War (1618–1648), when Hutterites were caught between opposing military and political forces. In the process thousands were killed and many recanted under heavy physical and social pressure. Protestant and Catholic armies ransacked Hutterite properties, pillaging, burning, killing, kidnapping, and raping. Many Hutterites lived for years in subterranean cave dwellings "with secret entrances and passages" until 1622, when all remaining Anabaptists were expelled from Moravia by the ascendant Catholic authorities.[41]

It was during the Thirty Years War that the German writer H. J. C. von Grimmelshausen visited a Hutterite community (probably a loosely affiliated commune near Mannheim, Germany) and pronounced it a kind of heaven on earth.[42] But the war had a devastating impact on Hutterite life. By 1631 only one thousand Hutterites remained, either in Slovakia, where the Sabatisch Bruderhof became the new Hutterite headquarters, or in then-Protestant Transylvania, where the Alwinz and Kreutz communes had been established in the 1620s.

During this period (1630–1662), a new elder, Andreas Ehrenpreis, provided strong leadership for the Hutterite communities. Ehrenpreis directed the process by which hundreds of Lehren (sermons) were written and gathered into a single collection. These sermons make up the bulk of contemporary Hutterite homilies. Thus, modern Hutterites are perhaps more the "children of Ehrenpreis" than they are the children of Jacob Hutter or Peter Riedemann.

Amazingly, the sixteenth- and seventeenth-century Hutterite sermons still account for more than 90 percent of the homilies that are read in colony church services every day. These sermons, considered specially blessed and inspired by God, consist of detailed analyses of Bible passages along with commentary and examples from daily life. At least 50 percent of the content in most sermons consists of lengthy quotations from the Old and New Testaments that are used to clarify the central (biblical) text or speak to contemporary issues, or both. Major emphasis is placed on Gelassenheit and the importance of living communally. Other prominent themes are humility, a life of suffering, refraining from sin, the importance of doing good works, and remaining faithful to the end. The sermons are hard-hitting in their assessment of Christians who do not live communally. For example, the Acts 2 Lehr includes this comment about noncommunal Christians: "They show us little of the new birth as a pig does or a dog. They are sitting in the nest of their own manure . . . which has been

made of human excrement."[43] The sermons were written just one generation before the Hutterites first gave up community of goods.

The Hutterites also compiled a large collection of hymns that were sung
at church services. Of the 347 songs in what became an 894-page Hutterite songbook, one-eighth were written by Peter Riedemann, and another fifty hymns were composed by Wolf Sailer. One of Sailer's hymns
contains more than five hundred lines and ten verses.[44] The hymns were
collected in handwritten volumes that were copied whenever there was
sufficient time (and resources) to do so. In many communities, ministers
were the only Hutterites who held transcripts. The hymns were not published in a single volume until 1914, when in *Die Lieder der Hutterischen
Brüder*, Hutterite minister Elias Walter positioned the hymns by date of
composition, beginning with songs written in 1527 by Swiss Anabaptist
leaders Felix Manz and Michael Sattler. The last song in the volume was
composed in 1725.

Hutterite hymns were sung according to at least one hundred different
melodies and included many fifteenth- and sixteenth-century German
folk tunes as well as thirty-three Lutheran chorales.[45] Musicologist Helen
Martens notes that forty of the original melodies are still sung by Hutterites in the 2000s.[46] The hymns remind members of the steadfastness
of persecuted ancestors. Many of them focus on Jesus's death and resurrection and the Day of Pentecost. Although one hymn consigns Protestant
persecutors Martin Luther and Ulrich Zwingli to hell, most offer prayers
of intercession for enemies as a preferred expression of Christian love.[47]

After Ehrenpreis's death in 1662, the Roman Catholic Church raised
the level of persecution and harassment throughout the Hapsburg Empire.
Hutterites Martin Roth and Joseph Kuhr wrote, addressing their persecutors, "You priests are such good Christians that when you see a light beginning to glimmer, you try to put it out."[48] The Catholic Church was in fact
very successful in its antiheretic program. As a result the Hutterites gave
up communal life entirely from 1690 to 1757 and dwindled at one point
to a membership of forty-nine people.

When communal life was resumed in Transylvania in the 1760s, only
nineteen of the participants were members of the original Hutterite group.
One of them, Susanna Zilch, left her husband and two children in order to
join the reestablished communal group.[49] The other forty-eight members
were converts from a group of Lutherans, who had fled to Transylvania

from Carinthian Austria in the 1750s. Unexpectedly, the expatriates were converted by the powerful communitarian message of the Hutterite sermons, which some of them had read. This occurred at a time when most traditional Hutterites had given up not only communal life but Anabaptist Christianity as well.

A handful of people resurrected communal life at Kreuz, Transylvania, but Anabaptism itself was illegal in the Austrian Empire. Pursuing religious freedom, the tiny Hutterite remnant moved eastward to Wallachia in 1767 and eventually to Russia. The late-1760s journey was not easy; at one point members of the group survived by eating weeds and tree bark. The few hundred noncommunal Hutterites (later called Habaner) who remained in Slovakia (few stayed in Transylvania) recanted and joined the Roman Catholic Church. They continued to live in small isolated and somewhat separate German-speaking villages, however, into the twentieth century.[50] In the late 1800s, a few Habaner descendants visited the Hutterites in South Dakota, and from time to time there have been other contacts. In the early 2000s, a Habaner descendant, Karel Fridrich, had a lengthy conversation with ex-Hutterite Peter Hoover.[51]

Resettling in Russia

In 1770 communal life was reestablished formally in north central Ukraine, at Wischenka. The new commune was built on the estate of Count Peter Alexandrovich Rumiantsev, a nobleman who invited the Hutterites to settle there to improve his land and make it profitable. Rumiantsev granted the Hutterites many privileges, including exemption from military service, control of their schools, and even the right to distill spirits. But after his death in 1802, Rumiantsev's heirs attempted to reduce the Hutterites to the status of serfs, with almost no economic or political rights.[52] The Hutterites appealed to the Russian government, which allowed them to settle on crown land eight miles away at Raditschewa. Here internal conflicts, economic problems, and a major fire caused the Hutterites to give up community of goods for a second time in 1819.

The first time in European Hutterite history that communal life was disbanded, in the seventeenth century, the cause was external: extensive religious persecution and the social and economic impact of the Thirty Year's War. This second dissolution, in 1819, arose primarily for internal reasons. It had no relationship to military conflict or outside harassment but resulted from interpersonal conflict, economic problems, and theological controversies, all of which led to the acceptance of more individualistic perspectives.

Karl Peter notes that, historically, whenever loyalties to individual Hutterite families superseded loyalty to the community-at-large, communal life slowly disintegrated.[53] When family values take precedence over religious positions, people sell goods and services on the side and pocket the money, instead of depositing it in the common treasury. James Stayer points out that although Hutterites struggled with this problem from the very beginning, they were usually able to forestall widespread complacency.[54] But at Raditschewa in the early 1800s, individual interests caused division of opinion on the necessity of communal life. Elder Johannes Waldner, a communalist and a chronicler, stood on one side of the debate; his assistant minister, Jacob Walter, who favored disbanding communal life, on the other.

After a terrible fire destroyed most of Raditschewa's buildings in 1819, the fate of community of goods was sealed. With the exception of the orchards, the woods, and a few common buildings, personal possessions and land were divided equally among the members. The fire started when the hot hoop of a newly constructed wooden barrel contacted an overhanging thatched roof above a door frame when the barrel was rolled out of the shop.[55] On return visits to the area in the early 2000s, Prairieleut descendant Wesley Tschetter discovered that the 1819 conflagration is part of the institutional memory of Raditschewa's present residents. It is noted in the village's history, published in 1999.[56]

Notwithstanding their economic problems and internal dissension, the Hutterites experienced significant population growth in northern Ukraine, increasing in numbers from the 67 who fled Transylvania and Slovakia in 1767 to a total of 415 by the mid-nineteenth century. Growth was primarily from within—a result of large families, the retention of young people, and immigration from Slovakia—but there were also a few Mennonite and Amish converts with surnames like Decker and Schrag.

In 1842 the Hutterites moved once again, this time south, to a region north of the Black Sea, where thousands of Dutch Mennonites had settled and prospered beginning in the late eighteenth century. Mennonite official Johann Cornies encouraged the Hutterites to join them. Appointed by the Russian government to chair the influential Agricultural Society, Cornies was also a member of the Supervisory Council for Government Lands.[57]

Johann Cornies was an influential and powerful man. He supervised land allocation and economic development involving the Mennonite colonies, and the Russian government placed him in charge of the Hutterites as well. Cornies provided considerable financial and organizational assistance to the Hutterites, including a fifteen-thousand-ruble advance. But he also controlled many aspects of Hutterite life, even specifying how houses were constructed and advising what crops to grow.[58] He also interfered in Hutterite social affairs and was responsible for ending the Hutterite practice of arranged marriages. Before Cornies stepped in, the communitarian Hutterites held that for true Christians, not even marriage was an individual decision. According to the Chronicle, "We should not be so arrogant and sure of ourselves, despite all good advice, and assert our own self-will, 'It must be this man or that woman and nobody else.' That is not right."[59]

This way of thinking made no sense to Cornies. He intervened after a Hutterite girl appeared at his door one evening, upset that she had been paired off with an older man (a widower) for whom she felt no attraction. Cornies allowed the girl to reject her marriage vows and hired her as a personal servant. He then informed the Hutterites that arranged marriages were not acceptable. The Hutterite Chronicle reports, "For a long time afterward a wedding could not take place . . . until the girl had affirmed either to Cornies or to reliable people in the community that she willingly consented to the proposed marriage."[60] Cornies also promoted education and placed some Mennonite teachers in Hutterite village schools.

By the 1860s Hutterites had established five noncommunal villages near the Mennonite Molotschna and Chortitza colonies. It was in southern Ukraine that the Hutterites, for the first time, became an almost exclusively agricultural society. Previously, at Raditschewa, they had reestablished many crafts industries and once again produced pottery, clocks, hats, cabinets, and fine linen.[61] They also operated two distilleries, which produced 61,500 liters of spirits annually.[62] But crafts industries meant marketing relationships with non-Hutterites and the development of a more capitalistic mind-set. A few of the industries became so large that, for the first time in Hutterite history, non-Hutterites (Ukrainian peasants) were hired to provide sufficient labor.[63] Much of this activity bothered Hutterite church leaders, who considered it subversive.

In southern Ukraine, however, most Hutterites became farmers. Many of the traditional crafts industries were not resumed and thus were not brought to North America in the 1870s. By the late 1800s, some historic abilities and proficiencies had been lost. There were still bookbinders, shoemakers, masons, leather makers, and furniture makers, but individuals with these gifts were not selling their products on the open market, and their skills were often not passed on to the next generation.

The Resurrection of Communal Life

Southern Ukraine is where communal life was successfully reestablished for the second time in Hutterite history. It happened first in 1859, at Hutterdorf village, under the direction of Michael Waldner and Jacob Hofer.

As long as Hutterites relied on the Lehren as the primary way of interpreting the Bible, they were constantly faced with the communal imperative. Hutterite hymns and epistles also supported community of goods, as did the Chronicle. Michael Waldner's communitarian interest was preceded by unsuccessful attempts to introduce community of goods by George Waldner between 1848 and 1856.

Michael Waldner was called back to communal life through a vision or trance that he experienced during an illness that occurred shortly after he was selected as a minister. According to his nephew, Peter Janzen (a Mennonite who joined the Hutterites), Waldner was "transported" in his dream by a spiritual guide acting on behalf of God, who showed him both heaven and hell.[64] Janzen reported that "God Himself" gave Waldner specific instructions on how to live his life on earth. When Waldner asked where his place would be in the afterlife, the guide responded with a question, "Can you tell me, whether at the time of the flood, anyone was saved from the judgment who was not in the ark?"[65]

Earlier, in the sixteenth century, Peter Walpot had compared the Hutterite community to Noah's Ark. So it is not surprising that the spiritual guide in Waldner's vision used the "ark" metaphor to indicate community of goods. Through this mystical encounter, Waldner became convinced that communal life was the only way to Christian salvation. According to his son, the vision ended as "My father felt as if he were flying and

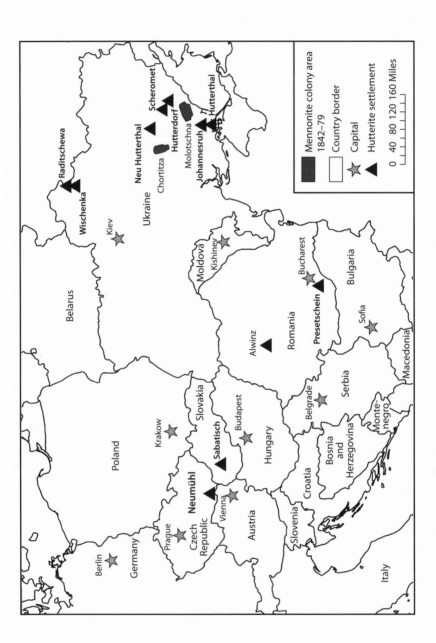

Hutterite settlements in Europe, 1528–1879. Courtesy of Stuart K. McFeeters.

Raditschewa

Wischenka

Kiev

Scheromet

Neu Hutterthal

Hutterdorf

Chortitza

Molotschna

Johannesruh

Hutterthal

Ukraine

Belarus

Moldova

Kishinev

Bucharest

Romania

Presetschein

Bulgaria

Sofia

Alwinz

Poland

Krakow

Slovakia

Budapest

Sabatisch

Hungary

Belgrade

Serbia

Bosnia
and
Herzegovina

Monte-
negro

Macedonia

Neumühl

Vienna

Austria

Slovenia

Croatia

Prague

Czech
Republic

Berlin

Germany

Italy

Mennonite colony area
1842–79

Country border

Capital

Hutterite settlement

0 40 80 120 160 Miles

then his guide disappeared" and a chorus of angels broke out in song.[66] Waldner had other prophetic dreams as well, many of which belong to a rich heritage of Hutterite folklore. In one of them, Waldner dreamed that Hutterites who did not live communally would end up in hell.[67]

During the 1860s and 1870s, two other communal experiments were also undertaken. One of these was in Waldner's own Hutterdorf village but under the leadership of the minister Darius Walter. Strong personality conflicts kept communal advocates, even those living in the same village, from forming a single church. The idea for yet a third communal group was hatched in 1864, when a teacher, Jacob Wipf, formed a minisociety in the village of Johannesruh. One family's home was converted "into a meetinghouse, another into a dining room for men, a third one for women, a fourth for a children's home."[68]

Despite renewed interest in communal life, two-thirds of the Hutterites in southern Ukraine refused to join any of the new groups. Oral history indicates that it was the wealthier Hutterites who were least attracted to community of goods. Whether or not this is true, the communalists were a distinct minority. Table 2.2 displays the ebb and flow of commitment to communal life among European Hutterites before the mass emigration to North America in the 1870s.

Table 2.2. Hutterites in Europe

Years	Place	Economy
1528–1621	Moravia	Communal
1546–1685	Slovakia	Communal
1621–1690, 1767	Transylvania	Communal
1685–1800	Slovakia	Noncommunal
1690–1800	Transylvania	Noncommunal
1767–1770	Wallachia	Communal
1770–1802	Ukraine (Wischenka)	Communal
1802–1819	Ukraine (Raditschewa)	Communal
1819–1842	Ukraine (Raditschewa)	Noncommunal
1842–1879	Ukraine (in Mennonite Chortitza and Molotschna Colony areas)	Noncommunal
1859–1879	Ukraine (in Mennonite Chortitza and Molotschna Colony areas)	Communal

Adding stress to the division in Hutterite society was a government edict issued by Czar Alexander II in 1870. New laws, to be enacted by 1880, were going to take away most Hutterite political and educational rights as well as some religious freedoms. The edict affected all ethnic German communities in Russia; a nationalistic and democratic spirit encouraged the assimilation (i.e., "russification") of foreigners throughout the empire.

Especially important to Hutterites was the loss of military exemption, which was central to their belief system. In return for this exemption they had agreed not to evangelize among Orthodox Christians. The proscription of missions did not bother the Hutterites, who by this time (like the Russian Mennonites) had become a closed ethnoreligious community. They rationalized the isolationist inward gaze by suggesting that God had called them to serve as models in a divinely guided remnant church. But they were unwilling to change their position on military service.

There were alternatives to serving in the Russian armed forces, but the Hutterites (unlike two-thirds of the Mennonites) viewed these options— for example, church-subsidized forestry and medical service assignments —as unacceptable compromises. They also feared the loss of their schools to teachers appointed by the Russian government, the loss of German as a semiofficial language, and the end of self-government in their villages, where some Hutterites were now serving as mayors.

Once again the Hutterites looked to other places, seeking freedom to practice their faith in whatever way they desired. Before they decided to leave Russia, at least two delegations were sent to St. Petersburg to request renewal of the pre-1870 privileges. These attempts were unsuccessful, and as a result the Hutterites turned to the west. After originating in Austria, thriving institutionally in Moravia and Slovakia, reestablishing communities in Ukraine following near extinction in Transylvania and Wallachia, the historically persecuted Hutterites were accustomed to fleeing from states, churches, and populations that despised them. In chapter 3 we discuss the Hutterite decision to relocate to the North American continent.

CHAPTER 3

Immigration and Settlement in North America

As guided by the Lord's hand
I must travel from this land
Into a strange place
To search for a homeland
—Paul Tschetter, "The Diary of Paul Tschetter," 1873

The Tschetters Visit North America

In the early 1870s, when the Hutterites were looking for a new place of refuge and exploring settlement options, two Hutterites were commissioned to accompany a Mennonite delegation of ten people on a study tour of the United States and Canada. The delegation is often compared to the group of twelve that Moses sent to "spy out" the "promised land" of Palestine in the Numbers account. The only two Hutterites willing to join the time-consuming exploratory expedition were thirty-one-year-old Paul Tschetter, a minister at the noncommunal Neu Hutterthal village, and his fifty-four-year-old uncle Lohrentz. From April to August 1873, the Tschetters were away from their families, traveling from Ukraine to the North American midsection and back.

Paul and Lohrentz Tschetter did not officially represent the communal Hutterite groups. While they were in North America, the communalists

sent their own three-man delegation to St. Petersburg to try, again unsuccessfully, to persuade the Czar to change course. But Hutterite communitarians held Paul Tschetter in high regard, and they anxiously awaited his
report.

During the visit to the United States and Canada, Paul Tschetter kept
a diary that includes a detailed analysis of the unsettled lands and peoples of midwestern North America, as well as critical deliberations on
late-nineteenth-century Western society.[1] The diary gives a clear view of
a minimally educated church leader's perspective on the non-Hutterite
world. Tschetter does not mince words or hide his negative opinions; he
expresses great dismay with aspects of secular culture such as smoking,
dancing, hunting, and musical instruments. After seeing men and women
dancing at a Hamburg, Germany, eating establishment en route, Tschetter
admonishes that they should "rather be praying than dancing."[2]

Tschetter also composed fourteen hymns that he interposed within the
diary text.[3] One of these, written in a small Chicago hotel after Tschetter
had strolled through the crowded streets of the city, is a theological analysis of the causes of the Great Chicago Fire of 1871. Tschetter did not like
what he saw and heard, and he developed a migraine headache, which
sent him back to his room. This is a translated stanza of the hymn:

> *In October of 1871*
> *The Lord punished this city*
> *Destroying her with fire,*
> *Judging her for her sins.*[4]

There was no doubt in Tschetter's mind that the Chicago fire was the
result of urban sin and debauchery. Widespread immorality had caused
God to impose a fiery and destructive judgment: Chicago's collective sin-
fulness led to physical catastrophe.[5]

While in the North American heartland, the Tschetters traveled from
Nebraska to what is now the province of Manitoba. Along the way Paul
conducted informal analyses of the soil, the climate, and the material resources and was especially pleased with the conditions he found in the
Red River valley of the northeastern Dakota Territory. But Tschetter also
sought guarantees from the federal government. Thus, before returning to
Russia, the Tschetters and Mennonite delegate Tobias Unruh requested a

1842. — Ältester Paul Tschetter. — 1919.

Paul Tschetter, a Hutterite delegate sent to explore settlement options in the United States and Canada in 1873. Courtesy of the Hutterite Mennonite Historical Committee.

personal hearing with President Ulysses S. Grant, and a meeting at Grant's Long Island summer home was successfully arranged by Jay Cooke, a major Republican Party contributor and a Northern Pacific Railroad trustee. The Northern Pacific had laid track between Minneapolis and the northern Dakota Territory and hoped to benefit financially from immigrant settlement in the Red River valley.

At their meeting, Paul Tschetter gave Grant a handwritten statement outlining the privileges he was requesting: a federal guarantee of military exemption and other special allowances, including permission to settle in separated, self-governing communities. He asked that Hutterites would be allowed to use German, operate their own schools, and be exempt from jury duty and swearing oaths in legal proceedings. He also wanted assurance that they would be allowed to leave the United States at any time. An artistic depiction of this meeting includes clear symbolism: the cannons surrounding the larger-than-life Civil War general, the dove positioned above the Tschetters, and the Bible in minister Paul Tschetter's hand.[6]

A couple of weeks after the meeting with Grant, Secretary of State Hamilton Fish responded to the Tschetters' requests, indicating that Grant could not provide federal assurances, owing to "the jurisdiction of the various states." Grant did believe personally that "for the next 50 years we will not be entangled in another war in which military service will be necessary." He reminded the Tschetters, however, that "should it be necessary there is little likelihood that Congress would find justification in freeing [the Hutterites] from duties which are asked of other citizens."[7]

Grant's response did not deter the Hutterites. On his return to Ukraine, Paul Tschetter held a meeting at the Neu Hutterthal village schoolhouse, where he gave a favorable report on his travels and recommended immigration to the United States. Canada had offered much more, including military exemption and large-scale coterminous land purchase opportunities. But Tschetter was not impressed with the Manitoba climate or its inhabitants. Most Hutterites, communal and noncommunal, agreed with Tschetter. They began selling properties and preparing to leave for the United States. Lacking a guarantee of military exemption, they accepted Grant's fifty-year prediction. In any case, they never anticipated that they would stay in one place for a long time. Throughout most of their history, the Hutterites had been sojourners without a country, relocating often and believing that true Christians should expect a life of suffering and turmoil.

A painting of the 1873 meeting between President U. S. Grant and the
Tschetter delegation. Courtesy of Chris Janzen.

Outside of the Slovakian Habaner community, not a single Hutterian living in 1873 had lived in one place for more than forty-one years.

By the 1870s, the Hutterite population in Russia had grown to 1,270
adults and children. Between 1874 and 1880, 1,254 people from this
group immigrated to the Dakota Territory. Contrary to their expectations,
they have lived in relative peace and isolation there, in other parts of the
United States, and in Canada ever since. Samuel Kleinsasser later evaluated the move, referencing the revolutionary developments of the next
century: "God took our church out of Russia just before all hell broke loose
over there."[8]

The first group of 384 Hutterites left Russia in 1874. Over the next six years the rest followed, at times in groups as small as five or six families. American Mennonite publisher John F. Funk, Mennonite relief organizations, and the Dakota Territorial Immigration Commission all advised the Hutterites to settle in the southeastern part of the Dakota Territory, near a group of Mennonite immigrants from the Crimea.[9] Most of the Hutterites homesteaded on land north of Yankton near the James River as it wound its way down to the Missouri.

Paul Tschetter had encouraged settlement five hundred miles north, in what is now northeastern North Dakota, but he did not accompany the first immigrant group; and intervening political and economic developments pushed the Hutterites southward. Influencing this decision were unsuccessful attempts by Senator Simon Cameron (R-Pennsylvania) to secure approval for immigrant purchases of large contiguous sections of land in the Red River valley. Agents of the Chicago and Milwaukee Railroad company also promoted settlement further south; this is where they had just finished laying track.[10] In the 1870s there was frenetic competition between railroad company land departments.

Nevertheless, it is ironic that the Hutterites settled in that section of the Dakota Territory. Paul Tschetter and most other Hutterites did not like the idea of putting down roots near a large Mennonite population. In southern Ukraine, many young Hutterites worked for wealthy Mennonites, and not all of them had good experiences. A few young Hutterites were even jailed for not fulfilling contractual obligations. For example, Zacharias Walter said that his daughter had been "shut up in a rank dungeon" for trying to run away from her employers.[11] Mennonites viewed themselves as culturally and educationally superior to the Hutterites, and they did not understand or accept the importance of ancient sermons, Ordnungen, and Tirolean cultural traditions. In his treatise "Why We Had to Leave Russia," Tschetter wrote that the Mennonites "lord[ed]" it over the Hutterites in many ways and had a negative impact on Hutterite spirituality.[12] But in North America the Hutterites settled near Mennonites once again.

Establishing Colonies in the Dakota Territory

On arrival in the Dakota Territory, 829 Hutterites, or about two-thirds of the group, decided to live on privately owned farms. This was the way all

Hutterites had lived from 1819 to 1859. Thereafter, the only Hutterites who had lived communally were members of the newly formed Waldner, Walter, and Wipf groups.

The noncommunal group, the Prairieleut (prairie people), organized three churches and numerous affiliated house congregations, and initially they retained traditional Hutterite beliefs and practices. They sang the Hutterite martyr hymns, spoke Hutterisch, ate ethnic foods, and read the sacred sermons. But most Prairieleut churches eventually joined Mennonite conferences; in the 2000s, the noncommunal Hutterians are quickly disappearing as a distinct ethnoreligious group.[13]

At the same time, the communal Hutterites (the Schmiedeleut, the Dariusleut, and the Lehrerleut), numbering about 425 people, established three colonies. The entire Schmiedeleut group, along with some Dariusleut and Prairieleut, were the first Hutterites to arrive in the United States. Under the leadership of Michael Waldner, this group initially looked for land in the state of Nebraska. They came to the Dakota Territory after a heart-wrenching experience in Omaha, where thirty-six children and a seventy-eight-year-old man died from an outbreak of dysentery. In the Dakotas, the Schmiedeleut purchased twenty-five hundred acres of land from Walter Burleigh, an American Indian agent. This very scenic property, called the Bon Homme Colony, sits on the bluffs overlooking the Missouri River, west of Yankton.[14]

The Dariusleut and the Lehrerleut settled fifty miles north of Bon Homme, building colonies on the banks of the James River. The Dariusleut community, led by Darius Walter, was called Wolf Creek; the Lehrerleut colony, under the leadership of Jacob Wipf, was named Elmspring. Throughout his life, all the way to his deathbed, Schmiedeleut leader Michael Waldner pushed hard for the unification of the three communal groups, but they could never agree on a central leadership structure.[15] Attempts to merge two of the groups nearly succeeded in 1876, when Waldner was elected and ordained as Hutterite elder by members of the Bon Homme and Wolf Creek colonies.[16] This happened while Waldner was in Russia, trying to persuade Hutterites still there to join the Bon Homme Colony. But when Waldner's election was later contested by a majority of the Dariusleut, the two colonies became permanently separate factions.

Each of the original colonies ultimately established hundreds of associated daughter colonies. All three Leut adhered to the Riedemann

Original limestone residences at the Bon Homme Colony in Dakota Territory, circa 1875. Courtesy of Tony Waldner. Photograph by Lawrence Anderson.

Original limestone barns at Elmspring Colony in Dakota Territory. Courtesy of Tony Waldner. Photograph by Lawrence Anderson.

confession of faith and other historic theological positions, and all were committed also to community of goods, but eventually there was little intermarriage and scant ideological cross-fertilization. As time passed, each group developed its own styles of dress, decision-making, and organizational structure. The three groups worked together only when they faced outside interference (for example, during times of war), in emergency situations, and in certain cases when it was financially beneficial. During the twentieth century, the three Leut established joint alternative service programs and a variety of insurance and marketing plans. They also created a central committee on which all three groups were represented, with one of the Leut elders acting as president. This inter-Leut governing structure never had much power, however, and the elder-as-president leadership structure was discontinued in 1990. In 1992 a fourth Hutterite Leut was created when the Schmiedeleut divided into two factions.

Differences between the communal Hutterite groups are based on distinctive social practices and idiosyncrasies that are often difficult for outsiders to discern. Unsuccessful 1870s-era attempts to unify the groups are described in the diary of Joseph "Yos" Hofer, a one-time member of the Dariusleut, Schmiedeleut, and Prairieleut.[17] The difficult-to-please Hofer had trouble deciding which Leut to join, and his diary provides important insights into the complexity of Hutterite interactions in the late 1800s. One significant obstacle was Dariusleut and Lehrerleut skepticism about the leadership abilities, financial acumen, and diverse interests of Schmiedeleut leader Michael Waldner. Waldner, in turn, complained about a lack of communal accountability, once noting that there was little cooperation among the three groups even with regard to "caring for the sick or replanting trees."[18]

According to Lehrerleut folklore, Waldner once visited the Dariusleut leader Darius Walter, at Walter's home, in an attempt to gain access to a chest full of money that had been left there by Lehrerleut founder Jacob Wipf while Wipf searched for a colony site. Waldner wanted to put the Wipf money in a common treasury, to symbolize the merger of at least two of the communal groups. When Waldner walked into the house and made his way toward the chest, however, Darius Walter's wife, Katherina, a large woman, sat on top of the trunk and would not budge, refusing to allow Waldner to take anything. To this day, many Lehrerleut and Dariusleut express skepticism not only about Michael Waldner's administrative abilities but also about the validity of some of his visions. "Some of it came from his own mind," says one Lehrerleut minister.[19]

The boundaries between the three Leut were fluid for a long time, though. During the first two decades in the Dakota Territory, dozens of marriages and much movement occurred between colonies. With friends and relatives in all camps, it was often difficult for Hutterites to decide what road to take. There was also movement across the communal-non-communal divide, with dozens of people changing affiliations. Some left the colony for a more individualistic life on the prairie; others moved into one of the colonies.

A good example of the crossover phenomenon is Michael Stahl, who had served as the (noncommunal) Hutterite elder in Ukraine. On arrival in the Dakota Territory, Stahl first homesteaded on private land. But in 1876, life-transforming visions convinced him that communal life was the true Christian way. In a vision that came to him while he was working in the fields, an angel told Stahl that noncommunal Hutterites were "all corrupt, even the ministers" and that they "will not last."[20] The emotionally shaken Stahl went home immediately and told his wife to pack up all of their belongings. Leaving wet clothes hanging on the line, the family left their farm and moved into the Wolf Creek Colony.

There are many stories of dreams and visions leading noncommunal Hutterites to join the colonies. Prairieleut settler Fred Waldner had a vision while taking a nap on a *Schlafbank* (sleeping bench).[21] In the dream he saw Jesus lying dead in one corner of his living room. Jesus then slowly resurrected, but in what Fred recognized as Bon Homme Colony, where he often visited friends and relatives. The meaning of the dream was clear: Jesus was coming to life at the colony, not in Fred's home. If he lived outside the colony, Jesus would, in a spiritual sense, be dead for him. In response Waldner gave up his private farm and chose communal life. Another version of the Waldner dream has Jesus flying through the air from one Prairieleut church to another, seeking true believers to direct to the colony.

The fluidity of movement came to an end in the early twentieth century, after the Dariusleut and the Lehrerleut left South Dakota for Montana, Alberta, and Saskatchewan, places where no Schmiedeleut settled. The Prairieleut were quickly Americanized and had limited interest in maintaining contact with communal relatives, who became an embarrassment for many of them. As a result boundaries solidified, although many communal Hutterites stayed abreast of noncommunal Hutterite affairs by reading the Freeman *Courier*, which was published and edited by Prairieleut Jacob J. Mendel from 1917 until his death in 1961. And on occasion communal life continued to be hard to resist. As late as 1932, Prairieleut Samuel and Susanna Hofer sold their farm and joined the Rockport Colony.[22]

The Dakota Frontier

Until the 1870s the Dakota Territory was a Native American frontier. The Appropriations Act of 1871 stripped the tribes of their official status as autonomous self-governing "foreign" countries and officially opened the eastern Dakota Territory to non-Indian settlement. The federal government limited Native American free movement to "reservations" (in the Dakotas, the western half of the Territory) and no longer signed treaties with them. But native people continued to traverse the entire Territory, hunting buffalo and other game. One Hutterite saw an Indian skinning a horse near Wolf Creek.[23] Many Hutterites found rock circles on their properties.[24]

When Mennonite Peter Jansen traveled through the Dakotas in the early 1870s, he saw abundant "wild game," "large herds of antelope," and many buffalo carcasses that had been left to rot.[25] Prairie chickens and ducks were everywhere, and there were almost no settlers. Novelist O. E. Rölvaag wrote in *Giants in the Earth* that the rolling hills of the prairies reminded him of waves on the ocean. For the Hutterites, the prairies brought to mind the steppes in southern Ukraine.[26]

The early years of settlement were difficult. The virgin prairie soil had to be plowed for the first time, residences and farm buildings constructed with locally available materials, gardens prepared for planting, and fences built to protect farmland from ranging animal life. There was plenty of tall grass for fuel, but few trees to provide lumber. Heavy winds brought dangerous accentuations of weather conditions harmful to crops and livestock. There were dust storms and insect infestations. Roads were few, often consisting of wagon ruts that connected government trading posts.

In addition, Hutterite settlement was undertaken during the economic "panic" (depression) years of 1873–1877, making things especially difficult for the new arrivals as prices dropped and markets for some crops evaporated. The pioneers had to adjust to language differences and an un-familiar system of weights and measures as well as new forms of currency and a democratic form of government. They had to plant the right crops, locate markets, and construct mills. The Hutterites and the Mennonites benefited by introducing Turkey Red winter wheat, a hardy variety they brought from Ukraine that did well on the Great Plains. Accompanying the wheat, though, was the dreaded Russian thistle (tumbleweed). Accord-ing to James Young, the first sighting of the tumbleweed occurred in the late 1870s on a farm in the Bon Homme area.[27] But this was of little impor-tance to the immigrants. Their main concern was putting food on the table.

In frontier life, chores were never-ending and all age groups were in-volved in the workload. The men of the Hutterite colonies took primary responsibility for the care of livestock and the planting, tilling, and har-vesting of crops. Hutterite women worked in the garden; prepared meals; made, ironed, and washed clothes; kept the residences clean; did most of the colony painting of buildings; and kept stove fires going with corn cobs and small pieces of wood. Buffalo chips (the "coal of the prairie") were also used as fuel, as were straw and hay twisted by hand into knots. Straw also provided bedding material for livestock. Children helped their parents wherever they were needed.

The first Hutterite homes had dirt floors. Large limestones were used to construct foundations with two-foot-wide walls. Cooking was done in earth-style ovens dug into the hillsides and lined with bricks. As the live coals were taken out, bread pans were shoved in.[28]

The riverbanks near the Wolf Creek Colony were covered with wil-lows and cottonwoods, which supplied small lumber. The creek also provided water for stock as well as a good supply of fish and crabs. Lush meadows on either side turned into hay for cattle. And there was wild fruit: chokecherries, plums, and different kinds of berries.[29] On the creek, colony members constructed a flour mill that was used by many local farm-ers and served as a source of income.

World Wars and the Lure of the Canadian Prairies

By the teen years of the twentieth century, most Hutterite colonies were doing reasonably well financially. Traditions had been maintained and be-liefs and practices transported to a new world. World War I presented a set of new challenges as President Grant's prediction of fifty years of peace was proved wrong for a second time. Previously, during the Spanish-American War (1898) and the conflict in the Philippines that followed, there was no mandatory military service. But in 1917, many Hutterite men were conscripted and ordered to report to military training camps. Written petitions requesting exemptions or alternatives received negative responses.

During the war, anti-German sentiment was especially strong in South Dakota, which had become a state in 1889. There were serious, if unwarranted, concerns about the loyalty of all of the state's German-speaking residents.[30] Patriotic citizens were especially angered by pacifists, and they harassed the Hutterites physically and verbally. South Dakota passed legislation that proscribed the use of German in large public gatherings (including church services), but both communal and noncommunal Hutterians disregarded it. Prairieleut minister Paul Tschetter explained, "In spite of the fact that this ordinance gave us much grief, we never abided by it in our Church, even though the minister of this particular day approached the pulpit with a heavy heart. The spirit of the Lord reminded us that we must obey God more than man." At this same time, distant Habaner relatives in Slovakia faced similar laws against the use of German.[31]

The Hutterites were uncompromising in their position against the use of force, and over the years they have maintained a consistent record, following their understanding of Jesus's life and teaching, confirmed by their sermons (for example, the Matthew 5 Lehr). In Hutterite history there is only one recorded incident of collective defense. It occurred in 1633, at Sabatisch, Slovakia, when a group of Hutterites wielded sticks, flails, pitchforks, and axes to resist local noblemen who were trying to requisition Hutterite horses to use against invading Turkish forces.[32] This action was deplored by church leaders, who passed a disapproving ordinance.[33] On occasion, there were individual aberrations. In 1764 Joseph Kuhr pulled down a colony house after its resident, an excommunicated member who had joined the Catholic Church, refused to leave.[34] In 1846 there was a "fracas" between Mennonite farmers and Hutterite laborers that came to "blows."[35] But these were exceptions.

Historically, Hutterites have also refused to pay "war taxes," that is, any tax specifically imposed to support a military effort. War taxes included those that would be used to pay for the manufacture of weapons, which

Peter Walpot and Andreas Ehrenpreis both wrote against. Following the same line of thought, many Hutterites refused to buy Liberty Bonds, which helped finance World War I. Justina Guericke, a granddaughter of Prairieleut leader Paul Tschetter, remembered that many Hutterite ministers consulted Tschetter on how to respond to the push to buy bonds, as well as the military draft and attacks from patriotic neighbors. Men "with long beards" visited the Tschetter home on a "daily" basis, and she was not sure what to make of them: "As a child," she said, "I thought they were Pharisees or High Priests from the Bible."[36]

Two Hutterite draftees from the Rockport Colony died as a result of mistreatment by military superiors at Fort Leavenworth, Kansas. Joseph and Michael Hofer were first court-martialed at Camp Lewis, near Seattle, after they refused to drill, carry weapons, and wear the uniform. The Hofers were then sent to the federal prison on Alcatraz Island, in San Francisco Bay, where they were forced to sleep "on a cold, damp floor in the stench of their own excrement."[37] Ultimately, the two were transferred to Fort Leavenworth, where they died as a result of forced exposure to cold weather.[38]

Almost every Hutterite draftee experienced humiliation in the military training camps. Many endured physical attacks as well as verbal taunting. Men's beards were removed after recruits first pulled on them or cut them into ridiculous shapes. Andrew Wurtz, later a Lehrerleut minister, was submerged in cold water in a bathtub, beaten in the stomach with fists, and hit over the head with a broom handle. He was also immersed in camp latrines.[39]

Especially difficult was the fraternal betrayal of Prairieleut Hutterians caught up in patriotic wartime fervor. Publisher Jacob J. Mendel, for example, served on the Hutchinson County Council of Defense, an organization that opposed family deferments for colony Hutterites and supported the same kind of mandatory military service laws that had caused Mendel's own parents to leave Russia forty years earlier.[40] One Hutterite sermon preface exclaims, "The world, or godless people, also meet from time to time for divine service in their churches . . . They also gather by the thousands to wage war, and are full of enthusiasm and unwearied in their deeds."[41] In the Hutterite view, Prairieleut like Jacob Mendel were exhibiting "godless" behavior.

The continuing impact of dreams and visions is evident in the 1917 account of draftee Jakob Waldner, who wrote: "I dreamt I came to the edge of a sea or river which was very wide. Standing there in my distress I saw a ship. The captain came to me and said, 'Here is your ship.' The man seemed so friendly and pleasant that I trusted him and told him my distress. He consoled me and said: 'I will give you the following advice: Keep on going eastward, do not go to the west, for there are many storms and lots of wind and very high waves.'" As a result Waldner did not follow orders to report to Camp Lewis. He took a train to Camp Funston in Kansas and reported there instead. Providentially, in his view, he did not end up like the Hofer brothers.[42]

But even those who were not drafted were harassed by local citizens. In South Dakota, thousands of head of sheep and one hundred cattle were stolen from the Jamesville Colony, north of Yankton, by a local mob that included a prominent physician. A photograph of the proud thieves was featured in a May 1918 article in the Yankton *Press and Dakotan*.[43] The Hutterite livestock were sold and the proceeds used to buy Liberty Bonds. While they were at it, the raiders also confiscated eighty-two gallons of colony wine, which they later distributed freely on Armistice Day.[44] The nonresistant Hutterites never went to court to recover any of these losses, either during the war or thereafter.

In the midst of nationalistic enthusiasm, very few colony Hutterites gave in to patriotic demands. They held to their conviction, as expressed in one of the sermons, that "the cross of Christ and the sword of this world are not in agreement any more than a sheep and a wolf would be in one barn."[45] Instead, most of the Hutterite colonies made preparations to leave the United States, or at least the state of South Dakota. In 1918 members of the Tschetter Colony left Kutter, South Dakota, for Redlands, Alberta. Sixteen colonies bought land in more-tolerant Canada; one moved to Montana, where two colonies had been established a few years earlier. A few Hutterite draft dodgers sneaked across the Canadian border in the middle of the war.[46]

Conditions for pacifists were much better during World War II and for the rest of the twentieth century, owing to officially recognized conscientious objector status and a variety of alternatives to military service. As a result, during World War II, 276 Canadian and American Hutterites engaged in public service work building dams, working in hospitals, and fighting fires.[47] Bon Homme Colony sustained a loss, however, when in

Sheep stolen from the Jamesville Colony in 1918. Three sheep are proudly held by prominent Yankton citizens. Courtesy of Robert Karolevitz.

1943 the U.S. Army appropriated sixteen hundred acres of the colony's land for use as a bombing field. The land was eventually returned in 1946.[48]

It was the more positive social and political climate in Canada that prompted so many Hutterite colonies to relocate there in the 1920s and early 1930s. During World War I, the South Dakota State Council for Defense tried to destroy the communal system completely by claiming that Hutterite colonies were not religious institutions.[49] By 1935, only two colonies remained in the state (Bon Homme and Rockport), and they were populated mainly by older people.[50] But in that same year, in response to out-migration and Depression-era economic devastation, the state of South Dakota, desperate to stop the exodus of its citizens, changed course and passed the Communal Societies Act. This act provided favorable tax rates and allowed Hutterite colonies to incorporate as communal organizations. As a result, many Schmiedeleut Hutterites returned, and by 1945 there were eleven South Dakota colonies.[51]

In the mid-twentieth century, the primary obstacle for Canadian Hutterites was Alberta's Communal Land Sales Prohibition Act, a law introduced by Mormon legislator Solon Low. From 1942 to 1974, it prohibited Hutterites from building colonies within forty miles of each other, limited total land sales to 2,072 hectares per community, and allowed no more than two colonies to be located in any municipality. Thus, when colonies branched out, friends and relatives often found themselves living hundreds of miles apart. The law was rescinded by the courts in the 1970s, but it showed that non-Hutterite Albertans did not favor the expansion of a pacifist, separatist, and communal sect.[52] The assimilationist platform of the Progressive-Conservative Party called for Hutterite children to learn to be civic-minded and patriotic Canadian citizens. The effect of the legal ruling was also mitigated somewhat, as "gentleman's agreements" continue to influence Hutterite land purchases. In South Dakota, similarly restrictive legislation nearly passed the state House of Representatives and Senate in 1955. A poll taken that year found that 87 percent of South Dakota citizens opposed Hutterite land expansion.[53]

The general Hutterite response to hostility and jealousy has been political withdrawal and social isolation. Until the later twentieth century, Hutterite colonies in North America shied away from most civic activities, focusing almost entirely on internal religious and social matters and making a simple living.

After the nineteenth-century Leut founders died, the most influential Hutterite leader during the early twentieth century was the Dariusleut elder Elias Walter (1862–1938). Walter, a nephew of Darius Walter, the Dariusleut founder, published Riedemann's confession of faith (in 1902), the Hutterite hymnal (in 1914), and the Chronicle (in 1923). Elias Walter also established an important archival center and an impressive library. Another important Dariusleut minister was Paul S. Gross (1910–1998), who wrote a book on Hutterite life and many widely distributed devotional pamphlets. Gross was committed to education and establishing closer relationships with non-Hutterites. Other prominent twentieth-century Dariusleut leaders include John Wurz, Martin Walter, and Michael Stahl.

Significant Lehrerleut leaders include Peter Entz, John Kleinsasser, Jacob Wipf, and John B. Wipf. Schmiedeleut leaders of note include Arnold Hofer, John S. Hofer, Leonard Kleinsasser, Mike Tschetter, John Waldner, and Samuel Waldner. Jacob Kleinsasser, an especially important force since the 1960s, is committed to resurrecting historical Hutterite principles, while remaining open to Holy Spirit–inspired innovations. Kleinsasser is updating the Hutterite Chronicle and has translated more than one hundred Hutterite sermons and many hymns into English.

Relationships with Other Communal Groups

In the early years of settlement, the Hutterites maintained close contact with Mennonite organizations, which provided tens of thousands of dollars in donations and loans. Mennonites in Pennsylvania and Indiana also hosted Hutterite immigrants—for months at a time if they arrived in winter—during their journey westward.

Relationships were also formed with two Radical Pietist communal groups: the Community of True Inspiration, or Amana Society, established by Johann Christoph Rock in 1708, and the Harmony Society, founded by George Rapp in 1804. Both groups spoke German. They gave the Hutterites thousands of dollars in donations and loans and provided expertise for the construction of colony buildings. The Pennsylvania-based Harmonists were especially interested in the Hutterites. By the 1880s, they held significant financial resources and much land, but they had a dwindling celibate membership that relied on new converts. In 1876 Harmonist leader Jonathan Lenz visited the Hutterites in the Dakota Territory to assess their financial needs and to discuss theological matters. Lenz then authorized the transfer of four thousand dollars to Bon Homme Colony "to help with start-up costs."[54]

In the 1880s the Harmonists offered the Hutterites twelve thousand acres of land in Warren County, Pennsylvania, if the entire group would settle there. Schmiedeleut leader Michael Waldner was unable to convince most Hutterites to join him, but in 1884 he and a group of forty followers took the challenge and moved to the Tidioute area, where they developed a small lumber industry and tried to transform the oil-rich territory into farmland. They were unsuccessful and were unwilling to develop other industries.[55] With the exception of a man named Samuel Kleinsasser, all members of the Waldner group returned to the Dakota Territory in 1886.

The Amana Society, which in the 1840s established communal villages west of Cedar Rapids, Iowa, also assisted the Hutterites financially. Gottlieb Scheuner, in his 1900 history of the Inspirationists, describes many Hutterite requests for material supplies and money. He notes that one "gift" consisted of two carloads of potatoes, flour, meat, and lard and that Amana also supplied cattle and sheep.[56] The Inspirationists taught the Hutterites how to construct a large mill and how to operate a steam engine. Hutterites also sought medical advice from Amana doctors, and when Hutterites were in Iowa, they attended Inspirationist church services.

One Hutterite, Michael Hofer (1859–1924), joined the Amana Society. It came about after Hofer sought medical treatment for eye problems caused by a Dakota dust storm. In order to pay for what turned out to be effective care, Hofer, a machinist, agreed to work for Amana for one full year. During that time he not only attended church services but met and eventually married Marie Stuck, the great-granddaughter of Christian Metz, who led the group from Germany to the United States in the 1830s. Hofer first laid eyes on his future wife when she was drawing water from a community pump.[57] He never left Amana, and many of his descendants are still members of the Inspirationist Church.

❧ ᕯ

IN THE 1870s, after nearly three hundred fifty years of residence in various parts of central and eastern Europe, the Hutterites put down roots in

North America. Here in the West, they once again encountered people and governments that did not appreciate their unique beliefs and practices. But in the United States and Canada, democratic political traditions and constitutional guarantees made it possible most of the time for the Hutterites to live in peace in their relatively isolated rural villages. The Hutterites were not successful, however, in healing the divisions that separated them. There were not only communal-noncommunal differences of opinion, but also institutional distinctions that separated those who chose to live in colonies. In chapter 4 we discuss similarities and differences between the four communal Hutterite groups.

Four Hutterite Branches

Since there was a longing for unity, it was decided to go back in time and start over.
—Joseph "Yos" Hofer, Hutterite diarist, 1877

In general theology, there are few differences among the four Hutterite Leut. But religious and cultural practices vary, and Hutterites spend considerable time making Leut comparisons, pointing to differences, laughing about points of contention, and most of the time presenting their own group in the most favorable light. In 1974 John Hostetler wrote, "The three Leut are differentiated from one another but accepting of the other's differences. Differentiations between or within the affiliations do not necessarily bespeak progressive or conservative tendencies: minor differences in customs can be attributed to leadership patterns and family traditions."[1] This statement bore some truth at the time it was written, but there has been considerable change in the past thirty-five years.

The Lehrerleut

The Lehrerleut are the most conservative and the least diverse of the Hutterite branches. They maintain the highest level of communal identity, have the tightest organizational structure, and are the most opposed to educational and technological innovations, changes in worship, modern dress, the use of English, and musical instruments. To some extent the Lehrerleut are also the least materialistic of the Hutterite branches. There are presently 139 Lehrerleut colonies: 72 located in the province of Alberta, 32 in Saskatchewan, and 35 in the state of Montana.

Some Lehrerleut distinctives are purely cultural. For example, Lehrerleut boys wear small cloth caps with a Neolite shield. These are not seen in other Hutterite groups. Lehrerleut women wear coverings that veil the head more completely than those worn by other Hutterite women, and they often wear blue long-brimmed bonnets when working outside, to protect their skin from the sun. Lehrerleut men have beards but no mustaches, because in Europe mustaches were associated with the military.

The Lehrerleut are the most centrally governed of the Hutterite groups. All Lehrerleut ministers (*Prediger*) meet biennially, and almost all senior pastors attend baptismal ceremonies and ministerial selection meetings whenever and wherever they take place. This practice requires thousands of miles of travel each year, but it ensures a strong sense of Leut unity. The Lehrerleut have also established a central Leut council, made up of two representatives from each colony, which approves all colony branching decisions.

When Lehrerleut colonies expand and establish daughter communities, they use the traditional process of casting lots. The colony council draws up two lists of people; those on one list will remain and those on the other will move to the new colony. Until the lot is cast, no one knows which list is which. Individual interests are not allowed to interfere with a divinely inspired procedure, even though this is not always a happy day for the people who are involved. In some colonies all families pack up their personal belongings the night before the lot is cast, in preparation for what could transpire.

All major Lehrerleut leadership positions in the new colony are filled by the governing councils of both "mother" and "daughter" communities. Parent colonies thus exert major influence over new colonies for at least a full generation. The Lehrerleut also commonly establish five to ten colonies in the same region so that individual communes do not operate too independently. Another way that the Lehrerleut preserve unity is by pooling some of their financial resources. A central fund is available to any colony with economic difficulties. A colony that takes money from the fund is subject to financial oversight, but the fund makes it unnecessary to borrow at high interest rates or to liquidate colony assets to reduce debt load.

The Lehrerleut are also the most cautious in forming relationships with

Lehrerleut toddlers in traditional dress, in Alberta. Courtesy of Max Stanton.

non-Hutterites. They are the most reclusive of the Hutterite groups and the least likely to invite nonmembers to stay overnight. The policy of Alberta minister Peter Waldner is "No more than two nights for each visit and even then be sure the visits are not too close together." In the 1970s and 1980s, the Lehrerleut were the most suspicious of the Hutterite relationship with the Bruderhof communities (now Christian Communities, International). They were apprehensive about merging with a group that had different cultural and theological roots and that was, in the words of Montana minister Jacob Wipf, "too utopian."[2]

The Lehrerleut also limit members' visits to colonies in other Hutterite branches. Although Dariusleut and Lehrerleut colonies are often only a few miles apart, many Lehrerleut individuals have never visited a Dariusleut community. The groups rarely worship together and spend little time discussing differences in beliefs and practices. When a Dariusleut or conservative Schmiedeleut minister visits a Lehrerleut church service, however, he is customarily invited to deliver the sermon.

Lehrerleut exclusivity has lessened a bit since the 1980s, as a result of common Lehrerleut, Dariusleut, and conservative Schmiedeleut dissatisfaction with the more liberal Schmiedeleut colonies. In addition, since the invention of the cell phone, the Hutterite grapevine crosses Leut lines regularly. Upon arrival at a Lehrerleut colony in Montana, Rod Janzen discovered that members knew exactly which Dariusleut colonies he had visited the previous three days. But the Lehrerleut continue to preach a gospel of separation, and they keep to themselves as much as possible.

Lehrerleut women have less public authority than do women in other Leut; and they less frequently accompany their husbands on business and church-related trips. The Lehrerleut monitor the behavior of young children more circumspectly and enforce a strong work ethic from the earliest years. Yet Lehrerleut males and females in their late teens and early twenties, before they take their baptismal vows, are given significant freedom, just as in other Leut. Rigid control of behavior between ages five and fifteen is followed by a "time of experimentation," even for those young people who never leave the colony. Adults often look the other way as their children experiment with tobacco, attend movies in town, and engage in various forms of sexual expression. In their late teens, a large percentage of males leave the colony for months or even years at a time, attracted to high-paying jobs in the oil and mining industries or on large corporate farms.

In most areas, however, the Lehrerleut exhibit caution. They have moved more slowly than other Leut in adopting technologies unrelated to agriculture and in establishing industries of any kind. Many colonies do not adhere to daylight savings, or what they call "fast," time. The Lehrerleut limit members' access to the media to a greater extent than other Hutterite branches do, and they live much more simply. At the Miller Colony, in Choteau, Montana, for example, outhouses were used until 1991. A few Lehrerleut colonies did not install indoor plumbing until the early 2000s. In general, the Lehrerleut are troubled by what they view as the more materialistic emphases of other Leut.

Ensuring equality is another important Lehrerleut standard. Joseph Hofer, a great-grandson of Lehrerleut founder Jacob Wipf, notes the importance of maintaining equality between individuals and families. At the Miller Colony, where he lived until 2009, when the colony branched, all of the new homes were built at the same time. They were designed identically in layout and furnishings, though with differences related to family size. In order to avoid feelings of jealousy and accusations of favoritism,

Greenwood Colony, Alberta, has very simple and humble residences that are almost identical. Courtesy of Max Stanton.

the colony did not mix old and new structures. The old buildings had to come down. Even in the colony's new homes, the minimal kitchen space, the small sink and counter, and the absence of couches or stuffed chairs convey a feeling of basic simplicity.

With the exception of ministers, Lehrerleut members eat three meals a day in the colony dining hall. The only exception is the light home-prepared Sunday evening meals that have become popular at some colonies. These in-house meals allow families to eat together as units, not segregated by sex or age.

The Lehrerleut view other Hutterites, except for those in conservative Dariusleut colonies, as too liberal in virtually all areas of life. They fear that most Schmiedeleut and Dariusleut are speedily turning their backs on historic Hutterite beliefs and practices.

The Dariusleut

The Dariusleut are generally viewed as the Hutterite moderates, but they are also the most diverse of the four groups. There is as much heterogeneity among individual colonies in dress, use of media, aesthetic sensibilities, and views of education as there is between the Dariusleut and Lehrerleut generally. The Wilson Siding Colony and the West Raley Colony, both in Alberta, for example, are more conservative than most Lehrerleut communities. The homes in these colonies are marked by simplicity and basic functionality. Inside Wilson Siding residences, simple linoleum is used as flooring material. Outside, there are no lawns or flower beds. At the liberal Warden Colony in Washington, in contrast, expansive residences have ornate staircases and hardwood floors. Warden lawns are well cared for and landscaped with flowers, bushes, and trees. Some progressive colonies have above-ground swimming pools, often in large tanks, whereas conservative colonies do not even allow children to ride bicycles.

It is often possible to categorize Dariusleut communities by looking at mother-daughter colony relationships and extensions. One finds conservative, moderate, and liberal colony lines. The latest edition of the *Dariusleut Family Record List* contains nine branching colony tree charts.[3] In virtually every case, the more conservative colonies have stemmed off from a common mother colony. In the branches, family ties are strong, with significant pressure for young people to marry within the group of related colo-

Warden Colony, Washington, a relatively liberal colony, has upscale residences. Courtesy of Max Stanton.

nies. Subtle intra-Leut ideological and cultural cliques result. Marriages between members of conservative and liberal clans occur but are viewed with some suspicion. Over the years, as the total Dariusleut population has grown at a rapid pace, internal subcultures have emerged, providing the same kind of social support system that the Leut as a whole did when it was much smaller. In this way the benefits of smallness are preserved.

Dariusleut Hutterites are divided ideologically. Traditionalists emphasize historic communal teachings in nonpietistic worship structures. Liberals are more ecumenical, more interested in higher education, and more open to new forms of technology. Evangelical-minded Dariusleut (who are found in both groups) emphasize the individual's personal relationship with God. Both traditionalists and progressives refer to evangelicals as "born agains" or "born against," the latter term indicating a position that is opposed to historic Hutterite beliefs and practices.

Dariusleut colonies are the most scattered geographically, from east-central Washington state, where they are the only Hutterite Leut, to all regions of Alberta; northeastern British Columbia, near Dawson Creek; central and southern Saskatchewan; many parts of Montana; and northeastern Oregon. The Owa Community in Japan (see chapter 10) is also associated with the Dariusleut.

Today there are 159 Dariusleut colonies, 102 in Alberta, 32 in Saskatchewan, 2 in British Columbia, 15 in Montana, 5 in Washington, 1 in Oregon, and 1 in North Dakota. Since colonies range from progressive to conservative, with great variation in practice, Leut leaders place significant emphasis on the "individual conscience" (or the individual colony conscience), and there is relatively autonomous community governance.[4] When a colony branches, decisions about who moves where are made within the colony and "by mutual consent," without reliance on the traditional lot-casting procedure.

The issue of Dariusleut identity is complicated. But all Dariusleut are tied together by a common and somewhat unique style of dress and strong family ties. Leadership at the Council of Elders level has traditionally expressed the views of the more conservative Dariusleut colonies, exerting a measure of restraint on forces of change.

Most Dariusleut view the Lehrerleut as rigid and restrictive. They say the Lehrerleut are legalistic and provide few educational and recreational opportunities for their children. Concurrently, although they are diverse

Young Dariusleut sisters in Montana. Courtesy of Max Stanton.

themselves, most Dariusleut have historically viewed the Schmiedeleut as too liberal. Since the 1990s, however, Schmiedeleut conservatives and progressive Dariusleut have discovered much common ground. A few marriages have even crossed Leut lines.

The Schmiedeleut

From the 1870s until the early 1990s, the Schmiedeleut was the largest of the three Hutterite groups. They were also known as the most liberal branch. Founder Michael Waldner was willing to take risks, such as moving to Pennsylvania, that no other Hutterite leader thought advisable. Waldner was also the most open to the direction of spirit-guided dreams and visions. Unlike the Dariusleut and the Lehrerleut, Schmiedeleut colonies are located in the states of South Dakota, North Dakota, and Min-

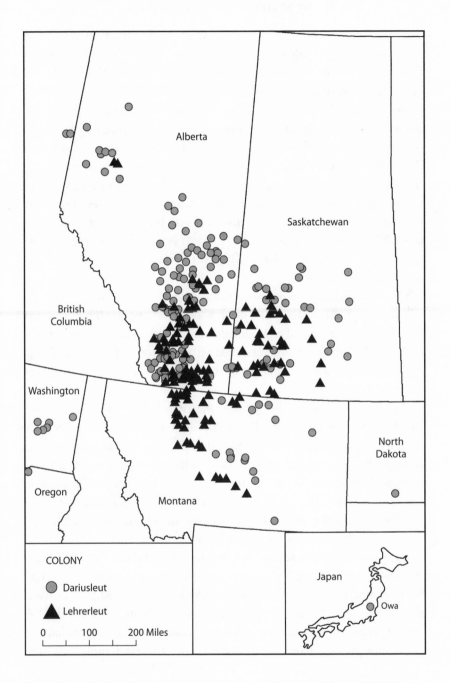

Dariusleut and Lehrerleut colony locations in 2009. Courtesy of Stuart K. McFeeters.

nesota, as well as in the province of Manitoba. Many of them are near population centers such as Winnipeg, Manitoba, and Sioux Falls, South Dakota, which exert strong secular influences and where there is significant interaction with outsiders.

Being liberal is a relative concept, however. In the Hutterite world it means slightly less conservative dress, head coverings that are placed farther back on the head, marginally greater openness to relationships with non-Hutterites, greater use of English, and more widespread use of musical instruments, cameras, and cell phones. Members of other Leut are alarmed that Schmiedeleut men and women and their families sit together in some colony dining halls. A Dariusleut man told us to watch carefully to see if Schmiedeleut men were holding hands with their spouses. Yet the most conservative Schmiedeleut differ little from the Lehrerleut and the traditionalist Dariusleut.

The Schmiedeleut were united until December 10, 1992, when, in a surprise move, the senior elder, Jacob Kleinsasser, was replaced in a contested vote of the council of Schmiedeleut ministers. The vote followed a day and a half of discussions centered on a series of prepared complaints against the elder and in response to the question "Can Jacob Kleinsasser continue to be our elder?"[5]

Among other matters, the opposing ministers believed that Kleinsasser had been unduly influenced by the Bruderhof, a twenty-six-hundred-member communal group with whom the Hutterites had merged in 1974. In 1990 the Dariusleut and the Lehrerleut had ended their own relationships with the Bruderhof and quit recognizing Kleinsasser as the common elder of all three Leut.[6] Many Schmiedeleut ministers believed that without the participation of the Lehrerleut and the Dariusleut, the Schmiedeleut might be unable to forestall a feared Bruderhof takeover.

Supporters of Jacob Kleinsasser rejected the validity of the ministers' vote and did not allow Kleinsasser to step down.[7] The meeting agenda had not indicated that a vote of confidence would be requested, and Edward Kleinsasser describes much of the discussion as "heated and unruly."[8] A second plebiscite was taken at a meeting where nine ministers changed their votes, giving Kleinsasser a close majority. The Bruderhof chipped in with proxy votes from their own Servants of the Word. But a majority of Schmiedeleut colonies refused to recognize the second vote. They complained that many conservative ministers were absent and that these men

Dariusleut and Schmiedeleut men visiting in Manitoba. Courtesy of Max Stanton.

were not allowed to vote by proxy. The dissenters were supported by the Lehrerleut and most Dariusleut colonies.

Since there was no clear winner, things began to get messy. The 1950 Hutterite constitution assumed that Leut elders would serve for life or good behavior; Kleinsasser's supporters did not believe he had done anything to warrant removal from leadership. Kleinsasser himself announced that only colonies that recognized his eldership were true Schmiedeleut, and he placed everyone else in *Meidung* (he shunned them).[9]

This step led to court battles, colony splits, family divisions, and theological controversies—the worst crisis in Hutterite history, at least since the communal-noncommunal divisions in Ukraine and the Dakota Territory in the mid-to-late nineteenth century. Instead of working out a compromise, both sides resorted to threats and counterthreats.

The Schmiedeleut who were more liberal tended to support the leadership of Jacob Kleinsasser. Some of them even viewed the break as a blessing in disguise. Kleinsasser supported the use of English and was open toward musical instruments, higher education, missions, and ecumenical endeavors. His supporters believed that they were resurrecting historic Hutterite positions and viewed the opposition as those for whom "traditions, culture, church laws and the old conservative ways of their forefathers seemed to be their route to finding spiritual salvation."[10] Colonies supporting Kleinsasser call themselves the Hutterian Brethren Schmiedeleut Conference or simply Group One. Other Leut refer to them as the Kleinsasser Group or the Jake K. Group after the elder or, derogatorily, the Oilers, a reference to a bad investment in oil wells (a few colonies were swindled by two men who in 1982 were jailed for fraud).[11]

More conservative Schmiedeleut supported the ministers who were opposed to Jacob Kleinsasser. This group, unofficially called Group Two, was and continues to be much larger than the other Schmiedeleut group. It is led by a committee of American and Canadian ministers instead of a single elder. Although they never formally imposed Meidung on Group One supporters, in November 1994 Group Two leaders instructed Group One colonies to quit using the "Schmiedeleut" name. Group One took this to mean that Group Two no longer recognized them as brothers and sisters in the faith. Group Two is also sometimes called the Gibbs because of its association with banker Donald Gibb, who took a strong anti-Kleinsasser stand in the 1990s. In a lengthy manuscript, Gibb described Kleinsasser's leadership as a "sordid story of deceit, deception and dissipation of Hutterian Brethren assets." The Group One Schmiedeleut responded with a statement from the accountant firm Meyers, Norris, Penny & Company, which accused Gibb of "mixing fact and speculation in the stating of his case." In this book we designate the two groups Schmiedeleut One (liberals) and Schmiedeleut Two (conservatives).[12]

In the early 1990s the anti-Kleinsasser ministers were concerned about multimillion-dollar investments (for example, in gold-mining equipment and a plastics plant), the more centralized governance structure that had developed, the increased use of English in church services, and ecumenical mission projects. They also disliked the Schmiedeleut participation in court proceedings against a recalcitrant member, Daniel Hofer, who accused Kleinsasser's colony (Crystal Spring) of stealing his unpatented wet and dry hog-feeder invention.[13] Crystal Spring disagreed, asserting that their product had its own unique features. For various reasons, Hofer was ultimately excommunicated and asked to leave his home at the Lakeside Colony. When he refused, Hofer and Jacob Kleinsasser ended up in court. Kleinsasser explained that he was "seeking the protection of the court to protect us from a rebellious, destructive situation."[14]

Trying to Find Unity with the Bruderhof

The Schmiedeleut division was tied to the relationship that all Hutterite branches established with a religious society called the Bruderhof beginning in 1931. In the mid-1920s, German Christian socialist Eberhard Arnold discovered that the Hutterites (whom he had read about) still existed. In 1930 he traveled to the United States and Canada to meet them. While in North America, Arnold visited all thirty-three colonies then existing and formally requested a merger between his own small communal group at Sannerz, Germany, and the Hutterites. Eighty-year-old Alberta Hutterite Maria Hofer recalls a tall handsome man who knew little about farming, suffered from eye problems, and was once caught smoking a cigarette. Hofer says that Arnold was sincere in his communal Anabaptist commitments.[15] He had extensive knowledge of church history and theology and he spoke German fluently.

What followed, in 1931, was an unusual merger between an Old Order Anabaptist society and a twentieth-century religious movement, leading to important and in some ways transformative developments. In 1935 Bruderhof members fled to England and Paraguay in reaction to Nazi harassment, and in the 1950s and 1960s they established communities in the eastern United States. But the Hutterite-Bruderhof relationship was always shaky because of ideological, organizational, and cultural differences. The Bruderhof supported ecumenical social and political activities, higher education, and extrabiblical sources of inspiration, for example, the writings of the German theologians Johann Christoph Blumhardt and his son Christoph.

The two groups severed their relationship in 1955 but reestablished it in 1974, when the Bruderhof asked forgiveness for previous actions.[16] The Bruderhof adopted Hutterite dress and expressed eagerness to learn from Hutterite traditions. Many Hutterites in turn believed that the Bruderhof might provide an important revitalizing force for their communities. But by the late 1980s, the Hutterite majority had come to view Bruderhof members as invasive and unwilling to conform to Hutterite cultural and ideological expectations. In 1990 the Lehrerleut and the Dariusleut cut off relations with the Bruderhof. When the Schmiedeleut divided in 1992, the conservative faction followed suit. Then in 1995 even the progressive Schmiedeleut, the biggest backers of the 1974 merger, severed their own organizational ties with the Bruderhof.[17] Table 4.1 summarizes the history of the Hutterite-Bruderhof relationship.

Today there are 61 Group One and 118 Group Two Schmiedeleut colonies. Of the Group One colonies, 50 are in Manitoba, 6 in South Dakota, 3 in Minnesota, 1 in Alberta, and 1 in Nigeria. Group Two has 57 colonies in Manitoba, 52 in South Dakota, 5 in North Dakota, and 4 in Minnesota. The total Schmiedeleut population includes 179 colonies. Map 4.2 shows North American Schmiedeleut community locations.

Schmiedeleut colonies were hit hard by the 1992 division. In some colonies, individuals and families took opposite sides. The Schmiedeleut One (the progressive Kleinsasser group) insisted that Schmiedeleut Two ministers could not perform marriages or carry out other church responsibilities. Some Hutterites switched colony residences; others left communal life, completely fed up with the whole situation. Many colonies split into factions, and at times the courts were asked to intervene to determine which group owned colony assets.

The critique of Jacob Kleinsasser's leadership is reminiscent of the

Table 4.1. The Hutterite-Bruderhof relationship

Years	Status	Group(s)
1920–1930	Unaffiliated	
1930–1955	Full	All Hutterite branches
1955–1974	Unaffiliated	
1974–1990	Full	All Hutterite branches
1990–1992	Affiliated	Schmiedeleut One
1995–present	Unaffiliated	

Johannes Waldner–Jacob Walter clash of the early nineteenth century, as well as the dissatisfaction with Michael Waldner in the 1870s and 1880s.[18] It created an environment in which any Hutterite who was dissatisfied about various matters could now find a reason for leaving his or her colony and joining the other side, or leaving colony life altogether. Many people grew tired of the unrelenting Leut-wide conflict, the personal attacks, the internal family disruptions, the lawsuits, and the threats.

Tension between the two Schmiedeleut groups remains and prompts accusations of impropriety on both sides. Most Dariusleut and Lehrerleut individuals and colonies take the Schmiedeleut Two side. Differences of opinion center on the following issues:

Bruderhof influences. Some Bruderhof influences on education, worship, humanitarian efforts, and aesthetics are noticeable at Schmiedeleut One colonies. Schmiedeleut Two minister John S. Hofer calls the overall influence "liberalization" and notes that it is "ongoing" and rapidly being "institutionalized." Many Hutterites believe that the Bruderhof was trying to remake the Hutterites in their own image. "They thought that we were too dumb and uneducated to stop them from controlling us," says Schmiedeleut One German teacher Dora Maendel, but she also recognizes the positive impact of the Bruderhof-Hutterite pact.[19] Young persons who visited the Bruderhof or hosted Bruderhof members are overwhelmingly positive about those interactions.[20] They liked the exposure to new ideas that broke the mold of the traditional culture. The Hutterites, for their part, "loosened up the Bruderhof," says Lucas Wipf, a one-time member of both groups: "You could always tell when you walked into a Hutterite home. You didn't have to be as careful about what you said."[21]

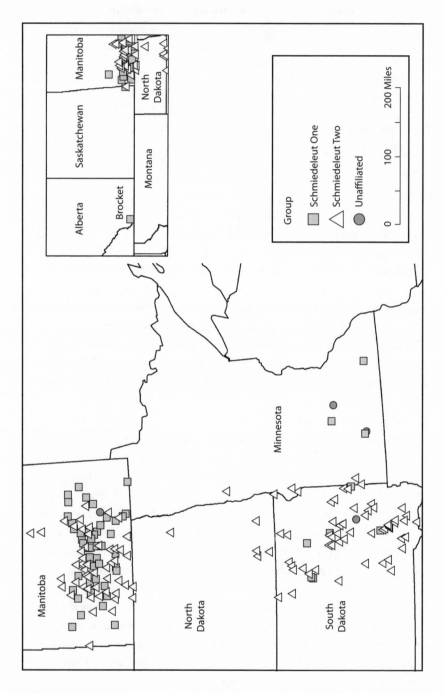

Schmiedeleut colony locations in 2009. Courtesy of Stuart K. McFeeters.

In 1993 Schmiedeleut Two minister Samuel Kleinsasser wrote a lengthy treatise on the Hutterite-Bruderhof relationship, titled "Community and Ethics." In this unpublished but widely distributed two-hundred-page statement, Kleinsasser, a brother of Jacob Kleinsasser, suggests that contact with the Bruderhof was dangerous because the "[Hutterites] had not yet learned the art of hiding their feelings, or of smiling when the heart was cold." Kleinsasser believes that Hutterites were "outwitted" by the Bruderhof and "threatened with acculturation."[22]

Organizational centralization. Schmiedeleut One leaders support a more centralized governance structure than has been traditional among the Schmiedeleut. Group One supporters believe that centralizing the Leut control promotes unity and offers economic benefits. It is reminiscent of Lehrerleut governance models, though the Lehrerleut are at the other end of the conservative-liberal spectrum.

Financial investments. During the 1980s, some progressive Schmiedeleut colonies made novel and often bad investments in stocks and bonds, mining, and oil production. The Schmiedeleut One position is that the colonies involved were just trying to find new ways to make a living in a changing economic environment.

Use of the courts. The Schmiedeleut One went to court to oust excommunicated church member Daniel Hofer, who refused to leave his home as ordered. The Schmiedeleut Two position is that colonies should not ask the government to remove excommunicated members.

Restrictions on colony visits. The Schmiedeleut One does not allow Schmiedeleut Two members to stay overnight, attend worship services, or eat with their members. At least in theory, Schmiedeleut Two does not hold the same restrictive position.

The Schmiedeleut One has placed Schmiedeleut Two members in Meidung, and Group One members refuse to shake hands with Group Two members. When a Group One woman marries a Group Two man, ministers from the bride's group do not attend the ceremony. One member says that "members of Group Two will never get to heaven because they have broken their vows," a comment reminiscent of Schmiedeleut founder Michael Waldner, who in 1875 placed the entire Dariusleut group under excommunication for not recognizing a decision to merge the Wolf Creek and Bon Homme colony governance structures.[23]

Both Schmiedeleut sides admit that mistakes have been made. Schmiedeleut One members regret not ending the Bruderhof relationship earlier. Schmiedeleut Two representatives wish there had been another ministers' meeting in the critical year of decision (1992). But the Schmiedeleut split has also had positive outcomes. By the early 1990s, the Schmiedeleut had grown to more than fifteen thousand members, in more than 150 colonies. Institutionally, it was hard to hold a group that large together. Traditionalists and progressives were engaged in heated conflict. Unlike the Dariusleut, who had their own liberal and conservative factions, the Schmiedeleut had no history of radical individual colony decision-making. After the division, each of the two smaller Schmiedeleut groups had the opportunity to reevaluate its place and purpose in the Hutterite world.

The Schmiedeleut break upended the balance between conservative and liberal colonies. It accelerated progressive tendencies in Schmiedeleut One and conservative directions in Schmiedeleut Two, although much diversity remains at the colony level.[24] In any case, each side has been released to go its own way. In a negative sense, this result works against the development of a spirit of moderation. Yet by providing the opportunity for the groups to move in different directions, the split has in many cases reduced rather than increased levels of conflict.

The break has also forced both groups to look carefully at Hutterite beliefs and practices: to evaluate weaknesses as well as strengths. In both Leut there is now a greater emphasis on understanding the history of the Hutterite church as well as social and theological issues that had often been taken for granted. The Bruderhof relationship, in an intriguing, unexpected, and ironic way, has promoted greater collective self-awareness among all the Leut, including the Lehrerleut and the Dariusleut, if only because these groups feel the need to defend their positions more knowledgeably and articulately.

This picture harks back to the 1870s, when three small groups, none bigger than a large colony today, held irreconcilable differences. Then, too, friends and relatives were positioned against one another in an extremely uncomfortable situation. An outside (Mennonite) force exerted considerable influence, especially on the fourth (noncommunal) Hutterian group. Yet all three communal Leut eventually thrived with separate organizations. It took a few generations for tensions to subside and for critiques to be iterated in cultural instead of theological language. But eventually stasis was achieved. If the experience of the three much smaller Hutterite

groups in the 1870s is repeated, Schmiedeleut reunification may never occur. But while family relationships remain close, there is always a chance
that Schmiedeleut reunification may occur in the years ahead.

Inter-Leut Contacts

Within each Leut there are many cross-colony relationships. One finds
intercolony male and female work crews engaged in building projects,
harvesting, slaughtering, and preparing for weddings and funerals. Much
visiting and many exchanges of information occur. Inter-Leut relationships are much less frequent, especially if they involve the geographically
distant Schmiedeleut.

When they live in the same area, colony leaders in different Leut sometimes visit with each other. There is also some inter-Leut contact at Hutterite educational conferences and in times of emergency. When a collapsed
hog barn needs to be rebuilt, a fire needs to be put out, or a few more laborers are needed in the garden, neighboring colonies help. The women of the
New Rosedale (Schmiedeleut Two) and Fairholme (Schmiedeleut One)
colonies help each other with baking whenever there is a funeral.[25] When
the Schmiedeleut Two James Valley Colony, in Manitoba, lost its kitchen
in a fire, the Schmiedeleut One Starlite Colony sent firefighters.[26] Weekly
donations of hot meals, food supplies, and kitchen equipment continued
until a temporary kitchen was constructed.

There are other contacts as well. In one case a Dariusleut woman consulted a Lehrerleut physical therapist. A girl at a Dariusleut colony in
Alberta is a pen pal of a Schmiedeleut Two girl in Manitoba. In 2005
a van-load of Dariusleut Hutterites from Washington visited a dozen
Schmiedeleut One and Schmiedeleut Two colonies in Manitoba. When
traveling, Hutterites often dine, worship, and stay overnight at the colonies of other Leut. Members also visit each other's book centers and occasionally share cups of coffee downtown. Dariusleut farm manager Paul
M. Wipf spent a week at a Schmiedeleut One colony exchanging ideas
on agriculture, new industries, and theology. Schmiedeleut One members
speak positively about the hospitality of Alberta Dariusleut members who
hosted a group of their vacationing youth.[27] In general, cell phone, e-mail,
and unlimited telephone plans are increasing communication across the
Hutterite world.

In solidarity, however, most Hutterites are critical of the directions in which Schmiedeleut One is going. They fear that more liberal practices may eventually affect their groups as well. The modern English hymns of Schmiedeleut One composer Butch Wipf, for example, are sung by young people across Leut lines. Further complicating matters, in 2005 the excommunicated Dariusleut colony Brocket, in Alberta, joined the Schmiedeleut One. It was the first time in Hutterite history that a colony changed Leut associations.

For a summary of the numbers and locations of Hutterite colonies of the four Leut, see table 4.2. Included are 179 Schmiedeleut, 159 Dariusleut, 139 Lehrerleut, and 6 unaffiliated colonies. Residency in all colonies is about forty-nine thousand.

Table 4.2. Hutterite colonies, 2009

	Dariusleut	Lehrerleut	Schmiedeleut		Unaffiliated	Total
			One	Two		
Canada						
Alberta	102	72	1	0	1	176
British Columbia	2	0	0	0	0	2
Manitoba	0	0	50	57	1	108
Saskatchewan	32	32	0	0	1	65
Total Canada	136	104	51	57	3	351
United States						
Minnesota	0	0	3	4	2	9
Montana	15	35	0	0	0	50
North Dakota	1	0	0	5	0	6
Oregon	1	0	0	0	0	1
South Dakota	0	0	6	52	1	59
Washington	5	0	0	0	0	5
Total USA	22	35	9	61	3	130
Japan	1	0	0	0	0	1
Nigeria	0	0	1	0	0	1
Grand Total	159	139	61	118	6	483

❦ ❧

NOTWITHSTANDING INCREASED DEFECTION RATES and smaller family sizes than in the past, the Hutterite population in all Leut continues to grow rapidly, more quickly than membership in most North American Protestant denominations. The return rate for unbaptized runaways exceeds 75 percent, and the average age of colony members is under twenty-one. When one visits a Hutterite colony, a striking impression continues to be the large number of children everywhere.[28] In addition to the 483 Hutterite colonies, there are also dozens of colony "farms," which are colonies-in-formation. Hundreds of Hutterites live there as advance personnel, setting up agricultural operations, building roads, and constructing houses, as they prepare the new commune for permanent settlement.

Hutterites comment often on the differences that set them apart. A Lehrerleut woman is asked if she knows anyone who has married into any of the Dariusleut colonies nearby. "None that I can think of," she says. "For myself, I really don't think I could have ever married a Dariusleut." When asked why, she replies, "Oh, it's just that the Dariusleut women dress so funny." In the 1990s, Ruth Lambach attended the wedding of a Schmiedeleut Two woman and a Dariusleut man. Lambach reported, "You would have thought she was being prepared to go live on Mars because she was going to have to get used to so many new and different habits."[29]

Even counting exceptions, the Lehrerleut is the most conservative branch of the Hutterites. The Dariusleut and Schmiedeleut Two hold the middle ground, while the Schmiedeleut One is the most liberal in cultural and religious matters. When it comes to foundational beliefs and practices, however, there is much more that ties the four Hutterite groups together than that which sets them apart, especially when Hutterites as a whole are compared to the more individualistic church and social groups that predominate in North America. Chapter 5 treats those unifying elements, Hutterite theology and ecclesiology.

CHAPTER 5

Beliefs and Practices

*Gelassenheit is the name of the refining fire that proves whether what
looked like faith was only a delusion.*
—Andreas Ehrenpreis, church elder, 1650

Community of Goods

ommunity of goods, the central identifying characteristic of the
Hutterites, is based on particular interpretations of the Bible that
are supported by Hutterite sermons and hymns. Arising from
these sources, Hutterite practices are backed up by the Ordnungen and by
a serious commitment to church discipline. Each Hutterite colony operates like a small, well-functioning village, with a strong sense of communal responsibility. Individuals willingly give up personal desires for the
good of the brotherhood-sisterhood, as expressed in a Hutterite sermon
on 1 Corinthians: "Just as wine is made of many grapes, pressed, crushed,
joined and merged together in one pure liquid, so also we have been called
together from many peoples with many opinions."[1] Although communitarian ideals are frequently emphasized in Hutterite sermons, they are
rarely discussed. Instead they are lived out through work, worship, and
social interaction. "Specific actions are judged by whether they are communal or self-serving,"[2] says Hutterite Patrick Murphy.

In the Hutterite view, everything that happens at the colony is part of
a divinely structured plan; all things have their proper place. Property is

shared; lives are lived in submission to others. The colony is the "gathered community of saints," and every person, regardless of personal idiosyncrasies, is valued and respected.[3] Hutterites believe they are engaged in a constant battle between good and evil, between the carnal (individualistic) and spiritual (communal) sides of men and women. The only way individualism may be overcome, the only way to experience a bit of heaven on earth, is to live communally. Hutterites remind each other that Jesus said to pray "*Our* Father," not "*My* Father."

Communal life is supported by the Ordnungen, which reflect organically the will of God at a particular time and place for a specific group of people. The Ordnungen preserve the proto-utopian plan even as they deal with apparently mundane matters. Hutterites believe that religious faith is a lifelong journey and adventure, essentially related to the community. Donald Kraybill asks a Hutterite whether he is "saved." He responds, "Ask my wife and some of the brothers."[4] God is the ultimate judge, but it is the community that decides whether to accept a person into the church, and the church holds the "keys" to the kingdom of heaven as God's representative on earth.

Kraybill and Bowman note that Old Order faith is practical, gentle, humble, constant, and all-inclusive. Communal living goes a step further, demanding and exhibiting unity more than any other socioeconomic structure. Jacob Hutter wrote, "He led us together to serve Him in unity and to show that God himself is one and undivided."[5] The words "Community in Unity," emblazoned on a sign at the entrance to a colony in South Dakota, appropriately characterize the Hutterite way of life.

Hutterites call non-Hutterites *Weltleut* (worldly people), outsiders, or "English." They hold an ethnocentric worldview that is infused with spiritual meaning and is similar to that found in many traditional societies throughout the world. In the United States and Canada it is an increasingly outdated notion, because of multicultural commitments and relativistic perspectives as well as widespread cross-ethnic marriage. But the Hutterites continue to view the world in culturally dualistic terms.

The Lehren

Of the many singular traditions the Hutterites have developed over the years, one of the most important is the practice of holding daily worship services. The focus of these meetings is to read the Lehren (sermons), which help Hutterites interpret the Bible and provide spiritual guidance. In the Hutterite view, Christian community of goods is founded on the Bible, and the Bible is best interpreted by sacred works like the Lehren.

Most of the four hundred sermons were drafted by Hutterite ministers in Slovakia between 1629 and 1665. Excerpts from the twenty-six sermons that are found in the second Chronicle (the *Kleingeshichtsbuch*) were written between 1652 and 1659, primarily at the Kesselsdorf community, which served as an unofficial seminary for Hutterite ministers. With a few exceptions, the Hutterite sermon canon was closed after the seventeenth century. Most of the Lehren were thus written right after the physical and psychological devastation of the Thirty Years War, a time when the Hutterite population decreased from forty thousand to two thousand. Survivors were trying to reestablish an earlier spiritual vitality, and the Lehren were central to this endeavor.

Hutterite elder Andreas Ehrenpreis coordinated the creation of the sermon collection in order to provide theological unity for those who remained in the communal villages. The Lehren not only review basic communitarian tenets; they are filled with attacks on spiritually weak members. While recognizing the torturous experience of physical persecution, the sermon writers rail against falling asleep in church, cursing, slander, holding individual property, greediness, ethical laxness, and spiritual apostasy.

Hutterites believe that the Lehren are inspired by God and continue to be the best way to find out what the Bible means and how Christians should live. A Lehr typically begins with lengthy passages from the Old or New Testament, followed by verse-by-verse exegesis and practical suggestions for daily life. Nearly 50 percent of the sermon content is iteration of biblical text.

Although the authors of specific Lehren are not widely known, major sermon writers include H. F. Kuentsche, Caspar Eglauch, Mathias Binder, Johannes Milder, Tobias Bertsch, and Andreas Ehrenpreis.[6] Because there are different authors, a few sermons are based on the same Bible text. Each of the Hutterite Leut also read slightly different renditions of the Lehren. Schmiedeleut sermons, for example, are often shorter than Dariusleut sermons.[7] The sermons are traditionally read in a chanting style that stresses the importance of words and concepts, not the individual delivering them.

At Sunday morning services, and also on special religious holidays, the sermon is preceded by a preface or foreword (*Vorred*).[8] Like the Lehr, the Vorred is an expository meditation on selected Bible verses, but it is less exegetical.

Analysis of the Schmiedeleut list of 378 sermons indicates that by a three-to-one ratio, Lehren texts favor the New Testament over the Old Testament. Among the 108 sermons from the Old Testament, the apocryphal books of Ecclesiasticus, Sirach, and Tobit, which emphasize the importance of good works, tradition, and peoplehood, are especially popular. The Psalms, with 44 sermons, are also prominent. The Schmiedeleut list includes 149 sermons based on the Gospels. Sixty-nine of these comment on verses from the book of Matthew, revealing the central place of Jesus's life and teaching in Hutterite theology. The New Testament epistles are the subject of another 119 sermons, with 1 John (21 sermons) the epistle used the most. By reading the Lehren at every church service, the Hutterites ensure that their beliefs and practices are clear and do not change. This practice and the maintenance of traditions make it easier to keep the Christian community unified.

Most Hutterite colonies possess at least one hundred of the Lehren. In the past most ministers copied the sermons by hand, simultaneously becoming familiar with the content. Others asked family members with good penmanship to make the copies, or they inherited collections from other ministers. Today most sermon compilations are photocopied, and in each Leut there are colonies that have collections for sale. In some cases the Lehren are scanned electronically and digitally enhanced. Ex-Hutterite Robert Rhodes wonders whether the move away from handwritten copies has decreased comprehension of Lehren content. Most Hutterite ministers do not share this concern, but lay members note that they can usually tell, by the way that the sermon is read, whether a minister has studied the content ahead of time.[9]

Because many of the sermons are long, it is common for ministers to spend five to six services on a single Lehr, beginning with a preface on Sunday morning and continuing with the sermon throughout the week. During the calendar year, each minister keeps a careful record of sermons read and hymns sung at each church service.[10]

The Lehren, which are considered specially blessed, are, with a few exceptions, the only sermons delivered in the colonies. Said one Hutterite woman, they "answer any question about any issue that is important for us in our daily lives."[11] For the most part, the sermons are delivered in German, although some progressive colonies use English translations when there are people present who do not understand German. Or in such cases the minister may deliver the sermon in German but use English in some other part of the service. Some ministers go a step further, at times breaking into English to "keep people awake." At one colony the minister read the sermon in German but switched to English when reading the Bible. Schmiedeleut One elder Jacob Kleinsasser has published English translations of dozens of the Lehren, using an interpretive process that takes seriously the nuanced theological meaning of each word of the text.[12]

Occasionally some ministers make contextual "transmediations" with comments "off the sermon" to elucidate main points. Dariusleut minister Paul S. Gross was well known for this practice. In summer 2006, Schmiedeleut One minister Mack Waldner interrupted his sermon-reading five or six times to make practical suggestions.

Exceptions to the seventeenth-century sermon canon include a few written in the sixteenth century and seven sermons composed by Lehrerleut minister Andrew Gross in the 1930s and 1940s. Gross's sermons are viewed as spirit-filled by all Hutterite branches despite their very recent origin. At some Schmiedeleut colonies, one Gross sermon is read every year.[13]

Hutterite sermons are not for the fainthearted; they are filled with hard-hitting commentary. The sermons make strong moral demands and assume that Christians will have to make great sacrifices. They are practical, down-to-earth, and filled with analogies from animal life, as in this communitarian entreaty from the sermon on Acts 2, the Pentecost Sermon: "For dogs and cats are unable to share. Bad music is there, for one can see with one's eyes and hear with one's ears how they share their drink and food with grumbling, showing teeth, biting."[14]

A sermon on Matthew 6 includes an attack on people who let their minds stray while sitting in church: "They sit during a sermon from the word of God, their hearts and minds wander[ing] after some other temporal things which they love." Another section of the same Lehr gets more specific: "In the same way . . . a woman who besides her husband, looks at young boys, hangs her mind on them and wants to love them, is not true, honest and right."[15]

Many sermons speak out against pride and arrogance. The Matthew 6 Lehr includes the following comment: "There is no creature in this world that makes such a pitiful mockery . . . as man. This praying, swearing, and cussing makes a poor harmony."[16] Another description of "Christian" self-ishness is found in the Acts 2 sermon: "As soon as the pigs are brought home from the field and driven to the trough, one hears and sees how they grunt, whine and scuffle, step into the trough, slobber and squeal so that others dare not approach. Therefore it is impossible for godless men to live together." In the same sermon the writer notes, "One cannot see any more evidence of rebirth in them than in a pig or a dog. They sit like the cowbird in their nests of human excrement, with their natural crown, their proud feathers."[17]

The Vorred to the traditional New Year's Day sermon, based on Sirach 2, begins with the statement "We should be conscious of our precious time and use it worthwhile while we can."[18] A sermon on 1 Thessalonians 5:1–11 asks members to avoid "carnal works," warning, "By the drunken ones we understand . . . all those that are led astray by false doctrine and are ensnared and entrapped by closed-mindedness and unbelief in their hearts."[19]

Reverence for the Lehren is criticized by ex-members who join evangelical Protestant churches. They believe that God continues to give ministers spiritually authoritative insights and see the Lehren as restrictive works that limit the leading of the Holy Spirit. Hutterites themselves admit that many members do not fully comprehend the sometimes archaic German that is found in the sermons (the Lehren employ the Froschauer translation of the Bible). It is also true that although standard German is taught in the Hutterite German School, it is not used in daily conversation. Neither do members understand some of the sermons' historical references. A widely distributed 2007 letter from a German teacher notes as well that the sermons have lost much of their significance for young people.[20] In response, other Hutterites claim that sermons delivered in other Christian denominations often praise God but do not emphasize the importance of following Jesus in daily life. Most Hutterites value the Lehren and say that, during the week, they reflect often on sermon content.

The Lehren have not traditionally been made available to the general public or even to church members,[21] but a change may come about in connection with a Schmiedeleut One project, Die Quelle, which is placing historical and theological materials on computer disks. At an October 2006 meeting, participants expressed differences of opinion on whether the sermons should be part of the project. Some suggested that the sermons' sacred character would be diluted; words and phrases might be taken out of context. One minister said that a wide distribution of the sermons might decrease church attendance. There was also concern that non-Hutterites might find theological inconsistencies or misread sermon sections owing to insufficient understanding of references. But German teachers in attendance said that access to the Lehren would make them better prepared to connect sermon content with the German School and Sunday School curriculum.

Hutterites also recognize the importance of four volumes of epistles written by early ministers and evangelists. According to Robert Friedmann, these epistles give the Hutterites "a higher education in the discipleship of Christ." In 2000 the Schmiedeleut Two published a sixty-four-page theological statement, *The Hutterian Church Responds to Questions of Faith*, which provides a detailed statement about the uniqueness of Hutterite faith and life in the twenty-first century.[22]

The Word of God

The Hutterites are Trinitarians with regard to the relationship between God, Jesus, and the Holy Spirit. They believe in the divinity and humanity of Jesus and adhere to all parts of the Apostle's Creed. For Hutterites, the Lehren, their confession of faith, and Hutterite epistles and hymns do not constitute the foundation of the Christian faith but instead are Spirit-guided elucidations of the "Word of God" that Hutterites believe is found in the Bible. The sermons ensure the existence of a stable and unified interpretation. But this does not mean that members do not revere the Bible. Some follow yearly reading plans, often using the seventeenth-century King James translation. Others are involved in small Bible study groups.

The Lehren's approach to biblical exegesis is based upon the following Anabaptist principles:

Progressive revelation. Structurally, the Bible is viewed progressively, with the New Testament taking precedence over the Old Testament as a kind of canon within the canon. Old Testament passages are read through the lens of the New Testament, and many teachings and events are interpreted figuratively. For example, Old Testament religious festivals are viewed as early forms of Christian celebrations. The Easter sacrifice of Christ is compared to the slaughter of lambs in the Old Testament Passover, while the Hutterite Easter sermon suggests that Moses prefigured Christ.[23] Old Testament books are also valued for their many practical teachings.

Christocentrism. The Hutterites believe that Old Testament verses have to be assessed on the basis of Jesus's life and teaching, since Jesus is the supreme revelation of God. Everything is evaluated in light of his teaching, which at times overrules Old Testament understandings. For example, in Matthew 5:38–39, Jesus says, "You have heard how it was said: *Eye for eye and tooth for tooth,*" but then adds, "But I say this to you: Offer no resistance to the wicked."

Hutterites recognize a hierarchy of teaching even within the New Testament. If Paul appears to contradict Jesus, Hutterites interpret his words on the basis of Jesus's own statements. The Sermon on the Mount is particularly important. As one sermon preface puts it, "Jesus has shown us the will of God very clearly in the Sermon on the Mount. Even if we would not possess anything else of the Holy Scriptures, this would be enough for us to know God's holy will."[24]

Direct experience. Hutterites believe that correct biblical interpretation is based on a personal experience with Jesus and on the continued direction of the Holy Spirit within the context of the church community. "Jesus shows us that all reading and explaining of the Scripture is of no help to a person unless he personally comes to Jesus Christ," exhorts a sermon preface.[25] Humility and ethical living are also essential to a correct comprehension of the Bible.

Communal accountability. Conclusions about the Christian faith reached by individuals must agree with those taught by Hutterite church leaders and those found in the confession of faith. All Hutterites listen to scripture readings regularly at church services. Young people study and memorize Bible verses in German classes and Sunday School. Aside from ministers, German teachers are the most biblically literate colony residents. They are the ones who explain the meaning of the sermons to young Hutterites.

Prayer

Like most Christians, Hutterites believe in the importance of daily prayer. Direct communication with God is essential to faith, and not only in a collective or public sense. Many Hutterite prayers are formulaic, for example, those said at mealtimes and bedtime. But the communication is personal and direct. In progressive colonies, prayers are more spontaneous. The authors have listened to hundreds of Hutterite prayers and find that a major theme is the importance of showing respect to others in order to bring honor to God.

Every Hutterite participates in morning and evening prayers. Prayers are also said before and after every meal and snack and (for some young mothers) before and after breastfeeding. The standard *Nachtischgebet* (prayer after a meal) reads as follows:

> *Gott lob und dank für Speis' und Trank.*
> *Gottes Segen hat uns gespeiset leiblich.*
> *So bitten wir Dich, speis' uns Herr auch*
> *Viel mehr geistlich, durch Jesum Christum. Amen.*
> (We praise God and thank Him for food and drink.
> His blessings have nourished our bodies.
> So now we ask Thee Lord, nourish us even more, spiritually.
> Through Jesus Christ. Amen.)[26]

Humility and Suffering

The Hutterites believe in an afterlife where individuals are rewarded or condemned for their actions on earth. The individual's eternal state is tied to present behavior, as God's grace and good works are sewn together in a seamless theological web.

According to Hutterite teaching, true followers of Jesus will imitate him and experience persecution. They expect to be harassed verbally and in other ways. Because they assume that life on earth will be filled with a certain amount of physical and emotional suffering, when criticism comes—and it comes regularly from neighbors, the media, and disaffected ex-members—they usually let it roll right off their backs.[27] Throughout their lives they have sung the stories of the Anabaptist martyrs from the

Hutterite *Gesangbuch* (songbook). In the Hutterite view, suffering with humility purifies the body and soul and provides a sense of joy if done for the sake of the gospel.

Humility extends to all areas of life. It is not acceptable, for example, to boast too much about personal accomplishments. The Matthew 6 Lehr teaches, "And because it is not pleasing to God, that one shall seek his own glory here on earth, Christ warns his own that they shall not do like the hypocrites and false clergy over which Christ spoke His woe, and that his own shall not seek outward glory and saintliness."[28] It is not appropriate to express the desire to serve in specific colony leadership positions. Although "it is permissible to think moderately well of oneself," there are significant social boundaries that impose much tighter controls on the ego than are found in most Western societies. These are similar to the forceful injunctions against pride and self-promotion found in traditional societies in many parts of the world. In Dympna Ugwu-Oju's book *What Will My Mother Say?* she notes similar communal strictures in the Nigerian village where she was raised.[29]

In the Hutterite context, humility even applies to the way hymns are sung: they are to be rendered with volume, power, and emotion, regardless of one's musical training or individual giftedness. Dora Maendel recalls: "As a child in German School one of the most frequently repeated admonitions we heard was about singing along whole heartedly—no matter where the singing was—in Sunday School, church, at home or even as a visitor in any of these situations. The expectation was that a child of God/a people of God should be known by the regularity of praise rendered."[30]

It is not easy to be humble. How does one exhibit this characteristic, for example, while confidently expressing the correctness of one's faith? Ideological certainty and social stability denote a measure of pride, but Hutterites must continually fight against this feeling. The conflict between *Hochmut* (pride) and *Demut* (humility) is ongoing. Hutterites like to be congratulated on their beautiful gardens and tasty food, but their response is usually to say that "anyone could do it" or to point to shortcomings such as an improperly weeded row of plants or an overcooked piece of meat.

Hutterites love to discuss controversial issues and often show unexpected flexibility in the course of these conversations. But a sense of community-determined correctness always places a brake on how far such discussions are allowed to go. Hutterites continue to view the world in fairly black-and-white terms.

In 2005 Dutch anthropologist Martine Vonk conducted research at dozens of Schmiedeleut colonies to determine what "values" Hutterites considered most important. She found that at the top of the list was a "spiritual life," defined as communally infused commitment to God and the church. Also important were "respect for tradition," "self-discipline," "accepting one's place in this life," "obedience," and "inner harmony," all necessary qualities in a commune.[31]

Worshipping God

There are two Hutterite worship service formats: the *Gebet*, a daily twenty- to thirty-minute service that precedes supper, and the *Lehr*, the ninety-minute Sunday morning service. Among the church services, the Saturday evening Gebet is especially important because, for Hutterites, this is when the day of rest begins.

The daily Gebet is scheduled as early as 5:00 p.m. during the winter and as late as 7:00 p.m. during the summer. In summer, and during other heavy work periods, the Gebet is often canceled if few men are able to attend; but colony practices vary. One Thursday evening in August, when a minister was asked whether the colony would be having Gebet, he responded, "We'll have it. We can spend at least twenty minutes of our day with God."[32] During the same month, however, another colony canceled the rarely skipped Saturday evening service. Church services are held most consistently among the Lehrerleut.

For Hutterites, every day of the week is sacred. Before moving to Russia in the late 1700s, Hutterites occasionally worked on Sundays, not considering it holier than any other day.[33] They rested only so that neighbors would not take offense at their way of doing things.[34] Sunday work was completely discontinued after the Hutterites moved to Russia, although farm animals were fed and distilleries and mills did not shut down. For modern Hutterites, the day of rest begins on Saturday evening and ends about twenty-four hours later. For most of them, Sunday evening is set aside for visiting friends and relatives. But other members change into work clothes after Sunday Gebet and return to regular tasks and functions, especially during planting and harvest seasons.

Hutterites leaving the Gebet (daily church) service. Courtesy of Max Stanton.

Attendance at church services varies depending on work responsibilities and personal interest. One of the sermons criticizes those who do not come to church, quoting five lengthy Bible passages and noting, "Often they have very little desire and love for God's Word . . . There are even those who have a hard time to walk across the yard [to the church service]."[35] Traditionally in North America, young boys and girls watched carefully to see when the senior minister left his house and started walking toward the church building. This was the signal for everyone else to follow. Today most colonies use intercom systems to call members to services. Hutterites wear their best formal dress to Saturday evening and Sunday morning services. During the week, they put on normal colony garb after changing out of their dirty work clothes. No one goes to Gebet straight from the hog barn or the fields.

The Hutterite worship service is simple but highly programmed, following an order that has changed little since the 1870s. During the service, the senior and assistant (second) minister sit on a long bench or chairs at the front of the church. Other members of the church council are seated to their right. Among the Lehrerleut, the German teacher also sits up front, in order to keep an eye on younger children, who are seated in the front rows. As people walk into the church, men move to the left and women to the right, and members take their seats according to age. Members under discipline sit in the church entrance or hallway. Visitors are seated in the back row.

A typical evening service begins with one of the ministers announcing, "We will begin our service in the name of the Lord with song," followed by a hymn. The minister (in this context called the *Vorsänger*, or song leader) lines out or recites the first line of the hymn, providing the words and the melody. The congregation sings out in response. Then a second line is read, and so forth. Lining out was introduced during an earlier era when hymn lyrics were sung from memory, but it is still an important practice because Hutterite hymnals do not include musical notation and there is no instrumental accompaniment, not even a tuning fork. Only by tradition would one know that the seventh line of hymn number 136 in the *Gesangbuchlein* is to be repeated before singing line eight. Hymns are selected based on their relevance to sermon content. Most consist of many verses, and it is common to hear congregants slow down as the hymn proceeds, or to slip into off-key modes. When this happens, the Vorsänger raises his voice to get the rest of the congregation to sing in key or faster.

After the hymn and opening words, one of the ministers reads from the Lehr. In liberal colonies, it is done with expression; in conservative colonies in a two-level monotone chant. The reading is followed by a prayer about five minutes in length, during which parishioners kneel on what is often a hard linoleum or tiled floor. This ends the Gebet. Colony ministers take turns reading the sermons. If a minister from another colony is present, he is usually asked to do the reading.

In North America Hutterites historically worshipped in schoolhouses and did not construct separate church buildings, but this practice is becoming less and less common. Some new colony churches seat 250 or more people to accommodate the large crowds that gather for weddings and funerals. Churches often have carpeted floors or rug samples to kneel on, and some have padded benches and air-conditioning. The Lehrerleut attach their chapels to colony dining halls so that members can walk directly from the church service to the evening meal without going outdoors.

The Gebet is an important part of Hutterite life and is woven into the fabric of what makes the Hutterites a unique people. It helps maintain a consistent spiritual focus for all colony members every day of the week. After a day of work, Hutterites of all ages (with the exception of infants, who are cared for by young babysitters) sit in the stillness of a simple building, waiting on God. They sing the lyrics of ancient hymns and listen to sermons that explain what the Bible means in everyday life. In this time of quiet contemplation, the Hutterites invite God to break into the environs of the natural world. The hauntingly melodic monophonic form of the hymns harks back to a different time and place; past and future are tied together in a separate realm that lies apart from the rest of human life. Former Hutterite Robert Rhodes recalls, "In the colony, I recall many evenings—there was a half-hour service most weekdays before supper—silently parsing recent concerns as we all sat in our church room, the winter wind fogging the row of darkened windows. I have heard many Hutterites say that *Gebet*, as the service was called, had salvaged for them many unpleasant days. I knew what they meant, having experienced such reprieves many times."[36]

Sunday morning church services are longer than those held on weekdays. Typically the Sunday Lehr begins with five or six verses from a song.

The interior of a modern Hutterite church. Courtesy of Max Stanton.

The service proceeds with a Vorred (sermon preface), prayers, the sermon, and a closing hymn. The Vorrede are more practical than the Lehren, containing many personal stories and words of encouragement. They are also less blunt in their critique of non-Hutterites and therefore less likely to offend the uninitiated.[37] At times, topically appropriate preface sections are also read at Gebet. There are special church services, with special sermons, for baptisms, weddings, funerals, and holidays.

Selecting Ministers

Hutterites choose ministers by casting lots, in a somewhat complicated procedure that they believe gives God a special and direct role in the process. The lot-casting process includes democratic elements, for example, in the nomination procedure and the probationary period that follows selection. Ordained Hutterite ministers usually serve for life. They are treated with great respect and wield significant influence within the colony.

Throughout most of Hutterite history, when a pastor was needed, the community held special meetings at which male members named those who had appropriate gifts. These names were placed into the lot. The process varied from time to time, and often a nominee was required to receive a minimum number of votes (perhaps five) before being presented. In 1782, for example, Johannes Waldner received twenty votes, while two other nominees received one or two votes each; the lot was then deemed unnecessary.

Astrid von Schlachta writes that during the Hutterites' first years of existence, the lot selection process was often bypassed. Founder Jacob Hutter, for example, was not chosen by lot; he was selected after "eight days and nights" of prayer. The church had just stripped leadership responsibilities from Simon Schutzinger, after discovering that Schutzinger's wife had held back money from the common treasury. A few years later, Peter Riedemann confirmed that having more than one nominee was not always necessary: "If . . . there is only one or just as many as needed, we need no lot, for the Lord has shown him or them to us."[38]

In the late 1500s, however, oral tradition suggests that the lot selection process was institutionalized and ministers were usually chosen this way until the late eighteenth century.[39] After the Hutterites moved to Ukraine, the record shows greater diversity. In 1857 the Chronicle notes that two men, Jacob Wipf and Martin Waldner, were chosen by a "majority vote," then confirmed "after a time of testing."[40] In North America the Hutterites resumed the tradition of casting lots.

With regard to this practice, the Hutterites emphasize two Bible verses. In the Old Testament, Proverbs 16:33 states, "In the fold of the garment the lot is thrown, but from Yahweh comes the decision." To Hutterites, this shows that God is the decision-making authority in the selection process. Similarly in the New Testament, the writer records in Acts 1:23−26: "Having nominated two candidates, Joseph known as Barsabbas, whose surname was Justus, and Matthias, they prayed, 'Lord, you can read everyone's heart; show us therefore which of these two you have chosen to take over this ministry and apostolate, which Judas abandoned to go to his proper place.' They then drew lots for them, and as the lot fell to Matthias, he was listed as one of the twelve apostles."

The ongoing attraction of lot-casting lies in the direct role that God is believed to play in the process. Outsiders may view it as a random event, but Hutterites believe that God is spiritually present in the room; there is no intermediary. In what they see as a sacred procedure, God, through the power of the Holy Spirit, makes the final determination concerning who becomes a minister, even if that person feels unworthy of the responsibility. Lot-casting is one of very few times in the Anabaptist or Hutterite experience when—according to Hutterites' understanding—God's direct power is seen and experienced in a public and unmediated way. It is an extremely powerful ritual, an observance with corollaries in the Roman Catholic celebration of the Mass, wherein the body and blood of Jesus are believed to be physically and spiritually present.

The lot selection process eliminates individualistic calls to ministry. Because church leaders are always chosen from within the colony, it also exemplifies the principle that the congregation should have detailed knowledge about their spiritual leaders; it is important to know their families, their general character, and even their youthful indiscretions. This public knowledge keeps ministers humble. Selection from within also ensures that there are church leaders in the making in every community. It is believed that God wants these men to be his spiritual representatives regardless of their past behavior. One new minister jokingly says that at the time he was chosen, his arm was in a cast because of an altercation that took place during an arm-wrestling contest.[41]

Hutterite ministers serve for the rest of their life unless serious moral infractions or health issues interfere. Selection by lot does not result in a life without sin, but the lifelong nature of the appointment means that differences of opinion and personal conflicts are usually worked out. A long-held custom has been that ministers ate their meals privately, to symbolize their special standing in the community. In Lehrerleut, most Dariusleut, and many Schmiedeleut Two colonies, the practice continues. Food is taken from the kitchen to the home of the senior minister. Colony guests are often invited to dine with the ministers.

In the early 2000s, Leut selection processes vary. When a minister is needed in a Schmiedeleut One colony, members of a special advisory board (the colony minister, the Leut elder, and members of the Leut's executive committee) nominate two candidates. A selection meeting follows. After a short sermon and prayer, male colony members and visiting ministers vote individually and vocally. A candidate must receive at least five votes to have his name placed into the lot. If only one qualified candidate emerges, either the process is repeated or the individual is selected without lot-casting.

Nominations to ministerial positions are based on the criteria enunciated in 1 Timothy 3, which include good moral character, sobriety, vigilance, and parenting skills. If two nominees qualify, the words *Du bist der Prediger* (you are the minister) are written or printed on a piece of paper, which is placed inside one of two or three Bibles or alongside one or two blank sheets under a hat. After prayer, the lot is cast as each nominee walks forward and selects a Bible or a scrap of paper.

Dariusleut and Schmiedeleut Two minister nominations are made by individual colony leaders after the male members place their votes. At least five votes are needed to become a candidate, and usually at least two qualified people are chosen as finalists. This choice is made prior to the annual meeting of the Leut ministers, where the names are reviewed before being placed in the lot. Among the Lehrerleut, the ministers of all of the Lehrerleut colonies are involved in the nomination process, and at least fifteen votes are required to qualify for the lot.

Once selected, the new church leader becomes a "second" or assistant minister, and there is a period of probation before formal ordination. Peter Riedemann writes, "no one is confirmed in his service unless he has first been tested and revealed to the church."[42] In some cases, the probationary period may last five or six years. The Hutterites want to be sure that the right person has been selected.

Ministers' responsibilities are varied, with spiritual and secular responsibilities intertwined. They organize church services, read the sermons, provide spiritual leadership, ensure church discipline, and give counsel. The sermons make it clear that their primary duty is to warn and admonish those who need warning or admonishment.[43] But ministers are involved in all aspects of colony life. Each morning after breakfast, the ministers meet with the business manager and the farm manager to discuss major projects and responsibilities for the day or the week ahead, as well as personal or social issues. Ministers cosign checks and are fully involved in colony decision-making. In years past, it was common for ministers to be honored by receiving better food and lodging than other members, a situation that resulted in criticism of the minister.[44] Ministers are no longer given higher-quality meals or living quarters than others, but they do have greater freedom of movement outside the colony.

Some ministers compare their roles to that of Old Testament priests, but all are integral parts of the colony labor force. They expect to be respected but know that they have to earn such respect. During times of heavy work responsibilities, seeding, and harvest, it is not uncommon to find ministers operating combines and other farm machinery. Many, especially younger assistant ministers, also take on special responsibilities such as beekeeping, wine-making, colony landscaping, or gardening.

During our visits to various Hutterite colonies, we have observed first-hand such participation by ministers. At one colony farm, a seventy-five-year-old Lehrerleut senior minister was leveling land with a scraper. He was doing this work in ninety-five-degree heat, occasionally stopping to rest and drink a cup of hot coffee inside a farmhouse that did not have air-conditioning. A Dariusleut minister in north central Montana was re-finishing furniture in a shop. An assistant minister at another colony was harvesting wheat.

Hutterites who become ministers have typically held at least one im-portant colony position beforehand. In 1982 David Decker Jr. studied the positions held by Schmiedeleut ministers before they were chosen by lot. Of 233 individuals surveyed, Decker found that 50 had previously served as farm managers, 35 as stewards, 34 as German teachers, 25 as carpenters, and 21 as cattlemen. Tony Waldner, who duplicated Decker's study for the years 1982–2002, found significant changes: percentage in-creases in hog men and German teachers and a marked decline in the per-centage of stewards and farm managers. In Waldner's study, electricians and mechanics are also represented. Table 5.1 compares the two studies.

Hutterite Spirituality

Spirituality is a complex quality that is difficult to elucidate. For Hutter-ites it is defined communally, practiced ritualistically, and infused with culturally unique observances, language, and idiosyncratic ways of think-ing. There is also ongoing debate among Hutterites in all the Leut about what spirituality means. Thoughts about spirituality are expressed in general conversation, at educational conferences, and in the songs sung by young people. Lehrerleut minister Jacob Wipf says that when he was young and the youth got together, they sang secular country-western and folk songs.[45] Now they sing contemporary Christian hymns. But this does not necessarily mean that today's young men and women are more spiri-tual. It all depends on how one defines the term.

Table 5.1. Schmiedeleut ministers' previous
colony positions

Position held	1874–1982	1982–2002
	%	%
Farm manager	21	12
Steward (Wirt)	15	12
German teacher	15	17
Carpenter	11	7
Cattleman	9	0
Blacksmith	9	7
Hog man	5	14
Chicken man	3	0
Turkey man	3	0
Electrician	0	11
Miller	0	6
Mechanic	0	6
Others	9	8
Total	100	100
	(N = 233)	(N = 166)

Hutterite faith is a communal faith. Hutterites know that individual Christians often desire things different from what the church discerns as the will of God. One minister noted, "If a young girl tells me that she has 'invited Jesus into her heart' this raises serious questions for me."[46] His point is that an individual cannot control what God does. The girl's experience might not reflect Christian Gelassenheit, since a true believer must turn his or her will over to God, simultaneously yielding to members of the church. One cannot be committed to God without being united with one's brothers and sisters. Hutterites do not consider a personal relationship with God unimportant, but it is always viewed communally, in the context of the church. There is no boundary between one person and another, between the spiritual and the secular, between personal interest and community interest, between profession and home. All parts of life are joined together holistically.

As in any large religious society, some Hutterites take the spiritual dimension of life for granted and are not much interested in theological matters. They retain a religious commitment that is cultural, one that they cannot even explain well. At some colonies it is not hard to find impious behavior, from tobacco use to immoderate drinking. The use of profanity is widespread in both English and Hutterisch. But such actions or language do not necessarily mean that those involved are not spiritually minded, at least most of the time.

There are different ways to explain and view the phenomenon of cultural religion. Critics call it "Christianity by birth." But in any religious society there are variations of spiritual commitment. Outside assessments rely heavily on non-Hutterite and noncommunal considerations, which have little bearing on Hutterite ethical issues or definitions of spirituality. Non-Hutterites often expect more from Hutterites than they do from themselves. Because the expectations are higher, deviations from what outsiders view as "good" behavior are quickly pointed out, especially examples of what is viewed as Hutterite hypocrisy.

The strongest attack on Hutterite spirituality comes from evangelistic evangelical Christians. Mission-minded people sometimes come from faction-ridden denominations themselves, and they are proficient at pointing out problems in other groups. All missionaries tend to maximize weaknesses and minimize strengths. If God is present in Hutterite lives, why would anyone want to leave and join a different, more spiritually enlightened group?

Hutterite Music

Vocal music represents one of the few forms of accepted aesthetic expression among Hutterites. Members sing hymns from three different books, *Die Lieder der Hutterischen Brüder* (Hymns of the Hutterian brethren), the *Gesangbuch* (The "Lutheran" hymnal) and the *Gesangbuchlein* (The small hymnal).[47] Musicologist Helen Martens, in her book *Hutterite Songs*, notes that most of the hymns were written in the sixteenth century.[48] Many colonies also sing from the *Unpartisch Passauer Gesangbuch* (a nondenominational hymnal) and other gospel song collections.

Die Lieder der Hutterischen Brüder is the oldest hymn collection. Before publication in 1914, these songs were preserved only in handwritten form. More than one-eighth of the 347 songs in *Die Lieder* were written by Peter Riedemann. There are also hymns by Swiss and Austrian Anabaptist leaders Felix Manz, Balthasar Hubmaier, and Hans Hut. Fifty songs were composed by Hutterite minister Wolf Sailer.[49]

Helen Martens explains that many of the hymns use fifteenth- and sixteenth-century folk tunes and that the texts are often not devotional in character. Instead, many hymns contain motivational (sometimes terrifying) stories of Anabaptist and Hutterite martyrs. Several deal with the Passion of Christ and the Day of Pentecost. *Die Lieder der Hutterischen Brüder* employs one hundred different melodies, all passed down via oral tradition. Thirty-three of the hymns are Lutheran chorales.[50]

The Hutterites never developed a tradition of four-part harmony. Instead, they sing in thirds and sixths, monophonically and melodically, using primary chords. At times men and women both sing the melody, one octave apart. Hutterites sing with great emotion and with fortissimo. At one Dariusleut colony the singing, especially by the women, is ear-shattering in the very small church building. The participants, uninhibited, hold nothing back, releasing themselves from all worries and doubts and expressing impassioned love for God and for each other.

In Larry Martens's study of Hutterite singing, he noticed a "suppression of individualism" and a piercing nasal quality.[51] Marcus Bach wrote that "the wailing strains overpower the room. The women's voices become more piercing, the men's weave their doleful spell."[52] Because most Hutterite voices are untrained, the regularity of tempo and rhythm is inconsistent. The singing is intuitive rather than time-based; in addition, pitch often changes as the singing moves slightly above or below the key in which it began. At other times one note slurs upward or downward.

One of the Hutterite hymns includes the following reference from the book of Acts:

> My heartfelt zeal compels me
> Dear God, give me the strength
> To sing a pure, new song
> Of true Christian community
> Which has suffered dire destruction
> Since Apostolic times
> Through violence and false teaching
> Suppressed and distorted
> Even to this day.

The same hymn also has a Genesis citation:

> *In God the Father's features*
> *The primal man was made.*
> *To him were given all creatures*
> *That he should be obeyed.*
> *He and his wife ruled them alone,*
> *Themselves without contention,*
> *Avoiding all dissension.*
> *Thus unity was shown.*

There is also a reference to Jesus:

> *Christ quite briefly gave command*
> *"If you would perfect be,*
> *Sell your goods on every hand.*
> *Come and follow me."*

And the hymn does not neglect the Hutterites:

> *Into one body is the wheat*
> *From many made to one.*
> *The Spirit draws and by its heat*
> *A single loaf is done.*
> *The grain which is not broken*
> *And is not in the bread,*
> *Will have to be forsaken.*
> *Its inner life is dead.*[53]

The Hutterites began to use the *Gesangbuch*, or "Lutheran hymnal," in the 1700s. This collection contains 730 German Protestant hymns. The third hymnal, the *Gesangbuchlein*, was compiled by Elias Walter in the early 1900s, originally for use in the German School and in Hutterite homes.

The development of a Hutterite musical canon occurred during the period 1589–1734 under the direction of various church elders.[54] In 1873 Paul Tschetter, a minister, composed fourteen additional hymns, which he included in his diary, but probably none of them were ever sung, except by Tschetter himself. In the early 2000s, the Schmiedeleut One published two new songbooks consisting of English and German hymns by composer Butch Wipf. Wipf, a credentialed schoolteacher, spent a year studying music theory and conducting at Brandon University in Manitoba. He writes that he is "add[ing] to our treasure" by resurrecting the lost art of songwriting. Informal analysis of the hymns reveals an emphasis on Gelassenheit and love for one's neighbor, for example in the song title "Everybody Is a Leader."[55] The theological content is orthodox Hutterian with an emphasis on discipleship (for example, "May I never treat my fellow man as an only") and following Jesus ("The Wood of His Cross was Real" and "What Would Jesus do?").

Wipf is opposed to instrumental accompaniment for his choral music, although he plays the guitar in other settings. He contends that "instruments can detract from the message of a song."[56] This view is in line with a Hutterite Vorred based on 2 Chronicles and Sirach that reads, "In the Old Testament, harps, lutes and cymbals as well as trumpets were used to praise God, but in the New Testament, the Lord requires a pure and genuine heart and consciousness."[57]

At church services Hutterites sing from the three approved hymnals. But young people everywhere, across Leut lines, also know the Wipf songs and many gospel songs, for example, "He'll Pilot Me in the Hollow of His Hand" and "In the Middle of the Road." Hutterites are also familiar with many black spirituals and contemporary Christian songs. Some colonies have compiled special songbook collections that are used when young people get together. Laura and Mary Anne Tschetter, of the Dariusleut, assembled an anthology that includes seventy-eight German and forty-seven English songs. The German songs are mainly religious, but they include a few folk songs, for example, "Tirol," "Gute Nacht," and "Schön ist die Jugend." The English songs are drawn largely from evangelical Protestant collections and include "Bringing in the Sheaves," "How Great Thou Art," "Amazing Grace," and "The Old Rugged Cross."

No Hutterites use musical instruments in worship services, but Schmiedeleut One colonies officially, and colonies in other Leut unofficially, allow guitars, harmonicas, and other instruments at youth gatherings. Some Schmiedeleut One children take piano lessons; one young woman was overheard playing a difficult Beethoven sonata. One of the authors sat around a campfire with a group of sixty Hutterites as a bluegrass-gospel group performed and colony members of all ages sang along. The music ensemble utilized guitars, an accordion, and hand-held drums.

Choirs are not part of Hutterite tradition, and there are no performances in church services, but beginning in the 1970s, singing groups were organized by young adults at many Schmiedeleut colonies and were unofficially blessed by many ministers. Now choirs are found throughout the Schmiedeleut world and also among progressive Dariusleut. The choirs, which provide recreational and spiritual outlets, are open to all of the colony's young people. At one colony a choir performed in the dining hall after lunch, singing three songs: a traditional gospel hymn, a "Negro spiritual," and a contemporary Christian song.

The one choir in which everyone is not invited to participate is the Western Manitoba Hutterian Choir, which requires auditions and has recorded two CD's. In this group specialized musical training and sophistication are apparent. Members sing in parts from written manuscripts and have a good sense of rhythm and timing.

There are no Lehrerleut and few Dariusleut choirs that perform at community events. But this does not mean that young men and women do not sing when they get together. The songs come from gospel radio stations, the Internet, or the Butch Wipf collection. At one Dariusleut colony in Alberta, two young women and one man sang a Wipf song with reverential emotion, their eyes peering off into the distance.

The musical boundary for most Hutterites takes in gospel and contemporary Christian songs, as well as historic Hutterite hymns. But many young people also listen to rock and roll; one twenty-year-old knew the music of rock legend John Lennon. When a guitarist introduced a group of Hutterite musicians to diatonic scales and chords, which are used in jazz, one girl commented that it was beyond her comprehension. "He [the guitarist] could talk and play all night; we'd never understand what jazz is." It was all "too heavy." But many young Schmiedeleut listen to popular music on their iPods, which are increasingly tolerated.

Music plays a vital role in every part of Hutterite life. One morning after breakfast in the dining hall, the entire community sang a hymn based on Psalm 63:7. It began this way:

> *Mein Gott! Nun ist es wieder Morgen,*
> *Die Nacht vollendet ihren Lauf,*

Nun wachen alle meine Sorgen
Auf einmal wieder mit mir auf,
Die Ruh' ist aus, der Schlaf dahin,
Und ich seh' wider, wo ich bin.
(My God, now it is morning again
The night has ended its journey
Now all of my cares awake
At once with me again
My rest is over, my sleep has ended
And I see again where I am.)[58]

Practicing Church Discipline

The Hutterites believe in the "binding and loosing" authority of the church. The body of believers decides whether someone has sinned, requests repentance, and offers forgiveness. Every Hutterite plays a role in ensuring the purity of the faith. The sermons emphasize the importance of recognizing and combating sin wherever it shows its face.

Church discipline, which prepares colony members for life beyond the grave in heaven, is exercised primarily to cleanse the soul and redirect the body and mind toward a life of honest discipleship. Admonition is part of everyday Hutterite life. In 1950 Clarence Jordan described this phenomenon among Hutterites as an "I am my brother's keeper" mentality.[59] Dariusleut Henry Wurz notes that the "severity" of a sin increases if it is overlooked and allowed to continue.[60]

Unacceptable behavior is handled in a very practical way. If you do something wrong, you admit it, stand up in church, show repentance and humility, and the ritual is over; the sin is forgiven and forgotten. The process is structured and predictable. Everyone knows exactly what is going to happen next. Because most Hutterites aspire to be self-disciplined, many problems are worked out in face-to-face discussions. The Hutterite Church also practices *Meidung* (shunning) and *Ausschlüss* (excommunication), but full-scale expulsions and excommunications are rare; when they occur, they are usually self-chosen. If a member sets up a private business and pockets the profits, he knows that his time as a Hutterite is coming to an end. Although shunning is more common, only a small percentage of Hutterites ever experienced it until the Schmiedeleut division in the 1990s.

A repentant individual may always return to the colony. One South Dakota Hutterite, Levi Tschetter, surreptitiously earned the equivalent of a master's degree and attended Lakota sweat lodge spiritual services. Tschetter was also known to overimbibe, but he was never expelled from the colony, where he served for many years as a schoolteacher. Speaking of church discipline, farm manager Paul M. Wipf says, "No one changed his beliefs and way of life after being lectured about his weaknesses and ripped apart in the process."[61]

Discipline for children in everyday life usually takes the form of a quick slap with a leather strap or the verbal threat of a future life in hell. Ex-member Clifford Waldner describes a life of unrelenting tattling, but many Hutterites are not overly concerned about what other people have to say about them.[62] In a small community, people are used to talking about other peoples' lives.

Hutterite discipline begins with one person confronting another and is based on Matthew 18:15−17: "If your brother does something wrong, go and have it out with him alone, between your two selves. If he listens to you, have won back your brother. If he does not listen, take one or two others along with you: *whatever the misdemeanour, the evidence of two or three witnesses is required to sustain the charge.* But if he refuses to listen to these, report it to the community; and if he refuses to listen to the community, treat him like a gentile or a tax collector." The Hutterites follow this teaching as closely as possible. If a person commits a sin that is not considered extremely serious, for example, lying, stealing a small amount of money, or overdrinking, a simple confrontation followed by repentance is as far as things go. If there is no repentance, someone else is brought into the conversation, and the entire church may eventually become involved.

The first step for a more serious sin, for example, fornication, adultery, or major theft, is a face-to-face meeting with the colony minister. Hutterites believe that ministers, in a mediational sense, "by ordination and laying on of hands, receive the power or spirit to bind or loose sins." A 2000 Hutterite document declares, "We are to obey them because they are accountable for our souls."[63] If this encounter does not lead to personal recognition of wrongdoing and redemptive action, or if the problem becomes endemic, the issue is brought to the church council and eventually to the colony's adult male population. Formal discipline, including shunning, may follow even if the individual is repentant. When shunned, a member is not allowed to work or eat with other colony residents for a prescribed number of weeks or months. She or he may attend church services but must sit in a hallway. The offender feels the seriousness of the infraction before being welcomed back.

One of the authors was touring a colony with a minister, when they came upon two girls and a few boys smoking cigarettes. The minister said hello and appeared to overlook what was transpiring. Later he confronted those involved, however, and they were instructed to tell their parents what they had done. Personal confrontation serves an important function, as do the harder instruments of shunning and excommunication. Because of the close connection between religious and secular domains of life, shunning and excommunication have social as well as spiritual implications. Since financial mismanagement is viewed as a serious infraction, a few colonies have been disciplined as collective entities.

Once full repentance has occurred and forgiveness has been offered, sins committed are never supposed to be mentioned again. Some ministers do record infractions, however, and their records may influence whether a person is later selected for a leadership position. This practice is criticized by most Hutterites. In theory, anger is never directed at the sinner, only at the sin. If a member repents and rejoins the church, all wounds are healed.

Hutterites emphasize church discipline, but there is less ethical rigidity than one might expect. There is a significant gap between the ideal and the real, and many ministers follow a "don't ask, don't tell" approach. On a particularly warm and humid summer evening, a Dariusleut teen sits in his bedroom playing the guitar. As he strums it, his uncle, a minister, walks into the bedroom, grabs the guitar, and breaks it over his knee. He then makes the following comment, "I don't want to have to ever do this to you again." When asked whether this means the end of his guitar-playing, the boy answers with a smile and the following statement, "No. You didn't catch what he meant. He was not angry that I was playing a guitar. Everybody in the colony knows that and I'm not the only one who does. It's just that I was playing loud enough for him to hear me when he was passing by. As the colony minister, he had no other choice but to take action."[64]

Ministers know about the omnipresent musical instruments at youth gatherings, the games of ice hockey, the radios, and the cameras; they were once young themselves and remember what it is like to test the social boundaries of the *Gemein* (community). In many colonies, electric guitars, televisions, laptop computers, and unapproved cell phones are hidden from public view, but everybody knows about them and where they are located. That nothing is done about them follows from the Hutterite view that a certain amount of deviance is expected; no one is perfect. The spirit of toleration serves as a social and psychological safety valve for many members. Doctrinal and practical rigidity is not allowed to stifle the creative aberrance of the human spirit. Some outsiders cry "hypocrisy" when they hear about this leniency. On an ideal-real continuum, they expect Hutterites to be closer to their proclaimed ideals, even if they themselves are not. Most Hutterites just smile in response.

While Hutterites do not anticipate perfection, and minor deviations are expected, church discipline ensures that members never get too far off the track. Even though most ministers deal with infractions with kindness and long-suffering patience, they take action when it is called for. From an early age Hutterites learn humility and develop what Jerald Hiebert calls "thick skins."[65]

Gelassenheit involves an ongoing struggle with one's self; it also means going along with decisions made by church leaders even if one disagrees with them, for the benefit of the communal order. It requires putting yourself in the shoes of other people, even though your natural tendency is just the opposite, as expressed in one sermon preface: "We are very sensitive to what others do to us, but oblivious to how we treat others."[66] Each year Communion is preceded by the *Veklarungs Lehr* church service, where each member confirms his or her unity in belief and relationships and confesses his or her sins publicly.

The Ordnungen

The Hutterite Chronicle states that when discipline is lacking, "we live as in a tumbledown house with no one repairing." The Ordnungen promote order with precepts and guidelines "not specifically covered in the Bible" that speak to different aspects of Hutterite life.[67] Ordnungen mentioned in the Hutterite Chronicle cover every conceivable practice, including how much to drink, conducting business with outsiders, witchcraft, the upbringing of children, professional obligations, and dress.

The Ordnungen are living statements that are continually revised to deal with specific needs at the discretion of Leut executive councils. Some regulations deal with seemingly minor issues. For example, a Schmiedeleut rule passed in 1876 stated that "kitchen utensils such as pails, pots, pans could not be taken out of the kitchen and into the home." This ordinance maintained order, however, and guarded against individualistic tendencies. Another regulation instructed that men's hair must be parted in the middle. "To avoid dishonesty," unbaptized members were not to mail letters unless they were first read by colony ministers. The 2008 Lehrerleut Ordnungen require that the entire Leut grant permission before an individual colony collaborates with a non-Lehrerleut church or organization.[68]

Evangelism

In general, the Hutterites have not engaged in active evangelism since the seventeenth century, when they were some of the most aggressive missionaries in Europe. Responding to cruel and relentless persecution and harassment in the following two centuries, the Hutterites turned inward and moved into survival mode. In the 1800s two mass migrations and internal discord sapped whatever evangelistic energies remained. Although the twentieth century saw a general stabilization and reinstitutionalization of Hutterite faith and life, there was little interest in missions. Many Hutterites are not overly concerned about this phenomenon. In customary Old Order fashion, they have come to see their role as models of countercultural Christian belief and practice and do not wish to push outsiders to join them. They expect the Holy Spirit to direct people to Jesus through their example. Hutterites follow the biblical injunction "Your light must shine in people's sight, so that, seeing your good works, they may give praise to your Father in heaven" (Matt. 5:16), but they do not expect many new or revitalized Christians to want to become Hutterites: communal life is hard and Hutterian cultural practices too embedded.

Other Hutterites are concerned about the lack of evangelism and would like to see the society's inward focus transformed. A Schmiedeleut One Web site says, "The Hutterian Brethren have felt somewhat guilty of their missionary efforts in the recent past."[69] The Lehrerleut are the least interested in evangelism, and conservatives in the Dariusleut and Schmiedeleut Two have similar views. Traditionalists are concerned that converts will bring new, more individualistic cultural values and that it will be difficult to control them. But an expanding group of younger Schmiedeleut Two, Dariusleut, and Lehrerleut take a different position, questioning the amount of money colonies spend on new buildings and residences while at the same time offering minimal support for mission projects. A Schmiedeleut Two theological statement declares, "We recognize that the church lacks in this area and that we will be held accountable."[70]

On occasion non-Hutterite individuals or even families visit a colony and ask to join. When this happens, if their sincerity is not questioned, the novices are asked to first establish residence for a few months or years, so that they can get a full sense of what it means to live communally. During this period, colony members will also have the opportunity to interact and get to know them and evaluate their levels of understanding and commitment.

Hundreds of outsiders have established temporary residence in the North American Hutterite colonies, and it is sometimes the most conservative colonies that host the greatest number of seekers. The conservative West Raley and Wilson Siding Dariusleut colonies in Alberta, for example, are noteworthy for their openness to inquisitive prospective members. These colonies were also the most enthused about the relationship established with the Owa Community in Japan, beginning in the early 1970s.[71] Owa members spent extended periods at West Raley and Wilson Siding, and eventually the Japanese communal group joined the Hutterites. But most interested outsiders leave colony life after a few months of residence; the Owa Dariusleut reside halfway around the world. Many seekers have difficulty with language and cultural issues; others miss the professional opportunities they left behind.

A renewed interest in Hutterite evangelism was energized by the Bruderhof relationship in the 1980s. A joint mission project in Nigeria (Palmgrove), for example, continues to be supported by the Schmiedeleut One. In this case, the Old Order Hutterites have stuck with a culturally demanding project even after the modern Christian group (the Bruderhof) bowed out.

The Schmiedeleut One define *missions* broadly to include basic humanitarian assistance. The Starland Colony in Minnesota, for example, has a large warehouse where material supplies and products are stockpiled and distributed freely to needy people. Many of the products come from thrift shops, but there are also Hutterite-made quilts and blankets and vegetables and fruit from colony gardens.

After Hurricane Katrina devastated New Orleans and the Gulf Coast in 2005, Starland shipped hundreds of blankets to victims; many of the blankets came from Schmiedeleut Two colonies. The Tschetter Colony in South Dakota donated six-by-nine-foot blankets imprinted with the words "Jesus Loves Me." Other humanitarian endeavors include Habitat for Humanity building projects and work in soup kitchens in Winnipeg and Minneapolis. Colonies in all Leut donate wheat, hogs, and money to the world relief efforts of the Mennonite Central Committee.

In Nigeria, the Schmiedeleut One have invested hundreds of thousands of dollars at Palmgrove, near Abak, constructing large Western-style buildings that have sometimes fallen victim to the climate, which includes rainfall exceeding one hundred inches per year. Wood rots, tiles are displaced, and cement foundations erode. The impact of environment on culture at Palmgrove reminds one of the tropical conditions described in Barbara Kingsolver's *The Poisonwood Bible* and Paul Theroux's *The Mosquito Coast*. But the Hutterites have shown unusual patience and tolerance in allowing Palmgrove to adopt its own styles of dress and even worship, including the use of electronic instruments and physical movement. Photographs of the community show television antennae outside individual residences. Western Hutterites who visit accept a diet that includes plantains, peanut spread, palm fruit, pineapples, and casaba.

❧ ☙

HUTTERITE BELIEFS AND PRACTICES ARE FIRMLY GROUNDED in historic sermons, hymns, epistles, Ordnungen, and ecclesial forms. Each Leut, and to some extent each colony, takes a slightly different view of what Christianity means in daily life, but all Hutterites are deeply committed to communal expressions of faith that emphasize simplicity, humility, stewardship, and devotion to God. Church discipline is a central Christian obligation for all Hutterites. Leut and colony differences center on how groups view the relationship between Hutterites and outsiders: progressives want more interaction; conservatives want less. These disparities are often reflected in lifestyle choices. The way church precepts and observances take on cultural form is the topic of chapter 6.

CHAPTER 6

Life Patterns and Rites of Passage

*A Hutterite is free to think what he pleases; as long as he behaves according to
prescribed and appropriate norms.*
—Karl A. Peter, *The Dynamics of Hutterite Society*

The Hutterite Family

Communal living has significant impact on Hutterite family values
and the way children are brought up. Hutterites view "family"
from a communal perspective. To some extent the entire Hutterite Leut, and especially one's colony, is a large extended family. This understanding is cemented by theological understandings as well as endogamous relationships. But the nuclear family is also very important.

The power of family identity runs deep, especially for Hutterite males.
In many cases, a man's father, sons, and uncles reside side-by-side in the
same colony for most of their lives. Since Hutterite women move to their
husbands' colonies, they are more likely to find themselves socially and
psychologically adrift, floating across the Hutterite landscape, away from
their mothers, aunts, and grown daughters. But members of the new colony are quick to welcome the new spouse and help her settle into the community's social environment. We were eating a picnic lunch under a shade
tree in eastern Washington state, when a woman told us that her husband
was from north-central Saskatchewan, nearly a thousand miles away. But
she is content with her plight. She and her children visit relatives and

friends at the home colony twice a year, and in Saskatchewan she was quickly accepted.

Each Hutterite family lives in a separate apartment, and husbands and wives are emotionally close to each other and to their children. To support family relationships, many colonies excuse married males from operating combines and performing other jobs at night so that they can spend time with their families. One Dariusleut farm manager asks family members to gather every Saturday evening for a time of collective spiritual assessment. There is open reflection on the "spiritual life" of each person present, including the farm manager.

Most importantly, Hutterite parents model communitarian commitment. Although fathers and mothers are intimately involved in the nurture of their children, the children know that they are also part of a larger extended macrofamily. Young girls and boys are cared for and disciplined not only by their parents but also by many other adults and older children. All follow the same pattern of getting up early, working hard during the day, eating meals in the dining hall, and attending Gebet. Every event has a prescribed time and place that change little from year to year.

Hutterite age groups mingle freely, with striking informality. On a Sunday afternoon one of the authors arrives unannounced at a Lehrerleut colony near Ryegate, Montana. A young boy wearing a small cap and carrying a German Bible welcomes him and leads the way to the minister's house. The child walks into the home without knocking and yells out "Jacob *Vetter.*" (*Vetter* is a term of respect, somewhat equivalent to "uncle." The comparable term for women is *Basel* [aunt.]) No surname is used, and the boy seems unconcerned that he has waked the minister from a nap. There are no apologies or reprimands. The minister walks into the living room with sleepy eyes and offers a handshake.

The Hutterites and Material Possessions

All Hutterites have some individual belongings, such as clothes, books, bedding, and toys. These denote personal identity and provide a measure of physical and emotional comfort. But they are few in number and there is general equality from person to person in the value of such items. Hutterites do not believe that God wants some people to have more possessions than others. It is not uncommon, therefore, to find all families in a colony receiving a new couch or set of chairs at the same time.

Communalism as a system represents an attack on social and economic inequality. Hutterites are much less concerned about personal possessions and material objects than noncommunitarians. But it does not follow that materialism has been eradicated, especially when colonies experience economic success. As collective wealth increases, ministers worry that material items are becoming more important than persons; furthermore, money for new furnishings eats into colony savings accounts.

Lack of Privacy

At a Hutterite colony privacy is hard to find. But it is not missed, because it has never been experienced by the members. Instead, emphasis is placed on what Carolyn Hartse calls "the collective self."[1] Even outsiders may walk up to a Hutterite home, knock on the door, and, if no one answers, walk in and see whether anyone is there. Whether working, worshipping, or playing, Hutterite males and females are always interacting with one another. There is constant intellectual and emotional stimulation in a highly relational and verbal environment. Non-Hutterites find themselves quickly caught up in the constant talk: the incisive comments, the witty insinuations, the immediate repartee.

One Hutterite who lived outside the colony for a few years said that what he missed most was the personal relationships that result from this constant togetherness. A Hutterite does not drink coffee by himself; neither does he weed the garden, paint the back bedroom, or go into town without other people. And there are always children running around underfoot. The beauty of this kind of camaraderie is difficult to explain. It is emotionally refreshing, and it combats and reduces feelings of personal and social alienation.

Hutterite colonies are secure places. In more than twenty-five years of short and lengthy stays at dozens of colonies, we have never had anything stolen, even though possessions are often left in unlocked rooms and vehicles. It is common, however, for colony stewards to lock their doors, since they often hold large amounts of cash.

Showing Self-Confidence

Hutterites are confident people. Hundreds of years of separated communal life in Europe and North America have had a positive impact on self-perception. They are also uninhibited. Lehrerleut minister Joseph Hofer picks up the text of an 1873 Hutterian composition that he has never seen before. Looking at the German title of the melody suggested, he sings out loudly and confidently.

Confident behavior is a Hutterite cultural trademark. Max Stanton, during one of his colony visits, was surprised to find a fifteen-year-old boy driving a truck with a large load of wheat. He made a comment, and the boy's surprised response was that he had been driving trucks for three years. And before that he had driven smaller vehicles: scooters, lawn mowers, and tractors. In another encounter, a young colony woman explained with aplomb how easy it was to prepare meals for 150 people at a time.

Birth

Officially, Hutterites do not believe in birth control unless it is recommended by a medical doctor. And if a contraceptive medical procedure is suggested, it is almost always women who undergo the operation. Very few Hutterite men have had vasectomies. However, Hutterite young people in the 2000s are delaying marriage by three or four years, in comparison to the norm fifty years ago. They are making personal decisions about children with little pressure to conform to a tradition of unfettered reproduction. It is thus increasingly hard to find women who have more than six or seven children.

Hutterites exhibit a greater level of modesty than is found in the predominant culture. Women talk little about pregnancies and childbirth in front of children, unmarried adults, or men in general. After delivering a child, Hutterite women, most of whom breastfeed, take six weeks off from work assignments and devote full attention to their newborn.[2] Meals are brought to their homes, and there is a special diet for new mothers that includes noodle soup, waffles, and a sweet dried bun (a kind of *zwiebach* called *Reascha*), which is often dunked in a cup of tea. Hutterite women of all ages, friends, and relatives drop by to hold the new baby. Both male and female infants are greatly cherished.

A few Hutterite families have adopted babies and young children. Childless couples who have worked with adoption agencies have often experienced lengthy waiting periods. But there are exceptions. In 1977 a family at Fairholme Colony took in twin boys, who were given the Maendel surname. Both married Hutterite girls and are, in the 2000s, colony members in good standing. Some colonies continue to be interested in adoption.

Taking Care of Infants and Children

Once new mothers return to colony work assignments, child care is provided by young females, who take on this responsibility as early as age ten. The *Sorgela* (babysitters) are chosen on the basis of age, personal character, and general reliability. It is a great honor to serve in this capacity, and the relationship between babysitter and child is usually remembered for life, even after the sitter's formal responsibilities end at age fifteen.

Hutterites believe that the will of small children must be trained so that they will not think their interests are more important than anyone else's. They believe that infants are born innocent but that around age two a Satan-driven individualistic and sinful spirit emerges and interferes with communitarian values. This drive must be redirected and self-will and egotism eradicated. The process is supported institutionally by the Hutterite kindergarten, the German School, and Sunday School.

One part of training children involves mild discipline with a leather strap. Hutterites believe that if corporal punishment is used appropriately when children first disobey, it will rarely, if ever, be needed later on. Most boys and girls are not punished physically after they reach age six or seven, and some never need the strap. In any case, Hutterite children develop an early taste for the communal experience and its anti-individualistic expectations.

By age ten Hutterite children dress much like adults. Girls replace their caps with shawls. Younger children dress more casually and liberally, with patterns, colors, and styles that are not allowed for adults. Many attend church in bare feet when the weather is warm. Traditionally, Hutterite children have been given Bible names: Jacob, John, Joseph, and so forth; but in the past few decades, one increasingly finds "English" names such as Tamara, Tanisha, and Teanna.[3]

The Kindergarten

The Hutterites claim that they invented the kindergarten in their Moravian communities during the sixteenth century. But the kindergarten (*Klanaschul*) as Hutterites define it is more like a preschool program. It is where two- to five-or-six-year-olds spend their days, Monday through Saturday, while their parents do other kinds of work. Kindergarten teachers are usually older women who have a special love for children. Much of the curriculum is unplanned, but it usually includes hymn-singing, Bible stories, and games, as well as instruction in how to get along with others. It is in the kindergarten that children learn to curb self-will and take responsibility for their actions. Here German and Hutterisch are the only languages spoken.

Kindergarten areas usually include playground equipment and a variety of toys. The children eat their noon meal in the Klanaschul building and do not attend church services. According to the Hutterite Easter sermon, "Little children . . . prevent the Word of God being rightly heard."[4] Some Schmiedeleut One colonies have a separate *Kinderlehr* service, where children listen to Bible stories and sing hymns.

Hutterite Children

As Hutterite children grow up, they naturally assume that the wisest people in the world are the men and women in their own colony. They do not attend school alongside non-Hutterites and so are not told daily that they are missing something important: for example, television shows or new styles of dress. In a world where all adults serve as surrogate parents, free to admonish and laugh with them, children wander at will in and out of different homes. With regard to discipline, Dora Maendel notes, "In an African village, when a child does something wrong, it's not just the parents who communicate their disappointment, but the close neighbours and the whole extended family, including uncles, aunts, grandparents and cousins. Just like on a Hutterite colony."[5]

On the colony grounds, Hutterite children are not overly protected; they are given extensive opportunities to take physical risks. In the evenings children above the age of six or seven are relatively unsupervised until about 8 o'clock. During this time, they wander onto the far reaches of colony properties. One colony rings a bell when it is time for children to return to the domestic courtyard, where they can more easily be observed by parents and siblings.

Hutterite children are typically at ease with adults, whether Hutterite or non-Hutterite. Boys and girls are confident, forward, and participatory. They make direct comments and let their feelings show without inhibition. They are inquisitive and hold strong opinions; these traits are especially noticeable in Hutterite girls. Children are frequently asked to sing songs for guests, and they do so unrestrained, loudly, and expressively.

Hutterite children are not influenced by television or video game—induced passivity, nor are they jaded by the constant rebroadcast of emotional sentiments. A nine-year-old girl, visiting from another colony, walks confidently into the living room, addresses people by their first names, with respectful appellations, then disappears into a bathroom. Fifteen minutes later she emerges with wet hair hanging down onto her face, sits down on the couch, and participates in the conversation. She exhibits little self-consciousness and much self-confidence.

Hutterite children do not have to confront the assimilationist demands of the public school system, where individuals must stand on their own and deal with debasing comments that, when said over and over, may destroy their confidence and affect their self-perception. Hutterites know they are different, and they hear prejudicial comments when they are in town. There are friendly and not-so-friendly wisecracks and side glances. Ruth Lambach comments, "As a teenager dressed as a Hutterite, I proudly walked down the street in Grand Forks, North Dakota, thinking myself the best dressed person on the sidewalk. I looked around and my eye was disturbed because I could recognize no pattern in clothing or hairstyle or hair covering. Everything seemed chaotic. There was no symmetry of design."[6] But Hutterite children go to public places in groups, carrying a strong social network of support with them. They know why they are different and that their difference symbolizes a special spiritual calling.

Hutterite children are jacks-of-all-trades. Accustomed to hard work and involved daily in various colony enterprises, they develop early a general sense of competence. In the summer especially, they are full participants in the colony work cycle, whether picking up nails from construction sites or helping in the community garden. During fall, winter, and spring they attend "English" or German schools during the day, do a few

Lehrerleut children in traditional dress, in Alberta. Courtesy of
Max Stanton.

chores in the late afternoon, and spend evenings on homework or engaged
in recreational activities.

The babysitting responsibilities that Hutterite girls often take on
around the age of ten are one example of useful work done by children.
A tremendous amount of trust is demonstrated in this assignment. Ruth
Lambach describes serving as a babysitter: "As the eldest I was responsible
for my younger brothers from the time they were about six weeks old.

From the age of nine I was not able to go anywhere without a little one. We got very handy at dragging babies along with us."[7]

In general, Hutterite children handle responsibility well and are very helpful. One afternoon, a Hutterite German teacher went into town to deliver potatoes to a local grocery. Three young girls rode along in the colony van. When they arrived, the girls quickly got out, pulled back the heavy back door of the van, and started carrying heavy boxes of potatoes inside. No one had told them to do anything.

Young People and Becoming an Adult

The fifteenth birthday is a special time for all Hutterite boys and girls. That is the day when they are publicly recognized as adults. There is nothing pointedly religious about the event, but it bears remarkable similarities to Jewish bar mitzvah and bat mitzvah observances and (for girls) the Catholic-influenced Mexican-American *quinceañera* celebrations.

At age fifteen non-Lehrerleut adolescents move from the *Essenschul* (children's dining room) and begin joining the adults for meals. Lehrerleut boys and girls start eating with the adults at age fourteen. They also quit attending German School and are no longer under the tutelage and supervision of the German teacher. This transition occurs at age fifteen in all Leut. Corporal punishment ends at this age, too, although in earlier times, it was prolonged well beyond age fifteen. According to a regulation passed in 1935, "Disciplining unbaptized young people 21 years or older shall be done by having them stand up throughout a church or prayer meeting service, instead of punishing them by spanking."[8]

Hutterite girls are usually given a large wooden hope chest at this onset of adulthood, while boys receive a colony-constructed desk. Both come with a lock and key. Young women use the chests to store fabric for new dresses, small gifts, photographs, toiletry items, simple jewelry, and correspondence. Schmiedeleut *Dienen* (unmarried young women) also receive elaborate, beautifully crafted dressers or tallboys, often with attached framed mirrors and matching bedside tables.

Adulthood brings new responsibilities. After school hours, boys begin working in a variety of colony enterprises, perhaps in the hog, dairy, or poultry operations. They are usually assigned work where they are most needed, but their individual talents and interests are always recognized.

Young males drive trucks and combines and learn welding and carpentry. Hutterite females are assigned to kitchen rotations, and some serve as teachers' assistants. In recent years, the Schmiedeleut and the progressive Dariusleut encourage teens to complete high school, delaying full-time commitment to particular jobs.

From age fourteen or fifteen until the time they are baptized and join the church, in their early to mid twenties, Hutterite males and females are given a great deal of freedom. Some look at different life options. The majority of Hutterite adolescents do not stray far from the nest, but a significant number test the waters outside the colony environment. The Weggeluffene (runaway) phenomenon is discussed in chapter 10. But even those who do not leave the colony often experiment with practices that go against the Ordnungen. Young people know that this is a time of introspection and exploration, that the decision to join the colony is a serious one that must be made by each person, and that this is the last time in their lives when they may transgress without serious repercussions. Many young Hutterites have lit up cigarettes, and some have smoked marijuana. A large number have gone to the movies or learned how to dance.

In the twenty-first century, as more and more Hutterite young people postpone marriage until their midtwenties, they also join the church later, so the time of testing is extended. This development concerns many Hutterite leaders. Even though the vast majority of Hutterite youth do not leave the colony permanently, runaways as well as the community's other unbaptized men and women are susceptible to questionable diversions. To make the time of transition easier, Manitoba German teacher Jonathan Maendel has created special spaces on the colony grounds: for example, a barbecue circle in the middle of an open field, where young people can talk, sing, and grill hotdogs if they wish. He is also designing and planting a beautiful line of trees with attractive walkways. He hopes such improvements will influence Hutterite young people to stay at home and out of trouble.

Overall, Hutterite young people exude an innocence of expression, demeanor, and understanding that is refreshing. They are both inquisitive and firmly grounded in colony values. They often seem younger than their peers in the outside world.

Baptism, the Lord's Supper, and Joining the Community

Contending that individuals should not be baptized and join the church until they fully understand the implications of communal Christianity, the Hutterites practice believer's, or adult, baptism. Unlike evangelical Protestants who also reject infant baptism, Hutterites rarely baptize adolescents. Most Hutterites wait until their early to mid twenties to join the church, often joining right before marriage, for which baptism is required. A baptismal service is held once a year on Palm Sunday. Those who want to join the church know that it is a lifetime commitment to God and to the Hutterite community, and the vow is not taken lightly.

When a young person wants to be baptized, she or he notifies the colony's senior minister, who begins an informal review. The person then receives six to eight weeks of religious instruction in early spring. About a week before baptism, each candidate confesses his or her sins to one of the colony ministers in a process of spiritual and emotional cleansing. Candidates also meet with members of the church council, who ask questions about their faith. The candidates' answers help determine whether they are ready to move forward. There are also lectures about the lifetime significance of the baptismal commitment. In the Lehrerleut, inquiries about the conduct of candidates are relayed to all member colonies, providing an additional check on those who are not considered qualified for baptism.

Interest in membership does not automatically qualify an individual for baptism, but most people who want to join are accepted by the church. Those that are refused have usually been involved in significant misbehavior, and the colony wants to spend additional time observing whether or not authentic change has occurred. Since each Hutterite's life is watched carefully and continuously, there are few surprises.

On Saturday afternoon of the Palm Sunday weekend, the candidates respond publicly to catechism questions and recite Bible verses or poems that summarize the Christian plan of salvation. This is a highly moving and enriching experience for the entire Hutterite community.

At the baptism service, a minister reads a sermon based on three Bible texts, one each from Genesis, Matthew, and John. The candidates stand in front of the congregation and recite a prayer and the Apostle's Creed, then kneel down. The senior minister cups his hands over the head of the man or woman to be baptized, and a second minister pours water from a china pitcher or basin into his cupped hands. As the hands are opened, water pours down onto the head of the new member. After the candidates have been baptized, they shake hands with or embrace other members of the colony.

Hutterite baptism is considered equal to a vow taken when a person joins a religious order. It is a covenant with God made through the community, a sacred pact that must never be broken. At Dariusleut and Schmiedeleut baptisms there are often many visitors, including friends, relatives, and ministers from other colonies.

One week later, on Easter Sunday, the colony observes the Lord's Supper, and the new members take part for the first time. Hutterites view Communion symbolically (the bread and wine represent but do not become Jesus's body and blood), but it has significant theological meaning and demonstrates the commitment of members to each other and to God. Easter is the only time the Lord's Supper is celebrated, giving it special importance. It is closed to nonmembers.

At a church service two weeks before Communion, every member participates in a congregational confession of faith and ministers say a special prayer. Hutterite men rise to their feet to signify that they are prepared to participate. Hutterite women usually remain seated, having confirmed their spiritual readiness before their husbands at home before the service. During the next two weeks, the Hutterites are to search their hearts for mistakes and wrongdoing and "to make things right" before observing the Lord's Supper. Some individuals confess wrongdoing to a minister; others approach people they have offended or who have offended them.

The Lord's Supper is the occasion when members recommit themselves to a life of suffering, following the example of Jesus. During the central observance of the three-hour Communion service, a minister first passes around the bread. Everyone breaks off a piece and eats it. A pitcher of wine is passed next, and each member takes a sip. A special thanksgiving song is also sung. Stanza 2 of the hymn reads as follows:

> The grain of wheat was crushed and broken;
> The price of all our sins was paid for;
> The bread of life of whom was spoken
> The truth foretold by all the prophets,

This bread of life to us was given
When Christ upon the cross was hanging.[9]

Dating in Hutterite Colonies

In a commune where everyone is closely watched and where there is little privacy, one might think dating possibilities would be limited. But for people who have grown up there, the matter is not troubling. Although Hutterite young people, compared to others, have fewer opportunities to spend long periods of private time with the opposite sex, and group dating is quite common, colony members accept this situation as a pattern of communal existence. Besides, there are always ways to get around the system. At most colonies there are many young people and a strong peer support system; thus it is possible to arrange secret meetings on and off the colony grounds. And dating options expand when colonies are located close to each other.

Dating is eagerly anticipated by young people and by their parents, and opportunities present themselves whenever there are mixed-gender activities. With the exception of the Lehrerleut, Hutterites usually do not marry within their home colonies; there are too many people who are either first or second cousins or who have at least come to be viewed as relatives. But in the evenings or on weekends, young people from two or more colonies often get together. Contacts are also made during family visits and labor exchanges and at baptisms, weddings, and funerals.

At some colonies there are unchaperoned visits between young males and females behind closed bedroom doors. Hutterite adults are likely to look the other way. This practice varies from colony to colony. In some colonies a "date" means two people alone in a room with the lights off. Hutterite dating is semiplatonic, consisting primarily of conversation, but there is also some physical contact.

According to informal assessments, sexual relations among unmarried young people are less frequent than societal averages but are nevertheless increasing. There is more privacy in bigger homes and greater media access to sexual images. Lesley Masuk, who lived at a colony for two months and later married an ex-Hutterite, writes that Hutterite young people have more dating freedom than her Prairieleut mother allowed. Masuk also notes that there is significant physical intimacy between young men and women.[10] Some Hutterites mention obtaining diaphragm prescriptions and condoms. When married couples use these devices for birth control or health purposes, ministers are consulted and a physician's recommendation is required. But wayward young people pick up contraceptives at convenience stores.

Many Hutterites are critical of what is going on and actively promote "hands-off" dating practices—the official position of the Schmiedeleut One. Commenting on such a policy, the wife of a colony minister exclaimed that if there was no touching, hugging, and kissing, a girl would never know someone was interested in her.

Hutterite dating often takes place over several years, so the pair gets to know each other well. If a Hutterite man is interested in a particular woman, perhaps someone he met at a *Hulba* (engagement party) or some other social event, he might request an opportunity to visit her colony, even if she lives hundreds of miles away. Dating from a distance is facilitated by cell phones, e-mail, and text messaging. Some young Hutterites have Web sites and chat rooms, where private and semiprivate conversations take place.

Marriage

"In the colony almost no one stays single," says the wife of a Dariusleut minister. If a boy or girl appears uninterested in marriage or seems not to be trying hard enough to find a match, there are always adults around with entreaties and recommendations. Colony women often assist the dating process as informal matchmakers: the only remaining form of the arranged marriage structure that existed into the 1840s. Parents also are actively involved in mate selection. One young person said, "I wouldn't think of dating someone my parents didn't approve of." One afternoon, an unmarried twenty-four-year-old was being teased relentlessly about his singleness. An older woman came by and interrupted with the comment, "Don't worry about it. God will find someone for you." Hutterites also often say that opposite personalities create the strongest marriages.

In the 2000s, the biggest problem for marriage-minded Hutterites is the rising ratio of young females to males. This is the result of male runaways' staying on the "outside" longer than in the past and many of them not returning to the colony. Margaret Hofer's study of members who joined the

Lehrerleut between 1990 and 2004 indicates that 1,300 females joined the church during this time, but only 1,050 males joined. The average age at baptism is also lower for women than for men. The upshot is that a growing number of women join the church before a marriage that might never occur. Young women may thus be tempted to leave the colony because doing so might be the only way they will have an opportunity to marry and have children.

As a result of the male-female population imbalance, which has hit the Lehrerleut especially hard, in some families unmarried daughters are asked to take care of aging parents for years at a time. It is rare for a Hutterite woman over age thirty to marry. But the same is not true for men. Because of the runaway problem, Hutterite men are in high demand and rarely have a problem finding a spouse.

As mentioned in an earlier section, a significant majority of Hutterites do not marry within their own colony, but the Leut differ in this respect. Our 2007 study of Dariusleut and Lehrerleut marriages indicates that 34 percent of Lehrerleut marriages, compared to only about 12 percent of Dariusleut marriages, are intracolony. The difference is explained to some extent by Lehrerleut branching practices, which are very much "by the book" and use the lot-casting system, making it more likely that a mix of unrelated people will be found in mother and daughter colonies. The Dariusleut, in contrast, often divide along strict family lines, so it is more difficult to find an unrelated mate within one's own colony. Dariusleut colonies are also smaller in size, further limiting dating options. Hutterites generally disapprove of first-cousin marriages; in 2003 leading Dariusleut ministers issued a statement against the practice. But second- and third-cousin marriages are common.

Hutterite marriage arrangements are standardized yet complex, with variations in practice. When two people decide to marry, something like this occurs: First, accompanied by a few friends, the prospective groom approaches the colony's senior minister. At the same time, the groom's father asks the bride's parents for their consent.[11] In most cases the couple are fairly certain that their parents are supportive, but the ritual is observed nonetheless.

The groom then submits a written request to the minister of the bride's colony, who calls for a special meeting (*Stiebel*) of the church's male members. They appraise the groom's request and discuss the character of both individuals. Sometimes there is a request for a background check, especially if either member has lived outside the colony, but for the most part the meeting is a formality. The same procedure is followed at the bride's colony.

If both colonies agree to the match, close friends and family members gather at the bride's home, where advice is again shared and blessings given. The bride and groom formally and publicly announce their engagement in a short ceremony that includes a toast with glasses of wine, and on the following Saturday a Hulba (shivaree) is held at the bride's colony. The couple's engagement lasts for at most a couple of weeks.

Although Hulba celebrations vary between colonies and Leut, those in attendance often include Hutterites from colonies near and far as well as non-Hutterite friends and business associates, colony teachers, store owners, and physicians. The Hulba is a huge social gathering where everyone relaxes and opens up and where alcohol sometimes flows freely. But the spiritual side of the human experience is also recognized through the singing of gospel hymns such as "The Old Rugged Cross" and "Amazing Grace" or the German hymn "Keiner wird zu Schanden" (None will come to shame).

At one Hulba, songbooks were distributed and the dining hall was filled to capacity. As the songs were sung, young men, wearing aprons designed for the occasion, served food, snacks, and drinks (wine, coffee, and sodas) into the early morning hours. There was also a full-course meal. The engaged couple sat at a head table, along with the bridesmaid, the best man, and both sets of parents. A second table was reserved for ministers.

In some Dariusleut colonies, the Hulba continues on Sunday evening, with family choirs, impromptu duets and trios, and instrumental performances. Here the main attraction is often the couples' friends and relatives. They recite well-worn poems and talk about the fun and mischief they had with either the bride or the groom while growing up. At one Hulba around midnight, a group of older uncles and family friends stood up, stomped on the table, and sang the Tirolean anthem "Tirolean Boy" at the top of their lungs.

The marriage ceremony usually takes place on the Sunday after the engagement week. It is held at the groom's colony, where the newlyweds will live, and where their new home has been cleaned from top to bottom. There is often a second Hulba at this colony, similar to the one at the bride's colony.

The wedding Lehr occurs on Sunday morning and is usually a ninety-

A newly engaged Hutterite couple at the bride's Hulba (shivaree) celebration. Courtesy of Max Stanton.

minute service divided into two parts. During the first half, the congrega-tion listens to the traditional wedding Vorred. The second part includes a wedding sermon directed at the young couple and the actual ceremony, which takes place during the last fifteen minutes. The bride usually wears a special dress, perhaps an iridescent blue that stands out from the darker, more subdued clothes of other women in attendance. In the Dariusleut, the groom often wears the same long black suit coat as the minister: the

An outdoor Hutterite wedding reception scene in Alberta. Courtesy of
Max Stanton.

"jacket with a skirt." The bottom of this jacket extends to just above the
knees. Schmiedeleut grooms wear a regular dress jacket.

At the banquet reception that follows the wedding ceremony, the new
couple is toasted with wine, and small gifts are placed at each table setting as mementos. There is also a chance to pose for photographs as ministers pretend not to notice. Wedding gifts are usually practical items such
as small appliances, lamps, ceiling fans, clocks, and linens. There might
be quilts, pieces of clothing, silverware, towels, and hand-stitched wall
hangings. Sunday evening is spent in the community kitchen, with more
singing and visiting. The dozens of Hutterite marriages that take place
each year provide many dating opportunities and highlight the Hutterites' love of celebrating.

Although Hutterite marriages exhibit closeness and caring, there is
not much public physical contact between husband and wife. Gertrude
Huntington says that the relationship between spouses, although important, is not "too strong," as the larger church family always overrides the

nuclear family.[12] Nevertheless, we do not believe that the average Hutterite husband and wife are more psychologically or socially distant than non-Hutterite spouses. Loving affection is demonstrated in various ways. A few families spend summer evenings at local parks or playgrounds or at favorite ice cream parlors or pizza places. More commonly, couples take strolls along country roads, near ponds or streams. Husbands and wives tease each other constantly, and like most farm families, they also often work side-by-side during the day.

Hutterite mothers often remind their children to show love and appreciation for their fathers when "dad comes home." Women stay up late to spend time with their husbands, offering snacks and colony gossip, especially when the husband has spent long hours in the field or making deliveries in town. On birthdays and anniversaries, spouses exchange practical gifts. The wife might make a favorite dessert or sew a new shirt. One husband made a jewelry box with a beautiful flower hand-carved on top. Women cross-stitch wall hangings that include marriage dates or the names and birthdays of children. Some of the hangings feature popular phrases such as "Love One Another," "Love at Home," or "Bloom Where You Are Planted." Men who have been away from the colony for a few days often return with small gifts.

Max Stanton and a Hutterite man once arrived at the man's residence at about nine o'clock in the evening. His wife immediately prepared a meal, even though she had just completed a long workday and had many young children. When Stanton thanked her for her effort, she responded bluntly, "Well, at least somebody appreciates what I have done!" Her husband's response: "Non-Hutterite men have to keep telling their wives how much they are appreciated, or else they might get up and leave, or even ask for a divorce." Both comments were delivered with humor and sarcasm but also with a grain of truth.

For Hutterites, marriage is a lifetime commitment; although there are some separations, divorce is not an option. If one spouse sues for divorce, she or he must usually leave the colony. In one case, a man married a non-Hutterite while living outside the colony. After fourteen years of marriage, his wife filed for divorce and he returned to the Hutterite community. He was accepted back but cannot remarry until after his divorced wife dies.

Sexual Relations

The Hutterite Church is opposed to premarital and extramarital sexual relationships, but as one might expect, some experimentation occurs. Hutterites confront and sometimes yield to the same temptations as anyone else. In the somewhat rare case of out-of-wedlock conception, marriage is usually required for the couple involved as soon as the pregnancy is recognized. The *Dariusleut Family Record List* includes a young woman who was baptized in mid-July, married on August 16, and delivered a baby three days later. Cases of sexual assault, incest, and rape are virtually nonexistent.[13]

Hutterites have traditionally spent little time talking to their children about puberty and physical maturation. In the 2000s, more parents discuss sex with their children, but at some colonies the discussion does not occur until the day of the child's wedding. Hutterites—except in some of the most liberal colonies—do not want schoolteachers to discuss the details and consequences of sex in health or science classes.

Since Hutterites live on farms, children observe much reproductive activity from an early age. They are well aware of the similarities between humans and other mammals. Even so, some children are naive when it comes to the "facts of life." Moreover, most Hutterites get married when they are many years past puberty and far from the physical and temperamental changes that accompany that transition. Recognizing the problem of premarital sexual problems, Jacob Kleinsasser published a short book in 2001 that includes the following admonition: "If you engage in sexual experimentation before you commit yourselves publicly in marriage, how can you be sure that you will stay true to each other later?"[14] Kleinsasser also confronts issues such as pornography and masturbation.

The New Family

After marriage, a bride joins her husband's colony and undertakes the sometimes arduous task of fitting into that community's unique social structure. With a twinkle in his eye, Tony Waldner said the general rule was that a bride in a new colony "should be shy for one year."[15] Before making too many critical remarks or working for change, she should learn the particular routines and ways of doing things at her new place of residence. Smiling, Sarah Hofer, a minister's wife, says that the period of shyness should last for at least five years.[16]

Although some Hutterite sisters marry brothers, thus easing residential transitions, most newlywed wives have only their husbands to rely on and confide in until they break into the female peer culture of the new colony. Each commune has its own way of doing things, even such tasks as baking and cleaning, and the new bride may initially feel lost and homesick. To counter feelings of social displacement, the woman's mother-in-law and sisters-in-law give helpful orientation and emotional support. Other women also try hard to ensure the quick assimilation of the new bride. Marriage means a private residence for the first time, a very special thing for newlyweds. Marriage also involves an official job for the husband and increased community status for both husband and wife.

Aging and Death

In Hutterite society, older people are valued and respected. Physical and psychological changes are fully recognized in ways that are rarely found in Western culture. Between the ages of forty-five and fifty, for example, women in most Leut gradually diminish their workloads. Many of them are no longer assigned to the regular kitchen rotation, and when they are relieved of cook-week (*Kuchwuch*) responsibilities, life is much easier. Hutterite men, too, between the ages of fifty and fifty-five, often relinquish colony management positions and related responsibilities.

Retirement ages, fifty for women and fifty-five for men, have advanced by about five years since John Hostetler's 1974 study. They also vary to some extent based on individual colony needs and interests. The move to older ages for retirement was precipitated by smaller family sizes, which have increased colony workloads, despite the advantages of modern technology. An increase in male runaways also affects retirement-age considerations.

After retirement (it is really semiretirement), many men and women continue to work almost as hard as they did before, but they do so by choice. When it becomes apparent that a younger man needs a position, an older man usually relinquishes his managerial responsibilities. Retirees fill in for colony members who are traveling, ill, or bearing children. They chip in wherever they are needed, and they have considerable time to de-

A Dariusleut woman and her grandson.
Courtesy of Max Stanton.

vote to grandchildren and great-grandchildren. Children's toys are found scattered around the homes of "older" people. Many women spend more time sewing during retirement than they did before.

Peter Stephenson describes Hutterite retirement as a "prolonged affair."[17] As time goes on, daily naps get longer, the walk to the kitchen less frequent. Perhaps food is brought to the house by a relative or friend. Tasks are less arduous and stressful as life gradually slows down. The change is not abrupt; there is no move from full-time work to full-time relaxation, as is often the case outside the colony. Occasionally individuals decide to delay their retirements. One Dariusleut German teacher continued teaching into his midsixties. When someone remains in a position so long, he prevents a younger man from moving into the position. The one formal exception to the retirement system is the colony's ministers. But by the time senior ministers reach their sixties and seventies, they have usually transferred their most time-consuming responsibilities to assistant pastors.

Most Hutterites do not fear death. It is not a taboo subject but is readily discussed. One Hutterite told Hanna Kienzler, "Hanna, as soon as a person is born he is old enough to die."[18] As part of the material world, the human body is not viewed as particularly important; furthermore, physical death is seen as an entrance into a more glorious form of existence. Although Hutterites do not believe in total "assurance of salvation," the general thinking is that those who have tried to live a good life and have developed a close relationship with God can be fairly certain that they will spend eternity in heaven. At the funeral of a young boy who died in an ATV accident, his father emphasized the importance of spending as much time as possible with one's children. At the same time, he rejoiced that his son was now in heaven.[19]

Hutterites prefer a death that does not occur too quickly. They want to have time for farewells and the confession of recognized sins. Mistakes can be admitted and quarrels ended; the dying process functions as a time of healing and transitional preparation for the next world. A drawn-out death also allows many people to visit the afflicted, exchange information, and perhaps sing favorite hymns. Special foods are prepared, and distant family members may be able to make one last journey to see their relative. Hutterites prefer to die at home. They despise the social isolation and bureaucratic impositions of hospital rooms.

Each death is followed by a wake held a day or two later. At the wake

Lehrerleut men with grandchildren of two of the men. Courtesy of
Max Stanton.

the remaining spouse, if any, and close relatives are consoled, and everyone
focuses on the spiritual side of human existence. Three or four hundred
people and as many as one hundred ministers attend some wakes. In many
Dariusleut colonies, the wake is held from 8:00 p.m. until midnight, with
ministers taking turns selecting and leading appropriate songs and offering supporting and encouraging words. There are also many short breaks
for coffee and snacks. A Schmiedeleut wake lasts about two hours and
consists of singing and a short meditation. It is followed by visiting, eating,
and more singing. A poorly attended wake is taken as a negative commentary on the life of the deceased.

The formal funeral service, held the day after the wake, is also an event
attended by hundreds of friends and relatives. The funeral is not only a
time for mourning but also a time to contemplate the better life that the
deceased is now experiencing. Since the church service emphasizes the
importance of being prepared for life after death, it has significant instruc-
tional value for the living. Numerous Hutterite sermons are used, which
incorporate texts from Genesis, Psalms, Philippians, and Revelation.[20]

In the 2000s, Hutterites embalm corpses, but they are opposed to cremation. Hutterites are buried in oak caskets made by colony carpenters. At the colony cemetery, the interment service is short, consisting of a simple statement from a colony minister. Traditionally, deceased colony members' graves were filled by hand while everyone watched, but in most colonies this practice is no longer followed. Those who attended the burial service usually leave after the casket has been lowered into the grave. Afterward Hutterite men use colony equipment to cover the casket with earth.

Hutterites are unusual in that males and females live to about the same age, whereas in almost all other populations in the developed world, women have a life expectancy five or more years longer than that of men.[21] Some scholars suggest that the shorter female lifespan is the result of high fertility rates and corporeal fatigue, which lower resistance to disease. Populations with large families often see increased postpartum physical and psychological problems in women. If that is a primary reason for the shorter lifespan, having smaller Hutterite families could affect it in the future. Other researchers emphasize genetic determinations such as the "founder effect" (see chapter 7).[22]

It is sometimes suggested that Hutterite women experience more stress than men because a greater number of them have to move away from friends and relatives. Peter Stephenson suggests that in addition, death at younger ages is the result of the lack of "value" ascribed to the work that Hutterite women do, especially as they get older. "There is almost nothing to do except eat and gossip," he writes.[23] In comparison, as Hutterite males age, they are automatically given elder status. Their opinions are valued as they participate actively in colony decision-making. Most men also reside in the same colonies as many of their children. Stephenson claims that Hutterite women are not given the same increased status as they grow older, that for them the colony becomes more like a Home for the Aged.

We strongly disagree with Stephenson's assessment. It is true that women do not hold official status as they get older. But they never did, during their entire lives. They exert influence informally from behind the scenes, and this role only increases as they age. Retired women share in the same enhanced status as their husbands; their views are highly valued, especially since Hutterites revere the opinions of those who are older. In any case, the communal extended family provides a great degree of comfort to women of all ages, especially in their later years. It would be difficult to

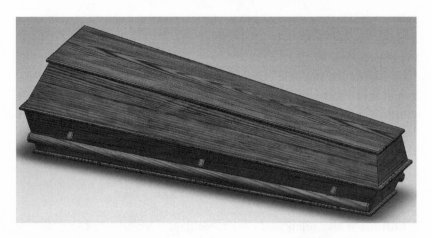

A handmade Hutterite coffin. Courtesy of Patrick Murphy.

find a more supportive social and economic environment for a person entering retirement than the colony.

Celebrating Holidays

Hutterites devote much time to communal observances and celebrations. In addition to Hulbas, weddings, wakes, and funerals, they celebrate many of the holidays commonly found on the Christian calendar. The way these are observed has been influenced by American and Canadian traditions. Small gifts are exchanged at most holiday occasions, for example, although greater numbers of presents are given at the birth of a child or at a wedding. Thousands of cards are sent at Christmas and also for birthdays, anniversaries, and baptisms.

EASTER

Hutterites have always given special attention to the Easter season. These are the "most important holy days," says one minister. Preparations begin on Palm Sunday with the annual baptism service and several important sermons. Formal Easter observances start on the morning of Good Friday with the reading of the "Crucifixion" Lehr. They continue through Tuesday, when the "Resurrection" sermon is read.[24] On Easter Sunday, members recall Jesus's resurrection from the dead, and the annual Communion service follows on Monday. Forty days after Easter, Hutterites celebrate Ascension Day.

Hutterites are not unaffected by the secular cultural traditions that surround them. Some colonies, for example, have Easter egg hunts for young children, using hard-boiled eggs. Nothing is wasted, since the eggs are later eaten for breakfast, and such festivities do not detract very much from the central, spiritual, Easter theme.

CHRISTMAS AND NEW YEAR'S DAY

Christmas is also celebrated over three days, December 25–27. Before Christmas, families clean the entire colony: residences, dining halls, church buildings, and laundry facilities. This is also the time of year when colony members butcher hogs. Traditionally, each family would receive an allotment of shampoo, deodorant, and other domestic supplies at this time, but at many colonies basic supplies are now requested and provided whenever they are needed.

On or near Christmas Day, some colonies schedule special programs. Young people might put on plays and sing songs; at one colony, Santa Claus made an appearance. Morning and late-afternoon church services are held on Christmas Eve and Christmas day. In the evenings there are visits with family members and friends from nearby colonies. Groups of people gather to talk and sing Christmas songs as young people move from home to home singing carols.

With regard to gift-giving, some Hutterites follow a unique version of the Continental Saint Nicholas tradition. A couple of weeks before Christmas, the colony steward distributes fruit, nuts, cookies, candy, popcorn, chocolate, soda, and maybe sardines and a ham, to each family.[25] These gifts are referred to as *Necklus*. At some colonies, family members also exchange small personal items on Christmas Eve. Hutterites give cards with religious themes as well as coffee cakes, poppy-seed rolls, pumpkin bread, and handmade items such as comforters for babies and special eight-inch-square potholders.

On December 26, Canadian Hutterites observe Boxing Day, usually without a special celebration, or even knowledge of the date's historical importance, although some colony cooks prepare a meal of homemade

Herzwurst (heart sausage). One of the Christmas sermons is read on either the twenty-sixth or twenty-seventh. More important is January 1, when Hutterites celebrate Jesus's circumcision and naming as a day of spiritual purification. They are admonished, "Let us circumcise our hearts so all that is evil, unrighteous and displeasing to God could be cut off from us and not be seen by us anymore."[26] The New Year's sermon thanks God for his ongoing faithfulness. On January 6, Epiphany, when the Hutterites remember the arrival of the Wise Men at Jesus's home, the sermon is from Matthew 2:1–23. Paul S. Gross describes this as the time when Jesus "meets the Gentiles."[27]

PENTECOST

For Hutterites, the Day of Pentecost, celebrated fifty days after Easter, carries special meaning because of its association with the establishment of community of goods. Hutterites recognize the Holy Spirit's arrival in Jerusalem and his mesmerizing and energizing power as a seminal event in church history. They believe that the ongoing guidance of the Holy Spirit is essential for the successful operation of community of goods. Six separate Lehren on the Acts 2:1–42 text are delivered at Pentecost, as well as on the three following Sundays.

OTHER HOLIDAYS

Hutterites also celebrate other American and Canadian holidays. Although many Hutterites discourage this practice, on Halloween some children go trick-or-treating at colony residences, usually without wearing costumes. Even here there are exceptions. William Allard noticed a girl at a Montana Dariusleut colony who was dressed as Britney Spears. A boy was wearing a New York Yankees uniform and a Coors Light baseball cap.[28]

In the fall Hutterites celebrate *Objinka* or *Dankfest*, their own rendition of a Ukrainian Thanksgiving celebration. It is sometimes combined with the American or Canadian Thanksgiving, but dates and practices vary. The feast is usually on the Sunday after harvest, and a special Thanksgiving sermon is traditionally read. The focus is on gratefulness to God. There is no set protocol, but some colonies hold a special program where children recite poems and stories or sing harvest songs. The menu for the

Children at the Objinka (Thanksgiving) meal in Manitoba. Courtesy of Dora Maendel.

feast is substantial and might include shrimp, spare ribs, roast duck, and hot wings. In the fall Hutterites also pluck geese and ducks and each family is given one of many allotments of beer and wine.

Celebration of Mother's Day and Father's Day has also become increasingly popular among Hutterites. At one colony a fourteen-year-old boy was found furtively weeding and watering flower plants late one evening. He said that earlier in the year he had purchased some seeds and was growing flowers to give to his mother on Mother's Day.[29]

❧ ❧

IN HUTTERITE COLONIES THE MOVEMENT from childhood to adulthood is relatively smooth, as social patterns developed over hundreds of years change little from generation to generation. The Hutterite life cycle follows regular and particular ritual patterns. Older people are treated with great respect and honor and are relieved of the most difficult colony responsibilities at relatively young ages. Along with the celebration of holidays in special ways, the predictable pattern of life ensures a strong sense of communal identity.

Hutterite life patterns exhibit communitarian social principles, which represent an alternative to the individualistic North American ways of doing things. In chapter 7 we look more specifically at Hutterite cultural forms, including ethnic identity, dress, food and drink, folk traditions, and health practices.

CHAPTER 7

Identity, Tradition, and Folk Beliefs

*A sister here had a spiritual dream. She saw three fountains. One belonged
to us [Schmiedeleut], one to Darius Walter [Dariusleut] and the other to
Jacob Wipf of the Lehrerleut Community. When they took water out one
from the other, they all three ran together. I was joyful about this,
interpreting the dream to mean a true unification.*
—Michael Waldner, Schmiedeleut founder, 1876

Ethnicity and Family Names

As an ethnoreligious group, the Hutterites have developed important sui generis identity markers. In addition to unique religious
beliefs and practices, Hutterites speak an Austrian dialect and
have developed distinctive styles of dress, culinary practices, and folk traditions.

Because the Hutterites have married almost exclusively within the community, over the course of time they have become a new and unique ethnic
group. Most modern Hutterites are the direct descendants of about ninety
individuals, a situation brought about by two facts: their minimal emphasis on evangelism since the late eighteenth century and their practice of
keeping themselves as separate as possible from non-Hutterites. The result
is a closed assembly of clans with fourteen predominant surnames, a group
described by Pierre Van den Berghe and Karl Peter as "nepotistic communists."[1]

Because of the limited gene pool, the average Hutterite husband and wife are very closely related, and people bearing the fourteen most common family surnames account for 97 percent of the Hutterites. More specifically, only eleven of the family names are found in the Schmiedeleut, ten among the Lehrerleut, and nine in the Dariusleut. In a genetic and cultural sense, the Hutterites are one of the few new ethnic groups to have evolved during the past five hundred years. In this way they may be compared to members of older ethnoreligions such as Judaism and Armenian Orthodoxy.

The creation of a new ethnic group does not take as long as one might expect. In his book *Before the Dawn*, Nicholas Wade notes, "The genome evolves so fast that whenever any community starts to breed in isolation, whether for reasons of religion, geography or language, within a few centuries its genetics assume a distinctive signature." He also explains that "one version of a gene, especially in small populations, can displace all the other existing versions of the same gene in just a few generations," a phenomenon generally called genetic drift. Drift, according to Wade, "can lead to a single version of a gene becoming universal, or fixed, and all other versions being lost." Moreover, "If a population gets squeezed down to small numbers by some calamity, and then expands, its gene pool will be an amplified version of that of the few individuals who survived the disaster."[2] Wade's model follows the "founder effect" theory, which emphasizes that small ethnic groups like the Hutterites are heavily influenced by the special genetic makeup of what might be a very small number of founding mothers and fathers.

The fourteen most common Hutterite surnames are listed in table 7.1. During the twentieth century, two Mennonite names, Baer and Teichroeb, also gained recognition as Hutterite names. Seven of the fourteen names (Gross, Maendel, Stahl, Tschetter, Walter, Wipf and Wollman) are considered Old Hutterite.[3] All but one of these family names (Gross) preceded the influx of ex-Lutheran Carinthians in the mid-eighteenth century. The Old Hutterite names are of Austrian, south German, and Czech origin, and most of them have been found in the Hutterite Church since the sixteenth or seventeenth century.

Another five Hutterite names (Glanzer, Hofer, Kleinsasser, Waldner, and Wurz) are Carinthian Austrian in background. These represent descendents of Lutheran families who fled to Slovakia and joined the Hut-

Table 7.1. Surnames and ethnic backgrounds

Surname	Ethnic background
Decker	Mennonite
Entz	Mennonite
Glanzer	Carinthian
Gross	Old Hutterite
Hofer	Carinthian
Kleinsasser	Carinthian
Maendel	Old Hutterite
Stahl	Old Hutterite
Tschetter	Old Hutterite (Czech)
Waldner	Carinthian
Walter	Old Hutterite
Wipf	Old Hutterite
Wollman	Old Hutterite
Wurz	Carinthian

terites in the 1750s. The remaining two surnames, Decker and Entz, are ethnically Mennonite and come from families who joined the Hutterites in Russia in the 1780s and 1860s, respectively. Although it is of relatively recent Hutterite lineage, Entz is one of the most common Lehrerleut names.

In Frederick Manfred's 1948 novel *The Chokecherry Tree*, two men traveling through southeastern South Dakota drive into a town they call "Free Men" (actually the Prairieleut town of Freeman). "Yeh, bo, this is quite a town. Quite a town," notes one of the characters. " 'Everybody in it is related. Full a Hofers and Kleinsassers and Tschetters.' Fats cleared his nose with a guggling sniff, 'Yeh, an' when the Hofers get t'huffin', an' the Kleinsassers t'sassin', an' the Tschetters t'spittin' seeds, you got somethin.' "[4]

Hutterites do not joke about the sound of family names, but informally they often ascribe psychological characteristics to them. Many Hutterites believe that the family line a person belongs to is a strong indicator of what a person is or will become. Karl Peter notes that this view makes it difficult for some Hutterites to escape being typecast.[5] Hutterite stereotypes vary depending on whom one asks, but they show many commonalities. The following are perceptions based on formal inquiries and confirmed by representatives from each Leut.

It is often said that Deckers are natural leaders but that they "go to extremes" theologically and do not always follow through on their ideas. Entzes are progressive and always pushing the boundaries. Grosses are sensitive, well-organized, and good businessmen, but they are viewed as less interested in spiritual matters. Hutterites admit that this description, like all folk characterizations, does not fit everyone with the Gross name. But many Hutterites recall from a Chronicle account that the patriarch of the contemporary Hutterite Gross line, a man named Andreas, watched as his wife and children joined the church but did not join, himself.[6] In such speculation about genetic-ideological fusion, one can see the continuing influence of folk beliefs. Also evident is the powerful influence of the Chronicle as a religious and cultural reference point. Hutterites often talk as if events reviewed in the Chronicle happened just yesterday.

Hofer, the surname of about one-quarter of all Hutterites, is associated with stubbornness as well as ambition. Kleinsassers, like Deckers, are viewed as gifted leaders, full of ideas and eager to begin new ventures. Maendels are considered innovative but somewhat impatient. It is also said that Maendels like to be in charge. Stahls are quick learners and easygoing but not good organizers. Tschetters and Walters are said to be the most intellectually gifted of the Hutterites, but like the Stahls, they are not viewed as efficient administrators.

The name Waldner is the one that elicits the most diverse opinion. It is often said that there are so many Waldners that it is difficult to characterize them. Walters, found only among the Dariusleut, are seen as generous and outgoing but too intellectual. Wipfs and Glanzers are unsophisticated but shrewd; Wollmans are reserved and soft-spoken but great entrepreneurs. Wurzes are often described as questionable financial managers yet tolerant, open-minded people and great conversationalists. Within the Dariusleut, the Wurzes are known as strict traditionalists.

The Dariusleut are divided into quasi-clans or extended family groups, many of which are named after an important personality. For example, the Jubaleut group was named after Joseph Wipf, the *Crischtjanleut* after Christian Waldner, and the Wurzeleut after John Wurz. Specific traits and characteristics are attributed to persons who belong to these clans.

One Hutterite folk tradition suggests that progressive Dariusleut colonies are indebted to one Paul (or "Red Paul") Waldner, who left the Hutterite community in Ukraine in the 1860s, moved to France, and was a participant in the socialist Paris Commune movement in 1871. According to this story, Waldner rejoined the Hutterite community in 1874, right before they migrated to North America, with a Bible in one hand and *Das Kapital* in the other. The problem with this tale is that no Paul Waldner is listed in Hutterite records from that time period.

Many Hutterites see little value in surname stereotypes. Manitoban Betty Murphy notes, "We are so mixed up, you can't really say anything." Yet, according to Peter Gordon Clark, many Schmiedeleut surnames correlate with positions of colony leadership. Clark's mid-1970s study showed that some surnames were more often found in influential positions (minister, steward, farm manager, and German teacher) than others. In his study, people with the surname Decker, for example, were the most often highly placed. The names Glanzer and Waldner were next in line, while the three names least associated with influential positions were Tschetter, Stahl, and Gross.[7]

Our own 2008 study of the Dariusleut and the Lehrerleut found something very different. Surnames not associated with influential positions in Clark's Schmiedeleut study (Tschetter was one) were prominent among Dariusleut ministers and stewards. Among the Dariusleut and Lehrerleut, we found only minor differentiation between percentages of people with specific surnames in leadership positions and the total percentage of Leut males with those family names. For example, among the Lehrerleut, 17 percent of the "leaders" have the name Hofer, and Hofers account for 18 percent of the total Lehrerleut population. We did not find more than a 3 percent differential with regard to any surname.

Because a Hutterite woman moves to her husband's community, surnames at particular colonies change very slowly. The same is true of associated mother and daughter colonies. It is common, therefore, for someone to tell you that a particular colony is a "Hofer" or a "Waldner" colony. Young children at one colony ask, "Are you a Hofer or a Decker?" Table 7.2 gives the surname breakdown for one colony from each Leut.

With reference to Hutterite first names, Lawrence Anderson's study of the period 1885–1985 discovered that the most common were (in order of preference) Jacob, Joseph, David, Paul, and Joshua. Biblical names

Table 7.2. Surname distribution in four colonies

Leut	Colony	Surnames	Resident Total
Schmiedeleut One	Crystal Spring, MB	Baer (21) Boller (4) Evans (4) Hofer (8) Kleinsasser (83) Maendel (21) McAdam (9) Waldner (24)	174
Schmiedeleut Two	Spring Prairie, MN	Kleinsasser (4) Waldner (79) Wipf (63)	146
Dariusleut	Little Bow, AB	Hofer (125)	125
Lehrerleut	Miller, MT	Hofer (63) Kleinsasser (21) Waldner (10) Wipf (43) Wurz (15)	152

dominated. For girls, variations of Mary, Susanna, and Katharina were the most popular, followed by Anna, Sara, and Rachel. But name choices have changed a lot during the past twenty-five years. One page of the *Dariusleut Family Record List*—not an atypical one—includes the names Melanie, Chad, Jessica, and Brittney.[8] Dariusleut leaders, concerned about the naming trend, recently issued a statement requesting that members quit giving children nonbiblical names.

For legal and identifying purposes, Hutterites sometimes use their mother's family name as a middle name.[9] Others use the first letter of their spouse's first name as a middle initial. Men and women are also known by their spouse's first name, such as "Sarah's John." John and Elizabeth Tschetter might be referred to as "John E." (husband) and "John Elizabeth" (wife). It is also common to name a child after a recently deceased relative so that the relative's name will live on.

Hutterites do not have a national homeland, but many feel strong emotional ties to the United States, especially, and to Canada, to a lesser extent. There are also residual symbolic ties to Tirolean Austria, as expressed in the singing of the nationalistic song "Tirolean Boy," with its ebullient stanzas and chorus. This song appears in many informally produced Hutterite song collections and is especially well-known by the Dariusleut. Here are the lyrics of stanzas 1 and 3:

> 1. *I'm a Tirolean boy*
> *Always happy and cheerful*
> *I'm a Tirolean boy*
> *With happy cheer*
> *I'm from a lovely land*
> *The land you know so well*
> *This is my homeland*
> *You're called Tirol, Tirol, Tirol.*

> 3. *And when at last I die*
> *Take me there to be buried*
> *And when at last I die*
> *Take me there*
> *Take me to my Fatherland*
> *The land you know so well*
> *This is my homeland*
> *You're called Tirol, Tirol, Tirol.*

> *Chorus: You my Tirol, Tirol*
> *You my Tirol, Tirol*
> *You my Tirol*
> *I'll see you never more.*

Nonethnic Hutterians

The Hutterites became a closed ethnic group in the eighteenth and nineteenth centuries, while they were living in eastern Europe. After adding a few Mennonites, the surname structure was closed. Since that time, with two exceptions, the additions of nonethnic members have been few indeed. Two Mennonite names, Baer and Teichroeb, are now entrenched in

the Schmiedeleut and the Lehrerleut, even though persons with these surnames did not join the Hutterites until the twentieth century. There are
presently ten Baer and twelve Teichroeb families; and one member with
the Teichroeb surname has been selected as a minister. People with other
surnames have lived in Hutterite colonies for long periods of time without
making life commitments. Some were baptized (or rebaptized) and joined
the church but still did not stay for more than a few years.

The experience of two families illustrates such fluidity. During the
1960s and 1970s, the Dale and Margaret Mowry family lived in various Christian communes in California, Minnesota, and elsewhere. In the
1980s, they joined the Hutterites at Riverbend Colony, in Manitoba. But
the Mowrys have been in and out of the colonies ever since. A few of their
daughters married Hutterite men, but these families have left as well.[10]
In the 1990s, journalist Robert Rhodes and his family joined a Hutterite
colony in Minnesota. Attracted by the communal Christian mandate, they
worked hard to find a place in what Rhodes continues to view as an admi-
rable attempt to create a spiritual society. Although his family left in 2003
because of "cultural" differences, Rhodes continues to appreciate the years
he spent as a Hutterite.[11]

Some people come from the outside and stay longer. Patrick Murphy, a
member of a Schmiedeleut Two colony in Manitoba, is a graduate of the
Mennonite Goshen College in Indiana. His parents, Don and Michi Murphy, who have had a lifelong interest in communal forms of Christianity,
started a no-longer-functioning Dariusleut colony, Fan Lake, in the state
of Washington in 1990. Like Robert Rhodes, Patrick Murphy is attracted
to the Hutterites because of their commitment to communal Anabaptism.
Murphy is fluent in German and Hutterisch. He is also forthright about
his concern that "some members are only cultural Hutterites, not followers
of Christ." But Murphy does not expect perfection, and he is trying to live
within the context of what is at least a vague approximation of what the
Kingdom of God will be like. He recalls, "Some told me not to join if I was
expecting a perfect church, but to join if my focus was to work with them
and build the Kingdom of God."[12] Murphy is married to Betty Hofer, and
as of 2009 they had three children.

Patrick Murphy is also a rare case of an outsider who joined the Hutterites and found white-collar work. Although he also assists with colony
farm operations, Murphy's primary responsibilities are computer-related,

Hutterites Patrick and Betty Murphy and their children. Courtesy of Patrick Murphy. Photograph by Jim Murphy.

and he has an office packed with computer software, hardware, and other paraphernalia. He has found creative ways to integrate academic interests with colony responsibilities. For example, when driving trucks on the harvest crew, he fills many twenty-minute waiting periods with extensive reading, usually in religious studies.

Language

The first language of every Hutterite is Hutterisch, an Austrian dialect to which many Russian and English terms have been added, showing the influence of the various places where Hutterites have lived. Hutterisch is derived from the German dialects spoken in the rugged Alpine regions of Tirol and Carinthia. Some linguists view speakers of these closely related regional languages as an interconnected speech community extending from the Jura Alps to the Danube River.[13] People as diverse as Arnold

Schwarzenegger and Pope Benedict XVI speak closely related dialects. All American and Canadian Hutterites speak with strong accents influenced by Hutterisch forms and pronunciations.

According to linguist Herfried Scheer, 81 percent of Hutterisch words are foundationally German.[14] All but forty words originate in Austria. The remaining terms are of Moravian, Slovakian, Transylvanian, Wallachian, Ukraininan, and English background. Scheer explains that many of the added words describe objects or concepts that were unknown to early Hutterites, such as the English-sounding "eksercais" and "frut kek."[15]

In 1997 Prairieleut linguist Walter Hoover published the first Hutterisch-English dictionary and lexicon with his own phonetic interpretations. He also began translating the New Testament into Hutterisch, a project that was later pursued independently by Wycliffe Bible Translators. Manitoba Hutterite Linda Maendel has assisted the Wycliffe organization by translating Bible stories into Hutterisch and helping to create a Hutterisch-English dictionary.[16]

Retaining the dialect is important to Hutterites. It creates a boundary between sacred (Hutterite) and secular (non-Hutterite) spheres of existence. Most Hutterites believe in forms of the Sapir-Whorf linguistic theory, which suggests that it is difficult to express certain beliefs and thoughts outside the boundaries of particular linguistic traditions.[17] To the Hutterites, Hutterisch grammar and syntax declare a worldview that they want to keep, a distinctive culture that is imbued with spiritual connotations. They believe that retaining Hutterisch helps preserve cultural and religious singularity and is a constant identifier and public witness. Its use enforces the distinctiveness of the Hutterite way of life. Hutterites hope that in the future Hutterisch will continue to be the primary means of conversation in their communities. When a young girl asks, "Can you speak our language?" she is referring to Hutterisch, not German.

The preservation of standard German is also important. It is taught in the Hutterite German and Sunday schools and used in daily church services and for most public prayers. The Lehrerleut are the strongest proponents of preserving the German language. Founder Jacob Wipf felt so strongly about this that he usually refused to speak even Hutterisch. Until recently, most Hutterite documents, including the confession of faith, the Chronicle, the epistles, and the hymns, were published only in German, giving the language a semisacred character.

Young children speak primarily Hutterisch until they begin school at age five or six. Public schoolteachers often criticize the Hutterites for making Hutterisch the children's first language, believing that it holds them back academically. Numerous teachers challenged Max Stanton when he expressed support for the Hutterite position at an educator's conference in the mid-1990s. While academic progress may initially be slower, competence in two or more languages is hardly an academic drawback.

Hutterites often mix languages, combining Hutterisch, German, and English in a single conversation. Even during presentations at educators' conferences, the three are constantly blended. German teachers say that Hutterite children increasingly think in English first before translating into standard German, and they view this as a dangerous development. The Hutterisch dialect itself is changing daily, as more and more English words get mixed in. The use of three different languages thus presents a great dilemma. English is important for business and new converts. The retention of German and the general use of Hutterisch are important for religious and cultural reasons.

In the mid-to-late twentieth century, the Bruderhof pushed hard for the translation of Hutterite documents and resources into English, for purposes of evangelism and so that their own members could understand what was being read and said. This process continues in the Schmiedeleut One. Their response to German-language purists is that Jesus spoke Aramaic, the common language of the Palestinian people, not Hebrew, the language of the Old Testament.[18] Progressive colonies are also committed, however, to improving Hutterite knowledge and use of standard German. Confirming this interest, some progressive colony members have sought formal linguistic training at universities and institutes, including the Goethe Institute in Germany.

Dress

As nonconformists, Hutterites dress distinctively and always plainly. This practice is based on New Testament teachings such as those found in Romans 12 and 1 Peter 3. 1 Peter 3:3–4, which is addressed to women, advises: "Your adornment should be not an exterior one, consisting of braided hair or gold jewellery or fine clothing, but the interior disposition of the heart, consisting in the imperishable quality of a gentle and peaceful spirit, so precious in the sight of God."

Uniform dress is found in many status-bound societies, and in nine-teenth-century eastern Europe, there was nothing unusual about the Hut-terite (peasant) costume. But in North America, the Hutterites refused to adopt what became the common dress of rural inhabitants. Here their plain style of dress became a distinguishing mark of the Hutterite Chris-tian faith. Plain dress defines sexual roles and status and de-emphasizes the importance of outward forms of physical beauty. It indicates that the wearer intends to follow Jesus within the context of a particular church commitment and also signals that Hutterites are uninterested in the chang-ing fashions of the outside world.[19] Plain dress is a protest against materi-alism, egotism, and planned obsolescence.

Hutterite sermons often speak of the ongoing struggle between the flesh and the spirit. In the Hutterite view, plain dress helps control the power of the body for men and women, concealing that which is physi-cally attractive and reducing the strength of sexual temptation as it honors personal character. Neither men nor women show much skin. Jewelry and makeup are also anathema because they bring special attention to indi-viduals, betraying the principle of communal Gelassenheit. To dress sim-ply and without undue adornment is also practical and economical, saving resources for other colony operations.

The Hutterites' distinctive and uniform style of dress is a constant public reminder of their Christian identity, a form of existence that be-gins in this life and continues into the next. Their personal appearance exemplifies deeply held nonconformist convictions and shows modesty, humility, and simplicity. It also helps the community maintain control over behavior outside colony boundaries, since watchful non-Hutterites recognize members by their dress and know how they are expected to act. Thus Hutterites are prompted to think twice about engaging in unaccept-able behavior.

Nuances in dress distinguish each Hutterite Leut from the others, and there are small dress differences between conservative and liberal colo-nies, but these are not immediately noticeable to an outsider. Most mar-ried Hutterite men wear beards that are cut short and carefully trimmed. In some conservative Dariusleut colonies, however, longer beards are worn. The Lehrerleut are unique now in not wearing mustaches, although at an earlier time all Hutterites held this position. In 1884, for example, the Schmiedeleut Ordnungen stated, "It is forbidden to wear a mustache, much less to twirl it."[20]

Hutterite males usually wear black or very dark-colored pants, long-sleeved shirts that button in front with large collars, in various patterns, and suspenders instead of belts. Lehrerleut men wear plaid shirts and button them at the neck. Progressive colonies allow men to wear short sleeves during the warmer months, and the younger men often wear T-shirts. During the week, many Hutterite men wear baseball caps issued by seed companies, whereas a more formal, dark hat is worn for church services. These are removed before entering the sanctuary. When working in the bright sun, Hutterite men wear dark glasses or sunshades.

Plain, uniform dress is not always what it seems. At first glance, for example, Hutterites appear to show little interest in personalized dress. Three brothers, ages eighteen to twenty-five, are introduced at one colony. They are dressed in identical black cotton pants, similarly designed blue-and-black plaid shirts, and black suspenders. They have similar haircuts and look like students at a Catholic secondary school with a strict dress code. The young men appear oblivious to the way they are viewed. But Hutterites express individuality in subtle ways. For example, among the thirty to forty girls in the Western Manitoba Hutterian Choir at a concert in 2007, no two of them wore dresses that were exactly alike. Some of the prints and colors were similar, but, looking closely, one could see that there were no identical dresses.

The Lehrerleut hold the most conservative position on dress, allowing a more limited selection of colors and print styles. Women wear more subdued, darker dresses, although many have calico, plaid, paisley, or floral prints. Older men in Lehrerleut and Dariusleut colonies in Alberta and Saskatchewan often wear cowboy hats, but they are not found among the Schmiedeleut in Manitoba and South Dakota. During the summer, some Schmiedeleut males wear sandals with socks. Samuel Waldner once wore sandals while delivering a sermon. Responding to critics, he asked, "What do you think Jesus wore on his feet?" One Dariusleut cattle boss says that he lets Hutterite women "put blue jeans on under their dresses when they are branding the calves."[21]

All Hutterite women wear long dresses or skirts that extend nearly to the ankles. Various colors are displayed, with an emphasis on blue, brown, and green. Dresses come in a variety of patterns, but younger girls typically wear brighter colors. With skirts, Hutterite women wear white or light-colored blouses that can be short-sleeved, except in the most conser-

A Dariusleut youth gathering in Washington. Courtesy of Max Stanton.

vative colonies. Traditionally, matching aprons were worn over the skirt; many Lehrerleut and conservative Dariusleut and Schmiedeleut Two women have kept the apron custom, but in more progressive colonies, the women no longer wear aprons, even at church services. Hutterite women also wear matching black vests and jackets and usually low black shoes and black polka-dotted kerchiefs. A bonnet is often worn at night.

Most Hutterite women never cut their hair, and all females cover their heads with a *Kupftiechle*, a usually black-and-white polka-dotted head covering or scarf. Girls under age ten often wear a bonnet (*Mitz*); most of them wear their hair braided. Girls and women older than age ten braid and tack their hair, placing it in a bun on top of the head. It is common for Dariusleut women to part their hair into four sections: they make a part from the middle of the forehead straight back, as well as across the top from ear to ear. The Schmiedeleut show more diversity, some of them brushing their hair straight back. Lehrerleut women wear starched Kupf-tiechlen with large white dots on a black background. Dariusleut women have smaller dots on their head coverings. Many of them start with a piece of black cloth, then apply small white dots with a fabric ink pen. A plastic stencil ensures that the dots are evenly spaced. Younger women wear head coverings with a geometric or floral design instead of dots.[22]

The meaning of a particular form of dress is subjective and socially determined. A non-Hutterite teen who saw a Hutterite girl remove her head covering said that it was shocking, almost as if she had taken off her blouse.[23] Slight modifications indecipherable to outsiders mean a great deal to Hutterites. They say a lot about personal character, demeanor, and position. The way one dresses may indicate a respectful or a disrespectful attitude.

Female (and male) dress is most relaxed among the Schmiedeleut One. But even in Schmiedeleut Two, head coverings have moved farther back on the head in recent years. The same is true for liberal Dariusleut. The head covering sometimes disappears completely inside private homes, or it is placed far back on the head. Liberal Hutterites attach their head coverings loosely with hairpins, leaving them untied under the chin, giving a winglike effect. At one colony a woman walks into the living room, where a group of adults is visiting, with freshly washed and uncovered hair. For another person, the head covering serves as little more than a support for a loose ponytail.

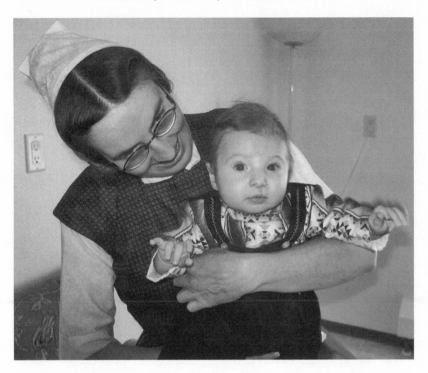

A Lehrerleut woman and her son. Courtesy of Max Stanton.

Before baptism Hutterite men and women have more freedom with regard to dress and hairstyles. And the dress code is not rigidly followed for children. In any case, change is in the air. Many older women now dye their hair, women of all ages shave their legs, and some Hutterite women use cosmetics, including small amounts of lipstick, nail polish, and blush. Some women wear sandals, and many Schmiedeleut One members wear wristwatches. Confronted by a member of a conservative colony, a Schmiedeleut One individual defended himself with the question "What's that long chain coming out of your pocket?" (other Leut allow pocket watches).

Although plain dress helps to conceal the female form, changes that occur over the years have tended to reduce this effect. For example, among the Schmiedeleut skirts have moved up from ankle-length to calf-length. In addition, there is increased interest in preserving one's looks with special diets and exercise, which are also popular because of health considerations. For some Hutterites, interaction with outsiders has created self-conscious discomfort with their traditional dress and appearance.

Most Lehrerleut clothing continues to be handmade from commercial cloth. The only clothing that is purchased regularly from stores is the special garb required for cleaning and disinfecting dairies, hog barns, and meat-processing facilities. Colonies in other Leut are buying more and more mass-produced clothing, especially for males. Many Dariusleut men wear black Levi and Wrangler jeans, which have a more tapered cut as well as pockets. "What does it matter," says one minister. "The pants are made by a sewing machine, not by God."

With the exception of underwear and stockings, most women's clothing continues to be made by colony seamstresses. Some communities also make their own shoes, gloves, and boots, but leatherwork is gradually becoming a lost art. Low prices in discount stores make it difficult to justify the time and effort colony craftsmen must invest to do the work.

Hutterite clothing is made from durable cotton and synthetics that do not fade quickly. Some "wash and wear" fabrics are purchased from Old Order Amish stores. Other textiles come from traveling salesmen, who spread out their large swaths of cloth and dry goods for Hutterite women to view in the colony kitchen. The *Hutterite Directory* carries ads from fabric stores that sell the kinds of cloth that are preferred by Hutterite clients.

Common dress and limited interest in individual expression does not mean that Hutterites do not have specific perceptions regarding what looks good and what does not. There are Hutterite styles and there is a Hutterite fashion sense, even if it operates only within the confines of the colony world. When he noticed fifteen-year-old visitor Annika Janzen wearing a long skirt, a smiling Hutterite male told a girl nearby, in Hutterisch, "You should put her [Annika] in a Hutterite skirt. She'd look better." The Hutterite girl responded sharply, "She's fine the way she is." But the man's comment indicates that there is indeed a Hutterite sense of style.

Sayings, Expressions, Humor, and Demeanor

Hutterites believe that you should be up-front and honest in personal relations and communication. Non-Hutterites are often taken aback by this modus operandi and think the Hutterites are rude or unsophisticated. But their manner is merely the result of the Hutterites' battle against hypocrisy, superficiality, and misunderstanding. They hold that an honest approach to all of life's contingencies encourages unpretentiousness and self-denial. Rod Janzen noted in an earlier work, "A critical approach to personal behavior and ideals is thought to foster humility and self-abnegation. People are not to think so highly of themselves that they take offense at straightforward personal comments." Evaluations of workshops at a 2007 Hutterite education conference elicited comments such as "The shorter the sweeter" and "Eve was led astray by one fruit. We have thousands in front of us."[24]

Donald B. Kraybill writes that Hutterites have "not been smothered by the superficial graces of middle-class culture."[25] Hearing that a young Hutterite woman and her aunt were going to accompany Max Stanton on his drive to another colony, a minister responded, "Well, I really don't see a problem here. But if anything happens to her [the younger woman], I'll chase you all the way to Africa if I have to!"[26] When asked about differences between the Israeli kibbutzim and the Hutterites, a Schmiedeleut minister said, "The kibbutz [sic] have guns under their beds." After Rod Janzen commented on the summer heat, he received the retort, "Hell will be hotter."[27] A common Hutterite saying is that you should not "speak negatively about your mother colony. She takes care of you." Another well-known saying contains a lesson about the importance of spiritual leaders:

> *Ein Schaff ohne Hirt*
> *Ein Schnaffner ohne Wirt*
> *Ein Schreiber ohne Feder*
> *Ein Schuster ohne Leder*
> *Ein volk ohne Lehr*
> *Ist nicht weit daher.*
> *(A sheep without a shepherd*
> *A worker without a leader*
> *A writer without a pen*
> *A cobbler without leather*
> *A people without teachings*
> *Is in no time not there.)*

And the linguistically mixed saying "Too soon *alt*, Too late *schmart*" speaks to the human condition throughout life.

Mennonite folklorist Reuben Goertz told the story of a Hutterite who, en route to North America in the 1870s, became terrified that during a storm on the Atlantic Ocean the ship was going to capsize. He appealed to the captain, who told him to go down to the boiler room, where workers were stoking the furnaces. These men had been in many storms, and the captain warned that they were a "wild and tough bunch . . . and they swear terribly." "But that's all right," he continued, "because once they stop swearing you'll know they are scared. When that happens you can start to say your prayers." The Hutterite went below and soon returned with a smile of relief on his face. "The Lord be praised," he exclaimed," they are still swearing."[28]

Karl Peter proposed that intense persecution throughout Hutterite history had created a people with "a high degree of uniformity in those psychological characteristics that were indispensable for defying the authorities." These included "courage, perseverance and obstinacy."[29] Perhaps, he concluded, "the no-holds-barred interactional structure . . . has a psychohistorical foundation in a history of unrelenting persecution and harassment."[30] Hutterites are not sure what to make of this kind of analysis. But they are committed to unpretentious speech and straightforward interpersonal relations, and in the Hutterite world "please," "thank you" and "I'm sorry" tend to be absent, especially in male environments. The tone of the voice conveys more, sometimes, than the words that are spoken.

Hutterites speak forthrightly about ideas and human actions. They often express personal opinions, stating them with what appears to be an air of confidence and finality—though they do not always mean what they appear to mean. There are comments about individual strengths and weaknesses, quality of work, decisions made or not made, and virtually anything positive or negative that takes place on the colony grounds. One might call this gossip. But it is an integral part of Hutterite life, and it has psychological benefits.

Gossip is a two-edged sword. Ruth Lambach says that in Hutterite society, "petty arguments and human likes and dislikes are often passed on, from one generation to the next." But gossip can also protect people from taking themselves too seriously. In a book on spirituality, Kathleen Norris writes that gossip can provide insights into what makes people tick.[31]

It also provides a forum for expressions of dissent. Among the Hutterites it does not really matter what you think or say, as long as your actions adhere to the Ordnungen. Gossip serves as an acceptable way for Hutterite women, in particular, to express their personal opinions. In a small, closed, patriarchal society women can exert significant social and political power by this means. Talk also plays an important role in the church discipline process.

Some Hutterite leaders do not like gossip and attack it forcefully. Manitoba minister Ben Maendel is known for the following comment: "Intelligent people discuss ideas, average people discuss other people, and below average people discuss themselves."[32] A sermon Vorred notes, "Indeed, gossip is among the seven things hated by the Lord," and the Bruderhof's "Law of Sannerz" forbade talk behind anyone's back (how successfully is debatable).[33] But gossip is a complicated phenomenon; even those Hutterites who have tried to eradicate it have not been very successful. In the highly verbal Hutterite culture, gossip is widespread and is fostered by new switchboard access systems, cell phones, and Internet chat rooms. Sooner or later most of what is said about a person gets back to the person.

The no-holds-barred Hutterite persona is an important cultural tradition. Hutterites often raise their voices and appear impatient. A woman sitting in the backseat of a car, tired of her mother's entreaty to keep her children quiet, responds (in Hutterisch): "Mom. Be quiet and stay up front."[34] One evening a young girl walks up to one of the authors and instructs, "We're leaving tomorrow morning at 5:30 a.m. and you're coming along."[35] Hutterites do not always wait patiently for someone to finish a sentence or gather her or his thoughts. Verbal apologies are rare, although if a gardener accidentally plows under a healthy two-hundred-foot row of ready-to-pick Chinese sugar peas (as once happened), regrets are offered.

Hutterites constantly tease and test each other with sarcastic wit, humor, and seriousness, woven together in a single conversation. A young man in a truck drives up to a group of Hutterites resting under a tree and says: "If anyone is getting too much shade, you can join us at the potato shed." He is helping construct a new one in the 95-degree heat. The man then requests sunblock.

While humor is important, loud boisterous laughter is not characteristic or much appreciated. Hutterite wit is rather expressed in words, with accompanying smiles, in comments that are filled with irony. At times it seems that every other statement has a funny or self-deprecating side. In the evening, young people move from house to house in search of new stories, new songs, or a new audience. Two Hutterite girls smile at the way a borrowed Hutterite coat looks on an outsider. "You better button it up, it doesn't look right," says one. At another colony, a ten year-old girl asks, in Hutterisch, if one of the authors is a "Christian." Everyone in the room smiles, but the question is a serious one. For the girl, "Christian" is synonymous with "Hutterite." In front of her is a man (Rod Janzen) dressed in black pants and a long-sleeved shirt, who has a trimmed beard. But he is also wearing a belt and has an English accent, and no one in the room is speaking Hutterisch. The girl's question is humorous to the listening Hutterites.

Some Hutterite humor is expressed in the widespread use of nicknames. A man called Five-Star likes a particular brand of whiskey. At one colony, one finds Tiger, Butch, and Happy. The latter is a man recognized for a rather unhappy personality. Some nicknames describe personal attributes or skills, for example, Shop Joe, Chicken Mac, and Preacher Joe. Others are forms of first names: Betts for Bethany, Lena for Helen. Still others are nonsensical and often derived from childhood experiences, such as Bamboo and Steam.

Humor is also helpful in getting a point across. Upset that ex-Hutterite novice Terry Miller is siding with the Schmiedeleut Two, Group One minister Arnold Hofer drives up to Terry's house to talk to him. According to Hofer, Miller confirms his position and bases it on a manuscript authored by Donald Gibb, with which both are familiar. "Do you really believe everything that Gibb wrote?" Hofer asks. Miller's response is "Probably 75 percent of it is accurate." Hofer retorts, "You know, Terry, the last time I was here you came walking out of the garden in your shorts and very tipsy." When Terry starts to protest, Hofer says "Well, wouldn't you say that at least 75 percent of what I just told you is true?"[36]

At the Forest River Colony, in North Dakota, Tony and Kathleen Waldner are congratulated for completing thirty-one years of marriage. Tony's response: "Well, the first thirty were the hardest."[37] Upon hearing complaints about a writer whose publications were duplicated and widely distributed by Hutterites, a minister quips, "He should feel honored. Plagiarism is the highest compliment a Hutterite can give you."

Hutterites combine honest reflection with a commitment to nonviolence. In Samuel Kleinsasser's words, "Passive virtues tend to oil the machinery of social intercourse. Generally applied they neutralize friction and disarm hostile situations."[38] In order to live communally, one must be a master of patience and have the ability to look at life's inconsistencies and problems with humor and humility.

Although Hutterites are busy people, there is always time to talk. There is much curiosity about "the world" and life in general, and talk with guests continues late into the evening. When Rod Janzen arrives at one colony, a woman asks, "What did you experience that was least expected, or the biggest surprise in those other colonies you visited?"[39] Questions asked reflect Hutterite understandings of life elsewhere. A fifteen-year-old visitor is continually queried about what she is going to do after completing high school: "What are your plans for the future?" Most Hutterite girls marry, raise children, and assume colony roles. The girls are aware that the outsider's options are different, and they want to know what she will choose.

At a Hutterite colony, Sunday especially is a day for visiting. Gatherings in homes exude a close family atmosphere, and guests are quickly drawn in and made to feel part of the group. This happened to a young girl in summer 2006. Arriving at a colony she had never visited, she was taken away by a group of young women and not seen again until the next morning. When asked how things had gone the following day, her response was that "it was awesome."[40]

Some Hutterites use mild forms of profanity or crudity, often in the Hutterisch dialect but sometimes in English. The word *hell*, for example, is frequently employed to stress the importance of a particular comment. And at a Lehrerleut colony, a middle-aged man exclaims, "The weather sure is shitty" (it is a very hot day). In James Michener's book *Centennial*, his Pennsylvania Mennonites use earthy expressions; he would find the Hutterites speaking the same way.

Eating and Drinking

Hutterite colony menus include a heavy dose of meat, potatoes, and fried delicacies. Hutterites eat a lot of beef, poultry, and pork, as well as homemade noodles, breads, fried potatoes, and dumpling soup. In recent years, pasta, pizza, chow mein, and crab salad have also started to appear at Hutterite meals.

At most colonies, males and females are seated on opposite sides of the community dining hall, or *Essenstuben*. most Hutterite children of ages five to fifteen eat separately in the Essenschul, under the supervision of the German teacher and usually his wife. Lehrerleut children eat in the main dining hall after the adults have finished. At certain times of the year, meals and snacks are carried to workers in the fields.

In the dining hall, members are traditionally served at long rectangular tables in groups of four. Each group shares serving dishes and takes bowls and utensils from a stack placed in front of them. Females clean up afterward, but in some colonies members take their plates and utensils to a central location before leaving the building. At colony tables, paper towels, Kleenex, and damp cloths often substitute for napkins.

Some dining-hall changes are in process. An increasing number of Schmiedeleut colonies, for example, serve meals buffet-style. This system eliminates the need for servers, and less food is wasted. The food is hotter, there are fewer dishes to wash, and it is also more sanitary because serving spoons are placed at each food site. In traditional Hutterite dining, members use their own forks and spoons to take food from the common serving bowls. But some Hutterites dislike the new buffet system. One man notes that the first people through the line always take the choicest pieces of meat.

In the 2000s one sees more healthful diets than the traditional ones: a greater assortment of salads, raw vegetables, and fresh fruit is provided. An afternoon snack at a Dariusleut colony in Washington consists of apricots instead of cookies. Lunch at another colony includes a whole-wheat sandwich filled with ham, turkey, cheese, avocados, lettuce, and sprouts. The meal is accompanied by a glass of orange juice and topped off with slices of watermelon. Hutterite desserts often consist of fresh fruit. Cakes, cookies, and other more traditional desserts are eaten at breaks or in the evening. Late-night snacks also include crackers, cheese, and meat.

Each colony has a large garden that provides most of the community's vegetables and fruit. Vegetable gardens produce tomatoes, peas, sunflowers, sweet corn, and radishes. Colony-grown fruit includes juneberries, raspberries, strawberries, grapes, and watermelons, as well as apples, cherries, pears, and apricots. Hutterites also collect wild fruit such as chokecherries and mulberries. Some colonies purchase additional truckloads of fruit and vegetables off-site at bargain prices. Costs are shared with other colonies, and the fruit and vegetables are canned, dried, or frozen.

Colonies also raise livestock and butcher and package their own meat. They are well-known for very lean bacon and commercial eggs that are packaged with distinctive labels. Colonies also produce milk, ducks, geese, hogs, and turkeys in quantities that often exceed the combined production of non-Hutterite growers in the states and provinces where they are located.[41] When Hutterites look down at their plates, they know that most of what they are about to consume has been grown or raised at the colony.

Breakfast at one Dariusleut colony includes a fresh peeled cucumber, raw broccoli, and cauliflower, accompanied by oatmeal topped with raisins and almonds, and a variety of pickled vegetables. At another colony breakfast is coffee, muffins, pancakes, eggs, and bacon. At mealtimes Hutterites eat quickly and consume relatively small amounts of food. But there is constant snacking, at midmorning and midafternoon coffee breaks and in the evening. More healthful diets mean thinner men and women. However, Hutterites still seem to be eating all the time.

Hutterite coffee breaks are important interruptions of the workday that energize the mind as well as the body because of the social interaction that occurs. Snack foods may include barbecue potato chips, candy bars, and tomato sandwiches. The fare varies greatly; a snack might also be raw vegetables, nuts, and raw sunflower seeds. Fresh fruit is served, as well as yogurt, cake, and packaged cookies. Coffee-break drinks are sodas, tea, strong coffee, and homemade herb teas. Packaged goods come from large-scale purchases at discount stores in nearby towns and cities.

Traditional Hutterite foods that continue to be popular include *Gashtel* (crumbled noodle soup), *Nukelen* (egg dumpling soup), *Kartoffelknedel* (potato dumplings), *Fleischkrapfen* (meat dumplings), *Griebenschmaltz* (goose or pork crackling spread), *G'schmolzmanudel* (large fried noodles), *Moos* (various kinds of fruit puddings), string-bean soup, fried cornmeal, pickles, and *Stritzel* (coffee cake).

At a colony in Minnesota, morning "coffee" consists of Reese's Pieces, cake, and a strong cup of coffee. The noon meal includes ribs, noodles, dumpling soup, carrots, peas, and homemade bread. At about two thirty it is time to snack again, with coffee, freshly baked chocolate chip cookies, and "smoothies" in the home of a colony member. A three-o'clock snack at another colony includes flavored, iced Starbucks coffee. At a third colony, coffee and cookies at eleven in the morning are followed an hour later by baked chicken and rice, boiled unpeeled potatoes, and cauliflower. Berry cobbler is served for dessert.

Every meal at a Hutterite colony begins with a standard prayer delivered by the field boss or one of the elders. In colonies where ministers eat in the dining hall, the minister delivers the prayer. The common blessing is

> Wir bitten Dich Herr Gott Himmlischer Vater
> Segne alle diese Deine Gaben
> die Wir von dir zu uns nehmen und empfangen werden
> Durch Jesum Christum. Amen.
> (We ask thee, dear God, heavenly Father
> To bless all of these, thy gifts, that we are about to partake of
> Through Jesus Christ. Amen.)

After the prayer, colony members eat very quickly and often in relative silence, especially if no guests are present. After ten to fifteen minutes, plates are emptied and a second prayer, of thanks, is said for the meal just consumed. Everyone except guests rushes off as Hutterite women gather around the tables, waiting to remove plates, glasses, and utensils. Many outsiders continue to sit before plates that are half full. When asked why there is a prayer after every meal, one Hutterite responds, "Since we ask God to bless the food before we eat it, isn't it even more important to thank God for it afterward, or are we saying that we didn't appreciate it?"[42] Prayers at some progressive colonies are extemporaneous and in English.

Alcohol and Tobacco

Hutterites drink alcohol in moderation, following Ecclesiasticus 31:27: "Wine gives life if drunk in moderation. What is life worth without wine? It came into being to make people happy. Drunk at the right time and in the right amount, wine makes for a glad heart and a cheerful mind." Furthermore, the Hutterite Chronicle notes that since Jesus in the New Testament commanded his disciples to drink wine, he expects his followers to do likewise when they meet him in heaven. The biblical support for this view, though metaphorical, is Matthew 26:29: "From now on, I tell you, I shall never again drink wine until the day I drink the new wine with you in the kingdom of my Father."

In the early nineteenth century at Raditschewa, the Hutterites produced twelve thousand liters of spirits annually.[43] Hutterites no longer make hard liquor, but most North American colonies have vintners who make the colony's wine. They use whatever fruit is available: rhubarb, chokecherries, raspberries, peaches, different varieties of grapes, and even dandelions; and sometimes they experiment by combining fruits. One of the Hutterite winemakers' experiments produced a rhubarb-raspberry concoction. In the evening guests are invited to sample a glass. After a particularly hard day's work, bottles of beer are placed on dining-hall tables.

Hutterite and non-Hutterite male guests are sometimes offered harder drinks, such as scotch, schnapps, or whiskey. This is a longstanding Hutterite tradition. Prairieleut minister Paul Tschetter, one of the 1873 delegates to North America, drank a jigger of schnapps every day before lunch as well as consuming a glass of wine before he retired at night.[44] Hutterites do not tolerate drunkenness, however, and at some colonies alcoholism is a problem because some members have a hard time limiting themselves to one or two drinks. Those people are not well respected in the Hutterite community. As a result a few Hutterite colonies have become collective abstainers; many ministers advocate less consumption of alcohol at festive events. There have even been a few dry Hulbas and weddings.

Tobacco use has always been an anathema for Hutterites. During Paul Tschetter's 1873 visit to North America, one of his major complaints about American Mennonites was that they smoked; even some of the women did. In the 1950s, theologian and Koinonia Farm founder Clarence Jordan developed a close relationship with the Forest River Colony, in North Dakota. But he did not like the Hutterites' no-tobacco position. Jordan said he "would rather have smoking than drinking," since "smoking doesn't destroy families."[45] He pointed out that alcohol was easier to hide and more easily abused than tobacco because it was colony-produced, whereas cigarettes had to be purchased with private funds from local stores. Forest River Hutterites told Jordan that he was just rationalizing his own love for tobacco. The stated Hutterite position does not mean that Hutterite colonies are smoke-free, however. By the early 1980s, so many Schmiedeleut men were smoking (as many as 25%, according to one minister) that Jacob

Kleinsasser launched a major no-smoking campaign, which significantly reduced the problem.

Recreation and Play

For most Hutterite adults, recreation consists primarily of visiting and traveling. Colony workloads are heavy and involve much physical exercise, so it is not considered appropriate for adults to engage in activities and games that are designed purely to entertain. Moreover, colony work is not viewed negatively and there is constant movement, as men and women go from one activity to another, fixing, cleaning, planning, and philosophizing. A conservative German teacher commented, "There is no time for sports. This takes time away from more important things."[46]

The Hutterite Ordnungen contain rules against listening to the radio or watching television or films. Many colonies discourage organized sports. But even the Lehrerleut allow their children to play softball, baseball, hockey, and kickball when the games are supervised by "English" schoolteachers. One Lehrerleut colony holds an annual "end of the school year" barbecue, where schoolchildren play softball after eating. No one keeps score, but everyone has a lot of fun. As long as the sexes are separated, most colonies allow young people to swim in local ponds or in dammed-up streams. At a traditional colony in Alberta, young boys were swimming in a canal.[47] A few Hutterite children have taken swimming lessons at public pools.

In any large community or social institution, there is always a gap between belief and practice. Many Hutterites, for example, listen to the radio every day. Farm equipment often comes equipped with radios as well as CD players, and progressive colonies do not always remove them. Many Hutterites are avid fans of local and national sports teams. In Canada hockey is especially popular; in the United States Hutterites listen to baseball and football games. In one schoolhouse a Hutterite teacher listens to Christian rock music on a tape player while her students are working on an assignment in an adjoining room.

At another colony a male runaway, Bobby Walter, became an internationally ranked bull rider. While he was away, Walter sent back some of his earnings. On one occasion many Hutterite friends and relatives attended a rodeo on a Sunday afternoon, right after the church service, to

Hutterite children on horseback. Courtesy of Max Stanton.

show support. That morning the minister reminded congregants that they should keep the Lord's Day holy, but he knew that two colony vans were leaving for the rodeo as soon as the service was finished. Walter eventually gave up the circuit, returned to the colony, married, and is now a committed member.[48]

Hutterites have an assortment of pets, including dogs, cats, and parakeets. Jacob Kleinsasser's friendly and full-of-life Pekingese follows a visitor in and out of buildings all around the colony. Dogs are also used for herding and guarding livestock, and cats keep the mouse population down. Some Hutterites use ATV's (All Terrain Vehicles) and snowmobiles for recreational purposes. At one colony a few boys ride BMX bicycles off the barn roof into a pile of hay.[49]

Hutterite children play with an assortment of dolls, building blocks,

Legos, and toy vehicles. Younger children are pushed around on traditional Hutterite-made two-wheel wagons with long handles (*Teichsel Veg-*
ela). Games of baseball, horseshoes, soccer, ice hockey, and even lacrosse
are popular, and some colonies have large sports fields that accommodate
these interests. A few colonies have gymnasiums with volleyball and basketball courts. Huttterite children also play cops and robbers and hide and
seek. A lot of teasing accompanies all of these activities.

The children are free to roam the colony grounds at will. They move
fearlessly across running creeks and rivers and along steep rocky banks,
where they encounter snakes and other wild animals as well as poison ivy.
In the course of an evening walk, Rod Janzen meets a fully clothed eleven-
year-old girl playing by herself in a shallow river. She is soaked but smiling, wrapped up in her own fantasy world. No one is monitoring her behavior. She is indeed a trusted babysitter. Jumping into bins of harvested
grain is another dangerous but popular pastime.

Recreational activities carry some risk, but early training in the practical arts and the imposition of serious responsibilities builds confidence
for Hutterite boys and girls at very young ages. Comfortable in all sorts of
physically demanding situations, they display little fear of the unknown
and little hesitancy to try something new, as long as they are on the colony
grounds. The unfortunate result, according to Victor Kleinsasser, is that
the accidental death rate for Hutterite children in Manitoba colonies is
higher than for rural non-Hutterite children in the area.[50]

Schmiedeleut One German teacher Jonathan Maendel suggests that
Hutterite young people need "watering holes," places where they can get
"refreshed" after work. At his colony (Baker, in Manitoba), members have
constructed walking and running paths through virgin forest, as well as
a hockey court—ice-skating rink, which serves as a tennis court part of
the year. A golf cart takes us quickly around those colony grounds. Some
colonies build ponds and stock them with fish, and the ponds also serve
as swimming holes. Other colonies have pool tanks with diving boards,
tubes, and other equipment. At one colony a small swimming pool was
heated by solar panels. Inflatable plastic pools are sometimes used by
young children.

Outdoor activities unrelated to work are novel for the Hutterites but
increasing in frequency. There are barbecues, organized hikes, and bonfire
services. At the Decker Colony, in Manitoba, ten to fifteen tents have been

set up in a wooded area, where the children are in the midst of a three-night campout. Each evening other members of the colony join them, all gathering around a campfire to sing. A small ensemble also performs gospel songs, including "In the Sweet Bye and Bye." Colony members sit on the ground or on folding chairs, while girls pass out potato chips, popcorn, and hot chocolate. Occasionally adults caution the younger children to "quit running." At Schmiedeleut One choral festivals, singing groups from various colonies perform for large audiences.

For Hutterites, travel continues to be one of the most popular forms of recreation. In the case of outings related to work assignments at other colonies, the trips might be combined with sightseeing in the mountains or visits to historic sites. Travelers stop at museums, zoos, large malls, and even water parks. One time a Hutterite woman bought a modern one-piece swimsuit. When confronted, she said, "This is better than going dressed as a Hutterite. I don't want to make a spectacle of myself."[51] One group of Hutterite youth visited the Old Order Amish in central Ohio. Ministers in all Leut drive regularly to meetings at other colonies. Their spouses often join them, and there are always a few older men and women who go along to visit friends and relatives. Weddings, funerals, baptisms, and hospitalizations bring a host of interested and empathetic visitors.

Hutterite women are often given two weeks in early spring, and sometimes another week or two in winter, to visit their home colonies. If they have young children, they take them along to see grandparents, uncles and aunts, and cousins. When a woman gives birth to a new baby, it is common for one or two unmarried sisters, cousins, or close friends to come and help out. They get rides with Hutterite men who are on the road selling products or buying equipment.

Among the Dariusleut, planting and harvest seasons vary with the differing north-to-south and east-to-west locations of colonies. The climatic influences of the Rocky Mountains and the Arctic north also affect growing seasons. It is thus quite common for teens and single adults to visit distant colonies for two or three weeks at a time to help with the planting or harvesting of crops. The matchmaking and dating possibilities of these visits are endless. Many Canadian and American Hutterites also travel to Mexico to seek special medical treatment. Some Canadian Hutterites visit the Mayo Clinic in Rochester, Minnesota, when the Canadian health care system (which they generally like) does not provide the services they want or asks them to wait too long to see medical specialists.

Business travel is increasing as Hutterites seek new markets for their agricultural and industrial products. Travelers save money on motels and restaurants by staying overnight at other colonies or with friends in other Old Order Anabaptist groups. In turn, Amish, Old German Baptist Brethren, and other travelers take lodging at Hutterite colonies. Some Hutterites have flown to Europe as guests of the John Deere Company and Case International. A few traveled to Hawaii to attend an agricultural equipment show. One group of men went salmon fishing in Alaska on a trip paid for by a farm machinery company. Hutterite work crews drive to Arizona to pick oranges and to Georgia for peaches.

A Hutterite man once entered a drawing at the Edmonton Mall in Alberta and won a vacation to Hawaii. When he asked his wife to join him, she refused and told him to give the funds to the colony. But he went anyway, taking a single adult daughter with him. On returning to Alberta, the two had to stand in front of the church and ask forgiveness, but for them the trip was worth it.

Some Hutterites have visited historic Anabaptist and Hutterite sites in eastern Europe. In 2007 Paul and Susie Hofer represented North American Hutterites at an event sponsored by the Austrian Government to recognize the 471st anniversary of Jacob Hutter's death. Others have returned to historic Hutterite villages, or their remains, in Ukraine, Hungary, the Czech Republic, and Slovakia. A few Hutterites have toured Israel. Many of these trips were associated with academic or church conferences.

Lehrerleut and conservative Dariusleut colonies often criticize the increasing travel and recreational involvements of other Hutterites. They believe that many of these activities are unnecessary, diversionary, too expensive, and not done for the glory of God. Not all recreational activities are accepted even in Schmiedeleut colonies. We once encountered a group of young Hutterites folk dancing in the dining hall. The activity was stopped immediately by the colony minister.

Some Hutterites also like to hunt, even though the church was historically opposed to it. The confession of faith and the Chronicle both speak against the use of guns. In 1633 Andreas Ehrenpreis wrote, "There is also a rumor that some brethren . . . own and use guns. This should not be, for what profit is a gun to the brother? It has never been permitted in the *Ge-*

mein in the past and shall also not be permitted in the future." After hearing about sales of elk meat by colony men, one Montana minister ordered that "every gun in the colony be put in a pile. The barrels were bent to uselessness."[52] But trapping foxes and shooting animals that are a threat to livestock are usually accepted.

In addition to visiting, a popular activity for all ages is the late-afternoon walk, especially the Sunday-afternoon walk. Women and children, and sometimes married couples, also take strolls around the colony on summer evenings, at times with flashlights in hand. Other forms of Hutterite recreation have a more practical angle. For example, Hutterite women are adept at crocheting, needlepoint, rug-making, and knitting.

Artistic sensibility is shown primarily in practical productions such as calendars, quilts, doilies, and black maple rolling pins. But students at one Manitoba colony, including Jacqueline Maendel, displayed their paintings at a Portage le Prairie gallery.[53] In 2008 Hutterite paintings were included in an exhibit named "Hutterite Life" at the Mennonite Heritage Museum in Winnipeg. Hutterites also make picture frames and do wheat-straw weaving, cake decorating, calligraphy, wood-burning, leatherwork, wood scroll art, and bookbinding. John Fleming and Michael Rowan feature Hutterite "folk furniture" in a 2004 publication.[54] They point out the distinctive and practical Hutterite design of the cradles, commode chairs, cupboards, bread boxes, stools, shelves, benches, tables, and chests of drawers that are pictured there.

Because Hutterite adults, especially women, are avid readers, most colonies subscribe to a daily newspaper and a weekly news magazine, for example, *McLeans* or *Newsweek*. Every colony has a library stocked with works in English and German. One library collection includes the Christian novels of Janette Oke and Christmas Carol Kauffman as well as books in the Hardy Boys and Nancy Drew series. Another colony library contains works on science, theology, and history, along with technical magazines dealing with sheep, dairy, and hogs. There are also back issues of the *Reader's Digest*, *National Geographic*, *Birds and Blooms*, and *Country Women*. Many Hutterite women read books and magazines on cooking and alternative medicine. Books and magazines are purchased at library and yard sales, and librarians at local public libraries say that Hutterite women also check out hundreds of romance novels each year.[55]

Music is an important part of the Hutterite recreational experience.

A handmade Hutterite quilt. Courtesy of Max Stanton.

Young people gather often to sing contemporary Christian songs. On Father's Day and Mother's Day, children drop by and sing for their parents. Hutterites sometimes adapt folk and gospel songs by changing the lyrics. For example, "What a Friend We Have in Jesus" has been transformed into a Mother's Day song called "What a Friend I Have in Mother." New lyrics have also been added to "Red River Valley." Art critic Michael Kimmelman writes that before the age of recorded music, families "listened to music by making it themselves."[56] The Hutterites continue this practice. Singing accompanies virtually every social gathering and major work project. A man at a Lehrerleut colony enjoys making music by hitting partially filled glasses of water, of different sizes, with sticks and small tools.

Photography is another entertainment form that is widespread, although it is not officially approved. In theory, photography is idolatrous; in practice, cameras are everywhere. In the 2000s, conservative Alberta Dariusleut contested a provincial law that required photographs on drivers' licenses.[57] Yet picture albums abound in most Dariusleut colonies; there are hundreds of prints of children and grandchildren. In moderate-

A colony business manager in Alberta at his Hutterite-constructed desk. Courtesy of Max Stanton.

to-liberal colonies, photographs are openly displayed on bedroom dressers. Lehrerleut members place theirs inside hope chests and dresser drawers. Since digital cameras and cell phones make images instantly accessible, it is difficult for even the most conservative ministers to control photography. At important events such as weddings, there are usually prearranged or serendipitous windows of time when ministers allow photographs to be taken, even in Lehrerleut colonies. An eighty-nine-year-old Hutterite woman said, "You know, older Hutterites do not allow themselves to have their picture taken. But if I am just sitting here talking to someone and a camera flash goes off—what can I do about that?"[58]

Hutterites also view work itself as recreational; it is not something to dread or complain about. Many Hutterites never take time to savor the moment, because there is always another interesting project to work on. But the most popular form of Hutterite entertainment continues to be conversation. Under a tree on a summer afternoon, a group sits and visits; men, women, and children of all ages drop by at regular intervals, and the group changes composition. People sit down and talk for awhile, then move on to the next work assignment. Topics discussed are diverse: children, farming, cults, politics, and theology.

Health and Well-being

Hutterites believe that God has reasons for allowing illness and suffering, so when someone gets sick, he or she is not usually blamed. Hutterites are also somewhat skeptical about modern medicine, feeling that doctors sometimes make mistakes and are often closed-minded. While Hutterites have good relationships with many physicians and nurses and speak favorably about them, they are always looking for a different and better way, and thus they are very interested in folk remedies and natural alternative medicines.

Salves of various kinds are used to heal wounds, although not nearly as much as in the past. One older Hutterian recalled that as a child, he gathered "sheep pebbles" in a half-gallon pail so that his grandmother could make a salve.[59] Salves were also made from cow udders, goose fat, and soft cow dung.[60] In the past, an Austrian herbal tonic called *Alpenkrauter*, which has a high alcohol content, was prescribed for intestinal problems. One folk practice was to have dogs jump over colicky babies to make them feel better.[61] A sick horse could be cured by pulling off one's shirt and wiping the animal with it. It was also believed that bloodletting would cure disease. Blood was removed from the body by leeches or by means of flexible cups with a lot of suction.

Although many folk remedies are no longer used, medicinal teas are a popular cure for gout, arthritis, and asthma.[62] Natural ointments for skin cancer that "draw out the cancer" are also prevalent. Hutterites use herbs, minerals, and vitamin supplements and take trips to Mexico for experimental cancer treatments that are not legal in Canada or the United States. Colony women often serve as uncertified nurses, masseuses, midwives, and chiropractors. Popular tonics include "ZMO Oil," a mixture of camphor and oil of eucalyptus; "Heilol," which has similar ingredients; and "Genuine Green Essence," used for stomachaches and head colds. Some Hutterites also buy homeopathic medicines. Hutterites frequent health food stores for special products, and they are especially interested in vitamin treatments and mineral additives. Many Hutterite women are experts on how these substances metabolize in the human body.

Some Hutterites go to psychics and seers who look patients in the eye and make diagnoses that some members believe are accurate. "There are many shysters around the colonies," says one minister, "but people still go to them." One seer swung a device underneath a table to determine which of an assortment of pills he had placed on the table should be taken. Some Dariusleut Hutterites have delayed immunizations for their children because they feared adverse reactions.[63] Hutterite individuals told a 2002 research team that some immunizations had caused weight loss, crankiness, and fever.

In the 2000s most Hutterite women consult doctors for prenatal care and have their babies in hospitals with their husbands present, but some colony midwives are still active. Hutterites are opposed to abortion unless the life of the mother is endangered. When they need to see a doctor, Hutterite women prefer female physicians. Hutterites accept blood transfusions and organ transplants and are willing to consider state-of-the-art medical technologies. There are no dietary restrictions based on religious principles.

Hutterites who are seriously ill receive many visitors. They readily accept home health care services and, as noted in chapter 6, they prefer to spend their last days at the colony. They donate blood when they learn that it is needed and tend to be well known at local clinics. Hutterites permit autopsies only if they are legally required; bodies are not customarily donated for medical research.

Hutterites with mental and physical disabilities are almost always cared for in the colony by members of the community. At one commune a boy with Down syndrome was asked to sing for us. He did so joyously and in tune; this was his gift to us. On another occasion, sign language was used to communicate with a boy who could not use his vocal chords. Persons with disabilities receive special care and much nurturing attention.

Beginning with the work of Joseph Eaton and Thomas Weil in the 1950s, researchers have generally found excellent mental health among the Hutterites. Eaton and Weil suggested that the Hutterites had "genetic or somatic immunity against certain mental diseases" owing to "a combination of genetic selection and the special cultural practices," that is, inbreeding.[64] They wrote that the Hutterites had one of the lowest incidences of schizophrenia on record but also a high rate of manic depression among women.[65] A 1963 study by Arthur P. Mange reported a mental illness rate of 41.5 per 1,000, a very low figure. Mange also thought inbreeding had affected Hutterite height and sex ratios, as well as facial features and body types. W. W. Howells found trunk expansion "unusually great" and noted higher-than-average obesity and arterial hypertension.[66]

In general, geneticists say that Hutterite inbreeding has produced few detrimental and many positive physical effects. Alice Martin ascribes this outcome to the particular genetic impact of the "founding" Hutterite families.[67] Sandra Hartzog agrees that inbreeding results are dependent on the genes present in a specific population and notes that "inbreeding is not necessarily detrimental of a population."[68] She explains further that intra-Leut marriages have created unique genetic characteristics for each Hutterite Leut. Hartzog writes, "The difference between Leut for blood type gene frequencies was as great as between any two distant European populations."[69]

In a 1990 study of Saskatchewan Hutterites, Peter Stephenson found high scores on body mass index, cholesterol levels, and blood pressure among the Dariusleut but did not discover the same characteristics among the Lehrerleut. There were no differences in levels of obesity or hypertension between the Lehrerleut and non-Hutterites.[70] Stephenson assumes that Leut differences are genetically determined, since the lifestyles are similar across Leut lines. He speculates that the Walter genetic line (this surname is only found in the Dariusleut) has introduced a critical transformative difference.[71]

Geneticist Carole Ober, in a more recent (1998) study, looked at the ninety Hutterite ancestors of present colony residents. She used the year 1910 as a starting point, since after this date marriages between communal and noncommunal Hutterites ceased to occur, as did most cross-Leut marriages. Ober searched specifically for human disease genes. To her surprise, she found that Hutterite "men and women appear to have avoided finding a mate with HLA (human leukocyte antigen) genes that resemble their mother's." In other words, very few Hutterite couples had the same HLA, allowing them to transfer "immune genes that provide resistance to certain diseases."[72]

Such findings present a huge puzzle for researchers, because having the same HLA is associated with many health problems, including a greater-than-average number of miscarriages. Hutterites have avoided this misfortune by having, without realizing it, what Meredith Small calls "love with the proper stranger."[73] The Ober study suggests that an encoded sense of smell may affect Hutterite mate selection as part of a unique evolutionary process. For whatever reason, Hutterite women for the past one hundred years have been giving birth to children who have important genetic immunities. Mystified by this and other studies, the Hutterites respond that God has blessed his people in a unique way.

In the 1980s, Karl Peter and Ian Whitaker described several psychophysical Hutterite characteristics that were the result of "the selective processes that led to this group's appearance in history." They pointed to qualities of "perseverance," "courage," "initiative," and "obstinacy" and strong personalities, related to historical persecution and migration—a kind of "psychological founder's effect."[74] Hutterite scores on the Myers-Briggs personality assessment test indicate a people who are extroverted; sensory, more than intuitive; feeling, as opposed to thinking; and judgmental, rather than perceptive.[75]

Anfechtung

Hutterites across the years have experienced high rates of an emotionally destabilizing form of depression called *Anfechtung* (literally, "temptation"). Not recognizing secular causes, the Hutterites usually pray for a person experiencing Anfechtung so that ultimately she or he will recognize her or his spiritual shortcomings and ask for forgiveness. Disruptive spiritual forces depart from the afflicted and life goes on.[76]

In the 1950s, the Anfechtung experience was studied by Bert Kaplan and Thomas Plaut as part of their assessment of Hutterite personality traits. They described it as a psychosis resulting from a heavy sense of guilt, leading to "a weakening of the ego's ability to deal with the moral struggle between ideology and impulse." Contemporary Hutterites view Anfechtung as a near nervous breakdown precipitated by a struggle to overcome a personal conflict, which is often spiritual in nature. Edward Kleinsasser calls Anfechtung "a mental/spiritual form of depression."[77] Hutterites do not consider Anfechtung to be part of the normal life struggle. It is a rare, temporary, albeit profound, spiritual defeat, wherein the individual feels abandoned by God. Those who are depressed receive many visits from family members, friends, and colony ministers. They are surrounded by a large group of caring colony members.

Peter Stephenson believes Anfechtung is the result of being cursed (*pschreied*), a concept and practice that is recognized by some older Hutterites. He says it is closely related to belief in the evil eye.[78] "Envy," Stephenson asserts, "is a serious antisocial emotion associated with the self-absorbed individual in this anti-materialist communal culture."[79] He also states that women are especially susceptible to Anfechtung and are often the persons accused of casting the evil eye. A focused gaze leads to panic or anxiety or "fear of an emotion (envy) rather than a focus on the material manifestations of envy (acquisition)."[80] Stephenson suggests that Anfechtung is a reaction to the demands of an equalitarian social existence, where personal scrutiny is constant and social withdrawal unacceptable.

Most Hutterites disagree with Stephenson's analysis. A significant number of them recognize the concept of being pschreied, and they confirm that short periods of ill health may result, but they do not relate it to Anfechtung, which they do not believe non-Hutterites fully understand. Hutterites believe that God uses Anfechtung to bring people with spiritual problems and personal guilt back to faith. It is a "spiritual" struggle, with unique causes. One person says that her Anfechtung was related to disagreements with colony leaders. "It is hard to live if you are not with the leadership," she notes. Another Hutterite says Anfechtung is the result of constant sermon admonitions to be watchful and busy, such as this one: "A Christian can never be idle . . . he is always in danger of losing his promised crown."[81] Many younger Hutterites associate Anfechtung with superstitious beliefs that they would like Hutterites to give up.

Folk Traditions

Hutterite folkways include numerous eastern European superstitions. In the eighteenth and nineteenth centuries, for example, Hutterite birth records often contained the signs of the zodiac.[82] Some older Hutterites continue to consult astrological charts. Older Hutterians recall that eggs thrown over a barn were believed to bring bad luck and that calves were castrated only when the moon was full. The gift of "water witching" (the ability to locate water sources) continues to be recognized.

Many Hutterites, as noted in the preceding section, accept the existence of *Pschreien*, a kind of curse. Hutterites interviewed can often name people they believe were unwilling targets of this occult phenomenon. Dariusleut Susie Tschetter says that Pschreien occurs when someone expresses too much admiration for particular human characteristics or accomplishments, or perhaps for animals or material objects.[83] If a person stares too long at a beautiful child, the child might become ill, some believe, even if the person staring does not intend that result. To forestall the curse, when someone calls a child pretty, another person might interrupt with "Phew, phew, phew" and make a gesture as if he or she is cleaning out the child's eyes. Hutterites are hesitant about saying too many nice things about babies and young children, believing that they are the special targets of Satan. Some older Hutterite women tie red ribbons around babies' wrists to protect them against evil forces, because they associate the color red with the protective "blood of the lamb" in the Old Testament.

There are many Pschreien stories to tell. A handsome man suddenly gets violently ill. The cause is an admirer who focused too intently on the man's good looks. "We immediately cleaned his eyes and he soon recovered from the sickness," says the storyteller. Another person reports that an openly admired stallion suffered strong spasms and loss of muscle control, symptoms that continued until he washed out the horse's eyes. In the mid-1990s, Prairieleut Lesley Masuk met a Lehrerleut woman who said that Lesley had "looked so beautiful" during her previous visit "that I thought I cursed you."[84] In the 2000s, a minister started sweating and was not able to continue his sermon after (he believes) a person in the congregation inadvertently thought too highly of him.

Hesitancy to say positive things fits well into the Hutterite communal ethic. Although most Hutterites do not make this connection and seem surprised that anyone else would, Pschreien belief does reinforce humility and Gelassenheit. Hutterite folk beliefs are not as powerful as they were fifty years ago, but there continues to be significant bias against self-glorifying stories or praising others. The caution that arises from Pschreien belief is an effective way to deal with the problem of naturally gifted individuals, whether the abilities are intellectual, artistic, or physical—anything that might cause a person to attract special attention. It provides strong support for a system of communal self-abnegation.[85]

Hutterites also continue to recognize the power of dreams and visions. It is said, for example, that Hutterite young people often have their future spouses revealed to them in the wee hours of the morning through the power of divine insight.

❦ ❧

HUTTERITE BELIEFS AND PRACTICES HAVE TAKEN on a variety of cultural forms, from speaking a distinctive dialect to wearing singular clothing and eating special foods. Hutterites maintain a separate identity by the way they live their lives every day. Folk sayings, health practices, and a closed ethnicity enforce their separateness. In every cultural domain, communal emphases predominate, for example, in the way Hutterite children interact on the playground and in the way colony members view their work. Each aspect of Hutterite culture reinforces communal Anabaptist principles and provides support for an intriguing and alternative form of existence that differs significantly from that of non-Hutterites who live and work nearby. In chapter 8 we continue to explore the phenomenon of prophetic separatism by looking specifically at Hutterite approaches to education.

CHAPTER 8

Education and Cultural Continuity

We have schools in which we bring up our children in the divine discipline, and teach them from the beginning to know God.
—Peter Riedemann, Hutterite elder, 1542

U ntil the past few decades, North American Hutterites did not support education beyond the elementary school level. Young people needed to learn to read and write and understand basic mathematical concepts and procedures, but nothing more. Twenty-first-century Hutterites want their children also to have a rudimentary understanding of how things work in American and Canadian society. But most do not believe it is important to nurture patriotism or prepare children for professional vocations, nor do they want the state to introduce their children to controversial issues or too many forms of creative expression.[1]

Hutterites know that compromise with the world is usually unidirectional. There are hundreds of stories about Hutterites who tried to integrate a broad inventory of "English" (non-Hutterite) customs into their lives, found it difficult to turn back, and eventually left the colony. Although Hutterites are aware that their way of life is anachronistic, they believe maintaining it is essential to preserve their religious identity and distinctiveness. A majority of Hutterites thus attend school only as long as state and provincial governments require them to do so. In most U.S. states, children are required stay in school through age sixteen. In Canada, the province of Alberta allows them to stop attending at age fifteen.[2]

The Lehrerleut continue to be skeptical about secondary education, as do Dariusleut and Schmiedeleut traditionalists. A different position is held by Dariusleut and Schmiedeleut moderates and liberals; it is in these colonies where major change is occurring. Hutterite progressives are interested in postelementary and even postsecondary study for at least some of their members. More and more colonies are sending gifted males and females to universities to earn teaching credentials. After they graduate, Hutterites can employ their own government-licensed schoolteachers.

The Public School at the Colony

In the sixteenth and early seventeenth centuries, the Hutterites established impressive school systems that were admired by their eastern European neighbors. Theirs was a highly literate society, with its own doctors, craftsmen, and teachers. Hungarian educator Jan Comenius visited Hutterite schools personally, and they influenced the development of his progressive pedagogical methods.[3]

Hutterite anti-education traditionalism is a post-nineteenth-century phenomenon. After the Golden Years period, Hutterites often found themselves on the run. In response they became cultural preservationists, uninterested in or afraid of educational developments in the Catholic- or Orthodox-administered schools in the various places where they lived. Recognizing the importance of literacy, they established private schools to provide instruction for boys and girls. But the quality of the schools was inconsistent. The Hutterite education system was dealt a particularly serious blow during the Raditschewa period (1801–1842), when economic and social problems made it impossible to maintain school standards and some Hutterites, as a result, were not even able to read or sign their names on official documents. An 1825 report indicated that the Hutterite school still functioned for children age seven and older but that male teachers were not being replaced when they retired.[4]

After moving to southern Ukraine, the Hutterites placed well-trained Mennonite teachers in their schools, and educational standards improved so that by the time the Hutterites immigrated to North America in the 1870s, they were once again hiring their own teachers, many of whom had studied at Mennonite high schools in the Molotschna Colony. But by then, Hutterites were no longer interested in anything beyond basic reading, writing, arithmetic, and Bible study. Hutterite schools remained at this level into the early 1900s, when state and provincial governments in the United States and Canada introduced mandatory attendance laws and required schoolteachers to have college degrees and credentials.

In response, most Hutterite colonies formed official and unique relationships with public school districts so that credentialed "English" teachers taught at the colony site. This is still the most common educational pattern. Every morning hundreds of public school teachers drive to colonies on gravel and dirt roads and instruct Hutterite children in colony-built schoolhouses. In some isolated areas, teachers stay in colony homes during the week or during cold winter months. Public school districts provide experts to assist children with special physical or psychological needs.

In sparsely populated areas, colony schools sometimes become their own school "districts" with colony-controlled school boards that hire teachers and make curriculum decisions. In north-central Montana, a colony member once served as the district superintendent. More commonly, non-Hutterite school boards establish the curriculum. Even so, when selecting textbooks they usually make concessions for the Hutterites in sensitive subject matter areas, for example, sex education and evolutionary biology. They also usually allow religious displays at Easter and Christmas. One American colony used "No Child Left Behind" federal grants to purchase eight digital keyboards to upgrade its music program.

Hutterite public schools are thus a distinct educational unit, what John Hiemstra and Robert Brink describe as "de facto reserved public school[s]."[5] These authors note that twenty-four of Alberta's forty-two school districts have Hutterite colony schools, which they describe as unusual "faith-based" public entities that are attended only by Hutterite students.

Although most colonies are satisfied with the teachers chosen by local school boards, they are concerned about the emphasis on nationalism and militarism in social science textbooks and how social issues are generally discussed. Many Hutterites believe that "English" teachers prepare children's minds for rebellious thought and behavior because they (often unintentionally) provide subtle rationalizations for what Hutterites consider "sinful" behavior. If nothing else, schoolteachers model individualism and want their students to be competitive and become high achievers. A primary goal of public school systems is to assimilate younger generations

A Hutterite colony school building in Manitoba. Courtesy of Max Stanton.

into a society's social, political, and economic life, something that Hutterites oppose when it contradicts their beliefs and practices. Non-Hutterite
schoolteachers are subversive in several ways. "English" teachers stress
competitiveness, creativity, and pride in individual accomplishment.[6]
Many of them help their Hutterite students sell black-market items to
non-Hutterites for cash that does not end up in the colony treasury.[7] One
"English" teacher (as a warning) showed the students what a marijuana
cigarette looked like.[8]

The majority of Hutterite schools hold classes in single- or double-class-
room buildings. Some instructors teach all the children together. More
commonly, there is a division between children in kindergarten through
grade four and those in grades five to eight. A typical Hutterite student
body numbers about twenty children. In larger schools, teacher aides are
assigned, and young Hutterite women assist as volunteers. Among the
more liberal Schmiedeleut colonies, one sees state-of-the art educational
centers, computers, and audiovisual equipment. The libraries there contain classic works like Hermann Hesse's *Siddharta* and J. R. R. Tolkien's
The Hobbit. One colony has a video-broadcasting studio. Many school districts fund colony library acquisitions, which are then, in a legal sense,
owned by the state.

Hutterites often express concern about the influence of "English" teachers. Nevertheless, one person told John Hostetler, "It is better to have the worldly school taught by a worldly person so that we can keep the lines straight."[9] A larger question is what Hutterites consider the purpose of education. In North America, Hutterites have over the years cared little for schooling that goes beyond literacy and math skills. With that much education, members could read the Bible and the Chronicle (a spiritual purpose) and understand work manuals (a practical consideration). Those involved in business would be able to converse knowledgeably with outsiders. The Hutterite German School has supplemented this training with language and Bible study. There is little interest, however, in helping colony members move into the professions or become active citizens.

Things are changing with the coming of new media and technology and the interconnected global economy. Many Hutterite leaders now see social and economic benefit in gaining a deeper understanding of language, history, science, and current events. Some also believe that increased academic proficiency gives Christians a deeper understanding of their own beliefs and practices.[10]

Many Hutterite children do well in public school programs. South Dakota Hutterite student Brenda Decker read so many books one year that she won a trip to the state capitol in Pierre, where she met the governor and received a small monetary award.[11] In the late 1980s, a Lehrerleut eighth-grader won a prize for the best science project in the province of Alberta. But because his colony would not allow him to travel to Edmonton to receive the award, the prize was given to a runner-up.

Every two years, Schmiedeleut educational committees convene a Canadian-American conference for persons who teach in Hutterite schools.[12] About half of those in attendance are Hutterites, a proportion that has increased as more members become credentialed schoolteachers. Of the Hutterites in attendance, most are Schmiedeleut, but there are always a few Dariusleut and even one or two Lehrerleut. Hutterite ministers and German teachers also attend the meetings. In 2006, five hundred people were at the conference, and evangelical social activist Tony Campolo was the keynote speaker.[13] Many Hutterites disliked Campolo's animated style and his challenge to their separatist ideology,[14] whereas others thought it was exactly what they needed to hear.

Semiannually, the province of Alberta holds its own colony schoolteachers' conference, which is attended by a much smaller contingent of

Hutterites. It is at this conference that one hears more teachers' complaints about Hutterite students: their lack of fluency in English and their non-competitive nature. Less affected by popular culture than non-Hutterites, the students are perceived by some teachers to be culturally short-changed.[15]

The Public School with Hutterite Teachers

In the 2000s, an increasing number of Schmiedeleut One colonies appoint their own credentialed Hutterite teachers. This development has revolutionary possibilities, since these teachers have the opportunity to clarify and integrate spiritual and secular information and perspectives. When Hutterites hire their own members as state-certified teachers, German teacher–"English" teacher collaborations are possible and can result in a greater amalgamation of Hutterite beliefs and practices. According to Manitoba instructor Karen Waldner, "Having our own teachers means we can do a better job of representing our culture."[16] But it also means that dozens of young Hutterites, to become certified teachers, must attend public colleges and universities, where they are introduced to secular perspectives in many subject fields.

Hutterite musician Butch Wipf earned a teaching credential in 1998. At a German teachers' conference, Wipf spoke with humility, good humor, and a solid command of subject matter. While describing curriculum options, he emphasized Hutterite-Anabaptist principles. The majority of Hutterites, however, see secular influences creeping into the colonies as young people pick up dangerous ideas while attending university and pass them on to students as well as other colony members. This view is most commonly associated with the Lehrerleut and Dariusleut but is also held by many Schmiedeleut Two, who see a seductive spirit of individualism creeping into the Hutterite community.

Educational choices vary. A majority of Schmiedeleut One colonies participate in Manitoba's ITV (Interactive Television) program.[17] Although supervised by credentialed Hutterite teachers, the ITV curriculum is controversial because it includes sex education and other sensitive topics.[18] The program also offers a sophisticated introduction to cultural studies, history, science, and languages. All of these elements fit a growing Schmiedeleut One interest in encouraging deeper academic understanding as well as general creativity. With regard to the ITV visual arts course, Anna Maendel notes, "The course increases the students' creativity in a number of areas including writing."[19] But most Hutterites think the ITV program is too secular.

Hutterite Private Schools

Some colonies have established private schools, because school districts will not allow their children to be taught separately. This is the case in the state of Washington, which defines colony schools as "religious" schools, and in some parts of Montana. These jurisdictions make the case that colony public schools abrogate principles of democratic equality and the separation of church and state. Non-Hutterite students, for example, do not have the option of selecting schools attended only by their friends and relatives. School districts that take this position refuse to send certified teachers to colony schools even if it means a loss of ADA (average daily attendance) funding. In these cases, the Hutterites operate their own schools, usually hiring credentialed non-Hutterite teachers and following state-approved curricula.[20]

A few Hutterite schools operate more independently, selecting curriculum materials from evangelical Christian publishing houses whose positions on abortion and premarital sex accord with their own—even though the curricula also promote a patriotic political agenda. One series contains the story of a Revolutionary War–era Protestant minister who tells his congregants to rip up their Bibles to provide fodder for cannons.[21] But these colonies also use educational materials from the conservative Anabaptist *Rod and Staff* and *Christian Light* series, which are less nationalistic.

In the state of Washington, where all colonies operate private schools, the mostly non-Hutterite ("English") teachers meet regularly to make teaching and curriculum decisions. Hutterite ministers are also involved in these conversations. Since Hutterites are denied access to public financing, these colony teachers do not qualify for medical insurance and retirement plans. Salary and benefit packages are lower, and there is little access to material resources from school district offices.

In most parts of the United States and Canada, however, rural public school districts need more, not fewer, students, and for this reason they

Members of a Schmiedeleut kindergarten class. Courtesy of Patrick Murphy. Photograph by Jim Murphy.

welcome the Hutterites, who show no signs of pulling up roots and migrating to the city. Significant controversy therefore arises when a colony establishes a private school within such a public school district. In 2003, the Riverside Colony, near Fort MacLeod, Alberta, started its own school; no other Dariusleut and Lehrerleut colony in the area followed suit. This move upset not only the local school district but other Hutterite colonies also, and in 2006 the Dariusleut leadership ordered the school closed.

In the Riverside case, other colonies had three concerns: they did not want to offend local politicians, fearing that the private school might influence future decisions affecting all Hutterites; operation of the school represented an additional cost to the Riverside Colony; and furthermore, the colony hired an uncredentialed teacher who used an evangelical Protestant curriculum. In the Riverside view, the more individualized curriculum led to improved academic achievement. There was also a strong Christian emphasis. But, following communal operational principles, the colony rejoined the school district. Most Hutterites worry that private schools introduce individualistic evangelical emphases that undercut communal principles. The public school does not pose the same challenge because no competing religious position is promoted there.

Public or Private? Hutterite or Non-Hutterite Teachers?

There is difference of opinion regarding who should teach in Hutterite schools. Colonies that have non-Hutterite teachers say this practice opens young people's eyes to world events and opinions from an outsider's perspective. It shows Hutterite boys and girls the difference between secular and spiritual worldviews. Many school districts have Hutterite parent advisory committees that review curriculum materials, giving colony members important input.

This position was not the one taken by Hutterites historically. In Europe, the Hutterites operated their own schools and hired their own teachers. In the one instance in which teachers were chosen for them (in Ukraine in the 1840s), those selected were Mennonites with similar Anabaptist perspectives. So in this respect, the progressive Schmiedeleut are resurrecting a Hutterite tradition. But prospective teachers must first attend secular universities to earn the required degrees; after the eighteenth century, Hutterites in Europe did not study at such institutions. Progressives see the benefit of more highly educated members and point to non-Hutterite teachers who encourage their students to leave the colony, on occasion even offering financial assistance; they also criticize education districts for placing their youngest, most inexperienced teachers in colony schools. Traditionalists respond that the higher-education trend is subverting Hutterite beliefs and practices.

The German School

The German teacher is one of the most important people on the colony grounds. He—in a few cases, she—is the one who spends the most time with young people. The German teacher is responsible for their understanding of Hutterite history and beliefs as well as their general behavior and moral development. Lehrerleut minister Jacob Wipf suggests that the German teacher has three main teaching areas: Hutterite beliefs and practices, German, and the "three R's." According to another minister, "He [the German teacher] must keep the children busy so that they do not get into trouble." Noah Entz notes that if Hutterite parents do not "support" the German teacher, the "battle" against bad behavior is sometimes lost, but even then the teacher's influential role is not diminished. German teachers are parental figures for all colony boys and girls, and they can be seen as the colony's most important disciplinarians. Eighty-four-year-old Maria Hofer declares that a good German teacher sets the behavioral tone for the entire colony and makes life easier for everyone, especially ministers—such as her husband, Peter Hofer.[22] In general, the German teacher encourages the development of patience, gentleness, modesty, self-control, and consideration for others. German teachers are selected on the basis of spiritual and relational talents, and many of them eventually find their names placed in the lot and end up as church leaders. Some continue as German teachers even after they become ministers.

The German School curriculum often includes Schmiedeleut Two minister John S. Hofer's book *The History of the Hutterites*, which traces the development of Hutterite faith and culture. Curriculum materials and a historical map accompany the book. Students in German School are given a variety of reading materials, including Hutterite martyr hymns, the Bible, the Chronicle, and books that contain strong moral messages.[23]

Every day before the "English" school begins, young Hutterites between the ages of five and fifteen attend a thirty- to sixty-minute German School session. A second class is held in the late afternoon, giving German teachers a second chance to teach German and ethics and to respond to questions and concerns that arise during the "English" school day. The German teacher has the final word, an arrangement that lessens Hutterite concern about the influence of outside teachers. In some colonies there is another hour or two of German School on Saturday morning.

There is no grading in German School sessions, and instruction is interwoven with singing and Bible verse memorization. By the time a young person joins the church, she or he knows hundreds of Bible verses. But the German teacher does not only teach ideas and principles in the school setting. He is also responsible for supervising young people after the school session is over. At meals, which children eat in a separate dining room, he teaches proper manners and general rules of behavior. Hutterite children in many colonies take turns saying memorized prayers before and after eating. The German teacher also directs children in after-school, Saturday, and summer colony chores, providing an initial orientation to work responsibilities and possibilities. This training often involves giving children jobs that could be done more competently by adults. It is in the areas of work and mealtime supervision that the German teacher's wife (or some other colony woman) plays an equally important role, as she focuses her attention on school-aged girls.

Work supervision is especially time-consuming during the summer months, when the "English" and German schools are not in session. The German teacher has to find practical things for children to do. At one colony children and early adolescents picked berries in the hot July sun, the German teacher and his wife working with them. German teachers' wives bear a particularly heavy load, since they are often at the same time caring for their own families, but they do not complain: all of these responsibilities are lightened by the communal character of colony child-rearing.

Summer and after-school chores often include gardening, but they can involve almost any aspect of the colony's operation, from using and repairing farm machinery to cleaning the hog and chicken barns. At a colony in northern Montana, the German teacher and the children, accompanied by many colony women, took an all-day trip to the Bear Paw Mountains to pick juneberries. They packed sandwiches for lunch, and a hot meal was brought out to them for supper.

Hutterite children posing during a work break. Courtesy of Max Stanton.

Since the late 1970s, the Schmiedeleut have scheduled annual German teacher conferences, where participants spend a weekend discussing
pedagogy, curriculum, and the use of technology. At a Schmiedeleut Two
German School conference in 2007, 275 people attended and there were
sixteen separate seminar sections.[24] There are now separate Schmiedeleut
One and Schmiedeleut Two meetings. Each group appoints an executive
committee that meets on a more regular basis. In October 2006, about one
hundred fifty people, most of them German teachers and their assistants,
attended a Schmiedeleut One meeting in South Dakota. A few ministers
also attended. The meetings lasted a day and a half and were structured as
a typical academic conference, with break-out sessions on music, children's
literature, Sunday school instruction, approaches to Bible study, the role
of the German teacher, and media and technology. There was ample time
for discussion, and a book center offered an array of material resources.

Participants at the conference studied and worshipped together, and
an evening meeting was devoted to missions. In one break-out session,
Manitoba minister Arnold Hofer emphasized the importance of teaching

with passion, which he also modeled, as he spoke on the practical nature of Psalm 119. He also talked about the beauty of the German language.

At a well-attended discussion on the Hutterite Sunday School, German teacher Jonathan Maendel described creative methods for teaching important principles. For example, Maendel had once taught the concept of peer pressure by getting up early one morning and digging a winding, circuitous path through the snow from the colony courtyard to the schoolhouse. Then he watched as every one of his students took the long path instead of following his own footsteps in a direct line. The incident led to an interesting and informative conversation. As Peter Walpot noted in the sixteenth century, "Let each schoolteacher deal with children as though they were his own."[25]

Other German teachers at the conference emphasized the importance of positive reinforcement and the negative outcome of unrelenting criticism. Maendel reported that when his students arrived one morning with their caps turned backward, he turned his own hat backward, causing the students to quickly turn theirs around. "They don't want to be like us," he explained.[26]

In the Schmiedeleut One, nearly 75 percent of the "English" schoolteachers are now colony members; in the Schmiedeleut Two as well, a growing number of colony members are earning teaching credentials. Both developments result in the placement of Hutterite members in both the "English" and the German school of a colony, where the teachers can work together cooperatively and innovatively, without the usual social and ideological barriers. Some Hutterites teach in both programs, merging the "English" and German school structures.

German School teachers are also typically responsible for the Hutterite Sunday School program. Beginning at about one thirty on Sunday afternoons, they hold a one- to two-hour session. All unbaptized Hutterites, ranging from five to twenty-five years old, walk to the schoolhouse for a discussion of Bible verses related to the morning's sermon. Sometimes the sermon content itself is reviewed or discussed, emphasizing practical implications of the text.

The Wild Years

The Hutterites, like many Old Order Amish, cushion youthful temptation by allowing a considered amount of adolescent misbehavior, especially for males. One Hutterite describes the way teens push social and ethical boundaries as "going up fool's hill."[27] When a minister discovers a group of girls and boys dancing in the dining hall, for example, they are engaging in "fool's hill" activity. But because none of the participants have joined the church, there is no specific abrogation of a religious vow, although most Hutterites do not condone the behavior.

Youthful indiscretions include going to town without permission, working for neighbors and pocketing the money, smoking cigarettes, drinking too much, going to the movies, or buying CD players and electric guitars. More serious offenses, such as viewing pornography on the Internet, drug use, and premarital sex, call for sharp discipline.

In some colonies, a significant number of young people experiment with at least one of these activities; at others there is little interest. In any case, the extent of involvement is probably below what is found outside the colony. Most participants eventually feel sorry for what they have done and ask forgiveness and at some point join the church. Many of the Lehren speak directly and knowingly to adolescent youth. One writer references the demeanor of the twelve-year-old Jesus in the temple in Jerusalem, stating that Jesus was "not like young people today, who enjoy themselves in frivolity, mischief, and gaiety. No, my dear young people! He was found in the temple of God."[28]

Inappropriate youthful behavior does not automatically disqualify a person for important colony positions. For example, one man, who is now a German teacher, is pictured as a fairly unrestrained character in the Michael Holzach book *The Forgotten People*. In the 1980s Holzach, a German journalist, lived with the Hutterites for a full year under false pretenses doing research. Holzach befriended the Hutterite teenager, who at one time was found drinking too much. But today the man is a transformed, committed, and highly respected colony member. Some youthful deviations are ideological. Beginning in the 1960s, many Hutterite young people took an interest in evangelical Christianity, which advocates greater informality in worship and questions the importance of Hutterite culture, the Lehren, and even communal life.

Ministers consistently say that the young people lack interest in their own history, but there is nothing unusual about such disinterest. It is to be expected in a society that separates itself from the outside world and where beliefs and practices are institutionalized. In an isolated traditional environment, everything is done habitually and predictably. Only when beliefs and practices are under attack does significant interest in the historical foundations emerge. Church leaders believe, however, that assaults on the culture can be forestalled if there is a greater understanding of what has made Hutterites unique through the centuries. When asked to describe the most important challenge for young Hutterites today, a woman in her midtwenties says, "We need to get back to our faith and take it seriously."[29] She thinks communal life should be lived on the basis of faith, not for reasons of tradition or basic economic or social security.

Taking a New Look at Secondary and Higher Education

Since the eighteenth century, Hutterites have generally opposed study at institutions of higher learning. In addition to persecution and harassment from educated churchmen and government officials, who used their intellect to justify theft of children and property, imprisonment, and torture, Hutterites have had negative experiences with members in good standing who left the community to attend university and never returned. In 1784, for example, Christian Wurtz defected after receiving permission to study medicine. This case and others are taken as important warnings. Hutterites often quote Ecclesiastes 12:12–13, which the King James Version renders, "Of making many books there is no end, and much study is a weariness of the flesh."

The first Hutterite to study at the college level was South Dakota Schmiedeleut David Decker Jr. in the 1950s. He first enrolled at Freeman Academy, a Mennonite secondary school located about fifteen miles east of his colony. Because Decker was married and had young children, he did not attend class sessions, instead picking up assignments periodically and working on a directed-studies basis. After graduation, he enrolled at Freeman College to prepare for teacher certification. Here he attended classes and at times even stayed for basketball games. During this same time period, Montana Dariusleut Annie Stahl ("Englische Annie") took accounting courses at Great Falls College. She too became a certified schoolteacher.

In 1961 Manitoba Schmiedeleut Peter Maendel followed suit, becoming the first Canadian Hutterite to earn a teacher's certificate.[30] Maendel was handpicked by the New Rosedale Colony council and accepted the decision in the spirit of Gelassenheit. During the past few decades, the move toward colonies' credentialing their own teachers has led dozens of Hutterites (mainly Schmiedeleut) to earn college degrees. In 2006 North Dakota Hutterite Jesiah Waldner completed the teacher education program at Mayville State University. Waldner stayed in university dormitories from Monday through Thursday, returning to his family on weekends.

In the 2000s many Schmiedeleut, liberal Dariusleut, and even a few Lehrerleut students earn high school degrees. These are often completed through correspondence courses, some of them online, that prepare students to pass graduation equivalency examinations. In the mid-1980s, Rod Janzen developed a program that provided on-site instruction at the Wolf Creek Colony in South Dakota.[31] Attendance demands upset many of the young men who attended the Wolf Creek "high school," but one, fourteen-year-old Nathan Hofer, later completed a college degree, taught school for a few years, and is now a colony minister. A few Hutterite colonies allow students to wear caps and gowns and walk through public high school graduation ceremonies.

The most organized Hutterite postsecondary endeavor is the Brandon University Hutterite Education Program (BUHEP), started in 1994 by forty Schmiedeleut One colonies.[32] The BUHEP is a combined undergraduate and teacher education program that prepares teachers for Schmiedeleut One colonies. Between 1994 and 2004, one hundred Hutterite men and women completed the program. Most Hutterites—and even some Schmiedeleut One—are skeptical about ideas presented in Brandon University classes.[33] But supporters believe it makes the students stronger as they juxtapose spiritual and secular ways of thinking and knowing. Program director Raymond Hoeppner notes the technological savvy of the students and says he overheard a minister tell one student "You may have a laptop—just don't let us see it."[34]

In addition to university studies, many colony members secure vocational licenses, which are essential for construction projects. Colonies have licensed journeymen as well as certified electricians, coolant technicians, and plumbers. These men are qualified to install, maintain, and repair most colony equipment. When Hutterites need a registered nurse, a certified public accountant, a doctor, or an attorney, they contact outsiders with appropriate degrees.

Colony Bookstores

Two Schmiedeleut colonies have large bookstores that also sell assorted school supplies. The Schmiedeleut Two James Valley Bookstore, in Elie, Manitoba, and the Schmiedeleut One Hutterian Brethren Book Centre at Baker Colony, MacGregor, Manitoba, both maintain large collections of historical works, confessional documents, fiction and nonfiction books for all ages, and curriculum materials. School supplies that they sell include pens, pencils, paper, and scissors. There are Bibles, hymnbooks, miscellaneous bookmarks, and greeting cards as well. The bookstores also carry an assortment of Mennonite, Bruderhof, and evangelical Protestant publications.

There is nothing equivalent to these stores in the Dariusleut and Lehrerleut world, and many colonies buy materials and supplies from the James Valley store. But both Leut have colonies where sermon copies are duplicated, deposited, and distributed and where one may purchase German Bibles and a variety of Hutterite historical works. A few colonies have large print shops. Individual Hutterites have small collections of books and articles for sale.

In 2007 a few Dariusleut published two issues of the *Rural Free Press,* a newsletter that bore similarities to the Old Order Amish *Budget.*[35] The newspaper included articles on Hutterite agricultural projects, history, theology, and legal matters. It contained a one-page "Kid's Corner" with puzzles and craft ideas. But because Dariusleut leaders disapproved of some of the content, the monthly ceased publication. In the Schmiedeleut One, the Fairholme Colony in Manitoba has published the bimonthly *Fairholme Focus* for nearly a decade. In 2010 the Schmiedeleut One plan to launch an academic journal. These two publications benefit from advanced word-processing technology.

❧ ❧

IN THE HUTTERITE COMMUNITY THERE ARE different perspectives on education and schooling, particularly at the secondary and university levels. But all

Hutterites agree that the primary purpose of any educational endeavor is to make young people more knowledgeable about the world and how it functions. Cultural knowledge and the practical skills that are developed as part of the learning process make it possible for Hutterites not only to put food on the table but to reach deeper understandings of and commitments to the communal Christian faith. In chapter 9 we look at how communal Anabaptist beliefs are reflected in the organizational structure of Hutterite colonies, with emphasis on governance and economics.

CHAPTER 9

Colony Structure, Governance, and Economics

No devoutness, no fear of God, no fruits of faith can develop without workers who cultivate, plant, water, and weed the fields and gardens of the human heart with the Word of God.
—Hutterite sermon preface, circa 1650

Work Patterns

For Hutterites work is life and is enjoyed for what it is. Hutterites engage in hard physical labor and for very long hours. They like to quote Ecclesiastes 9:10: "Whatever work you find to do, do it with all your might." Hard work is also often seen by the Hutterites as a form of discipleship, a core component of the Christian faith. One Hutterite story says that in the 1950s, a Canadian general supervising a flood control project yelled out, "Send us twenty men or ten Hutterites!" The notion of leisure time is almost nonexistent for the Hutterites. Most of them do not go as far as the man in Burton Buller's film *The Hutterites: To Care and Not to Care,* who when asked "What do you do for recreation?" responding by saying, "Work harder."[1] But there is a strong, Shakerlike dedication to busyness. Life on earth is short and every minute is important.

From an early age children are assigned chores; they help out in most of the colony enterprises. During the summer, there is no idle sitting and little time for reading books. Instead boys and girls clean, garden, and run errands. This work is not done for self or even just for one's family, but for the commune as a whole, and there is strong social resistance to any person or family that focuses too much attention on individual accomplishments. Hutterite colonies are full-employment operations. Proper order and suitable organization ensure a predictable rhythm of life in which everyone learns by taking action. As Michael Holzach notes, "I learned almost everything while doing it."[2]

With the heavy work load, one might expect colony members, especially children, to show signs of fatigue or to complain a lot. This is not the case. The authors have seen six-to-twelve-year-old boys and girls working in ninety-degree heat laying lines for new colony plumbing, mischievously kidding each other and telling stories as they do the work. Teenage girls pick raspberries in the middle of a hot summer afternoon, smiling as they relate stories and sing songs. We did not see emotionless people going through the motions with stern looks on their faces. At one colony a family discussion was interrupted at 11:30 p.m. when a load of cattle arrived. Two teenage girls immediately volunteered to get feed for the livestock. They ran into the basement, changed clothes, and were off in a hurry. There was no hesitancy, no complaining, even though both girls had just showered and prepared for bed and were expected to rise the next morning at six o'clock.

Mechanized farming has eliminated some of the work that was traditionally done in large groups. Still, outside of the necessarily isolated work of the combine operator and the hog barn manager, Hutterites usually work together. The work is done outdoors, and there is no differential in terms of economic compensation. In a fully communistic society, the business manager does not receive any more money than the mechanic.

Work is especially long and hard in the summer months and during the fall harvest. One young bride complained that she rarely got to spend time with her husband. The colony minister's response: "Be extra kind when you do see him." During the summer, children and adolescents get up as early as five thirty to work in the garden while the air is cool. Work on Sunday is acceptable if everyone agrees it is needed—especially after the Sunday Gebet, when the minister, business manager, and farm manager often sit down and discuss job assignments for the week ahead. In the winter there are more indoor projects. Women quilt, cross-stitch, varnish, and paint, while men do carpentry work, weld, and repair machinery.

The Natural World and Colony Aesthetics

Hutterites know the natural world intimately and feel an attachment to certain places and landscapes even though they do not celebrate nature in verse or song. While walking around her colony, Manitoba Hutterite Julia Hofer keeps picking up plants and insects and smelling them. She knows the name of every one.

Traditionally Hutterites have not given much attention to colony aesthetics. In the most conservative Lehrerleut and Dariusleut colonies, trees provide shade between the houses, but there are no flower beds or lawns. Some ministers have ordered members to uproot flowers after they were planted. But the natural beauty of hills, streams, woods, and mountains, or a wheat or corn field at sunset, are deeply appreciated as special gifts from God. The general simplicity of the most conservative groups brings as much contentment as is found in colonies that have ornate gardens and grounds. It all depends on how one looks at the natural order. A conservative Hutterite points to an older woman in a colony garden. He notes the joy with which she is admiring her plants as she weeds and waters them.

But the winds are changing. Colonies in all of the Leut are paying greater attention to aesthetics, and many Hutterites believe that the quality of their life is enhanced as a result. Manitoban Kenny Wollman describes nature as "a second Word of God"; Noah Entz speaks of the beauty of "God's creation"; and many Hutterite sermons and hymns discuss lessons that can be learned from nature.[3] Many colonies have built duplexes with front porches instead of the traditional four-family apartment complex. During summer evenings family members sit outside the front door visiting with their neighbors. On one porch, recycled and freshly painted tractor seats are placed alongside plastic lawn chairs.

Most colonies lay sidewalks in front of residences, and a majority now plant ornamental trees, flowers, and bushes. There are miniature fig trees, sweet peas, peonies, sedum, tulips, and columbine; some Hutterite homes have potted plants inside. One colony took the trouble to replant a row of semimature conifers when the trees interfered with the placement of a new house structure. The new residences are surrounded by a beautiful lilac hedge.

Environmental awareness is built into the social fabric of communal life. Recycling, for example, is an integral component of a simple lifestyle.

The sharing of meals, appliances, residences, and machinery is inherently conservationist.

Hutterite colonies occupy a variety of terrains, from the rolling hills east of the Rocky Mountains, in Alberta and Montana, to the flatter plains and prairies of the Dakotas, Manitoba, and Saskatchewan. In the province of Alberta, colonies are situated in three geographic zones, the northern arboreal forest, the central parkland, and the southern prairie. Rainfall amounts vary greatly, as do soil types; topography ranges from horizontal plains to steep mountains.

Some colonies have picturesque settings. The Miller Colony in western Montana is built on the edge of the Rocky Mountains and only sixty miles southeast of Glacier National Monument. The large Miller garden on a hillside is a striking and beautiful site. Members say that their close proximity to the mountains attracts visitors from various Leut. As we drove between Miller and its emerging daughter colony, Midway Farm, nine deer crossed the state highway in broad daylight. Beehive structures, painted white, were stacked up high, and there were shredded-wheat-style bales of hay in fields along the highway.

When Hutterites travel between colonies in north-central Montana and the city of Billings, they drive through wheat fields, open sagebrush desert, small pine forests, and a variety of hills, canyons, and gullies, with many striking ten-to-fifteen-foot-tall manzanita bushes. There are also miles of relatively flat, undeveloped terrain. Some of this land is privately owned and some of it part of the Fort Belknap Reservation. When we took this three-hundred-mile drive on a state highway, we saw only nine or ten vehicles. Colonies in the southwestern corner of Alberta are within sight of the Canadian Rockies' 8,000–10,000-foot snow-capped peaks most of the year. "It is the first thing I look at every morning and praise God for it," says one woman.[4]

The Forest River Colony in northern North Dakota lies in a valley surrounded by virgin woods and varied soil types. A small, decaying log cabin built in the 1880s remains on the property, as do a steep buffalo-jump area on the river bluffs and a plentiful supply of wild berries. The Forest River winds its way into the lives of all colony members as they cross it frequently to get to gardens and fields on the other side. At the Marble Ridge Colony in north-central Manitoba, the woods nearby are home to moose, elk, and deer.

New Rosedale Colony, in Manitoba. Courtesy of Max Stanton.

In some areas Hutterites have completely transformed the landscape. In east-central Washington, for example, a semiarid region has been turned into a successful communal farm. When the colony was first established, many Hutterites feared that they would not be able to survive economically in the extremely dry conditions, but irrigation systems and hard, unrelenting work have changed everything. The foundation is the Grand Coulee Dam, built in the late 1930s. What the Hutterites brought to the area was the insight that planting potatoes, not grain, was the key to financial success. As Albert Wollman puts it, "The only way to make a million dollars farming wheat and barley in eastern Washington is to start out with two million dollars."[5]

Architectural Patterns

Hutterites usually place barns, shops, and other farm buildings on the outskirts of their communities. Thus, hog and chicken barns, machine shops, and grain storage facilities are often the first structures that come into view when one approaches a colony. They surround and protect the more private environs of dwellings, dining hall, school, and church. In writing about this inside-outside construction plan, Deloris Hayden notes that the outbuildings form a barrier allowing Hutterites to live "in seclusion" as they "turn their backs on the world."[6]

Many Hutterite colonies appear hidden even when they are located near major roads. A colony might be placed in a valley behind a large grove of trees or on the side of a hill facing away from a nearby highway. It is possible to cross southern Alberta on highways 5, 52, and 61 and pass within five miles of more than thirty colonies. Yet only two of them, Silver Sage and Mayfield, can be seen clearly from the highway. Before the advent of satellite guidance systems and marked roads, even Hutterites sometimes had trouble locating other colonies. Not all communities are hidden, however. Some are built along major highways and are clearly visible, and many colonies place signs on country roads with arrows pointing toward their communities.

The Hutterite dining hall and kitchen are the functional center of every colony. This area is where Hutterites eat most of their meals and where important information is exchanged. Here everything is done communally by colony women, with rotational cooking, baking, and cleaning responsibilities, so that no one ever has to work by herself.

Hutterite women making cherry jam in the colony dining hall. Courtesy of Max Stanton.

The Hutterite kitchen contains modern stainless steel stoves, ovens, and appliances, all of them much larger than those found in non-Hutterite homes. They are cleaned thoroughly every week. The oversize ovens have sophisticated air cooling systems. A new kitchen at a Manitoba colony is innovatively designed so that all of the appliances are positioned in the center of the room. Marble counters line the walls.

The stainless steel equipment in colony kitchens is often designed and made by community craftsmen. Every kitchen also has a large pantry for canned goods as well as a large cold-storage area. There are automatic vegetable peelers, mixers, deep fat fryers, and enormous microwaves. The one appliance conspicuous by its absence is the dishwasher. In most colonies, the dishes continue to be washed by hand. Colony laundry facilities are customarily attached to the dining hall–kitchen structure. Here one sees large state-of-the art washing machines and dryers, reminiscent of a modern dry cleaning operation.

In decades past, Hutterites did not construct church buildings. Instead they held Gebet and Lehr services in the schoolhouse. But a majority of colonies now have separate chapels, indicating a certain shift in perspective. Instead of the full integration of life, as signaled by holding school and church in a single building, the distinct structure used for church services, which automatically takes on a more holy aura, indicates a step toward separation of the two spheres of Hutterite life. Some Schmiedeleut churches have ornate window designs and special acoustics. Even the Lehrerleut are building chapels, though they continue to be attached to the kitchen–dining room, making it possible for the overflow audiences at weddings and funerals to listen to the proceedings via speaker system. Some of the new Hutterite churches seat as many as three hundred people to accommodate the occasional large gatherings. Critics note that except during church services, the buildings stand empty.

Some colonies have constructed multipurpose buildings that are used for both educational and recreational purposes. The auditorium at the Hutterville Colony, in South Dakota, is an enormous structure with a high-tech sound system and recording options. The main meeting room can be used as a basketball or volleyball court. The building, which also serves as the colony school, has dozens of classrooms. One of the rooms is open twenty-four hours a day and is filled with new computers.

Leading the Community

In North America, the traditional practice has been for each Hutterite Leut to elect a senior elder as well as an executive committee made up of respected ministers. Leut elders typically served for life. The Dariusleut, Lehrerleut, and Schmiedeleut One still follow this practice. The Schmiedeleut Two, however, operates with an executive committee that has American and Canadian representatives. There are separate elders for Canada and the United States.

Each Leut's executive committee is responsible for assessing and enforcing the group's Ordnungen. The governing constitution of each group is also confirmed by this body. At present the Dariusleut, the Lehrerleut, and the Schmiedeleut Two recognize a constitution written in 1950 that was revised in 1993, after the break with the Schmiedeleut One.[7] They hold annual conferences where each Leut elects three ministers to the central Board of Directors, which exists primarily for legal purposes, presenting a united front to provincial and state governments. The 1993 constitution forbids a common senior elder (if one is selected in the future) to serve simultaneously as a Leut elder; such a dual position was possible under the 1950 constitution. The Schmiedeleut One continue to recognize the 1950 constitution.

Ministers in each Leut meet annually to discuss issues of general importance, but in a political and economic sense, each community is self-governing. At the colony level there is considerable flexibility, a preference for face-to-face conversations, and a general dislike for bureaucracy. If one colony fails because of bad management, the church as a whole is not directly affected. Although colonies experiencing problems are assisted by the rest, their unproductive (perhaps experimental) practices are not automatically applied to other communities.

In some ways a Hutterite colony functions like a Roman Catholic religious order. The 1950 constitution states that "each member in effect takes a vow of poverty," since the colony owns everything in trust on behalf of its members. In theory, the "spontaneous direction of the Holy Spirit" is foundational and everyone in the colony is treated as a member of a large family.[8] Each colony typically has two ministers who serve as the primary administrators, although new colonies operate with one minister, and there are a few small established colonies that have never selected a second minister. At one colony where there was temporarily no minister, the sermon was streamed in via telephone from its mother colony.

Hutterite ministers, traditionally called *Diener des Worts* (servants of the Word), wield both religious and economic authority, owing to the seamless web of spiritual-secular understandings and operations. Ministers, like other Hutterites, are jacks of all trades. Many assist with farm work and take on significant managerial and laboring roles. Assistant ministers often serve as German teachers, and as such they become involved in the garden and other areas, supervising work assignments for youth and colony women.

Each colony is governed democratically by the adult males, who elect managers to head the various agricultural departments. In early Hutterite history, all persons in important management positions were called *Diener des Notdurfts* (servants of temporal needs). Now this title is given only to the colony business manager. Hutterites are equalitarian in decision-making but conformist once decisions are made. Nevertheless, all members at every level discuss colony decisions openly without embarrassment or fear of reprisal, both before and after decisions are made.

Colony members choose the German teacher; the farm manager, who oversees the allocation of laborers and supplies; and the *Wirt* (business manager), who is in charge of the community treasury and makes most financial arrangements. For Hutterite males, these positions are the most important ones. Colonies also appoint department managers, who deal with cattle, hogs, chickens, and sheep. There are head mechanics and carpenters as well as beekeepers, shoemakers, goose bosses, vintners, and gardeners. Some of these work assignments are combined. The third level of leadership is the broader social association of baptized and unbaptized males, who constitute a large mobile labor force.

Next in importance after the colony minister is the business manager, or Wirt. This position is so important that if there is a tie vote, the lot is sometimes used to make the final selection. North American Hutterites used to call the business manager "the boss," denoting his extensive influence. But persons holding the position dislike this term, since it connotes power combined with a lack of accountability. Although the senior minister co-signs all colony checks and bears final responsibility for the commune's financial welfare, the Wirt ensures that everything functions properly on a daily basis. He is assisted by the farm manager (or farm boss), who is responsible for allocating work responsibilities and providing overall supervision. Like the ministers, holders of all other colony positions bear spiritual as well as material responsibilities.

At each colony, general governance is provided by the Council of Elders, which includes the ministers, the business and farm managers, sometimes the German teacher, and two or three older males. More influential on a daily basis is the smaller Executive Committee, or Board of Directors, which does not include the at-large council members. This group typically meets after breakfast at the home of the senior minister to discuss the day's work, transportation requests, and other important issues. The "breakfast cabinet" structure ensures that few problems are kept hidden. Generally no resident may take a colony vehicle into town, for example, without getting permission from at least one member of this group.

Below members of the executive committee, and directly responsible to the farm manager, are the heads of the various colony enterprises, including shops, carpentry, and the care and marketing of hogs and chickens. A new position, factory manager, has been added in some of the new industry-focused colonies. Schoolteachers can also be very influential on an informal basis. After joining the church, most Hutterite men are chosen for at least one of these positions. According to John Bennett, "The social management system of the commune-colony, at a population level of around 100, is more complex than the government of the typical town of 5000."[9] Every adult male has an important responsibility, involving constant personal involvement and consultation. Table 9.1 summarizes the leadership structure in a typical colony.

Colonies are organized hierarchically, and colony members treat with deference persons above them on the organizational chart. This tradition can be a problem if there is mistreatment or malfeasance, such as alcohol abuse or nepotistic favoritism, but such difficulties are usually dealt with satisfactorily through the intervention of ministers or other colony leaders. Colonies are small-scale enterprises, in which face-to-face encounters are the norm. Most Hutterite leaders minimize complaints and jealousy by establishing close personal relationships. Hutterites have lived communally for hundreds of years and are highly adept at mediation techniques. They know a lot about what it takes to work together effectively.

Hutterites in leadership positions take their responsibilities seriously. Practicing servant leadership, they are deeply concerned about the atti-

Table 9.1. Colony leadership structure

Executive Committee
    Minister
    Assistant minister
    Business manager (Wirt)
    Farm manager
Other important positions
    Assistant minister's spouse
    Carpenter
    Chicken man
    Dairy man
    "English" teacher
    Factory manager
    German teacher and spouse
    Head cook
    Hog man
    Kindergarten teacher
    Minister's spouse
    Seamstress (fabric buyer and distributor)

tudes held by those who are assigned jobs. But nothing works perfectly. Although the selection of ministers is to some extent protected from political intrigue by the use of the lot, questions remain. Are candidates nominated on the basis of spiritual or financial giftedness? Is preference given to friends and family members? Some spiritually gifted people are so good at the jobs they do that other members hesitate to nominate them for the ministry. Thus, their names never appear in the lot. It is also common for brothers (who often live at the same colony) to exert significant influence in the selection of ministers.

Certain colony positions are associated with special privileges. Members of the executive committee, for example, do more traveling, for church-related and business reasons, than most other Hutterites. They are also more likely to frequent restaurants or even hotels. With regard to nonministerial positions, typically at least one son is chosen to follow his father's colony occupation. Other selections are based on recognized gifts and apprenticeship training.

Economy of Scale

Sharing and diversification are key communal elements, and all colony operations benefit from a general economy of scale. For example, most communities own no more than ten vehicles, usually vans and trucks, for every twenty families. Non-Hutterite families own at least four times as many per capita. If you need a vehicle, you check out the keys and drive one that every colony resident owns. There is also economy of scale in food preparation and general purchasing.

Hutterites have well-insulated, comfortable homes and plenty to eat. Most colonies have up-to-date farm machinery, stainless steel dairy equipment, and air-conditioned combines. Their standard of living approximates that of non-Hutterites in many areas, although there are significant limitations and a commitment to general simplicity. In comparison to non-Hutterites, there are fewer material possessions and an absence of luxury items, such as jewelry, designer clothing, and costly knick-knacks.

Each Leut deals with financial problems in different ways. Lehrerleut colonies pay into a central fund that provides grants and loans to communities that need help, through an "equalization" policy. If a loan is needed to expand operations or construct new buildings, colonies borrow money interest-free and without outside supervision. If a colony incurs major indebtedness, a financial supervisor is assigned to administer its business affairs until everything is back in order.

In the Dariusleut there is no formal mutual assistance plan. Most colonies purchase insurance to protect buildings, livestock, and crops against fire, hail, flood, and drought that might affect financial stability. Loans from other colonies are made without administrative supervision, but they are often not interest-free. The Schmiedeleut groups have a mixed plan. They do not have a redistribution policy, but leadership committees approve large loans for heavily indebted colonies that agree to temporary financial oversight.

Colonies are not completely self-sufficient. Although communal, they are economically dependent on regional, national, and international markets. They sign marketing agreements and make purchasing arrangements with non-Hutterite private and public entities. The communist economies in the former Soviet Union and China operated similarly, prior to reforms in the 1980s and 1990s. And the Israeli kibbutzim have always functioned in this way. Although internally the social structure is equalitarian, it relies on competitive and unequal world markets to sell goods and raise money.

For many colonies, an important issue is the relationship between financial success and spirituality. Conservative Hutterites believe that there is always a connection, that colonies in financial distress are colonies with spiritual problems. Younger, more liberal Hutterites are not so sure; they wonder whether the accumulation of wealth might have a negative influence on spiritual health.

Farming

"It is an idyllic picture: fifteen to twenty Hutterite women of all ages, in long flowered dresses, lined up in rows, hoeing weeds in the enormous garden near the James River. The early morning sunlight, the moisture in the air, forms the illusion of a dream sequence. My first inclination is to suppose that this setting must be artificially created. It could have been a set from a movie portraying peasant life in the sixteenth century. The emotional sensation is the same one that occasionally hits a movie-goer in the opening scene."[10] This description was written by Rod Janzen in the mid-1980s, but it could just as well have been written twenty years later. Most colonies derive their income from farming operations that are highly diversified and involve everyone in the community. Grain products include wheat, canola, corn, malt barley, oats, alfalfa, timothy hay, and flax. Some colonies grow peas and soybeans. Corn, canola, and potatoes are also grown for seed. Livestock (for example, hogs, cattle, and sheep) and poultry (chickens, ducks, turkeys, and geese) are raised as well.

There are regional differences. In central Montana, for example, precipitation averages twelve inches a year, while in eastern South Dakota it is nearly double that amount. Some areas have cheap sources of irrigation; others do not. Soil types vary and government policies often have an impact on economic decisions. In Montana, the state pays farmers to set aside land to protect certain animal species. Hutterites must therefore decide whether it makes more sense to take these payments than to till the soil. In Canada there are provincial tariffs on chicken "positions" as well as on eggs laid. A productive egg farm in Alberta requires fifty thousand or more chickens; most colonies elsewhere in the early 2000s have at least ten to twenty thousand birds. At least $1 million is needed to secure an egg-production license, and there are also production quotas on milk, cattle, grain, and hogs.

One colony in Washington grows mint that is used in tea, potpourri, and as a flavor additive. A weed-free variety of timothy hay is exported to Japan for the specialty cattle market. Other colonies harvest potatoes (four thousand acres are planted at one community). Some of these are sold to potato-chip and french-fry manufacturers.[11] Hutterite colonies grow grass seed, sunflowers, and decorative flowers. Many communities keep bees, not only to make honey but to pollinate crops. Many colonies sell surplus produce from their large gardens.

A few Hutterite colonies have their own greenhouses, where flowers and plants are grown from seed and preserved during the winter, or both. Most of this operation is for internal use, but some colonies sell plants to outsiders just as they market honey commercially. Alberta Hutterites David and Helen Hofer constructed a greenhouse with a heating and humidifying system and grow tomatoes, bell peppers, cucumbers, and fruit organically in a soil-free medium. There is economic diversity across the Hutterite world. Some communities breed border collies for herding and protecting sheep. The Rockport Colony in Alberta makes and sells a product they call Coyote Pancake Mix.[12]

Farming involves not only planting, weeding, and harvesting, but also marketing whatever is grown. Quite a few colonies have joined dairy, grain, and egg cooperatives that help sell and distribute their products. In order to stay abreast of government policies—and in some cases to influence them—Hutterites also affiliate with local and regional agriculture and livestock organizations. In Canada, for example, where food production is highly regulated, Alberta's dairy board monitors milk-container cleanliness and milk temperature and transport time as well as the proper handling of cows and the composition of feed. Agricultural boards impose quotas on virtually everything that a farm produces, from grain, poultry, eggs, livestock, and potatoes to biofuels.[13] Hutterites do not serve as agricultural board members, but they do attend and speak at regional meetings and often dominate the membership of local cooperatives. In Alberta, twenty-five of the forty egg-growing and marketing cooperatives are Hutterite colonies. These organizations provide detailed national and international production figures and forecasts and aggressively promote the marketing and distribution of agricultural products. To compete successfully in a global market, Hutterites employ many non-Hutterite sales agents, attorneys, and accountants.

In the United States, there is less government control. But colonies are still affected by crop subsidies, quality control regulations on production and processing, and rules governing the toxicity and environmental quality of herbicides, pesticides, and fertilizers. Most American colonies are thus actively involved in crop and produce cooperatives. Between 1995 and 2005, total USDA subsidies for the Kingsbury Colony in Montana amounted to $1,277,918.[14] Two-thirds of the subsidy payments were for wheat and barley.

During harvest Hutterite men spend many long days and nights on the combine. This can be lonely work, although the cabs, now air-conditioned, are usually equipped with two-way radios. But the work never seems to end, and it is repetitive and mind-numbing. Drivers thus welcome riders who provide face-to-face diversions. "You girls should come more often," says a combine driver to two girls who join him for a thirty-minute ride. It is hard to forget the swishing sound of the harvester blades as a fleet of combines empties its harvest of grain into the huge trailers that await the load. After operating a large combine for eighteen hours without a break, one Hutterite dozed off and drove the vehicle into a small ravine.

Most colonies employ their own members, but in areas where the labor force is small or where too much land is under cultivation, others may be hired. In the state of Washington, for example, outside labor, primarily Mexican and Mexican-American, is relied upon during the harvest season. The workforce is completely non-Hutterite at the Schmiedeleut Dakota Turkey processing plant in Huron, South Dakota. The $45 million plant, which employs four hundred non-Hutterites, is a cooperative project of forty-four Schmiedeleut One and Schmiedeleut Two colonies. Here a communal organization that does not pay wages to its own members employs a large outsider workforce. The implications of Hutterites managing non-Hutterites in an economic operation have yet to be determined. A similar situation was found at a hog-processing plant that once functioned in Neepawa, Manitoba. These are unusual but growing developments.

Hutterites are successful farmers. In Montana, they produce more than 90 percent of the state's hogs and 98 percent of its eggs. In South Dakota, 50 to 60 percent of the state's hogs are raised at Hutterite colonies, and

Combines in the fields at Warden Colony, in Washington. Courtesy of Max Stanton.

this quantity represents 1 percent of total U.S. hog production. In Manitoba, Hutterites produce a significant percentage of the province's eggs.[15] The Hutterites have many advantages, including a large dedicated and industrious workforce of males and females who live in close proximity. Feed and seed are purchased in large quantities at low prices, and there is an important economy of scale in all agricultural processes, from slaughtering livestock and poultry to combining. Hutterites often have better machinery and more sophisticated farming operations than their neighbors, and they often barter with other colonies.[16] They exchange garden produce, machinery, and labor. In the process many non-Hutterite farm families cannot compete.

The amount of land owned by a colony varies depending on soil type, location, and crops. One colony in north-central Montana owns 20,000 acres of land. Much of it is not prime farmland, however, and it is not irrigated.[17] In 2006, 7,500 acres of this land was planted in wheat and barley. Another 7,500 acres lay fallow; undeveloped strips of land were everywhere. The remaining property was used for range cattle, chickens, geese, colony gardens, and recreational ponds.

Hutterites use up-to-date farming methods and equipment. Cultivators and seeders are getting bigger, as are combines, swathers, and trucks. Like their neighbors, Hutterites argue about the comparative quality of John Deere versus New Holland tractors and Peterbilt versus Kenworth trucks. Some Hutterites travel all the way to Tulare, California, to attend the annual agricultural equipment show. In 2007, en route to the show, six Montana Hutterites took a side trip to San Francisco, where they toured Alcatraz Island, where four Hutterites were incarcerated as prisoners of conscience during World War I.[18]

To increase production, Hutterites use herbicides and pesticides, and they interact regularly with machinery dealers, fuel suppliers, and fertilizer agents. At times, Hutterites volunteer to testify in front of agricultural review boards. In March 2007, Manitoba Hutterite Ricky Maendel argued against hog production restrictions, noting the colony's zero tillage practices, licensed pork-industry technicians, computerized hog production, and commitment to conservation.[19] Testimony by neighboring Hutterite Johannes Waldner described the environmental benefit of his colony's Better Air Systems hog barn ventilation equipment.[20]

Increasing numbers of colonies are accruing large debt loads as a result of high land prices, competitive markets, and rising energy costs. So some colonies have moved away from diversified agriculture on large acreages to livestock or poultry production, or both, on a few hundred acres. And because farming has become increasingly mechanized, diminishing the work load, many colonies have begun small industries or have established factories. Nevertheless, most colonies continue to rely on agriculture.

Outsiders often say that Hutterite colonies are bad for local economies. Sociologist Leo Driedger disagrees, noting that Hutterites use only one-third of the land per capita that other Canadian farm families do. As John Bennett points out, when Hutterites purchase land, they do it as a lifetime commitment.[21] Even with land-price inflation and difficult market conditions, they are not fair-weather farmers. Hutterite purchasing power is higher than that of previous landowners because of the larger number of people who live at each colony.

New Industries

Because of high land prices and competitive markets, many colonies have established small manufacturing enterprises.[22] In emergency situations, Hutterites have always repaired vehicles and equipment for their neighbors, but some now do it on a regular basis, and they also retrofit machinery for resale. Some communities are production centers for colony-specific products such as stainless steel kitchen equipment.

A few colonies have established larger operations, manufacturing hog feeders, barn ventilation systems, coal boilers, thermal heating units, and a variety of agricultural equipment, much of it patented. One Manitoba colony does demolition work in Winnipeg. The colony also repairs and rebuilds old vehicles at a noncolony site. Millbrook Industries in South Dakota builds the Hydron Module Ground Source Heat Pump, which uses the earth's warmth to heat and cool homes and businesses. It is sold in thirty-five states and Canada. Millbrook also has commercial feed, metal fabrication, and machine industries. The Newdale Colony, in South Dakota, specializes in metalwork and manufactures cladding for buildings as well as feed-mill equipment. According to a 2006 report, "The operations are state-of-the-art; equipment includes the latest in laser cutters, CAD/CAM software, robotic welders and more."[23] In Montana the Springwater Colony has a dozen wind-powered electric generators and sells power to the Montana Power Company. A South Dakota colony plans to build land-water vehicles for hunters.[24]

Colony carpentry work is also expanding. Hutterites have always made their own furniture, doors, and windows. Now some colonies are marketing these products. The Wolf Creek Colony, in South Dakota, constructed furniture for a large motel chain.[25] Wolf Creek also operates three large ovens that do rotational molding of plastic products such as corn combine guidance devices (head divider snoots).[26]

As they move into manufacturing, Hutterites have to decide whether they are willing to build items that are inferior in quality to those they make for themselves. Quality of workmanship is one thing; the value of materials another. Some colonies win furniture contracts by using compressed-wood materials that they would never use for their own needs. Hutterite furniture makers use the highest-quality oak, cherry, hickory, and maple to construct desks and chairs for their colonies. But when they produce for someone else, they may not choose the same materials. Critics inside and outside the Hutterite community question the impact of mass production on the group's historical reputation for quality over expediency.

One colony's response was to purchase state-of-the-art equipment from Germany and use only the best wood to build doors and cabinets. The work is done during the winter months when farm operations slow down. Other colonies do the same with less expensive machinery. Hutterites often say that they could accept more orders if they had a larger labor force.

In many shops, most of the varnishing and finishing work is done by Hutterite women.

A few Hutterite colonies make clocks. Others build modular homes from kits and resell them at a profit. A colony in Manitoba sells patio or yard "spinners." A Hutterite man in Alberta is well known for the quality of his leather products: shoes, boots, bridles, harnesses, and gloves. Some colonies have shoe-repair shops. Others install irrigation pivots. General self-sufficiency is shown by the continued presence of crafts such as shoemaking, tanning, bookbinding, rug-making, broom-making, and even soap-making, although these skills are slowly disappearing as mass production makes them less cost-effective. Shoemaker and minister Noah Entz, notes that it costs him about one hundred dollars in leather and materials to make a good pair of shoes.[27] In May 2008 Rod Janzen found Hutterite women at Pincher Creek Colony in Alberta still boiling soap in huge vats outside the kitchen.

Industry is moving into the colonies, but most North American Hutterites remain skeptical of large factory operations. They fear that cultural and religious change will follow as men and women work eight-hour shifts and have more free time on their hands. They wonder whether the overspecialized work might become tedious and socially alienating in ways that farm work is not. Advocates assert in response that industrial work involves more human interaction. While some people experience factory-line isolation, work-related social detachment also plagues certain agricultural pursuits. In the hog barn, for example, a man works in almost complete isolation and wears special protective clothing that covers most of his body.

At the prosperous Baker Colony, near MacGregor, Manitoba, little farm work or livestock remain, and there are no grain crops. Baker purchases its meat from local grocery stores. The colony engages in other enterprises. They build ventilation systems for livestock housing structures and potato storage buildings, manufacture heat exchangers, do custom rotational and injection molding, and construct and market picnic tables and lawn chairs.[28] Colony members thought long and hard about the impact of raising new generations that are separated from the land. Fearing that their children might never learn how to care for livestock, Baker constructed a miniature barn and stocked it with goats, chickens, rabbits, pigs, and horses. Hay is stored in a small loft. Colony children have the responsibility of caring for the animals.

In some ways, industrialized Hutterite communities hark back to the Hutterite past in Moravia, where small crafts trades abounded and were admired by neighbors. But factories require regular time schedules, and many colony leaders wonder what will happen if they develop diversified farm-industry economies, so that half of the colony members work nine to five in a factory and the other half follow the inherently irregular farming schedules. How will two very different labor forces interact? What activities will nonfarm workers engage in after the workday is done?

These questions are debated at Acadia Colony, in Manitoba, where a profitable truss-production factory is a major enterprise. Here the factory manager, Conrad Hofer, plays as important a role as the colony's farm manager.[29] He says that young males with a choice prefer farming. But he sees change coming as the more consistent factory work schedule allows married men to spend more time with their families. Jealousy between the two workforces is minimal, and the colony is considering rotating members between farm and factory jobs.

The movement from agriculture to industry was made earlier (in the 1970s and 1980s) by the Israeli kibbutzim.[30] It led rather quickly to the hiring of non-kibbutz members, because the communalists were not interested in nonagricultural work. Whether the Hutterite future will look the same is unknown. The Schmiedeleut colonies that run the Dakota Turkey processing plant view it primarily as a financial investment. They control the board of directors but delegate factory management and labor to outsiders. This is a model that other colonies might emulate. But industrialization does not automatically mean the employment of non-Hutterites. As colonies enlarge nonagricultural facilities, they could simply increase the size of individual colonies. That is how Hutterite communities functioned in the sixteenth century.

Paying Taxes

In the United States most Hutterite colonies file income taxes with the Internal Revenue Service as nonprofit 501(d) religious organizations with communal treasuries. They are assessed as collective "communal" entities, since the colonies do not pay individual salaries. Taxes are determined by dividing total colony income by the number of residents, then adding deductions. Most Hutterites do not pay social security taxes and do not collect from government retirement programs. Neither do they pay Workers' Compensation taxes or accept payments from this program. They pay property and sales taxes, as everyone else does.

In Canada, most colonies opted out of the national pension system in the late 1960s.[31] Before 1968, Canadian colonies also qualified for a special tax exemption as religious organizations, because members take vows of perpetual poverty, but they no longer qualify.[32] As in the United States, the colonies now compute their taxes by dividing total income by the adult membership (or in some cases, all residents over the age of eighteen), then subtracting exemptions.[33] Every adult Hutterite is treated as a self-employed worker. In effect, colonies incur an extra education assessment, since they are required to pay the salaries of public school teachers assigned to them and to provide buildings and educational supplies and materials, even though they also pay regular property taxes. This is the price of operating religious and culturally segregated schools.

In the late 1960s, when Alberta first quit recognizing Hutterites as a religious organization, the Lehrerleut were complacent, but the Dariusleut went to court, because of "war tax" considerations. They balked at paying taxes assessed for military purposes and took the position that they were as much a "religious order" as other groups that had been granted exemptions. Hutterites take vows of poverty, and many other religious orders had as much wealth as they had. In 1976 the Alberta courts ruled in the Hutterites' favor, but the decision was reversed in 1978, leading to a countersuit. In the end the Dariusleut agreed to pay provincial taxes but attached a note stating that the moneys were "not to be used for war taxes."[34]

With regard to insurance, there are various approaches. In 1980 the Canadian Schmiedeleut established a mutual insurance company. American Schmiedeleut did the same in 1983, and they added health insurance. Colonies in other Leut either purchase policies independently from private insurers or band together to purchase mutual policies at more favorable rates.

In general, Hutterite colonies deal with the same kinds of economic considerations, including taxes and insurance payments, as other farmers do. Paul Wipf summarized the Hutterite position: "I believe that God created this earth for all mankind. We don't really own any land. We're only stewards for the time that we are on this earth. We get paid the same amount for our produce as any other farmer. Colonies are under just as much financial stress as all the rest of the farming community. We aren't asking for any outside assistance to maintain our culture."[35]

Hutterite Women and Gender Relations

Hutterites believe that God has created a patriarchal social order that involves separate roles for men and for women. At the colony, this position influences work responsibilities and basic decision-making patterns.

The ordering of relationships places God over human beings, the old over the young, and men over women, in accordance with the Hutterite interpretation of 1 Corinthians 11:3, "But I should like you to understand that the head of every man is Christ, the head of woman is man, and the head of Christ is God." The head covering that females wear symbolizes their submission to men. In the Hutterite view, women, more than men, are motivated by emotion and intuition instead of rational thought.

Hutterites thus view gender the same way residents in most Western societies did before the twentieth century. At a Hutterite marriage ceremony, men are instructed to serve as models for their spouses. For women, an entire sermon focuses on the character of the prophetess Anna, in Luke 2. Anna exemplifies the virtuous woman who follows Jesus. Gertrude Huntington, Karl Peter, and more recently Hanna Kienzler and Lesley Masuk have done important studies of Hutterite women.[36] A few of their insights, along with many of our own, appear in the following paragraphs.

It is true that Hutterite women do not have the franchise and do not attend meetings where policy decisions are made. But they exert significant influence through the unregulated conversational grapevine. This line reaches behind-the-scenes and across colony and even Leut boundaries.

Hutterite women actively engage in mixed-gender discussions, offering strong opinions. Self-assured and full of ideas, they often interrupt Hutterite men in the middle of conversations. "I'm the one that makes sure that he is on time and gets things done," says the wife of one minister. Moses Stoltzfus, the leader of an evangelical group that has attracted many ex-Hutterites, describes Hutterite women as "vibrant," "strong," "self-confident," and "expressive." Manitoban Sarah Hofer puts it this way: "Women may not always be right but that doesn't mean that the men are right either."[37]

Each gender has a defined role. Adolescent males often ask their younger sisters to take dirty dishes to the kitchen or to clean up after a snack, and they comply. But the girls feel free to express personal opinions and make caustic remarks about male friends and relatives. Hutterite women are adept at multitasking and intellectual maneuvering. As Selma Maendel notes, "Not having a vote does not mean women have no power or say in what goes on, because most of the time, the voting is a formality."[38] Everything has been discussed at home before the men go to the meeting. Even earlier, the collective women's voice is discerned through hundreds of conversations. Women have major influence over colony decision-making.[39]

Hutterite women do everything. They rise early to get their children and husbands ready for the day. They sweep, scrub, sew, polish, mop, take family members to the doctor, and tend flower gardens. In many colonies, women mow the lawn and care for the trees, shrubs, and plants that beautify the courtyard. They hose down and sweep colony sidewalks, and they do much of the colony painting. Women also care for the elderly, the infirm, and colony members who are otherwise disabled, sometimes for years at a time. In the evening, they help their children with homework, especially with Bible verse memorization.

Hutterite women do not usually perform traditional male functions such as plumbing or electrical work, but young women check eggs, sort and load potatoes, and weigh grain trucks. Some women brand cattle and shear sheep. More than men, Hutterite women are the ones who rise at 5:00 a.m. to pick, clean, and can or freeze fresh produce. They are the ones who pull the down feathers off of ducks and geese for pillows, feather ticks, and quilts. Hutterite women pluck chicken feathers, clean the carcasses, and sanitize the flesh, alongside colony men.

In addition to sewing their own clothing and the pants, shirts, and dresses of their spouses and children, Hutterite women make most if not all of the colony's bedding and sheets. They paint houses and repair doors and windows. Some spend countless hours in the woodshop making gifts and toys for friends and relatives who are getting married or expecting a child. Hutterite women also assist in the cutting, sanding, painting, and varnishing of colony furniture, kitchen and bathroom cabinets, window frames, and podiums. Twenty-first-century Hutterite women are less involved in farming activities than their grandmothers were, because these

A wash line near a Hutterite residence. Courtesy of Max Stanton.

tasks have become less labor-intensive, but women continue to help in this area whenever they are needed. Many women work as dispatchers for vehicles and heavy farm equipment, and in some communities, women serve on emergency first aid teams.

Hutterite women are the dominant force within the walls of the family residence. But mothers and fathers work together raising children; they even share some household chores. Men often get up at night to help children who are ill or cannot sleep. Manitoba Hutterite Conrad Hofer dresses his young daughter every morning and even arranges her hair, placing it in a bonnet.[40] In the evening men serve wine and other beverages and help guests with their luggage.

Schmiedeleut One Hutterites are not feminists, but they have gone further than the other Leut in placing women in positions that were previously open only to men. At a fall 2006 German teachers conference, about one-third of attendees were females. Most were unbaptized women who work as German teacher aides, spending most of their time with the younger children. But a few women have been named to the position of German teacher, and in some colonies spouses of German teacher candidates are interviewed alongside their husbands before appointments are made.

Hutterite women working in the colony garden. Courtesy of Max Stanton.

At the conference, female participants did not speak during the general question-and-answer sessions. Neither did Hutterite women sit down with male outsiders in meetings or engage in conversations with them (unless Hutterite males were present) during breaks. But when the setting was more private, for example, in members' homes, the same women who were quiet in public became outspoken, opinionated, humorous, and even sarcastic. At a presentation at a Schmiedeleut Two colony in 2007, the women, seated in the back, whispered quietly every time a Hutterite man made a comment or asked a question.

Hutterite women exert their greatest influence away from public view. In the course of Hutterite history, their influence has been most pronounced in matters such as the design, construction, and equipping of houses; the placement of kitchens; the choice of flooring; and other domestic matters. But women also voice strong opinions about social, economic, and ideological aspects of Hutterite life. Many are better read than male Hutterites, and they are often aware of regional, national, and international developments.

Official leadership positions for women are limited to the elected positions of head cook, head seamstress (*Zeich Schneiderin*), and kindergarten teacher. In the Schmiedeleut One, the position of gardener, often a woman, is also elected. Women are named to head special work groups, for example the "geese" and "duck" ladies. Also important are ministers' wives, the German teacher's spouse (*Schulmutter*), and in some colonies the "English" teacher.

The colony's head cook coordinates cooking, baking, and soup-making and monitors the work of special-needs cooks, who plan and prepare meals for residents with specific dietary requirements. Until age forty-five (among the Lehrerleut and most Schmiedeleut) or fifty (for the Dariusleut), women participate fully in the rotational kitchen schedule. These Kuchwuch (cook-week) partnering assignments are usually long-term and therefore are made carefully. Every six to eight weeks, a pair of women are placed in charge of all cooking responsibilities. This is a huge task, since Kuchwuch lasts from early Monday morning until after supper on Sunday evening.

Every morning the cook-week partners arrive about four o'clock at the colony kitchen, where they work alongside the head cook to prepare breakfast. After breakfast, other women clean up and the Kuchwuch crew starts preparing lunch. A nap follows, but by three thirty the women are back in the kitchen making supper. Cook-week women do not attend Gebet, and most of them go to bed early so that they will be physically prepared for the next day.[41]

The head seamstress, or "colony mother," is the community's primary fabric buyer and distributor. She selects and allocates a variety of materials and related items. She also supervises female work assignments, making sure that the diverse needs of the colony are met.

Within colonies, assertive females and their friends create influential subcultures, a gender-specific power center that varies from colony to colony. This informal source of authority operates beyond the boundaries of nuclear families and fits well into the general communal structure. The female collective can increase its economic power through black-market activities (see a subsequent section of this chapter).

Women who do not hold formal positions often serve their husbands as assistant managers, accountants, and secretaries. Like males, young girls learn how to perform tasks through informal apprenticeships: by watching and doing. In addition to kitchen responsibilities, there are weekly cleaning, canning, and other work rotations, with the entire female population divided into two or three work parties (*Partei*). These work groups clean colony buildings, set and clear tables at mealtimes, and perform a variety of other jobs. At one colony, a group of fifteen- to twenty-year-old women served breakfast and then remained standing to meet the needs of those who were eating. The women filled coffee and tea cups, cleaned spilled liquids, and brought in freshly cooked pancakes, eggs, and oatmeal. If a person needed specific attention, he or she tapped lightly on a glass or cup with a spoon or fork.

The only women not usually assigned to work parties are those who are responsible for the long-term care of older or disabled individuals. The wife of the dairy boss is also at times exempted, because she customarily gets up at 3:00 a.m. to help her husband with milk-production chores.

In every Hutterite colony, there are also other, smaller, task-oriented work groups. For example, groups of two or three women clean the laundry room, prepare the butchering room, cut up chickens and ducks, and assist with baking responsibilities. Individual women clean and dust their own houses and coordinate doctor's appointments. In the Schmiedeleut, an increasing number of women serve as schoolteachers or as teacher's aides; and at both Hutterite book centers, women have served as book-store administrators.

Hutterite girls exhibit confidence and often hold a more serious and ironic attitude to life than Hutterite boys. These traits are seen in school, play, and work. Unlike boys, Hutterite girls take on babysitting responsibilities at very young ages, and they are also often assigned to help older women who have health problems.

One young girl told the following story that compares male and female attributes:

> I will tell you a joke. I mean it is a pretty stupid one, but it is true. Adam and Eve were together in the garden. One day God came along to visit them. He said that he brought them each a present, hidden in both of his pockets. One present was bulky and moving around, the other one was small. Adam, like all men do, wanted his present first. He chose, how all men would do, the big one. God reached into his pocket and gave him a bird. Since Eve did not get to choose, she waited for God to give her her present. God reached in his other pocket and gave her a brain.[42]

Like Hutterite males, young women often test colony rules, playing volleyball in mixed groups while wearing long dresses, or telling questionable stories. As early as the 1980s, Karl Peter noted a "newly accrued self-consciousness," a new individualism that was influencing the lives of Hutterite women as well as men. Peter stated that females were even starting to use sex to get power. He wrote, "This shift from an unquestioned sexual availability to that of sexual access depending on the behavior of the male is a pattern of behavior which simply did not exist in the past."[43] We strongly disagree with his assessment. In addition, Hanna Kienzler says that Hutterite women "flirt" in order to persuade men to stretch material and ideological boundaries. But there is nothing new about this observation; nor does it mean that Hutterite men are any less likely to flirt with or flatter colony women.

Shirin and Edward Schluderman found that Hutterite women were more introspective than men and described them as "sober," "sensitive," and "timid."[44] This is not our view. We find as many light-hearted women as those who are sober, as many who are outgoing as are timid.

In John Hostetler's 1974 work *Hutterite Society*, he wrote that Hutterite women "mildly dislike men as a group." In 1996 Patricia Looney agreed, adding that Hutterite women had "quick tempers." Without comparisons to non-Hutterite women, these assessments have little value; they seem ridiculous to us. In 1996 Gertrude Huntington, with John Hostetler, asserted that Hutterite women had "little to lose by complaining" and that a society comprised of very critical females had come about as a result.[45] We question the uniqueness of this characteristic. Everyone in Hutterite society, both genders, interrupts and makes critical comments. This behavior is an integral part of the Hutterite communal-cultural experience. Hutterite women do complain when they are asked to hoe weeds in the hot sun while colony males sit in air-conditioned combine cabs exchanging stories on their two-way radios. Hutterite men complain that modern Hutterite women have it "too easy" with their labor-saving appliances. Criticism is part of life, and with Hutterites it is reciprocal between men and women.

According to Karl Peter, modern Hutterite women also differ from those of an earlier time in other ways: greater material consumption, more labor-saving devices, greater concern with appearance (slimmer physiques and use of cosmetics), and more independence. These are accurate observations. Hutterite women also have more and more contact with non-Hutterite business associates. Hanna Kienzler notes that these relations start friendships, which in turn create new economic opportunities as businessmen and their families become prime contacts for the sale of colony goods. Some Hutterite girls clean outsiders' homes or do yard work, leading to more friendships and potential business contacts. In 2005 Kienzler observed the following price structure for handmade Hutterite goods: socks, $8–10; gloves, $20; queen-size pillows, $120–130; and feather quilts, $280–300.[46] Encounters with non-Hutterites provide insights about life outside the colony. In turn, these relationships give outsiders a more realistic and positive view of the Hutterites.

Houses and Living Standards

Standards of living are rising across the Hutterite world. There are more material goods, a greater concern for aesthetics, and a developing interest in recreational opportunities. Good times have also influenced architectural designs. On arrival in North America, Hutterites built in the longhouse apartment style first designed by ancestors in Moravia. The Lehrerleut and Hutterite conservatives in all Leut still generally construct this style of dwelling. But it is no longer possible to describe a "typical" Hutterite house.

Some colonies have randomly scattered clusters of duplexes. Others have parallel rows of 800–1,000-square-foot multiplex apartments. Mobile homes with storage sheds have become popular as temporary residences, since they can be moved and are relatively inexpensive. All Hutterite colonies are designed by untrained community architects, who copy the blueprints of other Hutterites. Non-Hutterite electricians, engineers, and plumbers are also often involved to ensure that government building standards are met.

There is much residential diversity across Leut and colony lines. Many conservative colonies, for example, did not install indoor plumbing until the 1960s; others not until the 1990s, long after progressive colonies had torn down their outhouses. In liberal colonies small kitchenettes first appeared in homes in the 1950s; they are now common in all Schmiedeleut, most Dariusleut, and many Lehrerleut colonies. Beginning in the 1980s and 1990s, some colonies installed heated pipes beneath the flooring in individual residences. Clocks that play Disney tunes have appeared in some colony living rooms. Many Hutterites have battery-operated alarm clocks that project the time onto the ceiling in easy-to-read large letters.

The most common colony residence continues to be a rectangular four-apartment lodge, although age and building styles vary, both externally and internally. Colonies that are two or three decades old often mix new and old structures, occasionally remodeling ranch-style farmhouses that were on the property when it was purchased. Many homes have been renovated with new paint and flooring as well as air-conditioning units.

Lehrerleut colonies show the most consistency in design and display characteristic order and cleanliness. Efficiency and functionality are central. The Lehrerleut kitchen-chapel is located in the middle of the housing complex, which itself follows a traditional building pattern of six to eight comfortable and well-built apartment-like dwelling units. The lack of residential diversity is ensured by Lehrerleut ministerial committees that make decisions about the general appearance and layout of new buildings. Each family home, planned for six to eight people, consists of a main floor and a large basement, with perhaps nine hundred square feet on each level. In addition, each family has access to individual cooler-freezer units in basement storage areas near the colony kitchen. These range from one hundred to two hundred square feet in size.

When a Lehrerleut colony in Montana rebuilt its living quarters in the early 1990s, all of the older buildings were dismantled to eliminate any semblance of inequality. The new houses are nearly identical even though family sizes vary. The new homes are larger than those replaced, yet extremely functional. Each dwelling has two stories, including the basement. The main floor consists of a living room with padded chairs, a sink and counter for the preparation of small snacks, a large rectangular dining room table, three bedrooms, and a large bathroom. One of the bedrooms can serve as an office or guestroom. In the basement there are an additional bedroom and bathroom as well as a storage room and a large open area.

Older Lehrerleut colonies often have smaller residences. At the Lehrerleut Vanguard Colony in Saskatchewan, for example, the minister Michael Entz, who appears in the 1983 Burton Buller film, lives in a very small apartment, with little space to move around. In Entz's view, this is all he needs.[47] Even in his cramped quarters, the well-read and articulate Entz maintains a library.

There is more diversity among the Dariusleut. In some of those colonies, there are new housing units with 2,400 to 2,500 square feet of living space on two or three levels. More typical is a multiplex unit containing four or five family apartments, where the basement has furnace rooms and water-heater closets. Some new residences include large sewing-quilting work spaces. But there are also older duplexes with small, atticlike upstairs bedrooms squeezed under the slope of the roof.

Older houses in all Leut have narrow, steep staircases with as little as four-and-a-half-foot-high clearances. Older apartments have crowded and musty basements filled with cast-off or seldom-used items. In one house, extremely worn and cracked linoleum covers the floor. Yet at the same colony there are modern three-level houses with triple-pane windows and vaulted ceilings. The new homes have large closets and individual kitchens, and some of the rooms are carpeted. There is marble on the stairway and tile on the walls. Conservative Dariusleut, like the Lehrerleut, adhere to an ethic of simplicity. But even the most conservative home is likely to have, built into one of the walls, a cooler that is hooked up to an elaborate system to keep food and beverages cool.

Schmiedeleut in both groups show significant diversity in housing. While one well-known minister continues to live in an older house with a window air conditioner, many of his colony's members have moved into newer, modern homes. In all Leut, colony managers usually set aside one room as an office. In farm manager Paul Wipf's office at a colony east of Edmonton, Alberta, there is a large Hutterite-built desk stacked with books, papers, and documents as well as a computer and several kinds of software. There is also a single bed for guests.

Tony and Kathleen Waldner's residence at the Forest River community, in North Dakota, is typical of many colonies in all Leut. The Waldner house has a tastefully posted name plate near the front door, and the two-level home has six small bedrooms, one of them kept as a permanent guest room. The home also has two bathrooms, both with tub-shower enclosures; a living room with a desk, couch, and chairs; and a small office for Tony, the colony's German teacher. In 2006 the eight members of Waldner's family shared four bedrooms. There is also a small storage room and a kitchen with a large table, a refrigerator, and a microwave oven.

With the exception of the Lehrerleut and the conservative Dariusleut, new Hutterite residences usually have central heating and cooling systems. There are small walk-in closets, and a few colony living rooms, and even kitchens, have hardwood floors instead of linoleum. Bedrooms are often placed in the back for greater privacy. Some residences have concrete tile roofing. Modern colonies have stuffed couches, play areas for children, and shelves lined with books and manuscripts. New houses at progressive colonies look like upscale condominiums.

Many newer Hutterite homes have central vacuum systems; long hoses that attach to inlets at the base of the wall in each room eliminate the need to move heavy vacuum cleaners from room to room. This arrangement also makes it possible to sweep dust and refuse directly into a suctioning system every day. Some new houses are carpeted, although there is controversy about carpeting since Hutterites associate rugs with dirt. Rugs stain easily, and many children walk through colony homes.

The windows and walls of Hutterite homes and community buildings are kept very clean; they are washed regularly. Even farm machinery is hosed down frequently. Little dust, few stains, and almost no crumbs can be detected. Hutterite homes are clean but not always tidy, because of the large number of people, especially children, who reside in and move through the houses every hour of the day. Some Hutterites are packrats who have a hard time getting rid of things.

In all Leut, bedrooms are filled with colony-made furniture, including beds with very soft mattresses. Bedding consists of colorful homemade quilts and northern-European-style *Federdecken* (feather ticks) made of soft goose down. Even in modern homes, full kitchens are rare and appliances scarce; there are no large ovens or stoves. Indoor plants, however, are increasingly common, including ferns, African violets, and cacti. Hutterite women exchange seeds and cuttings with friends and relatives. Some Hutterite homes have fish tanks and terrariums, and birdfeeders are common on colony grounds.

Even with changes in living standards, individual Hutterites have little privacy. Typically only older singles have rooms to themselves, and someone usually knows where people are, who is ill, and who is expecting visitors. At one colony, one day, everyone knew that the night before a sixteen-year-old male had met his girlfriend behind the hog barn.

Individual Possessions

All colonies try to ensure basic equality of living space, taking into consideration family size and other variables. But all Hutterites have some personal belongings, such as books, clothes, crafts, photographs, radios, clocks, and toys.

In the most conservative colonies, alarm clocks and wall calendars are often the only living room decorations. It is in the relative privacy of the bedroom that one sees a greater expression of Hutterite individuality. Especially for young men and women, this is where secrets are kept. The rooms of Hutterite girls contain bottles of perfume, lotions, women's magazines, and romance novels, alongside Bibles and devotional works. The Hutterite girl's personal chest is the place where photographs, letters, and small gifts are carefully hidden away. The bedroom of one Lehrerleut male was filled with pictures and knickknacks with an equine theme.

At some colonies men and women make decorative spice racks, rolling pins, bowls, picture frames, and children's toys. Some of them are made for their own use, but most are given away as gifts. Other Hutterites engage in scrapbooking or crewel embroidery or make stamped greeting cards. Many Dariusleut and Schmiedeleut own loudly chiming grandfather or cuckoo clocks.

Private purchases are often made at garage sales and thrift stores, where Hutterites find hot plates, tea sets, waffle irons, jewelry boxes, guitars, harmonicas, and ice skates. Some Hutterites own digital and other types of cameras, computers, CD and DVD players, and cell phones. Most items such as these are officially forbidden, but they are tolerated in all but the most conservative colonies as long as they are not displayed or used publicly.

Many Hutterite young men purchase stylish boots and footwear as well as Western hats. Some of them wear this garb to the Sunday morning Lehr, to weddings, and while courting. Hutterite men often receive personal gifts and prizes such as baseball caps, pens, and even barbecue grills from feed, seed, and implement dealers. It is hard to control the array of material products that move through the colony gates.

The Black Market

Most colonies tolerate the existence of officially unauthorized but small-scale private enterprises, established without formal permission, which provide personal income that is pocketed by individuals or families and does not end up in the colony treasury. Here one sees the impact of social materialism. The primary motive for selling on the side is to gain additional purchasing power. It is how many Hutterite families accumulate funds to buy an array of personal belongings, including microwave ovens, electric frying pans, coffee grinders, and toasters, which they often store discreetly in downstairs living areas. Each Hutterite family also receives a small weekly spending allowance from the colony, but this does not usually amount to more than a few dollars per person.

To counteract the Hutterite black market, some colonies co-opt the production process or persuade members to transfer most, or at least part, of the proceeds to the community's bank account. Schmiedeleut One ministers try to forestall individual sales by providing larger amounts of cash to individual families, along with strict accountability procedures. A different approach is taken at the Dariusleut Wilson Siding Colony. Here individualistic temptation is blocked by the elimination of lump-sum allocations. When individuals or families need special clothing items, for example, new shoes, they request specific dollar amounts from the colony business manager, who in turn requires receipts that authenticate purchases.

In general, a colony that is doing well financially is less likely to see private enterprise developing, and its members will have less desire to seek outside sources of income. Yard sales and "farmers' markets" may in fact benefit the colony as a whole. Some colonies have weekly markets during the spring, summer, and fall, where garden produce, baked goods, eggs, and meat are sold to the general public.

But in many communities, custom sewing and small craft production are treated as private enterprise. Quilts and blankets are easy to sell, as are tea towels, rolling pins, and some items of clothing. Each colony takes a different approach to the small but omnipresent underground economy. Some ministers battle against it. Most believe, though, that as long as it does not get out of hand, it can serve as a harmless safety valve for those who want a few additional possessions but are generally committed to community of goods. Most ministers insist that the amount of money accrued from private sales represent an infinitesimal sum compared to total colony income. Other Hutterites insist that most of the money earned from private sales be used to purchase gifts, items that are ultimately given away. One person says that the black market might thus be viewed as "the good fruit of a giving spirit."

The Hutterite black market is a female-dominated industry, since women do most of the craft work that mobilizes the shadow economy. At some colonies visitors are bombarded by sellers as soon as they exit their vehicles. At others a soft sell begins just before departure.

Young Hutterite males have their own temptations and ways to earn spending money. They are often approached by local farmers and businessmen who offer temporary work. These jobs pay well, and the boys are compensated with cash, which they often keep for themselves.

In theory, holding back money from the common treasury is a serious offense. Private ownership (*Eigennutz*) is attacked forcefully in the Lehren. Colony residents involved are compared to Ananias and Sapphira in the Acts 5:1–11 account. The 1950 constitution states, "No individual member of a Colony should have any assignable or transferable interest in any of its property, real or personal." But desire for private ownership has intruded throughout Hutterite history. An 1801 entry in the Chronicle notes: "It is well known that announcements have often been made against having money for oneself, and this practice has been abolished and the money called in."[48] One finds comments like these throughout the Chronicle and the Lehren.

When people cross the line by making too much money, ministers step in. In 2006 it was discovered that three Dariusleut men were undercounting the number of calves born at one colony, then selling the "extra" on the side. The church forced them to close their bank accounts and transfer the money to the colony treasury.[49] Other ministers deal with black markets by requiring that all personal items be sold in a certain place; in one case this was the basement of the minister's house. In the future Hutterites will likely continue to debate the black market issue. While in many ways it is an innocuous phenomenon and serves as a safety valve for individual desires and wants, it always carries within it the potential of undermining the entire Hutterite communal system.

❧ ☙

THE ORGANIZATION OF A HUTTERITE COLONY requires the active involvement of all community residents, men and women, adults and children. Specific functions are based on age, interest, experience, and gender. Hard work is a central Hutterite virtue and expectation. Gender roles are patriarchal and clearly defined, but Hutterite women find creative ways to exert considerable influence on all colony operations.

Although communalism is the guiding social principle of colony life, Hutterites accept a modicum of deviance from the communal norm as long as their foundational beliefs are not threatened. The way individual creativity is given expression within a communal context is remarkable and exemplary. But there are always some people who feel stifled, who want to change the Hutterite system or at least the way it functions in their own colony. Most dissenters remain and work for change within the community, but others decide to leave the Hutterite Church for a different life on the outside. Hutterite demographics, colony expansion, and issues of conflict, division, and defection are discussed in chapter 10.

CHAPTER 10

Population, Demography, and Defection

Therefore they all slipped away from community like an eel from the hand of the one who wants to hold on to it.

—Hutterite sermon on Acts 2, circa 1650

As the Hutterite Church continues to grow at fairly rapid rates, the Hutterites want to keep individual colony sizes small. But among the Leut and the colonies there are various expansion models. In addition, a significant 15 percent of residents decide not to stay in the community.

Hutterite Family Size

Every Hutterite is encouraged to marry and have at least several children. In 1954, Joseph Eaton and Albert Mayer conducted a study indicating that the average Hutterite woman gave birth to 10.4 children.[1] These authors suggested that Hutterites were some of the most prolific people on record. This assessment and the Eaton and Mayer figures have been quoted ever since in historical, psychological, and sociological works, without consulting later studies. The Hutterite birthrate is no longer so high.

Observers began noticing a decline in population in the late 1970s. In 1980 Karl Peter published an article, "The Decline of Hutterite Population Growth," on this issue. Studies by Bron Ingoldsby and Max Stanton in 1988 documented an increased use of contraceptives, tubal ligation, and hysterectomies as forms of birth control, leading to smaller families. One-third of the women referenced in the Ingoldsby-Stanton sample had used some form of birth control. Hutterite couples were also marrying later and purposely, with the official encouragement of doctors, spacing their children so that their families did not become too large. A 2002 study by Katherine White confirmed these findings.[2]

Since the 1960s, family size has diminished significantly. Our own study of Hutterite genealogical records found that the average number of births per Hutterite woman decreased from about 8.3 in 1960 to 4.8 in 1990 (see table 10.1). The most radical demographic change occurred during the 1960s, when birth control options first became widely available. This decrease in family size does not mean that the Hutterite population as a whole is declining. Karl Peter's 1980 study noted an annual population growth rate of 4.12 percent, compared to 2.9 percent for the general population.[3] Hutterite growth has now decreased to about 3.5 percent, still a fairly high rate, which leads to a doubling in population size about every twenty years.. Figure 10.1 provides a one-hundred-year overview of Hutterite birthrate statistics; figure 10.2 plots the age of Hutterite mothers when their last child was born.

Colony Size and Expansion

Unless financially strapped, Hutterite colonies rarely get larger than 150 to 160 people, the number that colony acreages can usually support. Small size also fosters close relationships between members of all ages, making

Table 10.1. Hutterite birthrates, 1954–1990

Year	Births per woman
1954	10.4
1960	8.3
1970	5.8
1980	5.3
1990	4.8

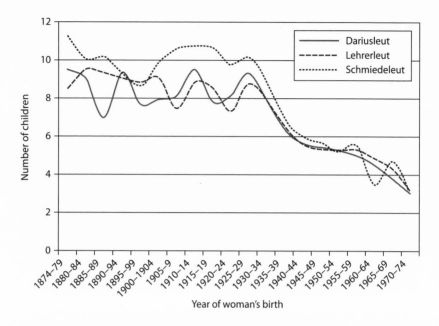

Fig. 10.1. Birthrate breakdown by Hutterite Leut.

it less likely that disruptive factions will emerge. Malcolm Gladwell, in his best-selling book *The Tipping Point*, notes that Hutterite colony size promotes social stability. Most Hutterites are very close to centers of power, hold important colony positions, and are personally empowered in a nonbureaucratic social structure.[4] Colony policies are analyzed informally via the gossip mill before decisions are made, before votes are ever taken. In a small community, it is not hard to discern the general will of the people.

Colonies start saving money for expansion, that is, the establishment of daughter colonies, as soon as their debts are paid off or the population exceeds one hundred. Hutterites are always saving money and looking for available land. Depending on numbers of children, male-female ratios, the number of runaway boys, and general retention rates, a colony that starts with fifty to sixty residents may grow to nearly one hundred within fifteen to twenty years. Expansion happens most quickly in colonies where there are large families, where most young people join the church, and where there are more male than female children. If a colony has a high

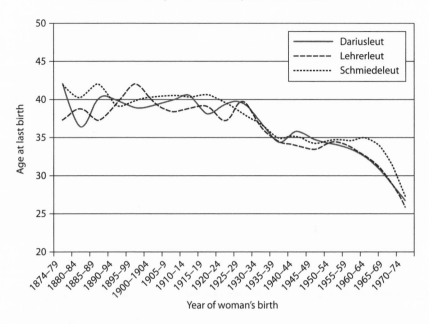

Fig. 10.2. Hutterite mothers' age at birth of last child, by Leut.

female-to-male ratio, it will automatically grow more slowly, since married women move to their husbands' communities.

Finding sufficient land for colony expansion can be difficult and often requires years of negotiating with more than one landowner. It is also necessary to wait until funds are available. As a result, not all colonies own properties that are contiguous. An emerging colony in western Montana consists of three separate family farms plus additional land, some of which is twelve miles away. Economic vitality is foundational for colony expansion. A community with 170 residents that has not expanded is a colony with major financial problems. To deal with this issue, the Lehrerleut have discussed pooling the resources of two or three colonies to provide the financial resources for the formation of one new colony. According to that plan, never yet implemented, the new commune might comprise a cross-section of members from each participating original colony.[5]

After land is purchased, colony residents start farming the new property and constructing roads, residences, and farm buildings. If the new property is located at a distance, a few families establish residence there or at least live there during the week. At first they might stay in already-existing farmhouses; this tends to be a temporary phenomenon, since these structures are usually difficult to convert to communal housing.

The more conservative colonies do not branch out until the new place is fully functioning and operational, and that process may take as many as six or seven years. Among the Lehrerleut, the establishment of daughter colonies must be approved by a committee that makes decisions on behalf of the entire Leut. The committee decides whether there is sufficient funding and whether the new property is likely to be profitable. It also reviews the economic and social impact on people who remain at the home colony. The mother community does not usually refurbish and renovate its own buildings until the new colony is able to operate on its own.

The decision about who moves to a new community varies depending on Leut and colony. Life in a new commune is often difficult during the first few years, with at least a few novice managers, new soil types, and houses and buildings to construct. The debt load is huge and the workload can be overwhelming. Thus moving is sometimes not the first choice of mother colony residents. On the positive side, new colonies have newer and often more comfortable residences, as well as the most up-to-date agricultural equipment. At one Alberta colony, most of the women wanted to move, because homes at the new site were larger, had more efficient heating and cooling systems, and were built with modern bathrooms, kitchens, and basements. The kitchen was equipped with newer and larger stoves and ovens. The men, who were also eager to move, were impressed with the state-of-the-art dairy, hog, and egg-producing facilities.

Traditionally, the lot was used to make all colony branching decisions. In the Hutterite view, this system allowed the Holy Spirit to make the final determination and helped reduce personal conflicts. The Lehrerleut still cast lots in establishing new colonies. After financial assets and liabilities are equally divided, two lists of families are drawn up by the church council, taking into consideration factors like age, sex, family, personality, and occupational gifts. A mix of people and interests is important to the spiritual and economic well-being of both mother and daughter colonies. The council also analyzes relationships between individual residents. Finally the names of all family heads are placed under the name of one of the colony's ministers, and the lot is cast. In traditional lot-casting, neither group knows which one will leave. Even an eighty-year-old minister might find his slate selected for the new community. The traditional custom was for all families to pack the day before the lot was cast, showing their symbolic and material acquiescence in whatever decision God was making.

Conservative Dariusleut and Schmiedeleut Two colonies employ a similar lot-casting process, but the majority of Dariusleut and Schmiedeleut communities use other approaches. In the Dariusleut each colony operates independently, and there is an emphasis on mutual decision-making within each community. Thus, branching decisions are often based on family considerations without involvement of the lot. If a senior minister wants to stay at the home colony, he does so. In at least one case, both ministers decided to stay, temporarily leaving the new colony without a pastor.

In the Schmiedeleut One, a different process is followed: At the beginning of the branching procedure, church council members use a chalkboard or a computer to divide up the names of residents, based on demographics, personal characteristics, and gifts. Sometimes the lot is used to determine which group leaves. But just as often the decision is made by the colony's church council. The Schmiedeleut One elder is also consulted.

The Schmiedeleut Two are much like the Schmiedeleut One in the way they make branching decisions. At a general meeting, two lists are drawn up, based on carefully discerned criteria. All decisions are made internally, however, without specific input from the Leut's elders. Both Schmiedeleut groups have developed the general criterion that no more than two brothers in a family (unless there are more than four) are placed on individual branching lists. Thus a majority of colonies have people with no more than two or three surnames. But there are exceptions: Crystal Spring Colony, in Manitoba, has five Hutterian surnames, as well as three families from Bruderhof, Mennonite, and other backgrounds.

Once established, a new colony operation opens up dozens of new and important managerial positions, presenting a great opportunity for persons who are tired of holding lower-level positions. This factor is especially important when a colony's male workforce has grown too large. Branching out is also an emotional time. There is always the possibility that one will lose some of one's closest lifelong friends. In summer 2006 a teenage girl at a recently divided colony unburdened herself. About half of the people she had spent her entire life with now live hundreds of miles away at a new colony. She was deeply distressed and near tears.

On occasion government policy has required that an entire colony be relocated. For example, in 2001 the Little Bow Colony, near Champion, Alberta, was forced to rebuild five miles away to make room for a dam and reservoir that were going to be constructed. The provincial government subsidized the construction of new homes, barns, and other structures, as well as all moving costs.[6]

Previous books describing the Hutterites have suggested colony branching rates of fifteen to twenty years. We assessed colony branching between 1990 and 2006. During this period, Dariusleut and Schmiedeleut communities started daughter colonies at a twenty-six-year rate, while Lehrerleut colonies branched out, on average, every twenty-two years. During the sixteen-year period studied, the quickest branching decision took place at the twelve-year mark, and the slowest took thirty-nine years. But a number of colonies have never branched off, even after fifty or more years of existence.

Looking at the most recent period, 2000–2006, branching interval rates have increased to thirty and twenty-six years, respectively, for the Dariusleut and the Lehrerleut, while decreasing to twenty-five years for the Schmiedeleut. These changes reflect the influence of later marriages, fewer children, longer "running away" periods, and higher defection rates. Unexpected in the 2000–2006 figures was the demographic stabilization of the Schmiedeleut. The general perception among Hutterites is that the Group One–Group Two division had a very negative impact on Schmiedeleut numbers. It did in the 1990s, but the situation has been reversed.

Leaving the Colony

Since immigrating to North America in the 1870s, the Hutterites have had an extremely high retention rate, which, combined with large families, has brought about remarkable population growth. In the 1950s researchers described Hutterite retention rates higher than 95 percent. In 1968 Victor Peters suggested that inbreeding added "genetic components favoring high fertility."[7] Although birthrates have decreased during the past fifty years, and defection rates for individuals and families have risen, Hutterites continue to have almost five children per family and to retain at least 85 percent of persons who are born and raised in the colony.

The 85 percent figure is based on a conservative analysis of colony records as well as interviews with dozens of Hutterite leaders and older colony members in all Leut.[8] Permanent defectors are sometimes designated in Leut family records. In the Lehrerleut record book, for example, some who have left are designated with the following statement (in German): "These people have rejected the community and have subsequently embraced the World."[9] More complicated is the informed speculation that is used in determining what percentage of Hutterite runaways will ultimately return to the colony.

A statistical analysis of marriage rates for the four Leut indicates almost no variance among the groups. Lehrerleut runaways stay away longer, however, and thus marry later. Informal assessments indicate that Lehrerleut defection rates are starting to exceed those of the Dariusleut and Schmiedeleut. For the Schmiedeleut, there is a slightly higher defection rate among the Schmiedeleut Two than among the Schmiedeleut One.

Even though only 15 percent of those born at Hutterite colonies decide to leave permanently, hundreds of young males (and many females) live outside the colony for one to five years before deciding to commit themselves to the church. Official colony statistics include these individuals in their population totals even though they are not in residence.

As early as 1982, sociologists Karl Peter, Edward Boldt, and others observed a rise in Hutterite defection rates. In 1993, Carolyn Hartse confirmed these findings and noted that beginning in the early 1970s, whole families, not just individuals, were beginning to leave the colonies in significant numbers.[10] Peter and Hartse used John Hostetler's fourteen-year population-doubling assumptions as a baseline for comparisons.

Late-nineteenth-century Hutterite defection percentages were likely even higher, but during the last twenty-five years of the twentieth century, rates did rise significantly. In 1974 John Hostetler suggested that 2 percent of the total population and 7 percent of those fifteen years and older left colony life permanently.[11] These figures have more than doubled in the past three decades.

Reasons for Moving "into the World"

Why do people decide to leave the Hutterite community? The main reasons are "born-again" Christianity, the Schmiedeleut division, the attraction of material goods and higher wages, individualism, perceived shortcomings in the Hutterite community, assimilationist pressures related to personal and social identity, and negative responses to church discipline.

BORN-AGAIN CHRISTIANITY

In the 2000s, evangelical Christianity is one of the most influential factors in decisions to leave colony life, especially for married men and women (and their families), but also for single adults. This development is the focus of Carolyn Hartse's doctoral dissertation. Hartse suggests that the attraction of conservative Christianity is closely related to the "perceived shortcomings" argument. For those who leave, there is cognitive dissonance between ideals and colony realities. This dichotomy provides an opening for evangelical Christianity, which reaches colony members via radio broadcasts, cassette tapes, the Internet, and "English" teachers and from Hutterites who have experienced a different spiritual reality.

Born-again Christianity is highly individualistic and pietistic. Many spiritually minded Hutterites are attracted to it because they desire a more personal relationship with God and want to spend more time studying the Bible. Some find theological support for evangelicalism in Hutterite sermons that preach against an overreliance on tradition and against general complacency. A sermon on Luke 2 includes the following injunction, related to the occasion when Jesus's parents lost him in Jerusalem: "Once we have received the Lord Jesus Christ into our hearts . . . through the word of God, if we thoughtlessly and carelessly turn away from Jerusalem, we can easily lose Christ again . . . If we look for Him among relatives and friends, we might not find him. There are many today who seek the Lord Christ among their relations and friends, saying 'This is the original faith; these are my friends and my parents; that is where I am saved.' But they have lost Christ in their hearts."[12]

The Lehren writers, who were not blind to the inherent problem of a traditionalist faith, asked Hutterites to "look at themselves in the spiritual mirror of the word of God."[13] A sermon preface teaches, "He [the Christian] must of necessity be reborn, renewed, changed, and turned around, if he wants to become an heir to eternal life."[14] In the Hutterite confession, Peter Riedemann includes a similar statement: "Whoever wishes to have Christ's nature and character must also be born of God."[15] Hutterite German teachers recognize and emphasize the importance of each child's developing an individual conscience and admitting to himself or herself and others when he or she makes mistakes. There are thus different forms of born-again thinking. Most evangelicals attack the Lehren and the confession of faith as dated and constricting, but Hutterite church leaders say that the born-again message in some form is at the very center of the Hutterite understanding of the Christian faith.

People who leave the colony desire something different from what the Hutterite Church has discerned to be the will of God. Even committed communalists sometimes question their place in the natural and supernatural order. A Hutterite sermon on Matthew 5 refers to such questioning: "Above all, the greatest and the most difficult are the inner trials, when the heart is in worry and torture." It is at this point that born-again Christianity, with its emphasis on a direct, self-proclaimed relationship with God, is so attractive. Hutterites insist that members who leave the colony have broken their baptismal vows. Evangelicals disagree, saying that they have broken only their vows to live communally, which they no longer accept as central to the Christian faith.

Evangelical Protestantism is not new to Hutterites. It affected Hutterite life soon after the group's arrival in North America. In the late nineteenth century, the Krimmer Mennonite Brethren (KMB) rendition of fundamentalist Christianity influenced both the Prairieleut and the communal Hutterites. Hundreds of Hutterians left the Prairieleut churches as well as the colonies to join the KMB Church.[16] Ukrainian-born John Z. Kleinsasser left the Elmspring Colony in the 1880s, for example. He later was the pastor of three KMB churches that emphasized the "new birth," including one that he established on his own land in Dinuba, California, in 1910.[17]

During the first half of the twentieth century, there were always Hutterites who listened to evangelical radio broadcasts; some of them developed an interest in the born-again emphases, but they usually did so within the context of communal life. Most Hutterites resisted evangelical individualism and extemporaneous worship forms and were successful in retaining a separate Anabaptist identity in their isolated rural communities.

In the mid-twentieth century, however, the evangelical message made new and more profound inroads via expanded access to radio and revival services and through "English" teachers, many of whom were evangelically minded Mennonites. In the 1960s, quite a few Hutterite young people were influenced by Canadian Mennonite schoolteachers Peter Boldt and Ann Voth. They joined the Hutterite Youth Movement, which crossed Dariusleut and Schmiedeleut lines, emphasized evangelical teachings, and caused some Hutterites to leave colony life altogether. Hutterite novice Terry Miller was one leader in this movement.[18] Evangelical interests have found a home among Hutterite individuals in dozens of colonies ever since.

In addition to those who leave the Hutterite community to join evangelical churches, hundreds of born-again advocates remain in the colonies, where they quietly—or not so quietly—promote a more emotional spirituality that emphasizes a personal relationship with God and often attacks specific social problems. This group is growing rapidly in the 2000s, leading to many conflicts within colonies.

The born-again influence is even apparent in the language of the Schmiedeleut Two confessional document, *The Hutterian Church Responds to Questions of Faith*. The statement identifies being "born again" as the place "where salvation begins" and continues with instruction in the faith process, including repentance and confession. But the Schmiedeleut Two document also proposes that a personal encounter with God will naturally lead to communal living: "Only if we meet the conditions set by Jesus Christ and do not waver from those conditions, only then do we remain in the glory of God."[19]

Some Christian leaders view evangelicalism as overly pietistic, incorporating what church historian Martin Marty calls a "retreat from responsibility." Robert Friedmann described the movement from Anabaptism to Pietism as "slip(ping) away from the narrow and difficult path of discipleship to the easier pietistic pattern." According to theologian Dale Brown, a pietist emphasis on "the heart" and the "inner word" does not necessarily de-emphasize the importance of works or of God as the foundation of the regeneration process. But traditional Hutterites see evangelical pietism as an easy road to a less rigorous faith. "I want them to *see* that I'm a Christian," says Hutterite Edward Kleinsasser.[20]

Hutterite traditionalists also accuse evangelicals of lacking humility and taking a stance of spiritual superiority when they focus on the "living power" of the Holy Spirit. They believe that at times this leads to a joyful preoccupation with self, since the "new Christian" believes that God's instruction is direct. He is thus less likely to listen to the teachings of the church. In the early 2000s, one Lehrerleut colony in Alberta lost nearly half of its members to a fundamentalist Christian group, and it was not an isolated case.

There are many born-again Hutterite communalists who are committed to working for change within the colony environment; one finds evangelicals in all Leut. Some refer to themselves as "Christians," to separate themselves from those who do not talk about a "new birth." Most Hutterites are upset by such talk, but even some church leaders resonate with the evangelical emphasis. One minister asserts that many "take religion for granted and live in the colony for the 'life' and nothing else." In his view, this "lukewarm Christianity" needs to be confronted more effectively to dispel the concerns of the more evangelically minded.[21]

Evangelical Hutterites who remain in the colony believe their movement represents an important corrective to cultural traditionalism. They emphasize that an "internal testimony of the Spirit" is essential to an adequate and constantly renewed understanding of the Bible. All Hutterites admit that reliance on the sermons can produce spiritual "deadness" if the teachings of Jesus contained in them are not followed. Ironically, this is a central theme of the Hutterite Lehren themselves.

Born-again Hutterites have started dozens of Bible study groups. Often it is younger people who request these groups, where personal faith is confronted and evaluated. At times ministers step in and stop the meetings, causing participants to say they are being persecuted. The ministers' response is that those who attend often believe that they have superior spiritual understandings. Ministers want to make sure that the Bible is interpreted according to communal Hutterian guidelines and that verses are not taken out of context. "The spirituality may be a good thing. But it is also disruptive," says one minister.[22]

Conflicts within colonies are growing. As a result, according to Manitoba minister Arnold Hofer, "Some of our brightest, best, most spiritual leave us."[23] In some communities, young and old are on different sides of the fence; in others, German teachers and ministers disagree. Sensing revolutionary developments, more and more Hutterite leaders accept at least some evangelical forms. "When young people get excited about their faith, is it my duty to tell them to shut up?" asks one. "Ministers shouldn't crack down on the evangelicals too hard," says another Hutterite. "They should direct the spiritual excitement back into the church."

Some ministers support Bible studies if the German teacher attends.

Other ministers lead Bible studies themselves. Montana minister Eli Hofer does this; he also integrates evangelical devotional material (for example, the writings of Josh McDowell and Charles Swindoll) with Peter Riedemann's Confession of Faith. In Hofer's view, Hutterites should respond with "gladness" when someone says she or he has made a commitment to God. His job, as minister, is to channel that commitment into the traditional Hutterite social structure, to redirect spiritual awakenings into Hutterite theological forms. Attending Bible studies gives ministers the opportunity to combat overly individualistic tendencies, misinterpretations, and the development of holier-than-thou cliques.

At times evangelicalism and traditional Hutterianism melt together. One seventy-year-old Hutterite woman is fully committed to communal life, but she also uses evangelical language. She describes three separate "spiritual" experiences in her life. The first came at age forty-five, when she "could not find Jesus" and felt dejected. Her "salvation" came through reading the Lehren, which released her from doubt. A few years later the woman went through the same experience, emerging once again with a stronger faith. In 2006 she was entering a third spiritual quest and used a derogatory term to describe Satan's involvement in testing her. This woman's experience sounds like Anfechtung, the psycho-spiritual condition discussed in chapter 7. But the woman speaks about her struggles using evangelical terminology. She talks about direct encounters with God but does so within the context of communitarian commitments. The sermons have been instrumental in helping her reclaim her faith.

The evangelical influence on Hutterite colonies is widespread. Historically, Hutterite funerals were somber and communal affairs. The worship service focused on God and the community, not on the person who died. Now many funeral services include personal comments about the deceased, and cemeteries are no longer just holes in the ground: they have gravestones with names attached. There is also an increasing use of gospel hymn collections such as the *Evangelisches Gesangbuch* (Evangelical songbook), which includes songs like "What a Friend We Have in Jesus," "Softly and Tenderly," and "Just as I am."[24]

Evangelicalism does not automatically destroy Hutterite culture or communal traditions. But it does represent change, and there is a strong correlation between colony evangelical movements and higher defection rates. This effect scares many ministers. At one colony a visiting pastor interrupted his reading of the sermon at Gebet to interject the following comment (I paraphrase): "If a young girl tells me that she has 'invited Jesus into her heart' this raises serious questions for me." In his view, individual Christians cannot control what God does. It was inappropriate for an individual to boast about her faith. The girl's experience also did not reflect the communal Gelassenheit that Hutterites traditionally preach, that an individual cannot be fully committed to God without yielding to the spiritual insights of other church members and exhibiting Christlike behavior. The minister did not mean that a personal relationship with God was not important, but he viewed it more communally.

Some evangelicals also emphasize an "assurance of salvation" position, suggesting that one can be "certain that one is 'saved' " and will spend life after death in heaven. Most Hutterites disagree. They believe it is blasphemous to claim a divine guarantee. With regard to the issue of assurance, Hutterites point to the Lehr on 1 John 5:1–3, which includes the following instruction: "Now if you get to be godly and change your life according to the word of the Lord, and capture the flesh as a captive of the Holy Spirit, and keep it bound with the fear of God, then you are prepared, and are assured in your faith."[25] In this reading, assurance comes as the result of a faithful following of Jesus, not by faith alone.

According to the Hutterite position, the colony provides a foundational kind of security, sometimes compared to Noah's ark in the Old Testament. Spiritual status is based on Christlike behavior and the willingness to share material belongings. Although God makes the final determination, and Hutterites do not claim to speak for God, most members feel secure in their faith, at least until evangelicals start questioning them.

Hutterites define Christian faith collectively. It is based not only on a personal relationship with God but is mediated by church members as representatives of Jesus. Evangelicals hold a more individualistic understanding of Christianity, stressing the importance of "having Jesus in one's heart." There is greater emphasis on self-development and less on communal commitment and humility. Listening to the wisdom of church members may be less important than listening to one's own heart.

Evangelicals often criticize the age and limited functionality of the Lehren and prefer worship services where members have the opportunity to share personal joys and concerns. They criticize the bad behavior of many Hutterites and speak of a lack of deep spiritual understanding.

Evangelicals talk about indiscriminate use of the media and alcoholism and about hypocrisy among the Hutterites; and since there are problems in any group, the evangelicals never run out of stories to tell. In fact, they help Hutterite leaders to pinpoint important problems. The Hutterite majority responds by saying that they can point to just as much hypocrisy in the born-again group and that it is even more distressing because evangelicals profess to be closer to God. They cite the Hutterite sermon that states, "Oh, yes, there are many lofty eyes who are raising their eyelids. They are always looking around afar to observe what is bad in others . . . thanking God they are not like other people." Evangelicals also condemn Hutterites for not engaging in evangelism, for turning their backs on people in "the world" who need their help.

In North America, born-again Christianity has subverted communal Anabaptism many times over. Hutterites who leave colonies and join other churches almost always give up communal life, pacifism, the German language, the sermons, and other traditions. An evangelical Hutterite asserts, "Many Hutterites have a low estimation of the transforming power of the Holy Spirit. They chide those of the born again group as deluded when they think that they have victory over sin." But traditionalists do not believe that the "victory over sin" evangelical experience necessarily makes a better Christian.

There are different ways to look at the effect of evangelicalism. In addition to conflict and tension within colonies and increased defection rates, there is also more religious talk and self-reflection. In the midst of conversations about people leaving, there is a strong interest in practical theology. It is evident not only in general conversation but in the songs sung by young people, and it occurs in all of the Leut, among progressives and traditionalists.

THE SCHMIEDELEUT DIVISION

A second reason for defection is specific to the Schmiedeleut. In 1992 the group divided into two factions as a result of differences that were partly connected to the 1974–1992 Bruderhof connection. Both Schmiedeleut sides accused the other of dishonesty, rule infractions, and power aggrandizement. The result was the breakup of many friendships and even extended families, as individuals found themselves residing in opposing

(Group One or Group Two) colonies. Brother went up against brother, grandparent against grandchild, in an intense internecine social battle. Especially difficult has been the formal shunning practiced by Schmiedeleut One, which has made it hard for some Hutterites to attend the weddings and funerals of friends and relatives.

Anyone dissatisfied with Hutterite life now had a reason to leave, and whole families often did so, many never coming back. If a person grew up hearing his parents constantly complain about a minister, or about uncles, aunts, and once-close friends, it was easy to think negatively about Hutterite life in general, especially if the individual's family seemed powerless to influence decisions made at higher levels. Recent trends, however, show that the population falloff from the 1992 break has reached its nadir and that the numbers are moving up.

THE ATTRACTION OF MATERIAL GOODS

A third reason for defection is the seductive attraction of material goods and higher wages. Most Hutterites have a good life, with plenty of food, nice clothes, and comfortable living arrangements. They do not, however, have the extra luxuries that are important to many middle-class families in the United States and Canada. Some Hutterites have a difficult time handling the contrast as they are bombarded with commercial enticements from the advertising industry.

The issue of material possessions and their relationship to spirituality is discussed often. Manitoba Hutterite Samuel Kleinsasser comments, "We spend money on buildings not missions and in effect condemn people to not hear the Word of God." But many Hutterites want even more material goods. In past centuries, Hutterites often left the community when economic times were bad. Now the situation has reversed, leading one minister to ask colony youth, "Will you flee when times are too good?" Dariusleut minister Paul S. Gross once warned, "Good times have never yet made good Christians."[26]

INDIVIDUALISM

A fourth reason for defection is the general attraction of individualism. The temptation to go out on one's own, find a job, rent an apartment, and not ask anyone's permission to do so is a powerful pull, especially for young males.

Hutterites who want to express themselves creatively also often feel socially and psychologically alienated in the colony. They want more opportunities, greater spontaneity, and fewer social controls. Many professional interests are not accommodated in colony life. Ex-Hutterite Ruth Lambach notes: "Here in the suburbs of Chicago, there is a Hutterite girl named 'Tschetter,' who is working on her GED . . . This girl is in weekly contact with her mother [in the colonies] through a cell phone connection. She tells me that Sioux Falls is filled with *Weggeluffene* (runaway) Hutterites."[27] Runaways and defectors want to experience life on the outside. One ex-Hutterite won a beauty pageant in Winkler, Manitoba.[28]

Most Hutterites have a strong sense of place and adhere to an ethic of communal responsibility. Old and young are valued and treated with respect, regardless of personal strengths, weaknesses, and idiosyncrasies. Eric Brende notes that the Old Order Amish have created a life that is "a means of embracing those who were different."[29] Hutterite colonies serve the same function. But nothing is perfect; not everyone fits in. Some Hutterites do not find acceptance within the communal order. They fall through the cracks and do not find meaning and purpose there. This is not to say that those who leave find life on the outside any easier, but many feel it is worth the risk.

HUTTERITE COLONY SHORTCOMINGS

A fifth reason for leaving the colony is related to real or perceived shortcomings in the Hutterite community. They may involve personal conflicts with other members, perceived hypocrisy, authoritarian leadership, and lack of spirituality. Many defectors experience dissonance between Hutterite theology and colony practices.

Marlene Mackie suggests that those who leave tend to hold low-status colony positions and that many male defectors are individuals who have not attained positions as important as those held by their fathers. But people leave for a variety of reasons. Mary Wipf left a South Dakota colony in the late 1970s because Hutterite leaders would not, in her view, deal forcefully enough with her husband's alcohol problems.[30]

More recently, many single Hutterite women are leaving because of limited marriage prospects. In the Lehrerleut, hundreds of young males live the runaway life for years at a time, and many never return to the colony. As a result more and more baptized Hutterite women are also leaving. They find work easily in restaurants, bakeries, food processing industries, and day cares. Like Hutterite males, they are trustworthy, industrious, and competent in many areas.

ASSIMILATIONIST PRESSURES

A sixth reason for leaving is the push to assimilate culturally, economically, and politically. Although social pressures vary, American and Canadian societies both encourage national identification. The capitalist superstructure, within which Hutterite colonies function economically, is especially seductive. With regard to political issues, one Washington Hutterite asked, "Why should I expect other people (i.e., nonpacifists) to provide protection so I can live in peace and security?" Listening to the radio, or even reading the newspaper, creates a desire in some Hutterites to be less isolated, perhaps even less Hutterite.

Some Hutterites tire of the constant reminders that they are different from their outsider neighbors. Why not just become a part of the group? Many non-Hutterite schoolteachers, evangelical Christians, and business associates actively push this sense of uneasiness.

CHURCH DISCIPLINE

Another reason for leaving the colony relates to particular cases of church discipline. Individuals who believe they have been treated unfairly sometimes react by moving into a world where they are not held accountable to church authorities. On the outside you can live the way you want to, although the consequences of such behavior may be unpleasant.

Those who leave the church usually contact friends and relatives who did the same thing earlier. There are dozens of small businesses in Calgary, Alberta, for example, that are owned or managed by ex-Hutterites. Hutterite members do not cut off relationships with residents who run away, and sometimes not even with those who leave communal life permanently. In January 2008, many colony members, including three Hutterite ministers, attended the funeral of a woman who had left a South Dakota colony at age seventeen, thirty-five years previously. One person present noted the "nonjudgmental participation on the part of the Hutterites" and "the human fellowship that took place after the service."[31]

There is no discernible correlation between defection rates and whether a colony is liberal or conservative. Examples of colonies that have almost perfect retention rates over the course of the past half century run the gamut from very conservative to extremely liberal.

"Renegade" Colonies

A few Hutterite colonies have left their Leut as total entities, yet continue to be structured communally.[32] Hutterites refer to members of these communities as "renegades." Examples of this phenomenon are the Elmendorf and Altona colonies, in south-central Minnesota. Both are former Schmiedeleut One colonies and both were influenced by born-again Christianity. They reject Hutterite ethnocentrism, worship more informally, and emphasize evangelism. But they retain communal life and are committed to Anabaptist theology. Recently the two have founded a third associated colony in Tasmania (Rocky Cape Christian Community), and they have been joined by ex-Hutterites from other church groups.

Members of the Elmendorf community are quick to name weaknesses in the Hutterite colonies and to justify their own positions. One leader, Peter Hoover, compares Elmendorf to one of the three original Dakota Territory colonies and suggests that the community may someday be recognized as the mother colony of a new Hutterian Leut or movement.[33]

Another Hutterite split-off group that continues to practice community of goods is the Fort Pitt Colony, near Lloydminster, Saskatchewan. This former Dariusleut commune was also influenced by evangelical Christianity. Many ex-Hutterites have also joined the charismatic Global Missions organization. Twenty ethnic Hutterian members of this group live on a single gravel road north of Sidney, Manitoba. Another one hundred ex-Hutterites attend the Global Mission church in Winnipeg; fifty are members in Winkler. Many of these individuals were influenced by Terry Miller, the one-time "youth movement" activist. Miller himself regrets his former lack of humility and forceful critiques of Hutterite belief and practice. In the 1990s, Miller contacted Hutterite leaders, asked for forgiveness, and ended all evangelistic efforts focused on the communitarians.[34]

In the early twentieth century, a few Hutterite colonies were excommunicated as total entities or were never accepted into any of the Leut. These include the Monarch, Felger, and Stirling colonies in Alberta. Another unaffiliated Alberta colony, Brocket, joined the Schmiedeleut One in 2005. Other Anabaptist communal groups, for example, Julius Kubassek's Community Farm of the Brethren, Bright, Ontario, also at one time had close ties with the Hutterites.

Charity Christian Fellowship

During the past twenty years, the most successful evangelistic assault on Hutterites has come from the Charity Christian Fellowship. Headquartered in Ephrata, Pennsylvania, the plain-dressing group has attracted hundreds of Hutterites who are interested in evangelical Christianity but do not want to discard traditional Anabaptist practices. Before the infusion of Hutterians, Charity was predominately an ex-Mennonite–ex-Amish church.

In 1988 Charity minister Moses Stoltzfus began holding tent meetings near Hutterite colonies. He also met with Hutterite "seekers," sometimes in their homes.[35] "God put this on my heart," says Stoltzfus, who is no longer welcome on colony grounds. He contends that there are "very few believers" in the colonies. Ivan Glick refers to Charity's work as "spiritual browbeating," but Charity holds conservative positions on social issues, demands plain dress, is pacifist, and is highly evangelistic. More than one hundred ex-Hutterites have moved to Pennsylvania to join the group. Others have joined Charity churches in Manitoba and South Dakota. At one Stoltzfus revival meeting in Winnipeg, Hutterite ministers tried unsuccessfully to intercept Hutterites who were going forward at the altar call.[36]

Individuals and Families Defect

Reasons for defection are complex and often involve a combination of factors. Elizabeth (Wipf) Flinn, for example, left the colony when she was twenty-one, not because she did not like life there but because community leaders would not allow her to continue her education.[37] Elizabeth's daughter Rebecca, an aspiring actress, works for a Los Angeles film-production company with an office near Hollywood and Vine.

On the outside many defectors do not connect with any church. Others join Christian groups that have as many rules and regulations as the colonies they left behind. The colony-world decision tipping point is different for each individual. Many Hutterites just want to try something different, and at the time of departure they are unsure about what path they will take. When married adults decide to leave, their children have no choice but to follow, regardless of how they feel about the decision.

Table 10.2 lists Hutterite surnames found in the telephone directories of three major cities located near large colony populations, including Saskatoon, Saskatchewan; Calgary, Alberta; and Sioux Falls, South Dakota.[38] The higher numbers in the Saskatoon and Sioux Falls areas reflect the presence of noncommunal Hutterites (Prairieleut) in those areas. There are also non-Hutterites of German background who happen to have the same surnames as Hutterites. Many of the Sioux Falls listings likely represent five or six persons in a household. In addition, many young men and women rely exclusively on unlisted cell phones. The total Hutterian population in Sioux Falls (runaways and defectors) might thus be as high as nine hundred people.

The experience of living on the outside can be shocking at first. Hutterites are not used to making very many individual decisions. Defectors have to find a place to live, set up a bank account, buy a vehicle and insure it, and find a job. Hutterites are accustomed to a highly ordered life, with set times for eating, work, and worship. Now everything seems out of control. Even after a Hutterite lives in the "world" for many years, the sense of loss, the disconnection from family and culture, can be heart-wrenching. One defector said, "The ark [referring to the Hutterite colonies] is so full of holes, if the flood came, it will all sink." But there are others, such as the Global Missions member who, after visiting a colony in South Dakota, wrote: "I have never in my entire life felt so sad at having to leave this community." She grieved over a life that might have been.[39]

Baptized ex-members who want to return are placed in Meidung for two or three weeks. They are then asked to kneel down in church and ask forgiveness from God and the community. Afterward they are accepted back by the laying on of hands. This mediating ritual allows former members to start recovering their lives as Hutterites. All wounds are healed, unless behavior on the outside has imposed serious consequences. For example, most colonies now require returnees to have physical examinations that include HIV/AIDS and hepatitis testing. One person who had con-

Table 10.2. Hutterite surnames in public telephone
directories, by city, 2007

Surname	Saskatoon	Calgary	Sioux Falls
Waldner	50	17	17
Walter	33	33	31
Gross	16	50	43
Wurz	17	8	8
Stahl	13	13	12
Decker	12	21	21
Tschetter	7	4	36
Wipf	5	0	23
Hofer	3	34	55
Kleinsasser	3	6	9
Wollman	4	4	20
Maendel	0	0	10
Glanzer	1	0	4
Entz	4	4	0
Total	168	194	289

tracted AIDS as the result of a sexual encounter was still accepted back, and he was treated with love and compassion all the way to his death-bed.

Hutterites who decide to leave permanently often make contact with other ex-Hutterites. Some establish semicommunal living arrangements, sharing houses and meals. Many socialize regularly with other ex-Hutterites and join the same churches. Tabitha Hofer, an ex-Hutterite who lives in Winnipeg, co-owns the Tall Grass Bread Company and Deli. When Hutterites visit her café, she gives them free coffee and cinnamon rolls.[40] They bring fresh produce and baked goods. Hutterites who seek medical care in urban centers often lodge at the homes of former members.

Implications of Running Away

The runaway or *Weggeluffene* phenomenon is an embedded Hutterite social institution. One study found that 27 percent of Hutterite males and 10 percent of females had left the colony at one time or another. Reasons for leaving varied: 29 percent indicated a desire for more individual free-dom and self-direction; 12 percent wanted to have unrestricted "fun," and they associated doing so with media access and the opportunity to make a lot of money; 11 percent listed problems with colony leaders; while an-other 11 percent expressed dissatisfaction with colony work roles. Most surprising is that few of the runaways surveyed mentioned religious rea-sons for leaving.

Many Hutterites suggest that runaways disproportionately represent the sons of members who hold lower-status colony positions. Runaway trends also run in certain families, indicating parental influence. Colony leaders believe that a lack of understanding of Hutterite history and be-liefs is another important reason for leaving.

Our own 2008 assessment found that nearly one-third of Hutterite males and about 10 percent of females leave the colony in their late teens or early twenties for at least a short period of time. In the Lehrerleut the percentages are highest (more than 40% for males). Between the ages of twenty and thirty, there is a particularly striking decrease in colony male populations.

At one Lehrerleut colony, so many young men have left that the last marriage was conducted in 1987; the last two children were born in 1993. When so many young men depart, some colonies, at least temporarily, do not have enough males to complete heavy manual labor requirements. Hutterite women pick up the slack. They paint, gather eggs, milk cows, feed animals, and assist in the birthing of livestock. Women clean garages, assist in the carpentry shop and barns, and wash vehicles. They also drive into town for vehicle and equipment parts. Some help with cattle brand-ing and garden plowing.

Young men in colonies with labor shortages sometimes use their clout to avoid doing undesirable jobs. Others engage in questionable activities that ministers are tempted to overlook. Some start small black market busi-nesses. In one case a young Hutterite started a lucrative beef-jerky opera-tion, so profitable that he left the colony and started his own company on the outside. On the other hand, in colonies where there are too many men, or where there is an aging membership, the runaway phenomenon creates good positions for the males who stay behind. This is also the case in colo-nies that have financial problems and are therefore not able to purchase sufficient land to start a new community.

When runaways grow accustomed to a world of individual freedom and choose not to return to the colony, it has a devastating impact on the lives of Hutterite women. Dozens of women may lose the opportunity to marry and have children. In past years, a greater percentage of male runaways returned, and they did not stay away as long. High wages in the mining, oil, and construction industries have changed these trends.

Hutterites have a strong work ethic, and being versatile, they learn new jobs quickly and effortlessly. They are thus in great demand. They often enter the workforce with skills that are not commonly found in people their age. Many men are experienced in plumbing, carpentry, cabinet-making, vehicle maintenance, animal husbandry, cement work, electrical wiring and repair, and heavy equipment operation. They are accustomed to taking orders from superiors and do not complain about wages or workloads. One Lehrerleut man, who left the colony at age seventeen and stayed away for seven years, did drilling and pipeline work in the booming Alberta petroleum industry. He says that many of the companies he worked for had Hutterite managers and that at one company, all the delivery truck drivers were runaways.[41] Hutterite female runaways also find jobs easily. They too are accustomed to long hours of work and find it easy to gain employment in rest homes, supervised living facilities, restaurants, and child-care centers. They generally move in with former Hutterites, who help them find jobs and provide orientation to a very different way of life.

Those who have run away and return for short visits with friends and family disrupt colony activities and social mores. Flashy cars and new technology are distracting, especially for impressionable Hutterite youth. Many colonies have rules limiting visits and do not allow runaways to stay overnight. But colonies also do not want to burn their bridges; they want the Weggeluffene to come back. At one Lehrerleut colony, when a runaway arrived, one of the ministers told him, "I don't want to see you"; but the minister had a smile on his face, showing ambivalence and hopefulness.

A large majority of runaways do return to the colony, and many end up in important leadership positions, including the role of minister. Significantly, since runaways are not church members when they leave, lifetime vows and commitments to communal life are not broken. And since most male runaways do not attend church on the outside, they have usually not been influenced by contrary theological or ecclesiastic traditions. There are many runaway stories and they affect virtually every Hutterite extended family.

Not everyone stays in the Hutterite community but leaving and staying away continue to be very much the exception to the rule. The vast majority of Hutterites do not want to explore alternative lifestyles. They like Old Order communal life in the quiet of the countryside. They have no interest in living in towns and cities with larger populations, no interest in giving up coffee every morning with seventy-five friends and relatives. In the colony they are confident and secure and are taken care of from cradle to grave. Most Hutterites are fully committed to communal values and practices and believe that this is the way God wants them to live. Most importantly, each Hutterite young person is asked to make a personal decision about whether to commit his or her life to communal Christianity. Nothing is forced; decisions are made with a full understanding of requirements and expectations. For prodigal sons and daughters there is always forgiveness and reconciliation.

❧ ❧

NOTWITHSTANDING INTERNAL DISSENSION AND DEFECTION, Hutterite colonies in all four Leut continue to experience significant population growth. Most members are very happy with the communal forms that have been created, refined, and institutionalized and which are constantly being evaluated. There is a significant Hutterite minority, however, who experience enough conflict with community ideals, practices, and persons that they decide to leave the Hutterite Church. Some of these decisions are affected by the growing influence of the media and technology. This phenomenon is discussed in chapter 11, which deals generally with how the Old Order Hutterites manage change.

CHAPTER 11

Managing Technology and Social Change

To support large growing colony populations on limited land areas, the
Hutterites have had to adapt to labor-saving devices and modern technology
to maintain their way of life.
—John S. Hofer, *A History of the Hutterites*

S ince the beginning of the group's existence, Hutterites have found
creative ways to manage social and economic change. They have
always tried to do so from a communal Anabaptist theological perspective. Dealing with change appropriately is a major concern of Hutterite leaders, especially in the rapidly changing environment of the twenty-
first century.

When discussing change and modernization, Hutterites refer to biblical
principles and examples and how these have been interpreted throughout
their history by confessional statements and the Lehren. The groups' Ordnungen derive from ideological principles, but they have undergone much
change much over time to accommodate social, political, and economic
trends. Such adaptation has always created tension within the Hutterite
community as it seeks to live apart from the "world" yet interacts with it
on a daily basis and is thus influenced by non-Hutterite ways of thinking. There is tension in thought and practice as Hutterites dress plainly,
live simply, and fight against individualism but at the same time sell their
products on the open market and listen to the viewpoints of non-Hutterites on the radio.

One of the most controversial issues in present Hutterite society is the use of technology and exposure to the mass media. Although Hutterites have always accepted the controlled use of the most up-to-date forms of technology, they have had more difficulty dealing with the mass media, especially since the advent of Internet and cell phone communication. The media are considered more dangerous than technology in general, and they have all along been viewed with greater fear and skepticism.

The traditional Hutterite approach to new technologies is to adopt them quickly, as long as they do not negatively influence Hutterite theology or culture. The Hutterites do not want the use of technology to change their social and cultural patterns too much. But they do not believe, as do the Old Order Amish, that speeding up farm work, revolutionizing agricultural production, or making life more comfortable for people inside their homes is necessarily bad. They are less concerned than many other Old Order groups about corollary social and ideological effects. "People lived differently during the nineteenth century," says one Hutterite minister, "but that doesn't mean that we have to live that way." Another minister offers, "You can't stop technology; you can just control it."[1] Hutterites generally view their managed use of technology as a strength, not a weakness.

But the Hutterites also know that some technological developments, along with closely related media innovations, need careful monitoring. These move quickly into the lives of Hutterite individuals and their families. Thus when Hutterites are asked to name the most important contemporary issues that require attention and clarification, they typically mention technology and the media, and more specifically, computers and cell phones.

When computers are used for egg-sizing, operating machinery, or filling out government reports, there is little controversy. When they are used by young Hutterites to surf the World Wide Web or to have long e-mail conversations with persons of the opposite sex, some of whom are not Hutterites, red flags go up. In colonies across the states and provinces, cell phones, computers, and digital cameras abound. This development is fraught with danger as well as opportunity. The effect of technology and media on younger Hutterites is hard to assess but also difficult to overestimate.

A girl at a Schmiedeleut Two colony understands word-processing procedures and uses this knowledge to assist in colony farm management procedures. She conducts colony business on the computer every day. This use of technology is viewed positively and is very beneficial to the Hutterite community. Two teenage boys at a Dariusleut colony listen to the music of Reggae artist Bob Marley and have learned that Jamaican Rastafarians use marijuana. Hutterites view the boys' use of technology negatively. At another colony, adolescents accumulate a large collection of iTunes on their individual iPod systems. Most of what they download is contemporary Christian music, but hundreds of other young Hutterites at other colonies probably download a much broader selection of music. The Internet provides access to widely diverse sites—from fundamentalist Christianity to rock and roll, chat rooms, and pornography—which can influence Hutterite culture from different angles.

Simplicity and Complexity

Hutterites believe that technology is essential to success in agriculture. Some technological innovations are also beneficial for the environment. The Turin Colony, in Alberta, for example, built a supplemental solar thermal heating system for their hog barn. The Pincher Creek Colony, also in Alberta, permits a private company to operate sixty windmills on community property.[2] This same openness to technology is found at colonies that are establishing small manufacturing enterprises. New industries require up-to-date equipment, technology, and applied media. Without them they cannot compete on the open market.

If farm machinery is not big enough or capable of performing necessary tasks, Hutterites build or invent their own, using the creative abilities of individual members.[3] In eastern Washington, two colonies were not satisfied with the size and efficiency of their potato-harvesting equipment. They approached a heavy-equipment manufacturer and requested a "super-digger." The result was the production of a self-propelled forty-two-foot harvester that handles potatoes with a very gentle touch. Hutterites travel across the North American continent and even to Europe, in search of the most modern and efficient equipment.

Hutterites also use the most up-to-date equipment in domestic arenas. Hutterite kitchens, laundry rooms, and residences have expensive modern appliances. Air-conditioning and indoor plumbing were once controversial but not any longer.

The use of modern technology results in the loss of many skills and craft traditions. An earlier generation of Hutterites forgot how to make pottery, quit sending its members to medical school, and watched its schools deteriorate. More recently, most colonies have ceased making their own brooms, shoes, soap, and butter. One forty-five-year-old Hutterite had difficulty moving a 1999 Toyota because it had a manual transmission. He said he had not driven a vehicle with a manual transmission for at least ten years. Hearing the story, the man's twenty-year-old son said to Rod Janzen, "You must have an old car."

The Hutterites move forward with caution, analyzing innovations from a religious perspective and relying on the wisdom of older members. Leut executive committees, ministers' councils, German teacher conferences, and colony church councils deal regularly with the issues of technology and the media. But it is difficult to control technological change and to know what the long-term effects of seemingly inconsequential decisions might be, especially if they involve the media.

Hutterites talk a lot about the interplay of religion, technology, and the media. They typically support change if it is economically profitable and there is no foreseeable adverse affect on religious beliefs. Hutterites are interested in efficient and productive agricultural and industrial operations. But most members worry about the social and ideological consequences of the many technology forms that entice them. One recent controversy involves the artificial insemination of cattle. While the Lehrerleut and conservative Dariusleut oppose this practice, it is commonly accepted by the Schmiedeleut.[4] Technology and media purchases are also costly. Buying expensive computer systems and paying high cell phone bills reduce the funds available for other colony purchases.

Exposure to the media introduces Hutterites to the temptations of more extravagant standards of living and a spirit of frantic competition. It opens the door to the world of sports, movie stars, and patriotic propaganda. All of this input concerns Hutterite leaders, who pose many important questions. Are there areas of Hutterite life that will be transformed in a negative, noncommunal direction if technology and the media are allowed to pursue their influential course? How many people should be given access to the Internet? Is there a correlation between higher living standards (often connected to new technologies) and increased defection rates? These are all questions under discussion in North American Hutterite colonies.

Telephones. The technology that Hutterites use most is telecommunication, which is available in an increasing variety of forms. As late as the early 1990s, a majority of colony homes did not have private telephone lines. Some colonies had central switchboards, so that one could call homes through an intercom system, often run by computer, but in most colonies the only way to talk to someone was to call the home of the minister or the business manager and hope that whoever answered could find the person you wanted. When you called, you knew that you were imposing on the time of whoever answered the phone. As a result, not only outsiders but also friends and relatives in other colonies were hesitant to call.

This system is still in place in many communities. But things are changing rapidly. There are now central switchboards in 75 percent of Schmiedeleut colonies, 73 percent of Lehrerleut colonies, and 27 percent of Dariusleut colonies.[5] Younger people especially are contacting persons inside and outside the colony via cell phone and e-mail. The cell phone makes it easy for Hutterites to make calls and send text messages whenever and to whomever they wish, facilitating private communication to an extent unimagined in the past. Intercom systems and cell phones mean more interaction between members of different colonies, across Leut lines, and with people in the non-Hutterite world. Unlimited-time telephone plans encourage longer conversations and an increase in the number of calls across great distances.

At times telecommunication can be a time-consuming distraction from work and other activities. At one colony the phone rang at least fifteen times during the course of an evening conversation. This would not have happened twenty years ago. At another colony, a girl in her early twenties was talking to her boyfriend who was three hundred miles away. One minister received so many calls from an older woman in another province that he simply quit taking them.

The introduction of the cell phone is especially revolutionary. On the positive side, the phones make it possible for Hutterites to contact each other even when they are miles away from home, for example, working in the fields or visiting other colonies or on business trips. But cell phones also increase the possibility of private conversations with persons not approved by the colony. According to a front-page story in the *Wall Street Journal*, cell phones allow Hutterite runaways to give their friends in the colonies "blow by blow accounts of their adventures: going to the movies, watching television, buying flashy clothes."[6]

Cell phone capabilities seem endless, and cameras are included in them without additional charge. Text messaging is used by many Hutterite young people and adults, and some of them own sophisticated models that provide access to the Internet. A Hutterite woman told Elizabeth Holmes, who wrote the *Wall Street Journal* article, that she had sent more than one hundred fifty text messages during the first two days after getting her new cell phone.[7] Many Hutterites receive free phones from local merchants or sales representatives. Others get theirs from family members who have defected or "run away."

Cell phone use is restricted most by the Lehrerleut, who in 2005 imposed a limit of five phones per colony. At some colonies cell phones are placed in a semipublic place, where they can be checked out on the honor system. These phones are used primarily by colony managers for business purposes. Members in all Leut are quick to tell you, however, about the dozen or so additional phones that are in the possession of colony members. On farm vehicles, CBs (citizen band broadcasting devices) and two-way radios are still the most common form of communication, but at the Warden Colony, in Washington, combine drivers have classy Bluetooth wireless headsets.

While most colonies still have large bells that call members to meals and work assignments, many communities now use intercom systems. They announce church services, births, marriages, deaths, and other news. At some colonies the intercom simulates the high ringing sound of the traditional colony bell.

GPS guidance systems. Colonies have also purchased GPS (Global Positioning System) guidance systems, which are costly but have important agricultural uses. With a GPS, fields can be planted in straight lines and at the most optimal depth. GPS's direct the movement of crop dusters and planters and are used for leveling fields and harvesting crops. Some GPS's turn tractors around automatically, making it easier to work in the fields. A GPS-guided combine or tractor can gauge exactly how much seed should be deposited in a specific row of a field. With this technology it is possible to sow seed twenty-four hours a day, since there is less worry about reduced sight in the darkness or operator fatigue. Many colonies also use infrared photographs to determine irrigation requirements. Global Positioning Systems help travelers locate businesses as well as other colonies.

Computers. Hutterite agriculture relies on sophisticated new machinery and computerized operations that provide exact production information on crops and livestock. In colony dairies, for example, each cow wears a necklace containing a computer chip that measures feed-consumption levels.

Hutterite colonies began computerizing farming operations in the 1970s and 1980s. To gain expertise, selected members took correspondence courses or learned how to use computers and the accompanying software by trial and error. Since then Hutterites have become very sophisticated and proficient in this area.

Because of the Internet, however, the computer is also a means by which the world, in a personal way, invades the protected space of the colony. It provides a pathway for consumerism, evangelical Protestantism, and nationalism to launch attacks on foundational Hutterite principles and cultural values. E-mail communications, which cannot be easily monitored, make it difficult for the colony leadership to maintain a protected, isolated social and ideological environment. For this reason, the Lehrerleut and the conservative Dariusleut use computers only for essential agricultural and accounting purposes; the Lehrerleut in 2008 began to phase out even these operations. Conservative Hutterites have always prohibited Internet access even though they lose some sales as a result.

In the nonconservative Dariusleut and Schmiedeleut colonies, however, use of the Internet is widespread, for business and for education. With the exception of ministers, stewards, and farm managers, computers are not officially allowed in individual homes; they are accessible only at the schoolhouse or in colony business offices. But in practice, more and more Hutterites are buying personal computers and discovering inexpensive ways to install wireless Internet-access software. Some Hutterites also own personal data assistants (PDAs), which help organize schedules and provide yet another way to reach the Internet. Many Hutterites also access the Internet at local public libraries.

Fax machines also continue to perform an important function, especially at Dariusleut colonies, where 73 percent of individual telephone calls still go through a central line located in the minister's or the business manager's home.[8] There is usually a five-to-ten-minute time limit on these calls, so the fax machine is an important alternative for social intercourse. It ensures rapid communication, although it is not private: at many colonies fax copies are placed in the colony kitchen, where dozens of people have an opportunity to read them.

Computers can be a blessing as well as a curse. The Schmiedeleut One

Die Quelle project, for example, makes it possible for anyone with a computer to access information about Hutterite history, beliefs, and practices. Die Quelle includes theological statements, historical documents, and even audio performances of Hutterite hymns. Many resources for German and "English" teachers are also contained on the disk. In addition, computers make it easier to archive genealogical information and to update colony address and membership lists.

Colonies with Internet access take various approaches to block unwanted Web sites. The Dariusleut make decisions on a colony-by-colony basis. Some communities have no built-in curbs, while others allow unblocked Internet use only on colony-owned units located in public places. These computers usually operate on very slow telephone lines and are often kept under lock and key. In 2006 the Schmiedeleut Two took steps to control unfiltered Internet use through the creation of an officially approved list of Web sites. The Schmiedeleut One use software to block pornographic and other undesirable sites.

Hutterite leaders, knowing that the Internet is easily misused, fear its influence. Not only does it provide access to modern music and sporting events; it also exposes Hutterites to noncommunal, non–Old Order forms of Christianity. It is even used to set up chat rooms where Hutterite issues are openly and honestly discussed. In her 2007 *Wall Street Journal* article, Elizabeth Holmes used a Hutterite chat room to gain insights from colony young people. Hanna Kienzler notes that many Hutterite females are establishing "virtual social networks" through e-mail communication.[9]

A more traditional form of communication, letter writing, also continues to be popular. Since a majority of Hutterites do not have access to cell phones or computers, or choose not to use them, they send thousands of letters and cards through the postal system every day. This is still the safest way to ensure private communication.

The media and other technology. Historically, Hutterite leaders have not (officially) allowed members to own or listen to radios. The same holds true for televisions, DVD players, iPods, and CD players. Outside of some Schmiedeleut One colonies, one rarely sees these items in public areas in homes.

In practice, however, radios are listened to every day by many people, in colony vehicles, in the shops, in bedrooms, and in the schoolhouse. There are fewer televisions, but most colonies have at least one hidden somewhere. At some colonies, television sets are covered up with a cloth cover sewn specifically for this purpose. A Hutterite man at a conservative colony told us about something that had been televised on the previous evening's 60 *Minutes* program. When asked how he would know this, he blushed and said that he had "seen it somewhere."

Radios, and often CD players, are now part of the standard accessory package in many trucks, vans, and combines. Conservative colonies ask that radios and stereos be removed before delivery, but there is diversity in practice in other communities. The influence of radio is evident in modern Hutterite musical and other tastes. In southern Alberta and Montana, for example, Hutterites like country-western as well as contemporary Christian and gospel music. Hutterites from Washington to Minnesota listen to radio talk show hosts Rush Limbaugh and Sean Hannity as well as National Public Radio. Anyone who goes into town can watch television broadcasts at bars and department stores.

One finds stereos, CD players, and digital cameras at most Schmiedeleut colonies. Some members have MP3 players. One of the authors was present when members of a Dariusleut community walked over to the schoolhouse to watch a VHS tape of a documentary on videotape. The official progressive Hutterite position is that stereos and DVD players, like computers, are used only for educational and business purposes and that they are kept in public places. But an increasing number of Hutterites have these devices in their homes.

Cameras are also omnipresent in the Hutterite world, even though they were historically banned and are still officially not approved, and photography is a popular pastime. Almost every Hutterite family, in all Leut, has a large collection of prints. The authors have often been criticized for not bringing along family photographs and for not having cameras in hand to take pictures when they visit. "Rod, I can't believe you didn't bring your camera along," exclaimed one minister. One also finds guitars in virtually every colony, even occasionally electric guitars, electronic keyboards, amplifiers, and percussion instruments.

Hutterite publications. The James Valley Colony, in Manitoba, publishes annual editions of the *Hutterite Directory.*[10] Other communities (the Lakeside Colony, in Alberta, and the Riverview Colony, in Saskatchewan) print their own address books. An online directory and a Hutterite map book are in the works. These publications give Hutterites up-to-date contact information. The James Valley book is financed by a small publication fee and by advertisements placed by livestock supply, seed, farm machinery, chemical, and fabric supply companies. Some of the advertisements announce colony-run businesses. The directory includes colony addresses and the phone numbers of at least the senior minister and the business manager of each colony. Some colony listings provide direct access to individuals and community shops. Each Leut also publishes annual editions of membership books for internal use.

FOR TWENTY-FIRST-CENTURY HUTTERITES, new technologies present opportunities as well as problems. The Leut, Leut subgroups, and individual colonies are adopting different approaches to new forms of communication. Hutterite leaders constantly debate ways that technology and media may be used in such a way that a communal and Christian way of life is not negatively influenced.

Other Twenty-First-Century Hutterite Issues and Concerns

North American Hutterites have established communal Christian enclaves that provide meaning and purpose for thousands of people. Most Hutterites are happy with their personal lives and with their work, and they try to live according to the teachings of Jesus as closely as possible. Not every society is perfect, however, and Hutterites are quick to admit that they have problems as everyone else does—the natural result, in their view, of humankind's sinful nature. The most important issues and concerns that confront contemporary Hutterites are discussed in the sections that follow.

The Schmiedeleut division. Accusations and negative appraisals continue from both sides. There are many pathways to reconciliation, and some leaders are trying desperately to find common ground. Others are pleased with the current situation and believe it frees both sides to move in directions they believe God wants them to go. The three much smaller communal Leut that existed in the 1870s never united, and the two Schmiedeleut groups may not reconcile in the 2000s.

Hutterite youth activities and runaways. Unsupervised youth gatherings are common in areas where colonies are located close together, causing Hutterite leaders concern about how the young men and women are spending their free time. Some worry about premarital sexual activities, others about alcohol and tobacco use. As one minister put it, in adolescence "the hormones take over, leaving the mind behind."[11] Many Hutterites are especially uneasy about the increase in the number of adolescent runaways and the influence this trend has on those that remain in the colonies. On the positive side, Hutterite ministers, German teachers, and other church leaders are developing creative approaches to deal with the problems that are specific to young people.

Passing along Hutterite traditions. Younger Hutterites, like young people in most societies, often have minimal interest in the group's history and beliefs. Furthermore, they sometimes lack personal commitment to distinctive Hutterite practices. Although this problem is not new—it has been present throughout Hutterite history, and young men and women in all societies test their cultural and ideological boundaries—Hutterite leaders are concerned that some colonies are spending too much time on business and not enough on spiritual matters. These problems and possible solutions are a central focus of Leut educational conferences.

Innovations. Schmiedeleut One innovations are rapidly being institutionalized. Included are English worship services, the use of musical instruments, openness to higher education, and various mission efforts. A Schmiedeleut One leader says, "If we are going too far, we can always step back." But the majority of Hutterites do not agree. They wonder whether other historic beliefs and practices will fall into disuse also, and they worry about the influence of the Schmiedeleut One on progressive colonies in other Leut.

Relationships with Non-Hutterites. Contacts are increasing as agricultural and industrial products are marketed nationally and internationally. Many Hutterites wonder whether increased relationships with outsiders will cause members to question the value of their traditions and to desire assimilation with the mainstream society. Will more contact with "the world" move Hutterite hearts and minds in noncommunal directions?

The rising standard of living. As living standards rise and Hutterites accumulate more material goods, how will their commitment to historic, plain Christian principles be affected? It is harder to preach a simple and humble faith and to focus attention on the supernatural realm of existence when one's community looks like a prosperous urban subdivision. On the bright side, growing prosperity makes it possible for Hutterites to donate more money to important social programs.

The spirit of individualism and the black market. Historically, the acquisition of personal property had a negative impact on Hutterite communal traditions. A Hutterite proverb speaks of this idea: "Communal life would not be so hard, if there were not such self-regard."[12] In 1926 the Schmiedeleut Ordnungen stated that chests and other furniture were to be painted one color, usually black.[13] Hutterites no longer insist on this level of singularity, but they continue to preach basic social equality, a value that the omnipresent underground Hutterite economy could subvert. Some Hutterites have small bank accounts; in one survey it was found that 80 percent of such accounts were in the names of Hutterite women.[14] As long as the black market stays small, as it is now, and everyone at least informally reaps benefits from it, it poses little danger. However, many colony leaders are experimenting with creative alternatives that will redirect the energy expended in this shadow economy to more communal activities.

Higher education. As more Hutterites pursue secondary school and college degrees, many members wonder how the additional education will affect their traditional beliefs and practices as well as their language and culture. There is concern about the influence of academic knowledge on issues of faith as well as the potentially subversive power of secular worldviews. Hutterite education committees and ministers' councils actively debate these issues and seek answers to the education question. Conservatives remain adamantly opposed to higher education, and liberals express cautious acceptance of it, at least under certain guidelines.

Evangelical Christianity. How will the Hutterite church respond to the "born-again" movement? More and more Hutterites are accepting the fact that other expressions of Christianity have value, and especially those with a pietist emphasis. The big Hutterite debate is whether to actively combat evangelicalism or to seek common ground by emphasizing similarities between evangelical emphases and the group's own theological traditions and practices.

Economic issues. Because of the globalization of agriculture, it is often difficult to purchase sufficient land to support Hutterite colony life. Profit levels are sometimes low and unpredictable because of commodity price volatility. Fuel and equipment replacement costs are rising. In response, as more colonies establish small industries, there are changes in workloads, daily schedules, and general lifestyles that affect Hutterite culture as a whole.

Evangelism and humanitarian service. Support for missions is increasing, especially in progressive colonies. Many Hutterites believe that God is calling them back to the kind of evangelistic witness that was exhibited by their sixteenth-century ancestors. But when these activities are done in association with non-Hutterites, they introduce members to different forms of Christian belief and practice. How will this contact change the way that Hutterites view themselves and others? Hutterite sermons include harsh words about noncommunal Christians, such as these criticisms in the Acts 2 sermon: "Their consciences are broad like the door of a cattle barn and they have the stomachs of ostriches which can digest iron. The old people, the lame ones, the cripples and the widows and orphans are deserted, and the pockets, satchels and chests of these people are filled."[15] But modern Hutterites often recognize the integrity of different Christian interpretations. They are experiencing less discrimination from non-Hutterites than at any other time in their history. At the same time, they are less sure that they are the truest believers, even as they continue to follow Jesus's ideal communal plan. The relationship between ethnicity and religion is ingrained in Hutterite life and taken for granted. But ethnoreligious fusion is a point of contention for other Christian groups. Evangelism in Nigeria, for example, has introduced the Schmiedeleut One to different styles of worship, dress, and even communal forms.

An aging population. Throughout most of Hutterite history, older people have accounted for a very small percentage of the group's population. But the current tendency to have smaller families and other demographics have created a higher adult-to-child ratio than in most earlier periods. The filling of colony managerial positions is affected, as well as the size of the workforce. The aging of the population also results in more health problems.

Response to change. The Leut and the colonies respond to change in diverse ways. One progressive minister suggests that God always works within the context of changing social, economic, and cultural conditions. He believes that instead of constantly fighting every innovation, Hutterites should respond with critical but open reflection. Not everyone agrees. The Hutterite majority believes that change in itself is more dangerous than advantageous.

All of the issues discussed in this chapter are hotly debated in colonies throughout the United States and Canada. Each Leut, and to a considerable extent each colony, is trying to find its own way of dealing with problems in a manner that preserves Hutterite beliefs and cultural practices yet does not, in the Hutterite view, close the door on the ongoing leading of the Holy Spirit.

❧ ❧

HUTTERITES MANAGE CHANGE BY DISCUSSING every technological, theological, and ecclesial innovation in great detail and by referring continually to the communal Christian principles they find in the Bible and which are supported by the Lehren, hymns, confession of faith, epistles, and Ordnungen. While nothing is set in stone, change comes slowly for Hutterites. New policies do not materialize overnight. The long deliberative process is intended to ensure that Hutterites find ways to introduce change without deviating too much from historically designed forms and patterns. Each Leut and each colony reach slightly different conclusions on what kind of social innovations are accepted.

The imaginative outcomes of the Hutterite deliberative process often provide ideas and applications that are also of benefit to non-Hutterites, for example, in conflict management and the efficient use of material and natural resources. The conflict between tradition and change is often precipitated by unavoidable relationships that Hutterites establish with non-Hutterites. Those relationships are the subject of chapter 12.

CHAPTER 12

Relationships with Non-Hutterites

Did Jesus teach and live in Gemeinschaft? We believe and openly declare that he did.
—Schmiedeleut Two Educational Committee, 2000

The World Outside

Hutterites interact with people of many different religious and cultural backgrounds. There are regular contacts with non-Hutterite businesspeople, teachers, and shopkeepers. Hutterites need and sometimes cherish these relationships, but they also maintain social barriers in order to protect their distinctive way of life.

Hutterites view the world from their own communal perspective and through an ethnoreligious lens. When they talk about someone who is not a Hutterite, they typically use the term "outsider" or *Weltmensch* (a person living in the "world"), or they refer to the person as "English." "Outsider" signifies that Hutterite and non-Hutterite ways of life are fundamentally different. The social environment outside the colony grounds is called the "world," based on the New Testament dualism that pictures believers as separate from "the world." What is seen here is the classic "two kingdoms" theological perspective. A member of the Hutterite Church is one of *unser Leut* (our people), that is, a member of a self-contained ethnoreligious family, one that it is difficult to become part of. When individual outsiders are better known, Hutterites substitute ethnic, religious, or ethnoreligious terms. One hears references to "the Catholic neighbor," "the Irish implement dealer," and "the half-Indian mechanic."

Except in emergency situations, Hutterites have not historically sought ecumenical relationships, nor have they participated in activities involving other Christian organizations. Hutterites had some contacts with Mennonites when they were in Russia, and those relationships have at times been renewed in the United States and Canada, because of their common theological roots. But in general Hutterites have remained separate.

Some of the Hutterites' isolationism has been challenged in the past few decades. One Dariusleut minister converses with Seventh Day Adventists, evangelical Protestants, and Tridentine Catholics, debating beliefs and practices. In all Leut there is more and more contact with non-Hutterite businesswomen and businessmen. There is growing curiosity about the wider Christian world, including "cults," with which the Hutterites do not want to be associated.

Most mainline Protestants and Roman Catholics leave the Hutterites alone. Conservative fundamentalist and charismatic groups criticize Hutterite spirituality and try to convert Hutterites. One large Protestant denomination issued a more subtle attack. In 1980 the Christian Reformed Church published a Sunday school study series entitled *Reasons*, which includes "challenges" from "sects and cults with Christian roots." "Challenge 7" is presented in a chapter on the Hutterites, who are described as "a Christian sect with a remarkable lifestyle but a flawed vision of the world." Instructors are cautioned, "Should it be apparent that your students are all too appreciative of the Hutterite lifestyle, that they are likely to leave your classroom thirsting for how wonderful, peaceful and heavenly it would be to live in such an ideal community, then conclude with a dose of realism."[1]

The Hutterites do not believe they are the only ones who will go to heaven. Committed Christians from other denominations will also be found there. But Hutterites believe that heaven will be communal and they will therefore have an inside track. One colony member speculates that in heaven, resurrected Hutterites are providing orientation for all of the holy city's noncommunitarian citizens, that is, most other Christians.

Professors and Academic Works

Hutterites say that sociologists and historians are pleased when they (the Hutterites) do not change, preferring a society that is frozen in time. When church services are unaltered, when there are no changes in dress or agricultural practices, it means to many writers that the Hutterites have successfully and admirably resisted the seductive forces of North American assimilation. It also makes it easier to describe and define them.

Professors who visit Hutterite colonies are often mistrusted or at least viewed as bothersome because they interfere with the work schedule. Hutterites have at times been quoted out of context or without permission. Non-Hutterites misunderstand the Hutterite basic beliefs as well as the rationale for many Hutterite customs. One Hutterite made the following illustrative comment:

> We are tired of college people dropping by for a week or so, taping some interviews and passing out some questionnaires for us to fill—and, usually talking so fast and with such big words that most of us just politely smile and agree with them without having any idea of what is going on. And then a few months later another gang of college people drop by with an article that visitor a few months before had published in some journal. Then they ask us if we really do "this and that" and when we say we don't know what they are talking about, they accuse us of holding back something from them because: "we know you know the answer, because look here, it's right here in this article!"[2]

Hutterites are committed to lives of humility and service and do not seek publicity. A minister tells his wife that he has been quoted in one of our books. She responds: "Well there's only one book that you should be concerned about having your name in: the book of life."[3] At a colony in Montana featured in a *National Geographic* photo essay, a minister exclaims that nothing else needs to be written about the Hutterites. Everything of importance has already been said.[4] A girl seated in the room tries to soften his comments, but this colony has been visited once too often. On our arrival at another colony, a thirty-year-old man sitting in a pick-up states, "We don't need another book about the Hutterites."

At some colonies one finds little curiosity about the outside world and a general annoyance with inquiries. But that is not the norm. Hutterites typically welcome outsiders who are sincerely interested in knowing more about them. Hutterites are not oblivious to popular opinion, nor are they uninterested in how they are viewed. In this regard scholars mediate between Hutterite faith and life and the outside world.

Many professors have helped collect, preserve, and translate Hutterite historical and theological works. Some are close friends and religious comrades. On numerous occasions, we have been asked to pray before eating snacks in Hutterite homes. Seeing black pants and shoes, plaid shirts and beards, Hutterite children ask, "What colony are you from?" In Canada, Mennonite historians and sociologists have lectured on Anabaptist history, beliefs, and practices at several colonies.

The Hutterites and Popular Culture

Unlike the Amish, Hutterites are rarely the focus of Hollywood films. There are a few exceptions. In 1941 a British film, 49th Parallel, included a lengthy section in which three Nazi infiltrators take refuge at a Hutterite colony in southern Manitoba.[5] The Hutterites depicted are good hosts but refuse to assist the soldiers in their assignment, even though the soldiers speak German. One of the soldiers defects after becoming the colony's baker. The Hutterites granted permission to film 49th Parallel at the Iberville Colony. According to Hutterite folklore, everything was moving along smoothly until one day a Hutterite woman saw actress Elisabeth Bergner painting her nails and smoking a cigarette. The Hutterite woman was so incensed she rushed up and doused the cigarette with a bucket of water, knocking it out of Bergner's mouth. Bergner was later replaced in the role by Glynis Johns.

A more recent film involving Hutterites is Leonard Nimoy's comedy Holy Matrimony (1996).[6] It stars Patricia Arquette as a very sexy thief who hides out in a colony with her ex-Hutterite compatriot, whom the Hutterites force her to marry in order to live in the community. The film seeks to contrast American and Hutterite culture, but it provides a very inaccurate portrait of Hutterites. For example, in the movie Arquette's new husband gets killed in a car crash. As a result Arquette is forced to marry the man's twelve-year-old Hutterite brother, a custom that is falsely presented as an expected Hutterite practice. Ex-Hutterites who accompanied Max Stanton to the film's premiere thought it was ridiculous in its characterizations.

Occasionally Hutterites also appear in popular magazines. In September 1994, for example, the Hutterites were featured in *Mirabella*.[7] There are also a few Hutterite documentaries. The best and most accurate is the Burton Buller–John Ruth 1983 production *The Hutterites: To Care and Not to Care*, an impressive fifty-eight-minute analysis of Hutterite life that includes interviews with Hutterites in all of the Leut. A more critical assessment is provided by ex-Hutterites Sam Hofer and Mary Wipf in the 1996 film *Born Hutterite*.[8] In the 1990s, the BBC produced a single-issue documentary, *How to Get to Heaven in Montana*, which details conflicts involving evangelicalism within the Flat Willow Colony. In 2004 German filmmaker Klaus Stanjek filmed a ninety-six-minute documentary at the Pincher Creek Colony in Alberta. *Commune of Bliss* explores Hutterite life there accurately and in great detail.

In October 2006 the Hutterites became the focus of the *Dr. Phil* television show, when a man from another Old Order Anabaptist group, the Old German Baptist Brethren, took his daughter from his estranged wife and asked to stay overnight at the ex-Schmiedeleut Elmendorf Colony in Minnesota.[9] This was unwanted publicity for the Hutterites, especially since Elmendorf, described by Dr. Phil as a Hutterite colony, no longer belongs to any of the four Leut.

Hutterites themselves stay informed of social, economic, and political trends by subscribing to news magazines, daily newspapers, and technical journals. Some listen regularly to the Canadian Broadcasting System and other news stations.

Colony Visitors

Non-Hutterite visitors are usually welcome at Hutterite colonies, but responses vary and are site-specific. Most colonies invite guests for meals, for worship services, and often for lengthy conversations. Some Hutterites see such hospitality as a form of evangelism. At times non-Hutterite visitors are even invited to stay overnight. There is no complaining when beds are given up, even when children have to sleep on the floor or on a couch. The occasion seems almost festive, especially for boys and girls.

Most visitors to the colonies, however, are friends and relatives from other communities, especially when colonies are located close to each other and during the summer months, when many women and younger children visit other colonies. Hutterite bathrooms are well stocked with toiletries and extra towels and bedding. For Hutterite children, visitors, Hutterite or non-Hutterite, constitute a form of entertainment, and young girls prepare the guest rooms with a sense of excitement. One asks her mother, "Why hasn't anyone stayed with us recently?"

Guests who are Hutterites do not interfere with daily operations. They know the colony routine and help with chores. No one has to be asked to do anything. But problems can arise when non-Hutterite visitors arrive. This issue, and the proximity of some colonies to major highways, has caused some colonies to establish organized paid tours that include noon meals. Some colonies, especially in Alberta, protect themselves from liability lawsuits with a sign near the colony entrance that reads, "Visitors welcome. Enter at own risk"—though many Hutterites dislike these signs. In Manitoba, the James Valley Colony paid a sixty-thousand-dollar settlement to a woman who broke her leg when she slipped and fell inside a colony freezer, even though she had been told not to enter.[10]

Hutterites are busy people. Visitors who stay more than a day are expected to join the workforce. The unskilled may be asked to pick up supplies in town or to transport older people to other colonies or to doctors' appointments. Visitors report a high level of acceptance as well as general Hutterite hospitality. One reserved sixteen-year-old said that he was fully "accepted" during the week he spent at a Hutterite colony. He did not dress as the Hutterites did, and he held very different perspectives on faith and life, yet he was accepted for who he was, with his own idiosyncrasies. Unrelenting pressures to conform are built into North America's various social institutions and are perhaps as strong, if not stronger, than those confronted at a Hutterite colony. One might anticipate that the separatist Hutterites would be less accepting than they are of people who are different from themselves.

Businesspeople as well visit colonies often, combining work and friendship in a social climate of mutual respect. Some accounting and consulting firms advertise openly for Hutterite clients.[11] An unusual enterprise is the Hutterite Prairie Market in Sioux Falls, South Dakota, owned by Prairieleut Obed Hofer. Forty-four Hutterite colonies participate by providing material products and fresh produce. These include meat and cheese as well as colony-built furniture and fancywork.[12]

Neighbors and Outsider Perceptions

Hutterites have good relationships with most of their neighbors, those who accept the fact that the communalists have chosen a radically different way of life. Since Hutterites believe and act counter to mainstream culture, however, some people feel uncomfortable with them. Discomfort leads to verbal attacks on those causing the irritation; it engenders negative appraisals and stereotypes. Not all rumors are groundless, though. Hutterites are not immune to human frailties and folly, and at times criticism is warranted and even helpful. Too often, however, characterizations of Hutterite are completely erroneous.

In 1976 Marlene Mackie conducted a study of outside perspectives of Hutterites that focused on cultural characteristics. Of those interviewed, 42 percent called the Hutterites "cliquish," a trait to be expected in a group that values separation. Closely following were "religious," "old-fashioned," "hardworking," and "shy." A scant 2 percent were concerned about the "plight" of Hutterite children.[13] In 1983 Rod Janzen studied Hutterite perceptions held by local businessmen and policemen in southeastern South Dakota. All were in towns located near Hutterite colonies. The study concluded that most of the individuals had subjective impressions not based on factual foundations.[14]

One common misperception is that Hutterites steal. Many store owners insist that Hutterites, especially children, shoplift regularly. It is true that Hutterite boys and girls do not grow up with a standard understanding of the private-property concept. On the colony grounds, everything is in some sense owned by everyone; Hutterite adults lock buildings and rooms that they do not want children to enter. In Hutterite schools, young children sometimes take pencils, paper clips, and paper without asking permission, but teachers say that this behavior is no different from that of any other group of boys and girls. When Hutterite children go to a store for the first time, it is sometimes difficult for them to keep their hands off the merchandise. But again, the same is true of most children; and Hutterite boys and girls are watched carefully by their parents, who do not allow them to take anything.

With reference to Hutterite adults, theft accusations by storeowners move into the realm of fantasy. For example, Hutterite women window-shop, as most other people do. But because they wear long dresses, non-Hutterites often think they hide store items underneath them. Retail managers insist that such theft is occurring, even though they have never caught anyone doing it. Before the era of bar codes, store managers commonly blamed product shrinkage on Hutterite shoppers, and many continue to watch Hutterite customers closely.

It is tempting to accuse people who look different and think differently of stealing something when it comes up missing. "I know it was the Hutterites," said an older Montana woman in the summer of 2006. A Hutterite man had once talked to her in her kitchen, and she was sure he had stolen a biscuit cutter that she could not find. But county sheriffs and policemen insist that they almost never arrest Hutterites for shoplifting (or anything else), even though many colonies frequent businesses in their areas of jurisdiction.

When confronted with the lack of evidence regarding theft, critics, often with annoyance, shift gears and accuse the Hutterites of being stingy. One businessman describes "extreme bargaining techniques." His assessment is likely related to the no-holds-barred Hutterite interaction style. Hutterites can be abrupt and demanding and often do not mince words. Like other farmers, some Hutterites go to town wearing dusty, stained work clothes. They do not dress or talk like white-collar workers. When Hutterites make large purchases, they expect to get a good deal. The "Hutterite wireless" spreads the word about where prices are lowest and where Hutterites are treated well. Accusations of bargaining are thus true, but Hutterites are not the only ones who bargain. At a local farmer's market, one woman accuses Hutterites of pricing garden items too high; another woman says angrily that it is cheaper to buy frozen peas than to buy fresh Hutterite peas. But the price is based on what the market will bear.

Hutterites are also accused of not supporting local economies. In some cases this accusation is true. Hutterites often shop in larger cities, but so do many rural and small-town residents. Locally, Hutterites conduct business with banks, hardware stores, pharmacies, lumber yards, fertilizer and chemical businesses, and machinery repair shops, as well as implement dealers, grain and livestock dealers, insurance companies, attorneys, and veterinarians. But they do not spend a lot of money on what they term "luxury" items, such as expensive toys, clothes, jewelry, or antiques. They also do not spend much at local shoe stores. Thus, whether a store owner or firm likes or dislikes Hutterites is often based on what kind of business it is and whether Hutterites like to shop there. Because they are a large, distinctively dressed, separatist group, they get stereotyped in ways that other citizens do not. Over the years, in Lethbridge, Alberta, the fifth day of the week was called "Black Thursday," since that was when the Hutterites came into town.

Another stereotype is related to Hutterite inbreeding. There is much talk, on the part of non-Hutterites, about mental problems and hereditary conditions having to do with the Hutterites. Studies show, however, that there is no greater occurrence of either mental retardation or hereditary disease among Hutterites than in the general population.[15] There is a greater incidence of certain illnesses, for example, heart disease, and there are more albino children and a higher occurrence of nearsightedness. But similarly idiosyncratic findings result from studies of other ethnic groups.

Conversations with non-Hutterites in twenty American and Canadian communities in 2005, 2006, and 2007 indicate that outsider opinions of Hutterites have changed little since the 1980s. If anything, complaints about Hutterites have increased. Neighbors continue to believe that Hutterites steal, suffer from inbreeding, do not invest in the local economy, and are uneducated.

On occasion Hutterite colonies are the victims of criminal acts, including vandalism and arson.[16] In 1998 the Montana Rights Network issued a report on a few arson cases and other crimes against the Hutterites. At one colony, a cistern was poisoned with pesticides. The report stated, "Resentment toward Hutterites appears to be growing." Antagonism stems from Hutterite economic success along with inaccurate stereotypes. In Montana, detractors say that Hutterites collect welfare and do not pay taxes, when in fact, since Hutterites pay corporation taxes, they "generate more revenue for the state." Hutterites do not collect food stamps or participate in cash assistance programs, and they rarely accept government benefits even when they qualify for them. The Rights Network asked law enforcement officials about Hutterite crime. They were told that "they did not know of any case" in which Hutterites had been charged with any crime.[17]

There has never been a murder in Hutterite history. In the early 2000s, a few sexual abuse cases did bring unwanted publicity as legal proceedings moved through provincial and state court systems. But in *The Courts and the Colonies*, published in 2004, Alvin Esau confirms that Hutterite crime in general is virtually nonexistent.[18] Historically, Hutterites were opposed to owning guns, but now, with the exception of the Lehrerleut, most colonies have a small number of rifles or shotguns. They are used primarily to kill small animals (coyotes, skunks, badgers, wolverines, gophers, squirrels, and muskrats) that attack Hutterite crops. Some men also shoot snakes and birds and hunt deer and pronghorn antelopes. The guns are kept under lock and key.

Another outsider complaint says that the Hutterites are able to outbid non-Hutterites for available farmland. This assertion is true. Hutterites save a lot of money. They are organized communally, work hard, recycle everything they can, make their own clothes, and repair their own machinery. They are often able to get the properties that they want. But when Hutterites purchase land, they live on it and farm it. It is kept in local hands, promoting economic stability in many isolated rural areas. Per acre, the Hutterite land supports three to four times as many people as the typical family farm does; yet local citizens dislike colony expansion because the Hutterites represent cultural and ideological difference.[19] Some people also do not like the large size of Hutterite families.

Most complaints are exacerbated because the Hutterites do not want to assimilate. They are different; they follow their own Old Order and communal Christian path. Hutterites do not dress like television personalities, and they go to church every day. They do not send their children to public schools in town, and they speak the Hutterisch dialect. When they use English, Hutterites do so with a pronounced accent, which non-Hutterites often make fun of. Although some Hutterites wear T-shirts and baseball caps, they also wear suspenders and very dark clothing.

In 2004 Montana novelist Peter Fromm published a short story with the derogatory title "Hoot," which reveals outsider stereotypes and includes a bloody physical attack on two Hutterite boys for no discernible reason. When asked, "What did you pound a couple of Hutterite kids for?" the main character's response was simply, "They were Hoots."[20]

Hutterites are particularly despised for being pacifists. Their sons and daughters do not enlist in the armed forces, and they do not support American or Canadian military ventures. They will not serve as policemen or in any public office. During the cold war, Hutterites were at times also associated with secular forms of communism. In the 1950s, when the Spokane Colony was established in Washington, local citizens feared the colony's proximity to the Strategic Air Command's Fairchild Air Force Base, and a major newspaper railed against them. During the 1960s, Hutterites were compared to countercultural hippie communitarians. Hutterites respond despondently to neighbors' complaints, but they are also quick to admit mistakes. There is a fragment of truth in some of the accusations. A few Hutterites blame negative publicity on the Hutterites themselves, believing there needs to be a more concerted effort to establish good relationships with members of local communities.

Notwithstanding the prejudicial examples given, a significant majority of Hutterite neighbors view the "colony people" positively. As one farmer says, "They will do anything for you in time of need." Most neighbors agree that when there is an emergency, for example, when a truck or a combine breaks down, or when a pipe bursts or floods threaten someone's property, Hutterites are there to help, often before being asked. In 2007 a Manitoba colony invited members of a non-Hutterite family into their own homes after the family's house and personal belongings were destroyed by fire.[21]

There are many commercial relationships between colonies and their neighbors. The Old Elm Springs Colony, in South Dakota, holds regular "bake sales" that include smoked meat, fryers, beef jerky, vegetables, and honey as well as breads, pies, and cookies.[22] Some colonies sell cabinetry, dressers, caskets, custom furniture, garden produce, beef and poultry. Many colonies service and repair their neighbors' machinery.

Hutterites also develop personal friendships with outsiders. According to one Hutterite, "There are few days when meals are eaten in the communal kitchen that an English friend isn't there to join us." Hutterites invite outsiders to weddings, harvest parties, and Hulbas. Non-Hutterites borrow tools and equipment, and Hutterites sometimes help their neighbors during calving, branding, seeding, and harvest. Whenever there is a problem, Hutterites come to the aid of their neighbors. In one Montana community, the Hutterites rebuilt a fire truck free of charge. The parts alone were worth five thousand dollars.[23] Hutterites participate in local fire departments and ambulance teams, and they make public presentations at church meetings.[24] In the 2000s, the Spring Prairie Colony, in Minnesota, twice hosted the annual Lion's Club breakfast.[25] One year four thousand people attended, and the colony almost ran out of food.

Friends of the Hutterites abound. One of them is Prairieleut Norman Hofer, a South Dakota farmer, who conducts colony tours and has spent much time studying Hutterite history and theology. Hofer is well liked and is often asked to speak at Hutterite education conferences. On one occasion he was visiting a community when members of the colony council were discussing the suitability of a man and a woman who wanted to get married. They invited Hofer to the meeting, where he listened as they discussed each person's good and bad points: their lifestyle, church attendance patterns, personalities, and families. Then they turned to Norman and asked for his opinion.[26]

Relationships with Other Ethnic and Religious Groups

Hutterites view people of other ethnic and religious backgrounds with a measure of suspicion. This tendency does not mean that they are uneducated about cultural and ideological differences. Among the Schmiedeleut One, Nigerian Inno Idiong has actively pushed multicultural understanding. His written statements castigate the paternalism of Western missions in Africa and point to the "pretense and standoffishness of missionaries" and their general ethnocentrism.[27] For three decades Hutterites have been connected to the Owa Community in Japan.

Some Hutterite colonies are located near Native American reservations and reserves. In southern Alberta, the Riverside, Standoff, Ewelme, Thompson, Deerfield, and Greenwood colonies border the Kainai and Pikani First Nations. At times colonies lease land from the tribes, and they interact on personal and professional levels. Cultural exchanges are few, but there are exceptions: for example, there is a common interest in natural health remedies. Hutterite herbalist Fred Tschetter notes that "These people [First Nations] have been here for thousands of years and through trial and error have had the opportunity to find out the healing potential of virtually every native plant. They know what works and how to prepare and use it."[28] Tschetter prepares and distributes natural medicines and has a large collection of herbs and concoctions for pain relief, fever reduction, prevention of illness, and use as food supplements. He consults regularly with a medicine man at the Kainai Reserve. Hutterite and First Nations students who attend classes together at Brandon University also often recognize communitarian commonalities.[29] Members of the Concord Colony, in Manitoba, are involved in prison ministries that have led to insightful exchanges with First Nations individuals.[30]

Some encounters between Hutterites and Native Americans are humorous. A few Hutterite boys in Washington came upon a group of American Indians standing by an injured horse. Assuming the godliness of the Hutterites, the Indians asked the boys if they would say a prayer before they shot it. The boys responded that they were not accustomed to praying for animals and could not pray in English. The young Hutterites ended up reciting the Hutterite mealtime prayer for the horse, in German.

Concerning other Christians, the Hutterite view is that noncommunalists do not understand the "fullness" of the gospel but that God blesses many of them anyway. A Hutterite minister told one of the authors that some non-Christians might even "make it into heaven." If people have never heard the "Word of God," how could they be held accountable? During the time of the Bruderhof alliance, some relationships were established between Hutterites and the Israeli kibbutzim.[31]

Relations with Anabaptist Christian groups are closer but not without critical assessments. Hutterites view Mennonites, for example, as materialistic, secular, and compromised on issues of military service, divorce, church discipline, and lifestyle. Nevertheless, colonies donate money to the Mennonite Central Committee (MCC), which provides material relief and professional expertise to poor people across the globe. At an annual MCC relief sale in Ritzville, Washington, a group of Hutterite children donated a scale model of a log cabin that sold for $950.[32]

Hutterites are less harsh in their appraisal of Old Order Anabaptist groups. Many Old Colony Mennonites from Mexico relocated to Canada in the late 1990s. The Hutterites criticize them for not living communally, but they respect their conservative positions on dress and lifestyle. They hold similar views of Holdeman Mennonites, Old German Baptist Brethren, and Old Order Amish.

A few Dariusleut and Schmiedeleut colonies have also developed informal relationships with the Aaronic Order, a Christian communal group with Mormon roots that is located in Eksdale, Utah. Many Hutterites have visited the community, and leader Robert Conrad has spent much time at Hutterite colonies.

There are also many connections with Latter Day Saints (LDS). In the 1990s, in ten large school districts in southern Alberta, 80 percent of the colony "English" teachers were Mormons. LDS teachers thus help shaped the way that Hutterite children viewed the world and even introduced them to LDS hymns. One person said, "In the 1950s if you took the Mormons and Hutterites out of this country [southern Alberta], all that would have been left would be a bunch of buffalos."[33] Mormons and Hutterites share a history of persecution and harassment based on unique beliefs and traditions. In the mid-nineteenth century, Latter Day Saints even developed their own communal "united order" villages. On one occasion in Alberta, almost all of the food served in the Cardston LDS Temple cafeteria came from a nearby Hutterite colony. But most Hutterites view Mormons as non-Christians and make negative comments about their beliefs and practices. Latter Day Saints, in turn, dislike Hutterite isolationism and pacifism; they are sometimes the strongest critics of the Hutterites.

Relationships with Non-Hutterite Teachers

One of the closest relationships with outsiders involves public school teachers. No single person from outside the colony has as much long-term, direct influence on Hutterite children, and even on the community's adults. A teacher's tenure is generally five to ten years, and during this time she or he sees students between 175 and 200 days a year. Hutterite children naturally respect teachers because of their age and subject-matter knowledge. If a teacher expresses support for military action or reflects positively on the use of force, students are caused to confront their own perspectives. A casual remark about a summer vacation or a television show, or what a teacher did over the weekend leaves a deep impression on a Hutterite child, leading to feelings of curiosity about life outside the colony. It is the German teacher's role to redirect this thinking within a Hutterite framework. He does so through careful questioning and occasional monitoring of schoolhouse activities.

Hutterites have mixed feelings about "English" teachers. One person notes frustration that teachers believe it is their duty to integrate Hutterite children into North American society. "We know they want to change our children and we don't know what to do about it," she says. Many "English" teachers say that their students are more serious about life than non-Hutterite children are. Others think colony children are closed-minded and lack initiative. In response, Hutterites claim that many of the teachers do not know enough about Hutterite life to make learning practical and relevant. Teachers work at the colonies for years without ever learning to speak Hutterisch, even for simple greetings. Many have never attended Gebet and have never read a book about Hutterite history and thought. But there are exceptions. At the Wheatland Colony, in Alberta, "English" teacher Betty Lou Mercer has designed a special course in Hutterite history.[34]

Non-Hutterite teachers who are evangelical Christians present an especially difficult dilemma. On the one hand, Hutterites like their ethical standards and their reverence for the Bible. But when these teachers share their evangelical perspectives with young boys and girls, the students sometimes become critical of their own traditions. Such has been the experience of Elaine Kroeker. Kroeker became interested in plain Christianity in the early 1970s when she lived briefly with an Old Order Amish as well as a Hutterite family as part of a college class assignment. In the early 2000s she taught school at a Hutterite colony in southern Minnesota. Kroeker has deep respect for the Hutterites and their communal way of life and she did not encourage students to leave the colony. But she also prayed with her students and discussed personal religious perspectives. Some young people visited her at her home to continue these conversations. They continue to regard Elaine as a close friend. This dynamic interchange of ideas is applauded by some Hutterites and disliked by others.[35]

Teachers become especially close to Hutterite individuals and families in isolated rural areas. Before the 1960s, a significant number lived in colony apartments for at least part of the week or school year. Many were married men whose children attended the colony school, played with Hutterite boys and girls, and learned to speak Hutterisch. During the day their spouses worked alongside Hutterite women and became their friends. For these women and for single female teachers, Hutterite women were often their closest acquaintances. Hutterite adults speak longingly and positively about past instructors with whom they sometimes developed lifetime friendships.

Max Stanton's 1992 survey of four hundred "English" colony teachers indicated primarily positive experiences. Criticism was directed at ministerial interference and the speaking of Hutterisch in the classroom. Some teachers expressed displeasure with German teachers' interventions. Since the two teachers use the same room, and German School begins right after public school is dismissed, "English" teachers are given little time to prepare their lessons inside the classroom or to talk to students privately.

Some teachers described a heavy workload, long commutes, and physical and professional isolation as they worked apart from other public school colleagues.

But teachers also reflected positively on personal friendships with students and their parents, uncles and aunts, and cousins. These relationships were much closer than in virtually any non-Hutterite school. Personal connections led to Hulba, wedding, and funeral invitations. The "English" teachers also ate noon meals with everyone else, and they received regular supplies of the community's garden produce and baked goods. One teacher's mother thought the relationships had become too close. She criticized her daughter for allowing her grandchildren to dress in Hutterite garb and learn to speak Hutterisch.[36]

Hutterites interact with a broad stream of humanity, and they are not unaffected by these encounters. Physicians, nurses, social workers, and other health care workers influence the way Hutterites view birth control, personal hygiene, child care, and nutrition. Agricultural marketing experts influence colony operations.

Hutterites and the Bruderhof

On two occasions during the twentieth century, the Hutterites affiliated institutionally with the Bruderhof society. No formal relationships continue, and few informal ones, but some influences remain. They are most evident in the Schmiedeleut One, where English is sometimes used in worship services and there is a more unified governance structure. There are piano lessons and theatrical productions and looser clothing regulations. In both Schmiedeleut groups, there is a growing interest in secondary and college education and in innovative teaching and curriculum development. Increased attention is given to the mass media, musical instruments have gained some acceptance, and manufacturing enterprises are being developed. Relations with non-Hutterites have also increased, not only via ecumenical mission projects but through strictly humanitarian efforts.

During the 1970s and 1980s, when the two groups were joined, Bruderhof publications gave the Hutterites significant public exposure, especially in the larger Christian community. The Bruderhof also promoted the translation, publication, and study of historic Hutterite documents, causing the Hutterites to look more deeply at their own history. Some Hutterite ministers had always pushed this agenda, and some of the changes were already in process, but social and ideological modifications moved forward more quickly with the influence of the Bruderhof association.

The Hutterites, in turn, influenced the Bruderhof. The Church Communities International (CCI) continues to utilize simple and relatively uniform clothing styles. The head covering is worn by women, and early Hutterite writings are honored, read, and studied. Perhaps most important is the presence of 450 ethnic Hutterites who are the offspring of twenty-two marriages across Hutterite-Bruderhof lines that occurred in the 1980s and 1990s. Many other Hutterites joined the Bruderhof in the 1950s and at the time of the break in 1995. Some children of prominent Schmiedeleut leaders are now members of the CCI.

In 2004 Bruderhof leader Christoph Arnold said that the Hutterites had brought a "freshness of spirit" to his religious society. But the Church Communities International is also trying to root out the very cultural isolationism that Hutterites exemplify. CCI teacher Chris Zimmerman says the group is in the process of separating "cultural baggage" from "Christian discipleship."[37]

Confused identification with the Bruderhof continues to plague the Hutterites. When Bruderhof representatives met with then Cardinal Ratzinger (now Pope Benedict XVI) in 2001, news accounts described the Bruderhof group as Hutterites. Hutterites were mystified by the encounter, as was the surprised and perhaps misled Ratzinger, who said, "We once persecuted you, now you want to have a relationship with us?"[38]

American-Canadian Differences

There are no ideological or cultural differences between Canadian and American Hutterites, and marriages cross national boundaries. But the different federal and regional laws and regulations and the differences in cultural and political traditions do affect the Hutterites.

For example, American Hutterites complain often about the high cost of medicine, which they compare unfavorably to its cost in the socialized Canadian system. Some Canadian colonies give financial assistance to American Hutterites who are hit hard by escalating health care costs. Yet when specialized medical procedures are required, Canadian Hutterites often come to American hospitals and medical centers.

There are also political differences. American Hutterites often express the nationalistic attitudes that permeate public school social science curricula. The fact that the United States is the world's most powerful country militarily, if not economically, affects the way American Hutterites view the world. Some Schmiedeleut One believe that the impeachment possibilities contained in the U.S. Constitution influenced some of the American Hutterites who sought to replace Jacob Kleinsasser as elder in 1992. In the United States there has also been a greater emphasis on cultural assimilation. Canada, in comparison, is more committed to bilingualism and multiculturalism and provides special funding for programs that benefit ethnoreligious groups. In general, Canada takes a more socialistic approach to economic and social issues.

Canadian Hutterites say too many of their American brothers and sisters are caught up in the national obsession with being the biggest and the best. Some American Hutterites believe that God created the United States as a special "nation under God" with a mission to perform, even though Hutterites themselves do not run for office or serve in the armed forces. Occasionally one sees American flags on colony grounds. American Hutterites counter that Canadian Hutterites often think they are intellectually advanced and culturally more sophisticated; they seem to exhibit social elitism. Canadian Hutterites attribute such national differences to their provincial schools, with their weightier curriculum, longer school year, and better pay for teachers. American school districts operate with greater autonomy, and educational quality varies more.

At times the U.S.-Canada divide influences marriage decisions. Especially for the Schmiedeleut in South Dakota and Manitoba, geographical distance is a major barrier. But in general, if two colonies have a mother-daughter relationship, American-Canadian location issues are irrelevant. They are also unimportant when one colony or the other is no more than one hundred miles from the border. There are also Leut differences. Among the Montana Lehrerleut, for example, only about 10 percent of marriages cross the Canada-U.S. line. The figure for the Montana Dariusleut is 49 percent.

Other differences affecting Canadian and American Hutterites are mundane. In Canada a biscuit is a light cookie, not a type of roll. Public facilities are called washrooms, not restrooms. Crossing the border is sometimes a harrowing experience, however, involving time-consuming questions and searches. Hutterites occasionally transport items illegally (for example, uninspected fruit, meat, and wine). They are also targeted because they make the crossing so often.

The Court System and Legal Controversies

During the twentieth century, Hutterites were involved in a few court cases that strained internal relationships and might portend future problems. Much of the legal history is reviewed in attorney Alvin Esau's 2004 book *The Courts and the Colonies*, where he documents a trend toward increased legal involvement, especially by the Schmiedeleut, during the mid to late twentieth century. Esau is concerned that Hutterites' involvement in the courts may compromise their theological principles and make it difficult to opt out of government-mandated programs. It may also encourage ex-Hutterites to take colonies to court seeking financial compensation for the time they spent living at and working for the colony. In 2008, two ex-Hutterites in North Dakota attempted to do so. Thus far, North American courts have backed the colonies in these cases, not requiring payments to those who leave.

The historical Hutterite position has been to observe the "law of love": to turn the other cheek and go to court only when they were sued or arrested. The Lehrerleut have been the most consistent in maintaining this policy, always refusing to take legal action, but this has been the approach taken by most other Hutterites as well. There are exceptions. In 1962, after the *Spokane Spokesman-Review* described the Hutterites as the "world's oldest communists" that operated "under a guise of religion," the Dariusleut sued for defamation of character and won three thousand dollars, a public retraction, and an apology from the newspaper.[39] Esau outlines a few Hutterite legal cases. But for the most part, instead of taking anyone to court, Hutterites in Europe and North America have defended their rights behind the scenes via contacts with influential political figures.

Beginning in the 1980s, however, more lawsuits were brought, beginning with the Lakeside Colony–Daniel Hofer case, discussed in chapter 4. In that case, related legal and investigative procedures publicized internal business practices and operations, with negative implications for the entire Schmiedeleut community. Esau admits that an offensive legal posture is often necessary when one signs agricultural and manufacturing contracts.[40] Legal contracts require the assistance of attorneys as Hutterites engage in large-scale agribusiness and stock-market investments. There are financial advantages to not turning the other cheek.

What most concerns Esau are occasions when colony leaders go to court to ask for the state's support, through its policing power, for decisions made on the basis of religious belief. An example would be asking the court to remove an excommunicated member from a colony. In Esau's view, such an action is a totally new phenomenon in the group's history. He fears it may cause courts to intervene in Hutterite internal affairs to an extent that they do not anticipate.

In 2005 the Montana Department of Public Health and Human Services cut medical benefits (Medicaid) to members of the state's Hutterite colonies, contending that each resident was making more than the maximum three-thousand-dollar qualifying amount. The state made this determination by using net-worth and net-asset figures. In response the Dariusleut went to court and lost.[41] In 2006 and 2007, conservative Alberta Dariusleut colonies won initial court cases contesting a provincial requirement that they carry drivers' licenses with photographs.[42]

Politics and Public Relations

Although the official Hutterite position is to avoid participation in politics, some members vote. In the United States, Hutterites often support the Republican Party because of its conservative stand on social issues such as abortion, the teaching of evolution, and homosexuality. In Canada, for similar reasons, most Hutterites support the positions of the most conservative political parties. In early 2005, Canadian Lehrerleut, Schmiedeleut Two, and Dariusleut took what the Canadian Broadcasting System described as "an unprecedented political stand" against same-sex marriage legislation.[43] Hutterite Paul Hofer expressed the Hutterite position: "Two men living together is not right; we are totally against that."[44] More striking was that in 2001 some Alberta Hutterite women (women cannot participate in colony elections) joined a group of men to elect a politician who opposed the construction of a large feedlot near a colony.[45]

There are exceptions to Hutterite support for conservative politicians. South Dakota Hutterites supported Senator Tom Daschle (1986–2004), a moderate-to-liberal member of the Democratic Party, because he opposed defense budget increases and supported South Dakota agribusiness.[46] In

Alberta one Lehrerleut colony supported a Liberal Party candidate because he was the colony's schoolteacher. A colony carpenter constructed a
stack of wooden holders for campaign posters, and the business manager
offered to post a row of placards on colony land.

It is nothing new for Hutterites to seek favorable advantages from governments. In Europe they negotiated with authoritarian rulers (kings,
princes, noblemen, czars, and Johann Cornies), and in North America with
democratically elected politicians (Ulysses S. Grant, Woodrow Wilson,
and, in South Dakota, Senator George McGovern). In both systems the
political winds change quickly. The Hutterite insistence on being a separate people always makes them a target for citizens of Western democracies who think the Hutterites receive unfair advantages, for example, military service exemptions or tax-funded public schools on colony grounds.
Minority-rights legislation usually protects the Hutterites, but exceptions
also exist, such as the treatment of Hutterite men during World War I or
the land-purchase restrictions of Alberta's Communal Properties Act.[47]

Hutterites attend the meetings of many professional and civic organizations: water advisory boards and councils, farmland and range management councils, rural electricity boards, and various agricultural associations. They participate and cooperate in irrigation development and
management councils as well as environmental preservation bodies. On
occasion, colonies have also donated money to educational institutions. In
1990 Hutterites gave fifty thousand dollars to the University of Saskatchewan for its agricultural college building fund.[48]

INTERACTION WITH NON-HUTTERITES PRESENTS important challenges for the
communitarians. Global economic conditions, interest in higher education, and continuing population growth lead to settlement near larger urban centers, which in turn leads to more contacts with outsiders. How
Hutterites deal with this development will affect their entire way of life
in the future.

As Hutterite relationships with outsiders proliferate and become more
intense, it becomes more and more difficult for the communitarians to retain a countercultural identity. Personal friendships and business relationships expose the separatist Hutterites to a multitude of ideas and practices,
some of which are extremely tempting as they simultaneously collide with

traditional cultural values and conventions. At the same time, these relationships provide serendipitous opportunities for non-Hutterites to learn about the many benefits of communal social and economic organizational designs.

Hutterite progressives view these relationships as hopeful, as long as new ideas and practices are evaluated carefully and are transformed and purified by communal Anabaptist principles and historical Hutterite life patterns. They also see unique evangelistic opportunities. Hutterite traditionalists view relationships with outsiders more negatively. They have less faith in the possibility of communitarian transformation of ideas and practices that have non-Hutterite origins, and they fear a dilution of historical Hutterite values in the process. Conservatives prefer to live in separated, isolated religious enclaves, having as little involvement with non-Hutterites as possible.

Conflict between progressives and conservatives is nothing new. Its presence has been felt throughout the course of Hutterite history. In North America, the perennial tension between old and new, within the framework of a communal and democratically governed Old Order society that remains institutionally unified and grounded in Anabaptist theology, has brought the Hutterites many benefits and is to some extent the reason for the society's ongoing demographic vitality.

CHAPTER 13

Facing the Future

No utopia, without Christ as head, can fully satisfy or fill Christ's place.
—Samuel Kleinsasser, "Community and Ethics"

A Second Golden Age

Even with all the many challenges that face them in the twenty-first century, the Hutterites are now living in a "Second Golden Age." It is not a period exactly like the sixteenth-century Golden Years experience, but there are widespread similarities. Consider, for example, that in the 1990s the Hutterite population for the first time exceeded levels attained in the sixteenth century. The population peak of forty thousand has now long been surpassed. Four hundred years after persecution and war destroyed the fabric of the earlier demographic high-water mark, the Hutterites, for the first time since the early 1800s, are taking a renewed interest in education and specialized training. They are resurrecting the industrial production processes and some crafts that were given up in the mid-1800s, although the commodities and economic structures are different. Agriculture continues to dominate the Hutterite economy, but new industries emerge every year. Many Golden Years Hutterites worked in shops, and the same is true for increasing numbers of twenty-first-century Hutterites.

All of this is taking place in North America, which has replaced Moravia as the Hutterite "Promised Land." Instead of being protected by members of the nobility in a feudal social order, where state churches hold significant power, Second Golden Age Hutterites thrive in Western Hemisphere democracies, where church and state are separate and religious and cultural minority rights are recognized.

In the 2000s, progressive Hutterites have a renewed interest in evangelism and mission projects.[1] Instead of turning in on themselves, according to an Old Order Anabaptist tendency institutionalized in the later seventeenth century, they are increasingly ready to engage people outside of the Hutterite community. The Hutterites are also an important and growing economic power, and the "world" is beginning to recognize Hutterite gifts and accomplishments in a broad range of areas, just as it did during the seventeenth century.

Ironically, some of what is transpiring is the result of critical and time-consuming analysis of the Hutterite past: thoughtful reading of the Chronicle and conscientious analysis of Lehren texts, the Hutterite epistles, and Peter Riedemann's confession of faith. For progressive Hutterites, the past serves as a motivational source for many of the changes occurring in the present. For traditional Hutterites, it serves as a motivational source for holding out against those very changes. But both liberal and conservative Hutterites see colony populations increasing, standards of living rising, and contacts with non-Hutterites moving forward.

There are also major differences between the Second Golden Age and the sixteenth-century version. Hutterites today face little political or religious persecution. Whereas modern Hutterites worry about required photographs on drivers' licenses, their ancestors feared that the government might throw them in prison and take away their children. As yet there is no large influx of nonethnics into the Hutterite colonies. Neither are Hutterite communities widely viewed as social laboratories that warrant emulation. Neighbors might take farm machinery to colony shops for repairs, but they do not send their children to colony schools, nor are there any Hutterite physicians to approach with medical questions and concerns. In contrast to the Hutterites of the sixteenth century, modern-day Hutterites are generally viewed as educationally backward and culturally unsophisticated. Hutterites also do not generally have a higher standard of living than their neighbors—although they may own more expensive farm machinery.

There are other differences. Many Hutterites say that twenty-first-

Schmiedeleut girls in Manitoba. Courtesy of Max Stanton.

century Hutterites do not have theologians and leaders who measure up
to Peter Riedemann and Peter Walpot and that Hutterite Christianity has
become formalized, with culture and religion intertwined in a way that
was not the case in the sixteenth century. Golden Years Hutterianism was
linguistically German, but no special language separated members from
the larger German-speaking communities of western and eastern Europe
as Hutterisch now distinguishes the Hutterites.

In addition, as yet modern Hutterite mission efforts are minimal. There
are no extensive evangelistic endeavors, no widely circulated epistles. During the Golden Years, Leonard Gross noted that dozens of total strangers
regularly arrived at and joined the community, bringing almost no material possessions with them.[2] Nothing similar is happening today. There is
also a general lack of unity, in contrast to the earlier period. There are four

separately governing Leut, with significant colony diversity within each group. Furthermore, the Lehrerleut and the conservative Dariusleut do not support—in fact they actively resist—the social and theological trends that are moving many colonies in some of the directions noted above. In the conservative view, God is calling modern Hutterites to go in a completely different direction than the progressives are taking; the Second Golden Age means something very different to them. And although farming continues to dominate the Hutterite economy, communities are much smaller than the one thousand who lived at the Neümuhl Bruderhof in the sixteenth century. Considering these various factors, some Hutterites suggest that the present can be compared to the sixteenth-century Golden Years only in terms of demographics and material success.

Hutterite traditionalists take a strong stance against many modern colony developments, as much as some of these might be reminiscent of Golden Years religious and social characteristics. In their view, the resemblances are superficial, de-contextualized, and inherently assimilationist. They do not see progressive Hutterites as restitutionists, but as a threat to sixteenth-century Hutterite theological and ecclesial traditions. They believe that progressives are quickly taking the Hutterite Church in the same direction that their Prairieleut relatives took in the late nineteenth century. In the conservative view, communal life, Gelassenheit, humility, a simple life, the central place of the Lehren and historic hymns, and basic Hutterian cultural and ideological distinctives are all under attack from liberal Hutterites who are using inaccurate historical comparisons and "wrecking our way of life."

Traditionalists seek to preserve an Old Order way of doing things, which they believe has tremendous value. They point out that it is the traditionalist Anabaptist groups, for example, the Old Order Amish, who are experiencing sizable population growth, not the more liberal Anabaptists such as the Mennonites and the Church of the Brethren. Hutterite conservatives believe that God has different things in mind for the twenty-first-century Hutterite Church. The sixteenth century is instructive but not a divine model for all historical eras, each of which is directed by the Holy Spirit in different pathways. For conservatives, the Second Golden Age is fraught with danger rather than creative possibility. They point to corollaries between modern trends and the individualistic developments that occurred in the midst of the first Golden Years. In their view, progressive developments often contain seeds of destruction.

But major changes are in the works. New hymns are sung, across Leut lines. More and more ministers are making remarks that are not in the script of the sermons—most of which were not written until decades after the Golden Years.

Some Hutterites say that there are too many conflicts in modern Hutterianism to make a credible comparison to the sixteenth century. Yet the Golden Years period was no utopia. It was not without its social problems, its conflicts and polarizing; there were members then who were attracted to heretical theological positions. Questions raised about community spirituality in the 1650s, the time when many of the Lehren were written, are similar to those advanced in the 2000s by Hutterite evangelicals. It was in response to the nonperfect nature of Golden Years life itself that Peter Walpot's *Great Article Book* was written, that so many Ordnungen were drafted, and that school regulations were first developed. In the 1570s there were many complaints about competitive individuals and even property theft, including barrels of beer and wood from the forest.[3]

Hutterites are divided on what the Second Golden Age should look like. Conservatives and liberals both often idealize the sixteenth-century Golden Years. But they interpret its relevance for the present in very different ways.

Dealing with Change

Throughout their history, Hutterites have confronted the challenges of societal change. On many occasions—even in the United States, during World War I—the entire community was forced to relocate in response to religious and political persecution. For the past eighty years, government-supported discrimination has been limited. During World War II and into the 1960s, many Hutterite men, single and married, served in conscientious objector work camps and on assignments that colonies were sometimes required to subsidize. But there has been no widespread persecution or economic and physical harassment. The changes that come from society are more subtle and perhaps more seductive. They include many of the issues reviewed in chapter 12, especially materialism, individualism, and nationalism. Both evangelical Christianity and consumer capitalism promote individualistic notions that are contrary to Hutterite communal understandings. New technology and media bring these ideas into colony residences and are highly influential as well as hard to control. Individualism is also promoted by public education curricula.

Hutterites have to decide what changes will change them too much and how far along a more individualistic pathway they wish to walk. The need to choose is not new, but North Americans Hutterites have never before been put in a position, in terms of numbers and economic power, where they had a realistic opportunity to influence the lives of non-Hutterites. During the Golden Years, Hutterites were convinced that they had discovered God's true plan for human life. They were confident and willing to suffer to spread this message. They were not seen as an "Old Order" preservationist sect that preached a "plain" lifestyle.

In the twenty-first century, Hutterites play completely different, though not less important, roles. Will Second Golden Age Hutterites continue to manage change by separation from the world, or will they change course and try to transform the world around them?

Reasons for Success

The longevity of the Hutterites' society and their continued demographic expansion are the result of a fervent commitment to a unique religious faith, one that is grounded in communal Anabaptism. This faith has been grafted onto what has become a unique ethnic stock of people who have lived in isolation for so long that their cultural mores are difficult to live without and now govern virtually everything that a Hutterite does. Within this socioreligious context, the following features of Hutterianism have been especially beneficial in keeping the group strong.

1. A strong and vital Christian faith that is institutionalized in unique ecclesial and cultural forms.
2. A communal way of life that incorporates a strong sense of collective identity and unity. By its very nature, communal Christianity tends to preserve traditional practices.
3. A strong and unrelenting work ethic that has a religious foundation.
4. Openness to technological innovations that create economic strength. Hutterites have not, however, allowed technology and the media to subvert their beliefs and practices.

5. Economic sophistication, demonstrated in increasing adeptness at dealing with national and international financial trends and developments.

6. Success in retaining large percentages of their young people. The defection rate remains at about 15 percent. This, combined with a relatively high birthrate (between four and five children per family), creates membership growth that exceeds most North American Protestant denominations, even those that emphasize evangelism. The Hutterite birthrate is double the Canadian and American average. Hutterite socialization is institutionalized and constantly reevaluated. Hutterites tolerate a certain amount of unacceptable behavior and experimentation before residents join the church. Thus, when religious vows are taken, they are self-chosen and taken with serious intent. Reconciliation with runaways and dissenters is ongoing and built into the social system.

7. Adaptable church discipline, so that even after becoming church members, Hutterites are not rigid and legalistic in applying all of the Ordnungen. Flexibility serves as a safety valve, allowing some subterfuge, some elements of individualism, as long as they do not get out of hand and disrupt the system.

8. Small size. Colonies stay small so that everyone in the colony has an opportunity to serve in an important position that is highly valued. Smallness also encourages close personal relationships.

9. An isolated existence ensured by the location of most Hutterite colonies in lightly populated rural areas. This feature assists in the preservation of a less capitalistic, less nationalistic, less materialistic way of life.

These positive features of Hutterite life create the strength necessary to solve the problems enumerated and reviewed in chapter 12. Hutterites are born and raised in a particular faith tradition. Since everyone in the colony is taught the same beliefs and practices, attends church services regularly, and is aware of the Ordnungen, there is little need for crisis-laden personal conversions to the Christian faith. Since culture and faith are intertwined, it is also easy to take both for granted—an ongoing dilemma for the Hutterites as for any other religious society.

An individual Hutterite may not be articulate or even knowledgeable about communal Anabaptist theology, yet he or she still exhibits piety that shows deep religious commitment. The same Hutterite man who curses (in Hutterisch) at a salesperson, smokes an occasional cigarette behind the barn, and listens to Seattle Mariners games on the radio, sits in contemplative silence at Gebet each evening. Here he enters a mystical and supernatural domain that calms his heart and mind as it focuses his attention. His faith might be expressed differently than some Christians or other religious individuals might wish, but it is a strong faith nonetheless. It is a plain, traditional faith, a faith that produces good works, which according to Hutterites are the mark of a true Christian. As Robert Rhodes notes, "Even in communities where the spiritual state is lacking, and there are some like this, the inclination toward community exists in virtually every soul, and dynamically so."[4]

For more than a century, scholars, Hutterites' neighbors, and others have been predicting the breakdown of Hutterite life. A 1950s-era letter sent to South Dakota government officials stated that the Hutterite system would fall apart within a matter of years, owing to high defection rates, rampant corruption, alcoholism, and a general lack of knowledge about their own traditions. In the eyes of Hutterite critics, the glass is always nearly empty; there is little hope for the future. Yet during the past sixty years, the Hutterite population has tripled in size.[5] A dynamic and enthusiastic commitment to communal Anabaptism remains even as the Hutterite engagement with change continues.

One progressive minister says that Hutterites should open the colony ecclesial gates and allow non-Hutterites to become associate members without living communally. This model has been adopted by other Christian groups that were once fully communal, such as Koinonia Farm, in Americus, Georgia, and Reba Place, in Chicago. We doubt that this kind of structure will ever be accepted by the Hutterites. We are confident, however, that the resilient Hutterites will continue to grow in size and perhaps in influence.

The Hutterites are the most successful communal society in modern history, and Hutterite cultural and spiritual health is unquestioningly vibrant in the 2000s. Pierre Van Den Berghe and Karl Peter describe the Hutterites and the Israeli kibbutzim as "the only two genuinely communistic utopias to have succeeded in establishing themselves in a non-parasitic manner within larger, stratified, state-level societies."[6] Only celibate religious orders have been in existence longer. At Hutterite colonies across the United States and Canada, we see strong commitment to communal Christianity and a growing interest in spiritual issues, and we see these elements everywhere in all of the Leut. They take on different forms and are expressed differently. But wherever one goes, there is forthright and thoughtful discussion of beliefs and practices. The Christian faith is taken very seriously, whether from the traditional or the progressive perspective.

The Hutterite Challenge to a Postmodern World

There is much that can be learned from the Hutterites. The importance of thinking collectively and globally makes sense in a world that is increasingly connected politically, economically, and ecologically. For Hutterites, religious and secular values are one, and the needs and interests of one person are just as important as those of another. Actions taken in micro form affect the lives of people thousands of miles away. This lesson is one that everyone is learning quickly in the early twenty-first century.

Hutterites are not materialistic in a wasteful, consumerist sense. They use and reuse everything, repairing items instead of replacing them. Hutterites make most of their own clothing and furniture and build most of their residences and shops. They frequent yard sales and thrift shops to find bargains on utensils, toys, and fabrics. Hutterites preserve and consume their own fruits and vegetables instead of buying packaged products laced with chemical preservatives and artificial colors and flavors. The Hutterites thus provide a valuable model for a world where natural resources are at a premium. By living communally and adhering to an ethic of simplicity and humility, they need fewer vehicles, appliances, and machinery. They use less energy per capita, and by working together collectively, they complete tasks more efficiently and with greater joy.

The innovative Hutterite village-colony that is never allowed to become too large can be seen as a prototype of a small community providing social and psychological balance—an important design for disempowered and alienated people in rural and urban settings throughout the world. Hutterites have also developed a remarkably effective approach to individual creativity and deviation in what has evolved into a loosely managed religious society.

Hutterite family members on an evening walk. Courtesy of
Max Stanton.

Hutterites model effective conflict-resolution techniques. Their commitment to nonviolence, modesty, and self-effacement makes it less likely that disagreements will lead to destructive behavior. Peacemaking and conflict-management skills are important in a dangerous and insecure world.

Hutterites are also open to technological innovations, which provide an economic foundation for their essentially spiritual existence. They model individual empowerment in the workplace via the provision of important colony positions for most members. And Hutterites take excellent care of older people. The early-retirement—part-time-employment option for men and women is exemplary, providing a creative pattern for dealing with problems of aging, including poor health, lack of purposeful work, and burdensome financial obligations. Older Hutterite men and women are cared for by a supportive and respectful community that encompasses all age groups.

The Hutterites are one of a very small number of North American communities that have successfully challenged the dominant consumer-oriented society. Quietly, since the time of their arrival in the Dakota Territory in the 1870s, they have created a unique ecological niche in the American and Canadian heartland. Men and women in the postmodern era are attracted to societies that can deal effectively with social and psychological alienation, fragmentation, loneliness, and nihilistic despair. Hutterites have not created a mini-utopia, but their colonies have built-in social and religious mechanisms that give purpose to the life of every member.

The Hutterites offer a creative alternative to individualistic capitalism, global militarism, and ecological catastrophe. On leaving colony life, Michael Holzach wrote these words:

Leaving one's possessions behind, liberating oneself from the weight of material things in order to work in the community together with other people, living no longer for the "I" but for the "We," no longer for having, but for being—all this seems like paradise to me. However, I am unable to live here forever because this Hutterite "being" actually begins only after the end of the earthly existence, i.e. after the death of the body. I am such an enlightened modern that I lack the faith needed for such a high goal in life; I just don't have it. I am looking for self-realization and not for self-surrender as baptism actually requires.[7]

As Holzach perceived, the Hutterite vision is tied to the recognition of a supernatural realm of existence. In the Hutterite view, Christian communalism on earth, in an ideal sense, points toward the communal utopia awaiting men and women in heaven. Hutterites are convinced that communism works only if it is guided by divine forces, that individual and collective moral commitment is not enough. They have no faith in communitarian political and economic systems that are based on secular principles. But even those who do not accept the existence of a life beyond the grave or the guidance of a divine being can stare in amazement at the social and ideological power and example of the Hutterite communal order here on earth.

Hutterite Colonies in North America, 2009

Schmiedeleut

Founded	Name of colony	Location	Prov./state	Parent colony	Group
2002	Acadia	Carberry	MB	Riverbend, MB	1
1971	Airport	Portage la Prairie	MB	New Rosedale, MB	2
2001	Altona	Henderson	MN	Fordham, SD	No affiliation
1988	Aspenheim	Bagot	MB	Huron, MB	2
1973	Baker	MacGregor	MB	Rainbow, MB	1
1920	Barrickman	Cartier	MB	Maxwell, MB	1
1958	Big Stone	Graceville	MN	New Elmspring, SD	2
1954	Bloomfield	Westbourne	MB	Riverside, MB	2
*	Blooming Prairie	Homewood	MB	Rose Valley, MB	2
1998	Blue Clay	Arnaud	MB	Blumengart, MB	2
1952	Blumengard	Faulkton	SD	Blumengart, MB	2
1922	Blumengart	Plum Coulee	MB	Milltown, MB	2
1918	Bon Homme	Elie	MB	Bon Homme, SD	2
1874	Bon Homme	Tabor	SD	Ukraine	2
1997	Boundary Lane	Elkhorn	MB	Plainview, MB	1
1995	Brantwood	Oakville	MB	Grand, MB	2
1987	Brentwood	Faulkton	SD	Thunderbird, SD	1
1959	Brightstone	Lac du Bonnet	MB	Maxwell, MB	1
1974	Broad Valley	Arborg	MB	Lakeside, MB	2
1948	Brocket	Pincher Creek	AB	West Raley, AB	1
*	Cameron	Viborg	SD	Rosedale, SD	2
2005	CanAm	Margaret	MB	Wellwood, MB	2
1994	Cascade	MacGregor	MB	Bon Homme, MB	1
1972	Cedar Grove	Platte	SD	Bon Homme, SD	2
1995	Claremont	Castlewood	SD	Poinsett, SD	2
1955	Clark	Raymond	SD	Jamesville, SD	2
1996	Clearfield	Delmont	SD	Greenwood, SD	2

continued

Founded	Name of colony	Location	Prov./state	Parent colony	Group
1983	Clearview	Elm Creek	MB	Whiteshell, MB	1
1959	Clearwater	Balmoral	MB	Poplar Point, MB	1
1962	Cloverleaf	Howard	SD	Graceville, SD	No affiliation
*	Collins	Iroquois	SD	Spink, SD	2
1987	Concord	Winnipeg	MB	Crystal Spring, MB	2
1988	Cool Spring	Minnedosa	MB	Newdale, MB	2
1954	Crystal Spring	Ste. Agathe	MB	Sturgeon Creek, MB	1
1975	Cypress	Cypress River	MB	Homewood, MB	2
1981	Decker	Decker	MB	Brightstone, MB	1
1959	Deerboine	Alexander	MB	Riverdale, MB	2
1971	Deerfield	Ipswich	SD	Plainview, SD	2
1987	Delta	Austin	MB	Sturgeon Creek, MB	2
1998	Elmendorf	Mountain Lake	MN	Upland, SD	No affiliation
1934	Elm River	Newton Siding	MB	Rosedale, MB	1
1992	Evergreen	Faulkton	SD	Blumengard, SD	2
1975	Evergreen	Somerset	MB	Rose Valley, MB	2
1959	Fairholme	Portage la Prairie	MB	New Rosedale, MB	1
1970	Fairview	La Moure	ND	Rockport, SD	2
1995	Fairway	Douglas	MB	Sprucewood, MB	1
1974	Fordham	Carpenter	SD	Huron, SD	1
1950	Forest River	Fordville	ND	New Rosedale, MB	2
1949	Glendale	Frankfort	SD	Bon Homme, SD	2
1966	Glenway	Dominion City	MB	Milltown, MB	1
1989	Good Hope	Portage la Prairie	MB	Poplar Point, MB	1
1948	Gracevale	Winfred	SD	Tschetter, SD	2
1959	Grand	Oakville	MB	Bon Homme, MB	2
1991	Grassland	Westport	SD	Long Lake, SD	2
1990	Grass Ranch	Kimball	SD	Platte, SD	2
1974	Grass River	Glenella	MB	Grand, MB	2
1991	Green Acres	Wawaneesa	MB	Spring Valley, MB	1
1955	Greenwald	Beausejour	MB	Barrickman, MB	1
1971	Greenwood	Delmont	SD	Jamesville, SD	2
1989	Haven	Dexter	MN	Rolland, SD	1
1996	Heartland	Hazelridge	MB	Lakeside, MB	2
1996	Heartland	Lake Benton	MN	Plainview, SD	2
1968	Hidden Valley	Austin	MB	Sturgeon Creek, MB	2
1979	Hillcrest	Garden City	SD	Riverside, SD	2
1958	Hillside	Doland	SD	Huron, SD	2
1958	Hillside	Justice	MB	Rosedale, MB	2
1975	Holmfield	Killarney	MB	Riverdale, MB	2

Founded	Name of colony	Location	Prov./state	Parent colony	Group
1962	Homewood	Starbuck	MB	Lakeside, MB	1
1918	Huron	Elie	MB	Huron, SD	2
1945	Huron	Huron	SD	Jamesville, SD	2
1982	Hutterville	Stratford	SD	Spink, SD	1
1919	Iberville	Elie	MB	Rosedale, MB	2
1961	Interlake	Teulon	MB	Rock Lake, MB	2
1918	James Valley	Elie	MB	James Valley, SD	2
1936	Jamesville	Utica	SD	Roseisle, MB	2
1997	Kamsley	Somerset	MB	Oakridge, MB	2
1993	Keystone	Warren	MB	Rock Lake, MB	1
1946	Lakeside	Cartier	MB	Maxwell, MB	1
1988	Lake View	Lake Andes	SD	Maxwell, SD	2
2004	Lismore	Clinton	MN	Big Stone, MN	2
*	Little Creek	Marquette	MB	Waldheim, MB	1
1967	Long Lake	Westport	SD	Pearl Creek, SD	2
1981	Maple Grove	Lauder	MB	Ridgeland, MB	1
1968	Maple River	Fullerton	ND	Blumengard, SD	2
1972	Marble Ridge	Hodgson	MB	Bloomfield, MB	2
1918	Maxwell	Cartier	MB	Maxwell, SD	2
1949	Maxwell	Scotland	SD	New Elmspring, SD	2
1973	Mayfair	Killarney	MB	Riverside, MB	2
1987	Mayfield	Willow Lake	SD	Clark, SD	2
1966	Miami	Morden	MB	James Valley, MB	2
1983	Millbrook	Mitchell	SD	Rosedale, SD	1
1949	Millerdale	Miller	SD	Milltown, MB	2
1994	Millshof	Glenboro	MB	Cypress, MB	1
1918	Milltown	Elie	MB	Milltown, SD	2
1996	Netley	Petrsfield	MB	Interlake, MB	1
1994	Neuhof	Mountain Lake	MN	Various Colonies	1
1974	Newdale	Brandon	MB	Bon Homme, MB	1
1993	Newdale	Elkton	SD	Hillside, SD	1
1936	New Elmspring	Ethan	SD	Alsask, AB	2
1977	Newhaven	Argyle	MB	Clearwater, MB	1
1988	Newport	Claremont	SD	Deerfield, SD	2
1944	New Rosedale	Portage la Prairie	MB	Rosedale, MB	2
*	Norfeld	White	SD	Spring Valley, SD	2
1993	Norquay	Oakville	MB	Milltown, MB	2
1998	Northern Breeze	Portage la Prairie	MB	Woodland, MB	2
1953	Oak Bluff	Morris	MB	Elm River, MB	1
1986	Oak Lane	Alexandria	SD	Rockport, SD	2
1969	Oakridge	Holland	MB	Barrickman, MB	2
1998	Oak River	Oak River	MB	Deerboine, MB	1

continued

Founded	Name of colony	Location	Prov./state	Parent colony	Group
1995	Odanah	Minnedosa	MB	Grass River, MB	1
1998	Old Elmspring	Parkston	SD	New Elmspring, SD	2
1995	Orland	Montrose	SD	Jamesville, SD	2
1964	Parkview	Riding Mountain	MB	Huron, MB	2
1949	Pearl Creek	Iroquois	SD	Huron, MB	2
1961	Pembina	Darlingford	MB	Blumengart, MB	2
1974	Pembrook	Ipswich	SD	Tschetter, SD	2
1972	Pine Creek	Austin	MB	New Rosedale, MB	2
1996	Pineland	Piney	MB	Iberville, MB	1
1977	Plainview	Elkhorn	MB	Waldheim, MB	2
1957	Plainview	Leola	SD	Spink, SD	2
1949	Platte	Platte	SD	Bon Homme, SD	2
1977	Pleasant Valley	Flandreau	SD	Big Stone, MN	2
1968	Poinsett	Estelline	SD	New Elmspring, SD	2
1938	Poplar Point	Portage la Prairie	MB	Huron, MB	1
1994	Prairie Blossom	Stonewall	MB	Oak Bluff, MB	2
1964	Rainbow	Lorette	MB	Elm River, MB	No affiliation
1967	Ridgeland	Dugald	MB	Springfield, MB	1
1997	Ridgeville	Ridgeville	MB	Maxwell, MB	1
1969	Riverbend	Carberry	MB	Oak Bluff, MB	1
1946	Riverdale	Gladstone	MB	James Valley, MB	1
1934	Riverside	Arden	MB	Iberville, MB	2
1947	Riverside	Huron	SD	Rockport, SD	2
1947	Rock Lake	Grosse Isle	MB	Iberville, MB	2
1934	Rockport	Alexandria	SD	Bon Homme, SD	2
1978	Rolland	White	SD	Gracevale, SD	2
2005	Rolling Acres	Eden	MB	Riverside, MB	2
1998	Rosebank	Miami	MB	Hidden Valley, MB	2
1918	Rosedale	Elie	MB	Rosedale, SD	1
1945	Rosedale	Mitchell	SD	Rockport, SD	2
1958	Rose Valley	Graysville	MB	Waldheim, MB	2
2003	Rustic Acres	Madison	SD	Wolf Creek, SD	2
1993	Shady Lane	Treherne	MB	Barrickman, MB	1
*	Shamrock	Carpenter	SD	Huron, SD	2
*	Shannon	Winfred	SD	Rockport, SD	2
1998	Silver Winds	Sperling	MB	Ridgeland, MB	1
1993	Sky View	Miami	MB	Miami, MB	1
1977	Sommerfeld	High Buff	MB	Rock Lake, MB	2
1977	Souris River	Elgin	MB	Maxwell, MB	2
1945	Spink	Frankfort	SD	Bon Homme, SD	2
1961	Spring Creek	Forbes	ND	Maxwell, SD	2

Founded	Name of colony	Location	Prov./state	Parent colony	Group
1950	Springfield	Anola	MB	Poplar Point, MB	1
1963	Spring Hill	Neepawa	MB	Sunnyside, MB	1
1978	Spring Lake	Arlington	SD	Wolf Creek, SD	2
1980	Spring Prairie	Hawley	MN	White Rock, SD	2
1956	Spring Valley	Brandon	MB	James Valley, MB	2
1964	Spring Valley	Wessington Springs	SD	Platte, SD	2
1976	Sprucewood	Brookdale	MB	Spring Hill, MB	2
1993	Starland	Gibbon	MN	Pembrook, SD	1
1991	Starlite	Starbuck	MB	James Valley, MB	1
1936	Sturgeon Creek	Headingley	MB	Blumengart, MB	2
1969	Suncrest	Tourond	MB	Crystal Spring, MB	2
1985	Sundale	Milnor	ND	Spring Creek, ND/SD	2
1942	Sunnyside	Newton Siding	MB	Milltown, MB	1
1977	Sunset	Britton	SD	Glendale, SD	2
1964	Thunderbird	Faulkton	SD	Glendale, SD	1
1984	Treesbank	Wawanesa	MB	Hillside, MB	2
1987	Trileaf	Baldur	MB	Parkview, MB	1
1941	Tschetter	Olivet	SD	Barrickman, MB	2
1997	Twilight	Neepawa	MB	Maple Grove, MB	2
1988	Upland	Artesian	SD	Spring Valley, SD	2
1985	Valley View	Swan Lake	MB	Elm River, MB	1
1989	Vermillion	Sanford	MB	Homewood, MB	1
1934	Waldheim	Elie	MB	Bon Homme, MB	1
1967	Wellwood	Ninette	MB	Spring Valley, MB	2
1992	Westroc	Westbourne	MB	Bloomfield, MB	2
*	Westwood	Britton	SD	Newport, SD	2
1964	White Rock	Rosholt	SD	Rosedale, SD	2
1962	Whiteshell	River Hills	MB	Iberville, MB	1
1984	Willowbank	Edgeley	ND	Fairview, ND	2
1981	Willow Creek	Cartwright	MB	Greenwald, MB	2
1979	Windy Bay	Pilot Mound	MB	Fairholme, MB	1
1991	Wingham	Elm Creek	MB	Sunnyside, MB	1
1963	Wolf Creek	Olivet	SD	Tschetter, SD	2
1971	Woodland	Poplar Point	MB	Rosedale, MB	2

		Dariusleut			
*	Albion Ridge	Picture Butte	AB	Keho Lake, AB	
1993	Alix	Alix	AB	Erskine, AB	
1964	Arm River	Lumsden	SK	Spring Creek, AB	

continued

Founded	Name of colony	Location	Prov./state	Parent colony
2007	Arrowwood	Blackie	AB	Springvale, AB
1962	Athabasca	Athabasca	AB	Rosebud, AB
1945	Ayers Ranch	Grass Range	MT	King Ranch, MT
1926	Beiseker	Beiseker	AB	Rosebud, AB
1990	Belle Plaine	Belle Plaine	SK	Holt, AB
2001	Bentley	Blackfalds	AB	Leedale, AB
1981	Berry Creek	Hanna	AB	Wildwood, AB
1984	Big Rose	Biggar	SK	West Bench, SK
1996	Birch Hills	Wanham	AB	Ridge Valley, AB
2001	Blue Ridge	Mountain View	AB	Waterton, AB
1996	Blue Sky	Drumheller	AB	Starland, AB
1960	Box Elder	Maple Creek	SK	Pine Hill, AB
1986	Byemoor	Byemoor	AB	Pleasant Valley, AB
1969	Cameron	Turin	AB	Ewelme, AB
1948	Camrose	Camrose	AB	Springvale, AB
1975	Carmangay	Carmangay	AB	Waterton, AB
1938	Cayley	Cayley	AB	West Raley, AB
2001	Cleardale	Cleardale	AB	Holden, AB
1961	Cluny	Cluny	AB	Tschetter, AB
2004	Codesa	Eaglesham	AB	Warburg, AB
1984	Craigmyle	Craigmyle	AB	Tschetter, AB
1947	Deerfield	Lewistown	MT	Wolf Creek, AB
1978	Donalda	Donalda	AB	Red Willow, AB
1958	Downie Lake	Maple Creek	SK	Wolf Creek, AB
1987	Eagle Creek	Asquith	SK	Sandhills, AB
*	Birch Meadows	Eaglesham	AB	Sandhills, AB
1997	Ear View	Gull Lake	SK	Downie Lake, SK
1918	East Cardston	Cardston	AB	Warren Ranch, MT
1981	East Malta	Malta	MT	Turner, MT
1996	East Raymond	Raymond	AB	Wolf Creek, AB
1979	Elkwater	Irvine	AB	Spring Creek, AB
1989	Enchant	Enchant	AB	Ewelme, AB
1976	Erskine	Erskine	AB	Stahlville, AB
1958	Estuary	Leader	SK	Riverside, AB
1927	Ewelme	Fort MacLeod	AB	East Cardston, AB
1944	Fairview	Crossfield	AB	Beiseker, AB
2000	Fallon (discontinued 2004)	Fallon	MT	Ayers Ranch, MT
1920	Felger (discontinued 1927)	Welling	AB	Beadle, SD
1949	Ferrybank	Ponoka	AB	Sandhills, AB
1980	Flat Willow	Roundup	MT	King Ranch, MT

Founded	Name of colony	Location	Prov./state	Parent colony
1980	Fords Creek	Grass Range	MT	Ayers Ranch, MT
1969	Fort Pitt	Lloydminister	SK	Ribstone, AB
1980	Forty Mile	Lodge Grass	MT	Spring Creek, MT
1987	Gadsby	Stettler	AB	Veteran, AB
1974	Gilford	Gildford	MT	Deerfield, MT
1977	Grandview	Grand Prairie	AB	Fairview, AB
1930	Granum	Granum	AB	Standoff, AB
1999	Green Leaf	Marcelin	SK	Fort Pitt, SK
1982	Hardisty (discontinued 2003)	Hardisty	AB	Standoff, AB
1996	Hairy Hill	Hairy Hill	AB	Plain Lake, AB
*	Hartland	Bradshaw	AB	Pleasant Valley, AB
1982	High River	High River	AB	East Cardston, AB
1969	Hillcrest	Dundurn	SK	Leask, SK
1994	Hillridge	Barnwell	AB	Lakeside, AB
1961	Hillsvale	Cut Knife	SK	Springvale, AB
1990	Hillview	Rosebud	AB	Rosebud, AB
1971	Hodgeville	Hodgeville	SK	Box Elder, SK
1970	Holden	Holden	AB	Cayley, AB
1949	Holt	Irma	AB	Granum, AB
1973	Hughenden	Hughenden	AB	Athabaska, AB
1959	Huxley	Huxley	AB	Stahville, AB
1979	Iron Creek	Bruce	AB	Camrose, AB
1981	Keho Lake	Barons	AB	Wilson Siding, AB
1992	Kilby Butte	Roundup	MT	Fords Creek, MT
1935	King Ranch	Lewistown	MT	Beadle, SD
1979	Lajord	White City	SK	Arm River, SK
1935	Lakeside	Cranford	AB	Wolf Creek, AB
1973	Lakeview	Unity	SK	Hillsvale, SK
1980	Lamona	Lamona	WA	Standoff, AB
1958	Leask	Leask	SK	Sandhills, AB
1977	Leedale	Rimbey	AB	Pine Hill, AB
1983	Little Bow	Champion	AB	New York, AB
2000	Livingstone	Lundbreck	AB	Spring Point, AB
1984	Lomond	Lomond	AB	Turin, AB
1982	Loring	Loring	MT	North Harlem, MT
*	Lost River	Dundurn	SK	Hillcrest, SK
*	Lougheed	Lougheed	AB	Veteran, AB
1988	Mannville	Mannville	AB	Vegreville, AB
1974	Marlin	Marlin	WA	Pincher Creek, AB
1981	Mayfield	Etzikom	AB	Wildwood, AB

continued

Founded	Name of colony	Location	Prov./state	Parent colony
1960	Mixburn	Minburn	AB	Holt, AB
1971	Morinville	Morinville	AB	Sandhills, AB
1984	Mountain View	Strathmore	AB	Cluny, AB
1924	New York	Lethbridge	AB	West Raley, AB
1960	North Harlem	Harlem	MT	Deerfield, MT
1957	O. B.	Marwayne	AB	Thompson, AB
1972	Owa	Owa	Japan	(original colony)
2002	Peace View	Farmington	BC	South Peace, BC
1953	Pibroch	Westlock	AB	Wilson Siding, AB
1927	Pincher Creek	Pincher Creek	AB	Felger, AB
1997	Pine Haven	Wetaskiwin	AB	Scotford, AB
1948	Pine Hill	Red Deer	AB	Lakeside, AB
1970	Plain Lake	Two Hills	AB	Scotford, AB
1970	Pleasant Valley	Clive	AB	Veteran, AB
1973	Pointeix	Pointeix	SK	Downie Lake, SK
2006	Prairie Elk	Wolf Point	MT	Surprise Creek, MT
1984	Prairie View	Sibbald	AB	Ferrybank, AB
1977	Quill Lake	Quill Lake	SK	Riverview, SK
1998	Rainbow	Innisfail	AB	Pine Hill, AB
2003	Raymore	Raymore	SK	Ewelme, AB
1949	Red Willow	Stettler	AB	Stahlville, AB
1960	Ribstone	Edgerton	AB	Camrose, AB
1977	Ridge Valley	Crooked Creek	AB	Spring Point, AB
1996	Riverbend	Waldheim	SK	Leask, SK
1939	Riverside	Fort MacLeod	AB	Standoff, AB
*	River Valley	Granum	AB	White Lake, AB
1956	Riverview	Saskatoon	SK	Fairview, AB
2005	Rockyview	Crossfield	AB	Little Bow, AB
1918	Rosebud	Rockyford	AB	Tschetter, SD
1936	Sandhills	Beiseker	AB	Springvale, AB
1979	Schoonover	Odessa	WA	Spring Creek, MT
1954	Scotford	Ft. Saskatchewan	AB	New York, AB
1997	Scott	Scott	SK	Lakeview, SK
2003	Shady Lane	Wanham	AB	Fairview, AB
2004	Silver Creek	Ferintosh	AB	Red Willow, AB
1961	Simmie	Admiral	SK	New York, AB
1969	Smoky Lake	Smoky Lake	AB	Beiseker, AB
1977	South Peace	Farmington	BC	Mixburn, AB
1960	Spokane	Reardan	WA	Pincher Creek, AB
1912	Spring Creek	Lewistown	MT	Wolf Creek, SD
1956	Spring Creek	Walsh	AB	Lakeside, AB
1991	Spring Lake	Swift Current	SK	Hodgeville, SK

Founded	Name of colony	Location	Prov./state	Parent colony
1960	Spring Point	Pincher Creek	AB	Granum, AB
2006	Spring Ridge	Wainwright	AB	O.B., AB
1982	Spring Water	Ruthilda	SK	Valley View, AB
1918	Springvale	Rockyford	AB	Jamesville, SD
1997	Spring Valley	Spring Coulee	AB	West Raley
1980	Stahls	Ritzville	WA	Huxley, AB
1919	Stahlville	Rockyford	AB	Spring Creek, MT
1918	Standoff	Fort MacLeod	AB	Spink, SD
2008	Stanfield	Stanfield	OR	Stahl, WA
1978	Star City	Star City	SK	Estuary, SK
1972	Starland	Drumheller	AB	Lakeside, AB
1991	Sunnybend	Westlock	AB	Cayley, AB
1990	Sunnydale	Perdue	SK	Hillsvale, SK
1956	Sunshine	Hussar	AB	Cayley, AB
1963	Surprise Creek	Stanford	MT	King Ranch, MT
1978	Swift Current	Swift Current	SK	Simmie, SK
1939	Thompson	Fort MacLeod	AB	East Cardston, AB
2006	Three Hills	Three Hills	AB	Wilson Siding, AB
1998	Tofield	Tofield	AB	Carmangay, AB
1948	Tschetter	Irricana	AB	Rosebud, AB
1971	Turin	Turin	AB	West Raley
1959	Turner	Turner	MT	Ayers Ranch, MT
*	Twin Rivers	Manning	AB	Huxley, AB
1971	Valley View	Torrington	AB	Huxley, AB
1973	Valley View Ranch	Valley View	AB	Thompson, AB
2008	Vauxhall Farms	Vauxhall	AB	Cameron, AB
1970	Vegreville	Vegreville	AB	Pibroch, AB
1956	Veteran	Veteran	AB	West Raley, AB
1985	Viking	Viking	AB	Warburg, AB
1964	Warburg	Warburg	AB	Ferrybank, AB
1972	Warden	Warden	WA	Spokane, WA
1913	Warren Ranch (discontinued 1918)	Utica	MT	Richards, SD
1961	Waterton	Hillspring	AB	Wilson Siding, AB
1993	Webb	Webb	SK	Box Elder, SK
1959	West Bench	East End	SK	East Cardston, AB
1918	West Raley	Cardston	AB	Beadle, SD
1998	Wheatland	Rockyford	AB	Stahlville, AB
1973	White Lake	Nobleford	AB	Granum, AB

continued

Founded	Name of colony	Location	Prov./state	Parent colony
1964	Wildwood (discontinued 1981)	Edson	AB	Red Willow, AB
1979	Willow Park	Tessier	SK	Springvale, AB
1918	Wilson Siding	Coaldale	AB	Richards, SD
2001	Wintering Hills	Hussar	AB	Sunshine, AB
1930	Wolf Creek	Stirling	AB	Wolf Creek, SD
2004	Wollman Ranch	Elgin	ND	Ayers Ranch, MT

		Lehrerleut		
1971	Abbey	Abbey	SK	Tompkins, SK
1954	Acadia	Oyen	AB	Crystal Spring, AB
2003	Armada	Lomond	AB	Spring View, AB
1968	Baildon	Moose Jaw	SK	Spring Side, AB
1981	Beechy	Beechy	SK	Main Centre, SK
1962	Bench	Shaunavon	SK	Old Elmspring, AB
1920	Big Bend	Cardston	AB	New Elmspring, AB
1978	Big Sky	Cut Bank	MT	Milford, MT
1986	Big Stone	Sand Coulee	MT	Cascade, MT
1948	Birch Creek	Valier	MT	New Elmspring, AB
2002	Bluegrass	Warner	AB	Elmspring, AB
1991	Bone Creek	Gull Lake	SK	Tompkins, AB
1964	Bow City	Brooks	AB	Sunnysite, AB
1968	Brant	Brant	AB	Rock Lake, AB
1994	Britestone	Carbon	AB	Rose Glen, AB
1991	Butte	Bracken	SK	Sand Lake, SK
2001	Camrose	Ledger	MT	East End, MT
1985	Carmichael	Gull Lake	SK	Cypress, SK
1969	Cascade	Sun River	MT	Glacier, MT
1965	Castor	Castor	AB	Hutterville, AB
1982	Clear Lake	Claresholm	AB	Rockport, AB
1971	Clear Spring	Kenaston	SK	Bench, SK
1975	Clearview	Bassano	AB	Newell, AB
2008	Cloverleaf	Delia	AB	Macmillan, AB
*	Cool Spring	Rudyard	MT	Rockport, MT
1930	Crystal Spring	Magrath	AB	New Elmspring, AB
1953	Cypress	Maple Creek	SK	Big Bend, AB
1992	Deerfield	Magrath	AB	Hutterville, AB
2002	Delco	New Dayton	AB	Sunnysite, AB
1978	Dinsmore	Dinsmore	SK	Glidden, SK
1963	Duncan Ranch	Harlowtown	MT	Birch Creek, MT

Founded	Name of colony	Location	Prov./state	Parent colony
1982	Eagle Creek	Galata	MT	Rimrock, MT
1977	East End	Havre	MT	Hilldale, MT
1987	Eatonia	Eatonia	SK	Haven, SK
*	Elk Creek	Augusta	MT	Milford, MT
1929	Elmspring	Warner	AB	Old Elmspring, AB
2008	Evergreen	Taber	AB	Midland, AB
1980	Fairhaven	Ulm	MT	Duncan Ranch, MT
1986	Fairlane	Skiff	AB	Rosedale, AB
1986	Fairville	Bassano	AB	Spring Side, AB
2002	Garden Plane	Fromtier	SK	Jenner, AB
1951	Glacier	Cut Bank	MT	Elmspring, AB
1969	Glendale	Cut Bank	MT	New Rockport, AB
1963	Glidden	Glidden	SK	Miami, AB
1978	Golden Valley	Ryegate	MT	Springdale, MT
1981	Golden View	Biggar	SK	South Bend, AB
2007	Grassy Hill	Gull Lake	SK	Carmichael, SK
2003	Green Acres	Bassano	AB	Newell, AB
1999	Greenwood	Fort MacLeod	AB	Big Bend, AB
1956	Handhills	Hanna	AB	Macmillan, AB
1999	Hartland	Havre	MT	Hilldale, MT
1967	Haven	Fox Valley	SK	Acadia, AB
1996	Hidden Lake	Cut Bank	MT	Big Sky, MT
*	Hillcrest	Gordon	MT	Springdale, MT
1963	Hilldale	Havre	MT	Rockport, MT
1951	Hillside	Sweetgrass	MT	Sunnysite, AB
*	Homeland	Falher	AB	Falher, AB
*	Horizon	Cut Bank	MT	Hillside, MT
1969	Huron	Brownlee	SK	Big Bend, AB
1932	Hutterville	Magrath	AB	Rockport, SD
1983	Jenner	Jenner	AB	Winnifred, AB
1981	Kingsbury	Valier	MT	Miller, MT
1976	Kings Lake	Foremost	AB	Elmspring, AB
*	Kingsland	New Dayton	AB	Miami, AB
1970	Kyle	Kyle	SK	Rosdale, AB
2003	Lathom	Bassano	AB	Bow City, AB
1999	Lone Pine	Botha	AB	Handhills, AB
1963	Main Centre	Rush Lake	SK	Rockport, AB
1959	Martinsdale	Martinsdale	MT	New Miami, MT
1937	Maxmillan	Cayley	AB	Big Bend, AB
*	McGee	Rosetown	SK	Glidden, SK
2004	McMahon	McMahon	SK	Waldeck, SK

continued

Founded	Name of colony	Location	Prov./state	Parent colony
1989	Mialta	Vulcan	AB	Brant, AB
1927	Miami	New Dayton	AB	Milford, AB
1981	Midland	Taber	AB	Miami, AB
2008	Midway	Conrad	MT	Miller, MT
2006	Milden	Dinsmore	SK	Dinsmore, SK
1918	Milford	Raymond	AB	Milford, SD
1957	Milford	Wolf Creek	MT	Milford, AB
1949	Miller	Choteau	MT	O.K., AB
1992	Miltow	Warner	AB	Milford, AB
1941	Monarch	Coalhurst	AB	BigBend, AB
2002	Mountain View	Brodaview	MT	Golden Valley MT
1992	Neudorf	Crossfield	AB	New Rockport, AB
2000	Neu Muehl	Drumheller	AB	Verdant Valley, AB
1950	Newdale	Milo	AB	Rock Lake, AB
1962	Newell	Bassano	AB	O.K., AB
1918	New Elmspring	Magrath	AB	New Elmspring, SD
1948	New Miami	Conrad	MT	Miami, AB
1948	New Rockport	Choteau	MT	New Rockport, AB
1932	New Rockport	New Dayton	AB	Rockport, AB
1994	Oaklane	Taber	AB	O.K., AB
1934	O.K.	Raymond	AB	Rockport, SD
1918	Old Elmspring	Magrath	AB	Old Elmspring, SD
1972	Parkland	Nanton	AB	Macmillan, AB
2002	Pennant	Pennant	SK	Abbey, SK
1975	Plainview	Warner	AB	O.K., AB
1989	Pleasant Valley	Belt	MT	New Rockport, MT
1994	Pondera	Valier	MT	Birch Creek, MT
1974	Ponderosa	Grassy Lake	AB	New Elmspring, AB
1997	Prairie Home	Wrentham	AB	Plainview, AB
1991	Ridgeland	Hussar	AB	Clearview, AB
1963	Rimrock	Sunburst	MT	Hillside, MT
1976	Riverbend	Mossleigh	AB	Newdale, AB
1985	River Road	Milk River	AB	Rock Lake, AB
1980	River View	Chester	MT	Sage Creek, MT
1935	Rock Lake	Coaldale	AB	Old Elspring, AB
1918	Rockport	Magrath	AB	Rockport, SD
1948	Rockport	Pendroy	MT	Rockport, AB
1953	Rosedale	Etzikom	AB	Hutterville, AB
1970	Rose Glen	Hilda	AB	Crystal Spring, AB
1970	Rosetown	Rosetown	SK	Milford, AB
1986	Rose Valley	Assiniboia	SK	Baildon, SK
1960	Sage Creek	Chester	MT	Miller, MT

Founded	Name of colony	Location	Prov./state	Parent colony
1966	Sand Lake	Val Marie	SK	Old Elmspring, AB
1983	Seville	Cut Bank	MT	Rockport, MT
1997	Shamrock	Bow Island	AB	Kings Lake, AB
1999	Silver Sage	Foremost	AB	Sunrise, AB
*	Silver Springs	Castor	AB	Castor, AB
*	Skylight	Vulcan	AB	Newell, AB
1968	Smiley	Smiley	AB	New Rockport, AB
1965	South Bend	Alliance	AB	Winnifred, AB
*	Southland	Herbert	SK	Beechy, SK
1995	Sovereign	Rosetown	SK	Rosetown, SK
1959	Springdale	White Sulphur Springs	MT	Milford, AB
1991	Springfield	Kindersley	SK	Smiley, SK
1955	Springside	Duchess	AB	New Rockport, AB
1979	Springview	Gem	AB	Bow City, AB
1982	Springwater	Harlowtown	AB	Martinsdale, MT
1987	Standard	Standard	AB	Arcadia, AB
1989	Starbrite	Foremost	AB	Crystal Spring, AB
1983	Suncrest	Castor	AB	Castor, AB
*	Sunnybrook	Chester	MT	Riverside, MT
1935	Sunnysite	Warner	AB	Elmspring, AB
1978	Sunrise	Etzikom	AB	Sunnysite, AB
1954	Tompkins	Tompkins	SK	New Elmspring, AB
1986	Twilight	Falher	AB	Macmilan
1998	Twin Creek	Standard	AB	Riverbend, AB
2002	Twin Hills	Carter	MT	Glendale, MT
2004	Valley Centre	Biggar	SK	Golden View, SK
1980	Vanguard	Vanguard	SK	Waldeck, SK
1974	Verdant Valley	Drumheller	AB	Handhills, AB
1063	Waldeck	Swift Current	SK	Elmspring, AB
1987	Wheatland	Cabri	SK	Kyle, SK
1990	Wild Rose	Vulcan	AB	Old Elmspring, AB
1995	Willow Creek	Claresholm	AB	Parkland, AB
1953	Winnifred	Medicine Hat	AB	Milford, AB
*	Wymark	Wymark	SK	Vanguard, SK
*	Zenith	Santa Clara	MT	Glacier, MT

*A colony-in-formation.

Glossary

Anfechtung: An internal spiritual struggle that leads to a state of emotional depression.

Aussiedler: An outsider, a non-Hutterite.

Basel: Literally, "aunt"; a term of respect for older female adults.

Brüderhof: Literally, "community of brothers"; a term identifying a Hutterite church community/village in Moravia and Slovakia during the sixteenth and seventeenth centuries.

Bruderhof: A communal Anabaptist society founded by Eberhard Arnold in Germany in 1920 that was merged with the Hutterites from 1931 to 1955 and from 1974 to 1995. In 2007 the Bruderhof, then numbering twenty-six hundred members, changed its name to Christian Communities, International.

Dariusleut: The Hutterite group that was founded by Darius Walter in Ukraine in 1860. The first North American community was the Wolf Creek Colony, near Olivet, South Dakota.

Demut: Humility.

Dienen: Young unmarried women.

Eigennutz: Private ownership of property.

Essenschul: The children's dining room.

Essenstuben: The Hutterite colony dining hall.

Fleischkrapfen: Meat dumplings.

Gashtel: Crumbled noodle soup.

Gebet: The daily colony worship service that precedes the evening meal.

Gelassenheit: Surrender of the will to God through the community.

Gemein: The German word for "community," often used to describe the Hutterite Church.

Gesangbuch: The songbook used by Hutterites; it includes many Lutheran hymns.

Griebenschmaltz: Goose or pork crackling spread.

G'schmolzmanudel: Large fried noodles.

Gütergemeinschaft: Community of goods.

Hochmut: Pride or lack of humility.

Hulba: A shivaree or engagement party, a celebration before a wedding; also called *Stubela.*

Hutterisch: The Tirolean-Carinthian-Austrian dialect spoken by Hutterites as their first language.

Kartoffelknedel: A potato dumpling.

Klanaschul, or *Kleineschul:* The Hutterite kindergarten or preschool.

Kuchwuch: The week when particular members of the colony kitchen crew, two at a time, are responsible for preparing all of the colony meals.

Kupftiechle: A black-and-white polka-dotted head covering or scarf worn by Hutterite women.

Lehr: The Sunday morning worship service or a single Hutterite sermon.

Lehren: The Hutterite sermons, most of which were written in the seventeenth century.

Lehrerleut: The Hutterite group founded by Jacob Wipf, a *Lehrer* (teacher), in Ukraine in the 1870s. The first North American community was the Elmspring Colony, near Utica, South Dakota.

Leut: One of the three original ethnoreligious clans within the Hutterite Church. The German word *Leut* is pronounced "loit." A fourth Leut was created in 1992 when the Schmiedeleut divided.

Lied: A song or hymn.

Meidung: The practice of shunning.

Mitz: A bonnet worn by young Hutterite girls.

Moos: Various kinds of fruit puddings.

Nachtischgebet: The traditional prayer after a colony meal.

Necklus: Holiday gifts given in December around Saint Nicholas Day.

Nukelen: Egg dumpling soup.

Objinka, or *Dankfest:* The Hutterite Thanksgiving, or harvest celebration.

Ordnungen: Hutterite rules and regulations, based on biblical interpretations made by the leaders of each *Leut.* In Hutterisch, the *Ordnungen* are called *Urnung.* They are also referred to as the *Gemein Ordnungen.*

Prairieleut: The term used to designate noncommunal Hutterites, those who, on arrival in the Dakotas in the 1870s, decided to live on private farms on the open prairie.

Prediger: A Hutterite minister or preacher.

Pschreien: A curse placed on an individual, often unintentionally, through the recognition of individual gifts or beauty.

Reascha: A sweet dried bun.

Schmiedeleut: The Hutterite group started by Michael Waldner in Ukraine, in 1859. The first Schmiedeleut community in North America was the Bon Homme Colony, near Tabor, South Dakota.

Schmiedeleut One: The Schmiedeleut branch that, since 1992, has continued to recognize the 1950 *Constitution* and is generally considered the most liberal faction.

Schmiedeleut Two: The Schmiedeleut branch that in 1993 adopted a revised constitution and is generally considered the more conservative Schmiedeleut faction.

Sorgela: A babysitter.

Stiebel: The Hutterite church council meeting.

Teichsel Vegela: A two-wheeled wagon with a long handle.

Vetter: Literally, "cousin" in German; in Hutterisch it is used as a term of respect for older adult Hutterite males.

Vorsänger: A song leader.

Weggeluffene: Hutterite runaways, those who leave the colony for a few months or years before deciding whether to join the church.

Weltleut: Literally, "worldly people"; the term is often used to refer to non-Hutterites; the singular form is *Weltmensch*.

Wirt: The Hutterite colony business manager or steward.

Notes

Preface

Epigraph: Kleinsasser, *Book 6*, 225.

1. Many specialized studies followed Hostetler's 1974 work. The most important are Gross, *Golden Years*; Stayer, *German Peasant's War*; and Packull, *Hutterite Beginnings*. Important analyses of contemporary Hutterite life include Peter, *Dynamics of Hutterite Society*; Kraybill and Bowman, *Backroad to Heaven*; and Schlachta, *Die Hutterer*. Two books published by Hutterites are also important: Gross, *Hutterite Way*; and Hofer, *History of the Hutterites*.

2. Manfred, *Sons of Adam*, 302. The character's name is "Red."

3. Horst, "Pieter Cornelisz Plockhoy."

4. Tony Waldner, conversation with Janzen, May 2006.

5. Gaddis, *Landscape of History*, 54.

6. Elshtain, "Religious Perspective of the Teacher," 195.

7. Norton, *Imagination, Understanding*, 6.

8. Geertz, *Interpretation of Cultures*, 14. An important source on anthropological research is Emerson, Fretz, and Shaw, *Writing Ethnographic Fieldnotes*. See also Macdonald, *Reimagining Culture*.

9. Gaddis, *Landscape of History*, 54.

10. Kraybill and Bowman, *Backroad to Heaven*. See also Redekop and Hostetler, "Plain People," 266–275.

11. Kraybill and Bowman, *Backroad to Heaven*, 15.

12. Redekop and Hostetler, "Plain People," 273.

13. Pitzer, *America's Communal Utopias*, 12.

Chapter 1. Communal Christians in North America

Epigraph: Wilder, *On the Way Home*, 20.

1. Ibid., 21.

2. Manfred, *Sons of Adam*, 300; Frederick Manfred, conversation with Janzen, July 1983. Manfred is the author of dozens of books dealing with the northern plains, including *Lord Grizzly* and *Conquering Horse*.

3. Wade, *Before the Dawn*, 44, 58, 160.

4. Hutter, *Brotherly Faithfullness*, 171.

5. The Prairieleut story is told in Janzen, *Prairie People*.

6. Eli Hofer, conversation with Janzen, August 2006.

7. Friesen, *Hutterite Confession of Faith*.

Chapter 2. Origins and History

Epigraph: Hutter, *Brotherly Faithfullness*, 153.

1. Packull, *Hutterite Beginnings*; Stayer, *German Peasant's War*.

2. Marx, *Critique of Gotha Program*.

3. All biblical references are from the New Jerusalem Bible unless indicated otherwise.

4. "Sermon on Baptism," in Hostetler, Gross, and Bender, *Selected Hutterian Documents*, 102.

5. Hutterite Educational Committee, *Hutterian Church Responds*, 39.

6. Stayer, *German Peasant's War*, 156.

7. Packull, *Hutterite Beginnings*. Packull's book is the most in-depth study of early Hutterianism.

8. Siegfried teaches at St. Louis University. Both of the authors have served or presently serve on the board of directors of the Communal Studies Association. Since 1999 Janzen has edited the organization's biennial journal, *Communal Societies*.

9. Hans Decker, conversation with Janzen, June 1988.

10. Walter, *Acts 2*, 110.

11. Friedmann, *Hutterite Studies*, 83.

12. Tony Waldner, conversation with Janzen, May 2004.

13. Tschetter, "Sermon on Acts 2," 5.

14. Engels, *Peasant's War*; Ehrenpreis, *Epistle on Brotherly Community*, 49.

15. Walter, *Acts 2*, xiv.

16. Hutterian Brethren, *Chronicle I*; *Chronicle II*.

17. Miller and Stephenson, "Jakob Hutter."

18. Packull, *Hutterite Beginnings*, 232.

19. Hutterian Brethren, *Chronicle I*, 418.

20. Packull, *Hutterite Beginnings*, 224.

21. Hutterian Brethren, *Chronicle I*, 145. Other important sources for information on the early Hutterites are Fischer, *Jakob Huter*; Packull, *Hutterite Beginnings*; and Stayer, *German Peasant's War*.

22. The most recent translation of this work is Friesen, *Hutterite Confession of Faith*. This book also contains valuable biographical information. Another important source is Friedmann, "Peter Riedemann." The most recent book on Riedemann is Packull, *Peter Riedemann*.

23. Hutterian Brethren, *Die Lieder*; Gross, *Golden Years*, 29.

24. Schlachta, "Against Selfishness," 270.

25. Friesen, *Hutterite Confession of Faith*, 121.

26. Friedmann, *Hutterite Studies*, 73; Hutterian Brethren, *Chronicle I*, 507.

27. Packull, *Hutterite Beginnings*, 74.

28. Gross, *Golden Years*, 195, 201; Stayer, *German Peasant's War*, 141.

29. Stayer, *German Peasant's War*, 147, 150.

30. Harrison, *Andreas Ehrenpreis*, 19.

31. Gross, *Golden Years*, 30—31.

32. Ibid., 198—199.

33. Friedmann, "Epistles."

34. Hostetler, *Hutterite Society*, 35.

35. Bender, "Hausbuch of Neumühl." An analysis of later Ordnungen is included in Anderson, "Hutterite Ordnungen."

36. Bender, "Rule of Teamsters," 243, quotation on 242.

37. Bender, "Hutterite School Discipline," 231—244.

38. Rothkegel, "Printed Book," 58.

39. Kalesny, *Habani Na Slovensku*, 367. Krisztinkovich, *Haban Pottery*, 24—38.

40. Buckwalter, "Review of von Schlachta."

41. Kalesny, *Habani Na Slovensku*, 366.

42. Grimmelshausen, *Adventures of a Simpleton*, 16.

43. Walter, *Acts 2*, 169.

44. Hutterian Brethren, *Die Lieder*, 286—293.

45. Martens, *Hutterite Songs*, 291—295.

46. Helen Martens, conversation with Janzen, March 2006.

47. Martens, *Hutterite Songs*, 296.

48. Hutterian Brethren, *Chronicle II*, 337.

49. Donner, "Report of Anabaptist Brethren."

50. Klusch, *Sieben Burgische Topferkunst*. See also Krisztinkovich, "Some Further Notes"; Waldner, "Among the Habaner"; and Kalesny, *Habani Na Slovensku*.

51. Peter Hoover, http://groups.google.ca/group/sunlit-kingdom/browse_thread/thread/e6adfc27f72a8ac# (accessed September 16, 2007).

52. Hostetler, *Hutterite Society*, 116.

53. Peter, "Instability of Community of Goods," 5.

54. Stayer, *German Peasant's War*, 145.

55. Wesley Tschetter, "Reflections on Paul Tschetter," 1974, Heritage Museum and Archives, Freeman, SD.

56. Kuleshov, *History of Raditschewa*. Wesley Tschetter purchased a copy while visiting Raditschewa in 2003. Wesley Tschetter, conversation with Janzen, May 2004.

57. Hutterian Brethren, *Chronicle II*, 606.

58. Urry, *None but Saints*, 120.

59. Hutterian Brethren, *Chronicle II*, 296.

60. Ibid., 638–639.

61. Ibid., 606.

62. Hostetler, *Hutterite Society*, 101.

63. Waltner, *Banished for Faith*, 102.

64. Janzen, "Diary," 67.

65. Friedmann, "Reestablishment of Communal Life"; Christopher, "Description of the Beginning," 2–3.

66. Friedmann, "Reestablishment of Communal Life," 150.

67. Christopher, "Description of the Beginning," 3.

68. Tschetter, "Biography of Paul Tschetter," 113.

Chapter 3. Immigration and Settlement in North America

Epigraph: Paul Tschetter, unpublished hymn found on page 25 of his 1873 diary, Heritage Museum and Archives, Freeman, SD.

1. Hofer, "Diary of Paul Tschetter." The original copy of the Tschetter diary is displayed in three small booklets enclosed in a simple manila folder, inside a glass-enclosed case, at the Heritage Museum and Archives, Freeman, SD. Though in somewhat fragile condition, the diary is legible and mildew-free.

2. Ibid., 116.

3. Some of these hymns, which had never been translated or published, appear in Janzen, *Paul Tschetter*.

4. Janzen, "Tschetter's Chicago Fire Hymn," 266.

5. Ibid., 271.

6. The Hutterites do not use the title "reverend" for their religious leaders; therefore, in this book we refer to the religious leaders as ministers.

7. Correll, "President Grant," 148, 149; Smith, *Coming of Russian Mennonites*, 74.

8. Kleinsasser, "Community and Ethics," 43.

9. Schell, *History of South Dakota*, 118; Unruh, *Century of Mennonites*, 25–27.

10. Harder, "Russian Mennonites and American Democracy," 58. Hutterite settlement decisions are discussed in detail in Janzen, *Paul Tschetter*.

11. Hutterian Brethren, *Chronicle II*, 652.

12. David P. Gross, "Report," in Hutterite Mennonite Centennial Committee, *Hutterite Roots*, 101.

13. Janzen, *Prairie People*. See also Hutterite-Mennonite Centennial Committee, *History of Hutterite-Mennonites*.

14. David Decker, "Bon Homme Gemeinde, 1874–1974," unpublished manuscript, 1974, Rod Janzen Collection. The articles of incorporation (in English) and other government documents are found Zieglschmid, *Das Klein-Geschichtesbuch*.

15. "Peter Janzen to *Mennonitsche Rundschau*, August 1890," in Voth, *House of Jacob*, 67.

16. Hofer, *Diaries of "Yos" Hofer*, 341–342.

17. Hofer, *Diaries of "Yos" Hofer*.

18. Friedmann, *Hutterite Studies*, 110.

19. Throughout this book, in order to honor requests for anonymity, many Hutterite people who contributed insights are not identified.

20. Janzen, *Prairie People*, 198.

21. Sources for the Fred Waldner story include Hans Decker, Arnold M. Hofer, Michael Waldner, and Tony Waldner. Janzen, *Prairie People*, 197–198.

22. Kleinsasser, *Our Journey of Faith*, 12.

23. Guericke, *Precious Memories*.

24. Notes from Jacob W. Tschetter's conversation with Wesley Tschetter, 1974. Guericke, *Precious Memories*, 41. An important contemporary non-Hutterian account is Beadle, *Autobiography*, 13, 22.

25. Jansen, *Memoirs of Peter Jansen*, 39.

26. Zempel, *Wind Is in the South*, 14.

27. Young, "Tumbleweed," 82–87.

28. Gross, *The Hutterite Way*, 21.

29. Jacob A. Tschetter, "Family History," n.d., provided by Wesley Tschetter, Brookings, SD.

30. Rath, *Black Sea Germans*, 350–356.

31. Gross and Hofer, "Neu Hutterthaler Record Book"; Waldner, "Among the Habaner," 89.

32. Hutterian Brethren, *Chronicle I*, 243.

33. Friedmann, "Hutterite Ordinances," 117.

34. Esau, *Courts and the Colonies*, 42.

35. Urry, *None but Saints*, 132.

36. Guericke, *Precious Memories*, 3.

37. American Industrial Committee, *Crucifixions in 20th Century*, 4.

38. In 2007 San Francisco attorney Susan Cohn petitioned the National Park Service to install a plaque on Alcatraz to recognize the mistreatment of the Hofers. Susan Cohn, conversation with Janzen, July 2007.

39. Youmans, *Plough and the Pen*, 26, 43.

40. Funk, "Divided Loyalties," 30.

41. Kleinsasser, *Book of Prefaces*, 155.

42. Schlabach, "Account by Jakob Waldner," 78.

43. Photograph in *Yankton Press and Dakotan*, May 4, 1918, in Karolevitz, *Yankton*, 156.

44. Zieglschmid, *Das Klein-Geshichtsbuch*, 487.

45. Kleinsasser, *Book 6*, 230.

46. Annie Walter, conversation with Janzen, July 2007.

47. Hofer, *The Hutterites*, 104.

48. Kriszintovich, *Annotated Hutterite Bibliography*, 130.

49. Hostetler, *Hutterite Society*, 131.

50. Unruh, *Century of Mennonites*, 122.

51. The last remaining Dariusleut colony, Rockport, relocated to Raymond, Alberta. The land was sold to the Schmiedeleut, who kept Rockport as the colony name.

52. For detailed information on the Communal Properties Act, see Janzen, *Limits on Liberty*; Flint, *Hutterites*.

53. Untitled article, no page number, *Sioux Falls Argus Leader*, 1955, Heritage Hall Museum and Archives, Freeman, SD.

54. Mendel, *History of East Freeman*, 106.

55. Janzen, *Prairie People*, 68–69; Arndt, *George Rapp's Successors*, 129–136.

56. Scheuner, *Inspiration Historie*.

57. Hoehnle, "Michael Hofer."

Chapter 4. Four Hutterite Branches

Epigraph: Hofer, *Diaries of "Yos" Hofer*, 5.

1. Hostetler, *Hutterite Society*, 174.

2. Peter Waldner, conversation with Stanton, July 2003; Jacob Wipf, conversation with Janzen, July 2005. In 2007 the Bruderhof changed its name to Church Communities, International. Since the group was called the Bruderhof when it was affiliated with the Hutterites, that is the name we use in this book.

3. Wipf and Wipf, *Dariusleut Family Record List*.

4. Eli Hofer, conversation with Janzen, July 2005.

5. John S. Hofer, interview by Janzen, May 2008; "Signatures of Ministers Supporting Jacob Kleinsasser," 1993, James Valley Colony, Elie, MB.

6. "Hutterian Brethren Church of the Darius & Lehrerleut Conference to the Society of Brothers Who Call Themselves Hutterian Brethren, December 11, 1990," Rod Janzen Collection.

7. Arnold Hofer, John S. Hofer, Edward Kleinsasser, interviews by Janzen, May 2008.

8. Edward Kleinsasser, e-mail message to Janzen, June 2008.

9. Jacob Kleinssasser, correspondence with "Servants of the Word," August 4, 1992, Archives of the Mennonite Church, Goshen, IN.

10. Edward Kleinsasser, e-mail message to Janzen, June 2008.

11. Gibb, "Hutterite Business Ventures," 1, 5.

12. Ibid., 1; J. G. Cristall, "Meyers Norris Penny & Co., 'To Whom It May Concern, re; Donald Gibb,'" July 16, 1992, 3, provided by Samuel Waldner, Decker Colony, Decker, MB. Names for the two groups have been in flux since 1992. A progressive Schmiedeleut Web site refers to the two groups as the "Schmiedeleut Hutterites" (the progressives) and the "Committee Hutterites" (the conservatives). While many traditionalists do not mind being called *Gibbs*, progressive Schmiedeleut do not like the term *Oilers*. In summer 2006, the authors found Alberta Dariusleut and Lehrerleut joking that they were now "all Oilers," referring to the success of the Edmonton Oilers hockey team.

13. Daniel Hofer, conversation with Janzen, May 2007; Jacob Kleinsasser, conversation with Janzen, May 2008. Crystal Spring Colony constructed its own unique hog feeder that Daniel Hofer says he invented but never fully patented because it was in continuous development. Crystal Spring patented the invention and sold it to a private company for a profit. Hofer was excommunicated after he persuaded the Lakeside Colony to "stop payment" on the use of what he says was his own hog-feeder invention.

14. Esau, *Courts and the Colonies*, 130.

15. Maria Hofer, conversation with Janzen, July 2006.

16. Janzen, "Hutterites and Bruderhof."

17. Today twenty-six hundred Bruderhof members live in communes in Pennsylvania, upstate New York, New Jersey, Germany, England, and Australia. There is no longer any formal association with the Hutterites.

18. The clash between elder Johannes Waldner and Jacob Walter was one reason for the disintegration of communal life at Raditschewa in 1821.

19. John S. Hofer, conversation with Janzen, July 2006; Dora Maendel, conversation with Janzen, July 2006.

20. This statement is based on interviews with sixteen Hutterites who visited Bruderhof communities during the 1980s.

21. Lucas Wipf, conversation with Janzen, March 2004.

22. Kleinsasser, "Community and Ethics," 35.

23. Hofer, *Diaries of "Yos" Hofer*, 39.

24. A Schmiedeleut One minister refers to an associated colony as "new age" because of its more radical approach to education.

25. Dora Maendel, e-mail message to Janzen, March 2008.

26. Dora Maendel, "Hutterite Colony Loses Its Kitchen," 24, Rod Janzen Collection.

27. Paul M. Wipf, conversation with Janzen, July 2006; Dora Maendel, conversation with Janzen, July 2006.

28. Cobb, "Color Them Plain," 5.

29. Sarah Gross, conversation with Stanton, July 2006; Ruth Baer Lambach, e-mail message to Janzen, January 2008.

Chapter 5. Beliefs and Practices

Epigraph: Ehrenpreis, *Epistle on Brotherly Community*, 47.

1. Kleinsasser, *Teachings for Easter*, 240. This quotation accompanies the 1 Corinthians Lehr text.

2. Patrick Murphy, e-mail message to Janzen, February 2008.

3. Hutterian Educational Committee, *Hutterian Church Responds*, 53.

4. Kraybill and Bowman, *Backroad to Heaven*, 207–212.

5. Ibid.; Hutter, *Brotherly Faithfullness*, 171.

6. Friedmann, *Hutterite Studies*, 184.

7. Patrick Murphy, e-mail message to Janzen, April 2007.

8. Phillip Gross, conversation with Janzen, August 2005.

9. Robert Rhodes, conversation with Janzen, May 2003.

10. Handwritten listings for three Manitoba Schmiedeleut Two colonies, 1998, provided by Patrick Murphy.

11. Katherina (Kay) Wollman, conversation with Janzen, July 2005.

12. Herman Wollman, conversation with Janzen, May 2004; Dora and Anna Maendel, conversation with Janzen, August 2006.

13. Mike Wipf, conversation with Janzen, April 2006.

14. Walter, *Acts 2*, 15.

15. Hofer, "Sermon on Matthew 6," 6.

16. Ibid., 8.

17. Kuentsche, "Pentecost *Lehren*," 278–282, 345.

18. "Sirach 2 Sermon," in delegate Paul Tschetter's (1842–1919) sermon book collection, 1870, n.p. The original copy of the only existing Tschetter sermon book is in the possession of Gideon Bertsche, Menno, SD.

19. Gross and Bender, "Hutterite Sermon," 62, 67.

20. Tony Waldner, correspondence with members of the Schmiedeleut Two Hutterite Educational Committee, February 12, 2007. Copies in Rod Janzen Collection.

21. Dariusleut minister Paul S. Gross's personal collection of sermons and prefaces is in the Archives of the Mennonite Church, Goshen, IN.

22. Friedmann, *Hutterite Studies*, 179, 187. See also Friedmann, "Hutterite Worship and Preaching," 10–12. Hutterite Education Committee, *Hutterian Church Responds.*

23. Kleinsasser, *Book 6*, 110.

24. Kleinsasser, *Book of Prefaces*, 177.

25. Ibid., 33.

26. Translations of non-English materials are by the authors unless indicated otherwise.

27. Kleinsasser, *Hutterite Sermon on Luke 23:24–26*, 10.

28. Hofer, "Sermon on Matthew 6," 5.

29. Kleinsasser, "Community and Ethics," 47; Ugwu-Oju, *What Will My Mother Say?*

30. Dora Maendel, correspondence with Janzen, April 2008.

31. Vonk, "Schwartz Values." A good introduction to traditional folk society characteristics is Redfield, "Folk Society."

32. Samuel Waldner, conversation with Janzen, August 2006.

33. Riedemann, *Account of Our Religion*, 126.

34. Hutterian Brethren, *Chronicle II*, 469–470.

35. Kleinsasser, *Book 6*, 175.

36. Robert Rhodes, editorial, *Mennonite Weekly Review*, November 1, 2004.

37. "Die *Quelle* project" seminar, Hutterville Colony, Stratford, SD, October 2006.

38. Schlachta, "Searching through the Nations," 34; Hutterian Brethren, *Chronicle II*, 103–105; Packull, *Hutterite Beginnings*, 227; Riedemann, *Account of Our Religion*, 110.

39. There have been a few exceptions. In 1952 Jacob Waldner was chosen as minister at Bon Homme Colony, Tabor, SD, without casting lots. There were other nominees, but the ministers present rejected them. Because of this unusual occurrence, the Schmiedeleut leadership decided that in the future, if there were not at least two acceptable nominees, the process would start over.

40. Hutterian Brethren, *Chronicle II*, 664–665. "Church Ordinances of the Hutterian Brethren, 1651–1873" is found in *Chronicle II*, 761–834.

41. David Walter, conversation with Stanton, July 2007.

42. Riedemann, *Account of Our Religion*, 112.

43. Kleinsasser, *Teachings on John*, 3.

44. Gross, *Golden Years*, 173.

45. Jacob Wipf, conversation with Janzen, July 2006.

46. Mack Waldner, sermon comments, Decker Colony, Decker, MB, August 2006.

47. Hutterian Brethren, *Die Lieder; Gesangbuch; Gesangbuchlein.*

48. Martens, *Hutterite Songs*, 291.

49. Hutterian Brethren, *Die Lieder.*

50. Martens, *Hutterite Songs*, 291, 295; Hutterian Brethren, *Chronicle II*, 297.

51. Larry Martens, conversation with Janzen, May 2005.

52. Bach, *Faith and Our Friends*, 117.

53. Bainton, "Frontier Community," 36. Dora Maendel, Fairholme Colony, Manitoba, German teacher, assisted in the translation of this hymn.

54. Friedmann, *Hutterite Studies*, 192.

55. Butch Wipf, conversation with Janzen, November 2007; Wipf, *Hutterian Songs: Book 1*, 170.

56. Wipf, *Hutterian Songs: Book 1*, 170.

57. Kleinsasser, *Book of Prefaces*, 53.

58. *Lutherische Gesangbuch* (Milwaukee: G. Brumder, 1870), hymn no. 376, translated by Max Stanton.

59. Lee, *Cotton Patch Evidence*, 100.

60. Hiebert, *Hutterite Story*, 289. Adherence to authority is discussed in Boldt, "Acquiescence and Conventionality."

61. Levi Tschetter, conversation with Janzen, July 1983; Paul M. Wipf, conversation with Janzen, July 2006.

62. Clifford Waldner, unpublished paper, 1984, Rod Janzen Collection. Waldner is an ex-Hutterite who lives in North Dakota.

63. Hutterian Educational Committee, *Hutterian Church Responds*, 33, 37.

64. Samuel Hofer, conversation with Stanton, July 1985.

65. Hiebert, *Hutterite Story*, 317.

66. Kleinsasser, *Book of Prefaces*, 159.

67. Hutterian Brethren, *Chronicle I*, 423; Hutterian Educational Committee, *Hutterian Church Responds*, 58.

68. Anderson, "Hutterite Ordnungen," 1, 2, 3; John Gross, conversation with Stanton, July 2007.

69. Hutterian Brethren, www.Hutterites.org, "Frequently Asked Questions," number 5.

70. Hutterian Educational Committee, *Hutterian Church Responds*, 59.

71. Hofer, *Japanese Hutterites*, 65.

Chapter 6. Life Patterns and Rites of Passage

Epigraph: Peter, *Dynamics of Hutterite Society*, 200.

1. Hartse, "On the Colony," 164.

2. Stanton, "Hutterite Way."

3. Wipf and Wipf, *Dariusleut Family Record List.*

4. Kleinsasser, *Teachings for Easter*, 12.

5. Dora Maendel to Darla Penner, executive director, Ukrainian Adoption Services Inc., December 30, 2005, Fairholme Colony, Portage la Prairie, MB.

6. Ruth Baer Lambach, e-mail message to Janzen, January 2008.

7. Lambach, "Colony Girl," 246.

8. Anderson, "Hutterite Ordnungen," 9.

9. Kleinsasser, *Teachings For Easter*, 266.

10. Masuk, "Patriarchy, Technology," 73.

11. Tony Waldner, e-mail message to Janzen, September 2005.

12. Huntington, "A Separate Culture," 3. Other works on Hutterite women include Lambach, "Colony Girl"; and Huntington, "Supplementary Essay."

13. Wipf and Wipf, *Dariusleut Family Record List*; Hiebert, *Hutterite Story*, 305. Hiebert notes thirty-eight counts of sexual assault, touching, and incest levied against one Hutterite in the early 2000s.

14. Kleinsasser, *Seeking Purity*, 10, 17.

15. Tony Waldner, conversation with Janzen, July 2006.

16. Sarah Hofer, conversation with Janzen, July 2006.

17. Stephenson, "He Died too Quick!" 128.

18. Kienzler, *Gender and Communal Longevity*, 75.

19. Hilda Entz, conversation with Janzen, May 2008.

20. Kleinsasser, *Funeral Teachings*.

21. Stephenson, "Gender, Aging, and Mortality," 359, notes this statistic. Eaton and Mayer, "Social Biology"; Morgan, "Mortality Changes."

22. Martin, "Founder Effect."

23. Stephenson, "Gender, Aging, and Mortality," 360, 361.

24. The Lehrerleut celebrate Communion on Easter Monday.

25. Maendel, "Hutterite Christmas Traditions," 7.

26. Kleinsasser, *Book 6*, 15.

27. Hofer, "History of Neu Hutterthaler," 51; Gross, *The Hutterite Way*, 96.

28. Allard, "Solace at Surprise Creek," 140.

29. Ron Waldner, conversation with Stanton, July 2007.

Chapter 7. Identity, Tradition, and Folk Beliefs

Epigraph: Friedmann, "Reestablishment of Communal Life."

1. Martin, "Founder Effect." Genetic studies on the South Dakota Schmiedeleut are being conducted by the Department of Human Genetics at the University of Chicago. Van Den Berghe and Peter, "Hutterites and Kibbutzniks," 522.

2. Wade, *Before the Dawn*, 10, 54, 120, 253.

3. The surname Gross is Old Hutterite ethnically, but some Hutterites speculate

that contemporary members with Gross ancestry are descendants of Prussian Mennonite converts. As Hutterite genealogist Tony Waldner puts it, "We don't know for sure." E-mail to Janzen, September 2009.

4. Manfred, *Chokecherry Tree*, 198.

5. Peter, *Dynamics of Hutterite Society*, 122–124.

6. Hutterian Brethren, *Chronicle I*, 510.

7. Betty Hofer Murphy, conversation with Janzen, May 2007; Clark, "Leadership Succession," esp. 297. See also Mackie, "Ethnic Stereotypes and Prejudice."

8. Anderson, "Hutterite Names"; Wipf and Wipf, *Dariusleut Family Record List*, 125.

9. Tony Waldner, e-mail message to Janzen, September 2005.

10. Dale Mowry, conversation with Janzen, May 2004; Arnold Hofer, conversation with Janzen, October 2006.

11. Rhodes, "Road of No Return," 100. Robert Rhodes, conversation with Janzen, May 2003. Rhodes, *Nightwatch*, 37.

12. Murphy, "Warum ich Hutterer wurde."

13. Lorenz-Andreasch, *Mir Sein Ja Kolla*.

14. Kriszintovich, *Annotated Hutterite Bibliography*, 273.

15. Scheer, "Hutterian German Dialect," 229, 232.

16. Hoover, *Hutterian-English Dictionary*; *Hutterian Language*; Linda Maendel, correspondence with Dora Maendel, February 2008, Fairholme Colony, Portage la Prairie, MB. In 2002 the American Bible Society published *Hutterische Bibl Tschiehten I* (Hutterite Bible stories I). Janke, "They're Here," 5.

17. Whorf, *Language, Thought, and Reality*; Sapir, *Culture, Language, and Personality*.

18. Some scholars (for example, theologian Randall Buth) suggest that Jesus spoke as much Hebrew as Aramaic. Randall Buth, "What I Learned about Jesus from the Rabbis," presentation, Fresno, CA, November 2007.

19. Scott, *Why Do They Dress That Way?* Stephen Scott, conversation with Janzen, January 2004.

20. Anderson, "Hutterite Ordnungen," 6.

21. Sam Waldner, conversation with Janzen, August 2006; Sam Hofer, conversation with Stanton, May 2002.

22. Stanton, "By Their Dots."

23. Chad Miller, presentation, Iowa Mennonite School, Kalona, IA, March 1987. For another reflection on Hutterite dress, see Ingoldsby, "Group Conformity."

24. Janzen, *Prairie People*, 231; "German School Inservice Summary, Bloomfield, Manitoba, October 2007," unpublished document provided by John S. Hofer, James Valley Colony, Elie, MB.

25. Kraybill and Bowman, *Backroad to Heaven*, 46.

26. Stanton, "Why I Love Hutterites," 12, Max Stanton Collection.

27. Comment overheard by Rod Janzen, New Elmspring Colony, Ethan, SD, July 2003.

28. Goertz, *Princes, Potentates,* 215–216.

29. Peter, *Dynamics of Hutterite Society,* 130.

30. Janzen, *Prairie People,* 232.

31. Ruth Lambach, e-mail message to Janzen, March 2004; Norris, *Dakota.*

32. Kenny Wollman, e-mail message to Janzen, June 2007.

33. Jacob Kleinsasser, *Book of Prefaces,* 164.

34. Esther Walter, conversation with Stanton, July 2002.

35. Young woman at Greenwood Colony, conversation with Stanton, July 2001.

36. Arnold Hofer, conversation with Janzen, May 2007. Terry Miller, conversation with Janzen, February 2010, contests the validity of this story. According to Miller, he never goes barefoot, does not own a pair of short pants, and does not recall other details.

37. Tony Waldner, conversation with Janzen, July 2006.

38. Kleinsasser, "Community and Ethics," 223.

39. Betty Hofer Murphy, conversation with Janzen, August 2006.

40. Annika Janzen, conversation with Janzen, July 2006.

41. Cobb, "Color Them Plain."

42. Joseph Wipf, conversation with Janzen, July 1985.

43. Hostetler, *Hutterite Society,* 101.

44. Tschetter, "Die Auswanderer," 91.

45. Amon Baer, conversation with Janzen, May 2007. Amon's Mennonite parents brought the Baer family name into the Hutterite community.

46. Henry Wurz, conversation with Janzen, May 2008.

47. Henry Wurz, conversation with Janzen, July 2006.

48. Bobby Walter, conversation with Stanton, July 2007.

49. Stanton, "Why I Love Hutterites."

50. Victor Kleinsasser, presentation on farm safety issues, International Hutterite Teacher's Conference, Aberdeen, SD, 2004.

51. Maryann Tschetter, conversation with Stanton, August 2003.

52. Brock, *Pacifism in Europe,* 244; Allard, "Solace at Surprise Creek," 138.

53. Harry and Cynthia Stahl, *Blessings 2007* calendar, 2007, Hutterian Brethren, Odanah Farms, Minnedosa, MB; Shannon Vanraes, "An Art Exhibit Providing Glimpse into Hutterite Life," *Central Plains Herald-Leader,* September 23, 2006, 3.

54. Fleming and Rowan, *Folk Furniture.*

55. Marlene Bogard, Martha Graber, Deborah Janzen, and Bernice Koller, conversations with Janzen.

56. Martens, "Musical Thought and Practice," 32; Kimmelman, *Accidental Masterpiece,* 33.

57. "Alberta Hutterites Balk at Driver's License Photos," *Mennonite Weekly Review*, May 29, 2006.

58. Anna Entz, conversation with Stanton, June 2007.

59. Marie Waldner, conversation with Janzen, July 1987.

60. Hutterite Mennonite Centennial Committee, *History of Hutterite Mennonites*, 126.

61. Arnold M. Hofer, conversation with Janzen, July 1987.

62. Janzen, *Prairie People*, 192.

63. Kulig et al., "Refusals and Delay," 109.

64. Eaton, Weil, and Kaplan, "Hutterite Mental Health Study, 57. See also Bleibtreu, "Marriage and Residence Patterns."

65. Hostetler, *Hutterite Society*, 362.

66. Mange, *Population Structure*, 75; Howells, *Hutterian Age Differences*, 122.

67. Martin, "Founder Effect."

68. Hartzog, "Population Genetic Studies," 1.

69. Ibid., 137, 140, quotation on 137.

70. Brunt et al., "Hutterite Heart Health Surveys," 514–519.

71. Stephenson, "Hutterite Colonies," 114, 117.

72. Ober, "Complex Trait Mapping."

73. Small, "Love with Proper Stranger."

74. Peter and Whitaker, "Hutterite Perceptions," 7, 6.

75. Hostetler, *Hutterite Society*, 246.

76. Siegel, "Deference Structuring."

77. Kaplan and Plaut, *Personality in a Communal Society*; Edward Kleinsasser, statement at Schmiedeleut One Education Committee Meeting, Acadia Colony, Carberry, MB, May 2008.

78. Stephenson, "Hutterite Belief in Evil," 259.

79. Stephenson, "Hutterite Colonies," 112.

80. Stephenson, "Hutterite Belief in Evil," 259.

81. Kleinsasser, *Book 6*, 8.

82. Hutterite Mennonite Centennial Committee, *Hutterite Roots*.

83. Susie Tschetter, conversation with Stanton, July 2007.

84. Lesley Masuk, conversation with Janzen, May 1998.

85. Janzen, *Prairie People*, 190.

Chapter 8. Education and Cultural Continuity

Epigraph: Riedemann, *Account of Our Religion*, 130.

1. Janzen, *Limits on Liberty*, 160.

2. Rob Ficiru, conversation with Stanton, November 2007. Ficiru has taught at Lehrerleut colonies in Alberta for two decades.

3. Kriszintovich, *Annotated Hutterite Bibliography*, 95.

4. Jacob A. Tschetter, "Family History," n.d., provided by Wesley Tschetter.

5. Hiemstra and Brink, "Faith-Based School Choice."

6. Janzen, *Perceptions of Hutterites*, 24.

7. Mann, "Functional Autonomy." This statement is also based on conversations with dozens of "English" teachers between 1983 and 2008.

8. Stanton, "Current Status of Teachers." See also Stanton, "Stranger in Their Midst."

9. Hostetler, *Hutterite Society*, 261.

10. Janzen, *Limits on Liberty*, 143.

11. Jeremy Waltner, "Wolf Creek Student Reads Her Way to Pierre," *Freeman Courier*, April 2004.

12. Stanton, "Current Status of Teachers."

13. Robert Rhodes, "Popular Author to Speak to Hutterite Educators," *Mennonite Weekly Review*, August 14, 2006.

14. Eli Hofer, conversation with Janzen and Stanton, August 2006.

15. Hugh Smith, Rob Ficiru, Craig Whitehead, and Sjeord Schaafstema, conversations with Stanton in August 2002, August 2004, August 2005, and August 2006, respectively.

16. Rhodes, "Popular Author to Speak," 3.

17. Sam Thompson, "Hutterites Wired with TV teacher," *Portage le Prairie* (MB) *Central Plains Herald-Leader*, March 2, 2007.

18. Dora Maendel and Anna Maendel, conversation with Janzen, August 2006.

19. Shannon Vanraes, "An Art Exhibit Providing a Partial Glimpse into Hutterite Life," *Central Plains Herald-Leader*, September 23, 2006, 3; "Geography with Our Feet," *Fairholme* (MB) *Focus*, September–October 2004.

20. A detailed discussion of the Canadian educational scene is found in Janzen, *Limits on Liberty*, 142–162.

21. Tony Waldner, conversation with Janzen, July 2006.

22. Jacob Wipf, conversations with Janzen, July 2006 and July 2005; Noah Entz, correspondence with Janzen, April 2008; Maria Hofer, conversation with Janzen, July 2006.

23. Group One Schmiedeleut Educational Committee, correspondence with Peter Bjournson, February 2008; "Resources Presently Used in Hutterite Schools," unpublished document provided by Edward Kleinsasser, Crystal Spring Colony, St. Agathe, MB.

24. "German School Inservice Evaluation Sheet, Grass Ranch Colony," November 14–15, 2007, provided by John S. Hofer.

25. Peter Walpot, quoted in Jonathan Maendel, "Historical Guidelines for the Hutterite School," October 2006, 2, Rod Janzen Collection.

26. Jonathan Maendel, statement at "German School" seminar, "Herbst Deutsch Versammlung," Hutterville Colony, Stratford, SD, October 2006.

27. John S. Hofer, James Valley Colony, Elie, MB, uses this description.

28. Kleinsasser, *Book 6*, 156.

29. Rebecca Wipf, conversation with Janzen, July 2006.

30. Lindsey Maendel, "Sarah 'WurtzSarah' Maendel September 17, 1919–November 9, 1970," *Fairholme (MB) Focus*, January–March 2006.

31. Janzen, "Hutterite High School Experience."

32. Michael Thibault, "Hutterites Head to BU," *Winnipeg Free Press*, December 11, 1994; *Brandon University Hutterian Education Program General Information* (Brandon, MB: Brandon University, 2007). See also John Longhurst, "Hutterites Opt for High Tech Education," *Christian Week*, May 6, 2007.

33. Anna Maendel, conversation with Janzen, August 2006.

34. Raymond Hoeppner, conversation with Janzen, July 2007.

35. *Rural Free Press*, September 2007.

Chapter 9. Colony Structure, Governance, and Economics

Epigraph: Kleinsasser, *Book of Prefaces*, 48.

1. Buller, *Hutterites*.

2. Holzach, *Forgotten People*, 209.

3. Kenny Wollman, e-mail message to Janzen, June 2007; Noah Entz, conversation with Janzen, May 2008.

4. Jacob Gross, conversation with Janzen, May 2008.

5. Albert Wollman, conversation with Stanton, July 2005.

6. Hayden, *Seven American Utopias*, 57. See also Thompson, "Hutterite Community."

7. Hutterian Brethren, *Constitution* (1950); *Constitution* (1993); Esau, *Courts and the Colonies*, 213.

8. Hutterian Brethren, *Constitution* (1950), 44, 46.

9. Bennett, "Communes and Communitarianism," 81.

10. Janzen, *Perceptions of Hutterites*, 5–6.

11. Richard Read, "The French Fry Connection: Following One Globe-Hopping Load of Northwest Potatoes Reveals a Lot about the World Economic Crisis," *Portland Oregonian*, October 18, 1998.

12. David and Helen Hofer, conversation with Stanton, July 2006; "Coyote Pancake Mix," *Rural Free Press*, September 2007, 7.

13. Farm bosses in twenty Dariusleut, Lehrerleut, and Schmiedeleut colonies in Canada, interviews by Max Stanton. See also Agriculture and Agri-Food Canada, 2007, www.agr.gc.ca/index_e.php.

14. "The Environmental Working Groups: Farm Subsidy Data Base," USDA, Washington, DC, 2005, in Max Stanton Collection.

15. Cobb, "Color Them Plain."

16. Bennett, *Hutterian Brethren*, 270.

17. Eli Hofer, conversation with Janzen, July 2005.

18. Susan Cohn, conversation with Janzen, July 2007.

19. CEC Manitoba Hog Industry Review Board proceedings, March 14, 2007, provided by Jonathan Maendel, Baker Colony, MacGregor, MB.

20. CEC Manitoba Hog Industry Review Board proceedings, April 25, 2007.

21. Driedger, "Hutterites," 680; Bennett, "Communes and Communitarianism," 79.

22. Susan Zielinski, "Colony Industry on the Move," *Portage le Prairie (MB) Herald Leader Press*, December 22, 1999.

23. Cobb, "Color Them Plain," 3, 4.

24. John Wipf, conversation with Janzen, April 2007.

25. Rick Schrag, "Colony Expands Industry," *Freeman (SD) Courier*, June 6, 1990.

26. Norman Hofer, e-mail message to Janzen, December 2007.

27. Noah Entz, conversation with Janzen, May 2008.

28. Kenny Wollman, e-mail message to Janzen, November 2007.

29. Arnold Hofer and Conrad Hofer, conversation with Janzen, May 2007.

30. Oved, *200 Years of Communes*.

31. Janzen, *Prairie People*, 258.

32. Hofer, *The Hutterites*, 175; Janzen, *Prairie People*, 262.

33. Driedger, "Hutterites," 680; Hofer, *The Hutterites*, 175.

34. Hiebert, *Hutterite Story*, 304.

35. Paul M. Wipf, e-mail message to Janzen, July 2006.

36. Harrison, "Role of Women"; Kleinsasser, *Book 6*, 157–167; Huntington, "A Separate Culture"; Peter, *Dynamics of Hutterite Society*, 197–207; Kienzler, *Gender and Communal Longevity*; Masuk, "Patriarchy, Technology." Two important Hutterite works are Maendel, "Women in Hutterite Culture"; and Stahl, *My Hutterite Life*.

37. Moses Stoltzfus, conversation with Janzen, April 2004; Sarah Hofer, conversation with Janzen, May 2007.

38. Maendel, "Women in Hutterite Society," 21.

39. Hartse, "On the Colony," 51.

40. Conrad Hofer, conversation with Janzen, May 2007.

41. Laura Tschetter, conversation with Stanton, November 2007.

42. Kienzler, *Gender and Communal Longevity*.

43. Peter, *Dynamics of Hutterite Society*, 200, 201.

44. Schluderman and Schluderman, "Personality Development."

45. Hostetler, *Hutterite Society*, 165; Looney, "Hutterite Women and Work," 82; Hostetler and Huntington, *Hutterites in North America*, 35.

46. Kienzler, *Gender and Communal Longevity*, 83.

47. Michael Entz, conversation with Janzen, August 2006.

48. Hutterian Brethren, *Constitution* (1950), 36–37; Hutterian Brethren, *Chronicle II*, 828.

49. John E. Stahl, conversation with Stanton, July 2006.

Chapter 10. Population, Demography, and Defection

Epigraph: Walter, *Acts 2*, 110.

1. Eaton and Mayer, *Man's Capacity to Reproduce*.

2. Peter, "Decline of Population Growth"; Ingoldsby and Stanton, "Hutterites and Fertility Control"; White, "Declining Fertility," 63.

3. Peter, "Decline of Population Growth," 104. Hartse, in "On the Colony," provides similar figures.

4. Gladwell, *Tipping Point*, 180–181; Olsen, "Demography of Colony Formation."

5. Noah Entz, conversation with Stanton, July 2007.

6. Webber, *World Within*, 9–10.

7. Peters, "Pockets of High Fertility."

8. The three Leut family record books are Lehrerleut Hutterian Brethren, *Lehrerleut Hutterian Brethren Church*; Wipf and Wipf, *Dariusleut Family Record List*; and Gross, *Schmiedeleut Family Record*.

9. Lehrerleut Hutterian Brethren, *Lehrerleut Hutterian Brethren Church*, 142, 506–510.

10. Peter et al., "Dynamics of Religious Defection"; Hartse, "On the Colony," 2. Edward Boldt is the son of Peter Boldt, who for many years served as an English teacher at a Dariusleut colony in Alberta.

11. Hostetler, *Hutterite Society*, 273.

12. Kleinsasser, *Book 6*, 181–182.

13. Kleinsasser, *Book of Prefaces*, 30.

14. Ibid., 183.

15. Riedemann, *Account of Our Religion*, 110.

16. The most detailed study of Prairieleut influence on the Krimmer Mennonite Brethren is found in Plett, *Krimmer Mennonite Brethren Church*. The attraction of the Krimmer Mennonite Brethren, as well as movement between communal and noncommunal Hutterites groups, is discussed in Janzen, *Prairie People*.

17. Janzen, *Prairie People*, 120–122; "Jacob D. Hofer"; Nachtigall, "Mennonite Migration and Settlements."

18. Janzen, *Terry Miller,* 23–24.

19. Hutterite Educational Committee, *Hutterian Church Responds,* 8, 13.

20. Marty, *Short History of Christianity,* 275; Friedmann, *Hutterite Studies,* 33; Brown, *Understanding Pietism,* 30, 49; Edward Kleinsasser, conversation with Janzen, May 2008.

21. Herman Wollman, conversation with Janzen, May 2004.

22. Arnold Hofer, conversation with Janzen, May 2007.

23. Ibid.

24. Waldner, *Evangelisches Gesangbuch.*

25. Hofer, *I John* 5:1–3, 5.

26. Samuel Kleinsasser, conversation with Janzen, May 2007; Joseph Hofer, conversation with Janzen, August 2006; Gross, *The Hutterite Way,* 12.

27. Ruth Baer Lambach, e-mail conversation with Rod Janzen, July 2006.

28. Kirkby, *I Am Hutterite.*

29. Brende, *Flipping the Switch.*

30. Mackie, "Defection from the Colony"; Mary Wipf, conversation with Janzen, October 2007.

31. Ruth Lambach, e-mail message to Janzen, January 2008.

32. Rocky Cape Christian Community, "Who We Are," www.thecommonlife.com/about.

33. Peter Hoover, conversation with Janzen, May 2004.

34. Terry Miller, conversation with Janzen, August 2006.

35. David Penner and Jerald Hiebert, conversation with Janzen, July 2006. Penner is a member of the Charity Christian Fellowship in North Carolina.

36. Ivan Glick to John A. Hostetler, August 31, 1997, Archives of the Mennonite Church, Goshen, IN; Terry Miller, conversation with Janzen, August 2006.

37. Elizabeth Wipf Flinn, conversation with Janzen, March 2007.

38. *SaskTel Phonebook* (Saskatoon, SK, 2006).

39. Mack Waldner, conversation with Janzen, March 1984; Edna Hofer, "My Visit to Bon Homme Colony," 1980, provided by Terry Miller.

40. Dora Maendel, conversation with Janzen, August 2006.

41. Arnie Waldner, conversation with Stanton, May 2005.

Chapter 11. Managing Technology and Social Change

Epigraph: Hofer, *History of the Hutterites,* 81.

1. Hans Decker Jr., conversation with Janzen, July 1986; Eli Hofer, conversation with Janzen, July 2005.

2. Debbie Olsen, "Bring on the Wind," *Rural Free Press,* September 2007, 1.

3. Laura Rance, "Capitalism on the Colony," *Winnipeg Free Press,* May 19, 1987.

4. Joseph Hofer, conversation with Janzen, December 2007; Paul M. Wipf, e-mail message to Janzen, December 2007; "Is It Morally Right to Artificially Inseminate?" January 2008, provided by Henry Wurz.

5. Murphy, 2008 *Hutterite Directory*.

6. Holmes, "For Montana Sect, Cellphones Send Mixed Message," *Wall Street Journal*, September 4, 2007, A-14. Elizabeth Holmes, e-mail message to Janzen, July 2007.

7. Holmes, "Cellphones Send Mixed Message"; Holmes, conversation with Janzen, August 2007.

8. Murphy, 2008 *Hutterite Directory*.

9. Holmes, "Cellphones Send Mixed Message," front page; Kienzler, *Gender and Communal Longevity*, 81.

10. Murphy, 2008 *Hutterite Directory*.

11. Joseph Wipf, conversation with Janzen, April 1985.

12. Stephenson, *Hutterian People*, 61.

13. Anderson, "Schmiedeleut Ordnungen," 8, Rod Janzen Collection.

14. Student survey data from the course "Minority Group Relations," Brigham Young University—Hawaii, May 1995, Max Stanton, instructor.

15. Walter, *Acts* 2, 7.

Chapter 12. Relationships with Non-Hutterites

Epigraph: Hutterite Educational Committee, *Hutterian Church Responds*, 31.

1. Evenhouse, *Reasons II*, 91–102.

2. John E. Stahl, conversation with Stanton, July 1996.

3. Mrs. Eli Hofer, interview by Janzen, July 2005.

4. Samuel Hofer, conversation with Janzen, July 2006.

5. Powell and Pressburger, *49th Parallel*.

6. Nimoy, *Holy Matrimony*.

7. Wilson, "A World Apart."

8. Hofer, *Born Hutterite*.

9. Robert Rhodes, "'Dr. Phil' Visits Hutterites, Belize on Search," *Mennonite Weekly Review*, October 30, 2006.

10. Patrick Murphy, e-mail message to Janzen, January 2008.

11. Meyers Norris Penny, "Cultivating Our Relationship with You for over 45 Years," *Rural Free Press*, September 2007, 2 (advertisement).

12. In 2009 the Hutterite Prairie Market temporarily closed down.

13. Mackie, "Ethnic Stereotypes and Prejudice."

14. Janzen, *Perceptions of Hutterites*.

15. Eaton and Weil, *Culture and Mental Disorders*.

16. Beth Hanson, "Religious Community Struck by Crime Wave," *Fresno Bee*, May 9, 1995.

17. "Network Meets with Hutterites," *Montana Human Rights Network News*, May 1998.

18. Esau, *Courts and the Colonies*, 52.

19. Douglas Cobb, "Jamesville Bruderhof," 71, Rod Janzen Collection. Cobb noted 20.65 acres per person at Jamesville, compared to an average of 77.85 acres per person for non-Hutterite families in the same area.

20. Fromm, "Hoots," 161.

21. "Hutterites Take in Fire Victims," *Winnipeg Free Press*, July 27, 2007.

22. Old Elmsprings Colony, Ethan, SD, advertisement in *Freeman (SD) Courier*, September 6, 2006.

23. "Arson Smacks of Religious Bigotry," *Montana Human Rights Network News*, May 1998.

24. For example, Cleo Heinrichs, "Storytellers Share Stories of Conscientious Objectors," *Winkler (MB) Times*, March 2, 2007.

25. Amon Baer, conversation with Janzen, May 2007.

26. Norman Hofer, conversation with Janzen, May 2007.

27. Idiong, *We Failed*, 44. See also Idiong, *How to Live Wisely*.

28. Fred Tschetter, e-mail message to Stanton, July 2007.

29. Raymond Hoeppner, conversation with Janzen, July 2007.

30. Samuel Kleinsasser, conversation with Janzen, May 2007.

31. Van den Berghe and Peter, "Hutterites and Kibbutzniks." See also Oved, *Witness of the Brothers*.

32. Phyllis Franz, "Washington Sale Raises $115,000," *Mennonite Weekly Review*, October 22, 2007, 7.

33. Stanton, "Hutterites and Mormons," Max Stanton Collection.

34. Betty Lou Mercer, conversation with Janzen, May 2008. The curriculum materials were reviewed on-site.

35. Elaine Kroeker, conversation with Janzen, May 2004; e-mail message to Janzen, July 2009.

36. Stanton, "Stranger in Their Midst, 3.

37. Johann Christoph Arnold, conversation with Janzen, April 2004; Chris Zimmerman, e-mail message to Janzen, August 2006.

38. Chris Zimmerman, e-mail message to Janzen, August 2005.

39. Youmans, *Plough and the Pen*, 79.

40. Esau, *Courts and the Colonies*.

41. *King Colony members v. Montana Department of Public Health and Human Services*, No. 04-395, Supreme Court of Montana 2005, MT 302.

42. "No Photo Required for Some Hutterite Drivers," www.cbc.ca/canada/

story/2006,05/10/hutterite-photos-drivers.html (accessed July 2007); "Appeal Court Decision Favours Hutterites," *Rural Free Press*, September 2007, 2; Mike Gross and Henry Wurz, conversations with Janzen, May 2008.

43. Canadian Broadcasting System report, "Hutterites Take Rare Political Stand against Gay Marriage," www.cbc.ca/canada/story/2005/02/17/hutterite -050217.html.

44. "Hutterian Brethren Church of Canada, Statement on Bill C-38: Same Sex Marriage," 2005, Rod Janzen Collection.

45. Mike Byfield, "The Politics of Stench; Alberta Moves toward Provincially Related Siting of Intensive Livestock Operations," *Report News Magazine*, November 2001.

46. Terry Miller, conversation with Janzen, August 2006.

47. Byfield, "Politics of Stench," 37.

48. Hofer, *The Hutterites*, 175.

Chapter 13. Facing the Future

Epigraph: Kleinsasser, "Community and Ethics," 47.

1. Jesse Hofer, "Rediscovering a Tradition."

2. Gross, *Golden Years*, 48.

3. Zeman, *Anabaptists and Czech Brethren*, 262–269.

4. Rhodes, "Road of No Return," 101.

5. Boldt, "Death of Hutterite Culture."

6. Van Den Berghe and Peter, "Hutterites and Kibbutzniks, 523.

7. Holzach, *Forgotten People*, 247.

Bibliography

Publications

Allard, William A. "The Hutterites, Plain People of the West." *National Geographic,* July 1970, 98–125.

———. "Solace at Surprise Creek." *National Geographic,* June 2006, 132–147.

American Bible Society, ed. *Hutterische Bibl Tschiehten I.* New York: American Bible Society, 2002.

American Industrial Committee, ed. *Crucifixions in the 20th Century.* Chicago: American Industrial Committee, 1919.

Anderson, James. "The Pentecost Preaching of Acts 2: An Aspect of Hutterite Theology." Ph.D. diss., University of Iowa, 1972.

Anderson, Lawrence. "Hutterite Colonies: Toponymic Identification," 1983. Tony Waldner Collection, Forest River Colony, Fordville, ND.

———. "Hutterite Names, with an Emphasis on the Knels Family Name," January 1985. Tony Waldner Collection, Fordville, ND.

———. "Hutterite Ordnungen: Sixty Years of Direction from the Early Hutterite Church in South Dakota, 1876–1935," 1984. Tony Waldner Collection, Fordville, ND.

———. "The Hutterites: Spatial Considerations," 1987. Tony Waldner Collection, Forest River Colony, Fordville, ND.

———. "Prudent Plain People on the Plains and Prairies of North America: The Hutterian Brethren," 1983. Tony Waldner Collection, Forest River Colony, Fordville, ND.

Arndt, Karl J. *George Rapp's Successors and Material Heirs, 1847–1916.* Cranbury, NJ: Associated University Presses, 1971.

———. "The Harmonists and the Hutterites." *American-German Review* (August 1944): 24–27.

Bach, Marcus. *The Dream Gate.* New York: Bobbs-Merrill, 1949.

———. *Faith and Our Friends.* New York: Bobbs-Merrill, 1951.

Bainton, Roland. "The Frontier Community." *Mennonite Life,* January 1954, 34–41.

Beadle, William. *Autobiography of William Henry Harrison Beadle.* Pierre, SD: State Historical Society, 1906.

Bender, Elizabeth, trans. "The Hausbuch of Neumühl, 1558–1610: The Oldest Land Register of the Hutterian Brethren." *Mennonite Quarterly Review* (April 1974): 215–236.

———, trans. "Rule of the Teamsters." *Mennonite Quarterly Review* (April 1974): 237–245.

Bender, Harold S., ed. "A Hutterite School Discipline of 1578 and Peter Schorer's Address of 1568 to the Schoolmasters." *Mennonite Quarterly Review* (October 1931): 231–244.

Bennett, John C. "Communes and Communitarianism." *Theory and Society* (April 1975): 63–94.

———. *Hutterian Brethren: The Agricultural Economy and Social Organization of a Communal People.* Stanford, CA: Stanford University Press, 1967.

Bleibtreu, Hermann. "Marriage and Residence Patterns in a Genetic Isolate." Ph.D. diss., Harvard University, 1964.

Boldt, Edward D. "Acquiescence and Conventionality in a Communal Society." *Journal of Cross Cultural Psychology* (July 1976): 21–36.

———. "The Death of Hutterite Culture: An Alternative Interpretation." *Phylon* (October 1980): 390–395.

———. "The Recent Development of a Unique Population: The Hutterites of North America." *Prairie Forum* (1983): 235–240.

Boldt, Edward D., and Lance W. Roberts. "The Decline of Hutterite Population Growth: Causes and Consequences—A Comment." *Canadian Ethnic Studies* (1980): 112–117.

Brednich, Rolf. *The Bible and the Plow.* Ottawa, ON: National Museum of Canada, 1981.

Brende, Eric. *Better Off Flipping the Switch on Technology.* New York: HarperCollins, 2004.

Brock, Peter. *Pacifism in Europe to 1914.* Princeton, NJ: Princeton University Press, 1972.

Brown, Dale W. *Understanding Pietism.* Nappannee, IN: Evangel, 1996.

Brunt, Howard, Bruce Reeder, Peter Stephenson, Edgar Love, and Yue Chen, eds. "The Hutterite and Rural Saskatchewan Heart Health Surveys: A Comparison of Physical and Laboratory Measures." In *Agricultural Health and Safety,* edited by Helen H. McDuffie, James A. Dosman, Karen M. Semchuk, Stephen A. Olenchock, and Ambikaipakan Senthilselvan, 513–520. New York: Lewis, 1995.

Buckwalter, Stephen. "Review of Astrid von Schlachta, 'Hutterische Konfession und Tradition (1578–1619): Etabliertes Lebens zwischen Ordnung und Ambivalenz.'" *Mennonite Quarterly Review* (October 2006): 691–693.

Chmielewski, Wendy, Louis J. Kern, and Marlyn Klee-Hartzell, eds. *Women in Spiritual and Communitarian Societies in the United States.* Syracuse, NY: Syracuse University Press, 1993.

Christopher, Stefan C., ed. "A Description of the Beginning of True Christian Community among the Schmiedeleut Hutterians, as It Began by the Power of the Spirit," 1972. Heritage Hall Museum and Archives, Freeman, SD.

Clark, Peter Gordon. "Leadership Succession among the Hutterites." *Canadian Review of Sociology and Anthropology* (Summer 1977): 294–302.

Cobb, Kathy. "Color Them Plain but Successful: Growing Hutterite Colonies Find Successful and Sizable Niches in District Economy." *Fedgazette*, January 2006, 1–5.

Correll, Ernst, ed. "Mennonite Immigration into Manitoba: Sources and Documents, 1872, 1873." *Mennonite Quarterly Review* (July 1937): 196–227; (October 1937): 267–283.

———. "President Grant and the Mennonite Immigration from Russia." *Mennonite Quarterly Review* (April 1935): 144–152.

Cross, David. *Hutterite CO's in World War One.* Hawley, MN: Spring Prairie, 1998.

Donner, Heinrich. "Report of the Anabaptist Brethren at Wishink in the Ukraine." In Hutterite Mennonite Centennial Committee, *Hutterite Roots*, 119–127.

Driedger, Leo. "Hutterites." In *Encyclopedia of Canada's Peoples*, edited by Paul Magocsi. Toronto: University of Toronto Press, 1999.

Eaton, Joseph W., and Albert Mayer. *Man's Capacity to Reproduce: The Demography of a Unique Population.* Glencoe, IL: Free Press, 1954.

———. "The Social Biology of a Very High Fertility among the Hutterites: The Demography of a Unique Population." *Human Biology* (January 1950): 206–264.

Eaton, Joseph W., and Robert J. Weil. *Culture and Mental Disorders.* Glencoe, IL: Free Press, 1955.

Eaton, Joseph W., Robert K. Weil, and Bert Kaplan. "The Hutterite Mental Health Study." *Mennonite Quarterly Review* (January 1951): 47–65.

Ehrenpreis, Andreas. *An Epistle on Brotherly Community: The Highest Command of Love.* Rifton, NY: Plough, 1978.

Eichler, Evan. "Hutterian Surnames," 1998. Rod Janzen Collection.

Elshtain, Jean Bethke. "Does, or Should, Teaching Reflect the Religious Perspective of the Teacher?" In *Religion, Scholarship & Higher Education: Perspectives, Models, and Future Prospects*, edited by Andrea Sterk, 193–201. Notre Dame, IN: University of Notre Dame Press, 2002.

Emerson, Robert M., Rachel I. Fretz, and Linda L. Shaw, eds. *Writing Ethnographic Fieldnotes*. Chicago: University of Chicago Press, 1995.

Engels, Friedrich. *The Peasant's War in Germany*. Moscow: Foreign Languages, 1956.

Epp, David H. *Johann Cornies*. Winnipeg: CMB, 1995.

Esau, Alvin. *The Courts and the Colonies*. Vancouver: University of British Columbia Press, 2004.

Evenhouse, Bill. *Reasons II: Sects and Cults with Christian Roots*. Grand Rapids, MI: Christian Reformed Church, 1981.

Fischer, Hans. *Jakob Huter: Leben, Froemmigkeit, Briefe*. Newton: Mennonite Publication Office, 1956.

Fleming, John, and Michael Rowan. *Folk Furniture of Canada's Doukhobors, Hutterites, Mennonites, and Ukrainians*. Edmonton: University of Alberta Press, 2004.

Flint, David. *The Hutterites: A Study in Prejudice*. Toronto: Oxford University Press, 1975.

Friedmann, Robert. "The Epistles of the Hutterian Brethren." *Mennonite Quarterly Review* (July 1946): 1–31.

——. *Hutterite Studies*. Goshen, IN: Mennonite Historical Society, 1961.

——. "Hutterite Worship and Preaching." *Mennonite Quarterly Review* (January 1966): 5–26.

——. Introduction to "Article Three of the Great Article Book: A Notable Hutterite Document concerning True Surrender and Christian Community of Goods." Translated by Kathleen Hasenberg. *Mennonite Quarterly Review* (January 1957): 22–62.

——. "Peter Riedemann: Early Anabaptist Leader." *Mennonite Quarterly Review* (January 1970): 5–44.

——. "The Reestablishment of Communal Life among the Hutterites in Russia (1858)." *Mennonite Quarterly Review* (April 1965): 147–152.

Friesen, John J., ed. *Peter Riedemann's Hutterite Confession of Faith*. Scottdale, PA: Herald Press, 1999.

Fromm, Peter. "Hoots." In *The Best of Montana's Short Fiction*, edited by William Kittredge and Allen Morris Jones, 151–170. Guildford, CT: Lyons Press, 2004.

Funk, Merle J. F. "Divided Loyalties: Mennonite and Hutterite Responses to the United States at War, Hutchinson County, South Dakota, 1917, 1918." *Mennonite Life*, December 1997, 24–32.

Gaddis, John Lewis. *The Landscape of History: How Historians Map the Past.* Oxford: Oxford University Press, 2002.

Geertz, Clifford. *The Interpretation of Cultures.* New York: Basic Books, 1973.

Gibb, Donald. "Hutterite Business Ventures and Dealings, 1981–1997," 1997. Patrick Murphy, James Valley Colony, Elie, MB.

Giesinger, Adam. *From Catherine to Khrushchev: The Story of Russia's Germans.* Lincoln, NE: Society of Germans from Russia, 1981.

Gladwell, Malcolm. *The Tipping Point: How Little Things Can Make a Big Difference.* New York: Back Bay Books, 2002.

Goertz, Reuben. *Princes, Potentates, and Plain People.* Sioux Falls, SD: Center for Western Studies, 1994.

Grimmelshausen, H. J. C. von. *The Adventures of a Simpleton.* New York: Frederick Ungar, 1962.

Gross, David, ed. *Schmiedeleut Family Record.* High Bluff, MB: Sommerfield Colony, 2006.

Gross, David P., and Arnold M. Hofer, eds., "The Neu Hutterthaler Church Record Book," 1997. Heritage Hall Museum and Archives, Freeman, SD.

Gross, Leonard, ed. "'Concerning the Sword': A Hutterian Apologia of 1577." Translated by Elizabeth Bender. *Mennonite Quarterly Review* (January 2009): 49–112.

———. *The Golden Years of the Hutterites.* Scottdale, PA: Herald Press, 1997.

Gross, Paul S. *The Hutterite Way.* Saskatoon, SK: Freeman, 1965.

Gross, Paul S., and Elizabeth Bender, trans., "A Hutterite Sermon of the 17th Century." *Mennonite Quarterly Review* (January 1970): 59–71.

Guericke, Justina. *Precious Memories of a Historical House.* Freeman, SD: Self-published, 1985.

Harder, Leland. "The Russian Mennonites and American Democracy under Grant." In *From the Steppes to the Prairies* (1874–1949), edited by Cornelius Krahn, 48–64. Newton, KS: Mennonite Publication Office, 1949.

Harrison, Wes. *Andreas Ehrenpreis and Hutterite Faith and Practice.* Kitchener, ON: Herald Press, 1997.

———. "The Role of Women in Anabaptist Thought and Practice: The Hutterite Experience of the Sixteenth and Seventeenth Centuries." *Sixteenth Century Journal* (Spring 1992): 49–69.

Hartse, Carolyn M. "On the Colony: Social and Religious Change among Contemporary Hutterites." Ph.D. diss., University of New Mexico, 1993.

Hartzog, Sandra Hitchens. "Population Genetic Studies of a Human Isolate, the Hutterites of North America." Ph.D. diss., University of Massachusetts, 1971.

Hayden, Deloris. *Seven American Utopias: The Architecture of Communal Societies, 1790–1975.* Cambridge, MA: MIT Press, 1976.

Hiebert, Clarence. *Brothers in Deed to Brothers in Need: A Scrapbook about Mennonite Immigrants from Russia, 1870–1885.* North Newton, KS: Faith and Life Press, 1974.

Hiebert, Jerald. *The Hutterite Story of a Pure Church: A Story of Dariusleut Alberta Hutterites, 1918–2000.* Raymond, AB: Self-published, 2006.

Hiemstra, John L., and Robert A. Brink. "Faith-Based School Choice in Alberta: The Advent of a Pluriform Public Model?" 2007. Max Stanton Collection.

Hoehnle, Peter. "Michael Hofer: A Communitarian in Two Worlds." *Communal Societies* (2002): 83–86.

Hofer, Arnold M. *The Diaries of Joseph "Yos" Hofer.* Freeman, SD: Hutterite Mennonite Centennial Committee, 1997.

Hofer, Jacob E. "A History of the Neu Hutterthaler Church, Including the European Background," senior seminar paper, Goshen College, Goshen, IN, 1953. Heritage Museum and Archives, Freeman, SD.

Hofer, Jacob M., ed. "The Diary of Paul Tschetter." *Mennonite Quarterly Review* (July 1931): 112–127; (October 1931): 198–219.

Hofer, Jesse. "Rediscovering a Tradition & Vision for Hutterite Mission." *Preservings* 27 (2007): 71–78.

Hofer, John S., ed. *I John 5:1–3: The Victory of Faith Sermon.* Elie, MB: James Valley Colony, n.d.

———. *A History of the Hutterites.* Winnipeg: W. K. Printers, 1982.

Hofer, Joshua. *Japanese Hutterites: A Visit to the Owa Community.* Elie, MB: James Valley Book Centre, 1981.

———, ed. "Sermon on Acts 2:40–42," unpublished translation, 1985. Elie, MB: James Valley Colony.

———, ed. "Sermon on Matthew 6," unpublished translation, 1985. Elie, MB: James Valley Colony.

Hofer, Samuel. *The Hutterites: Lives and Images of a Communal People.* Saskatoon, SK: Hofer, 1998.

Holzach, Michael. *The Forgotten People: A Year among the Hutterites.* Sioux Falls, SD: Ex Machina, 1993.

Hoover, Walter. *Hutterian-English Dictionary.* Saskatoon, SK: Walter Hoover, 1997.

———. *The Hutterian Language.* Saskatoon, SK: Walter Hoover, 1997.

Horsch, John A. *Hutterian Brethren.* Scottdale, PA: Herald Press, 1931.

Horst, Irvin B. "Pieter Cornelisz Plockhoy: An Apostle of the Collegiants." *Mennonite Quarterly Review* (July 1949): 161–185.

Hostetler, John A. *Hutterite Society.* Baltimore: Johns Hopkins University Press, 1974.

Hostetler, John A., Leonard Gross, and Elizabeth Bender, eds. *Selected Hutterian Documents in Translation.* Philadelphia: Temple University Press, 1975.

Hostetler, John A., and Gertrude Huntington. *The Hutterites in North America*. New York: Harcourt Brace, 1996.

Howells, W. W. *Hutterite Age Differences in Body Measurements*. Cambridge, MA: Peabody Museum, 1970.

Huntington, Gertrude. "Children of the Hutterites." *Natural History* (February 1981): 34–47.

———. "A Separate Culture: Hutterite Women in the Colony," 1995. Archives of the Mennonite Church, Goshen, IN.

———. "Supplementary Essay: A Comparison: Hutterite Women and Their Families." In *Working Together*, edited by Seena B. Kohl, 110–125. Toronto: Holt, Rinehart, and Winston of Canada, 1976.

Hutter, Jacob. *Brotherly Faithfulness: Epistles from a Time of Persecution*. Rifton, NY: Plough, 1979.

Hutterian Brethren. *Brothers Unite*. Rifton, NY: Plough, 1988.

———. *The Chronicle of the Hutterian Brethren I*. St. Agathe, MB: Crystal Spring Colony, 1987.

———. *The Chronicle of the Hutterian Brethren II*. St. Agathe, MB: Crystal Spring Colony, 1996.

———. *Constitution of the Hutterian Brethren Church and Rules as to Community of Property*. Winnipeg: E. A. Fletcher Barristers and Solicitors, 1950.

———. *Constitution of the Hutterian Brethren Church and Rules as to Community of Property*. Calgary: MacLeod Dixon Barristers and Solicitors, 1993.

———. *Das Kleine Gesangbuch für Allgemein Gebrauch*. MacGregor, MB: Baker Colony, 1995.

———, ed. *Die Lieder der Hutterischen Brüder Gesangbuch*. Scottdale, PA: Herald Press, 1914.

———. *Gesangbuch: Eine Sammlung Geistlicher Lieder*. Aylmer, ON: Altkolonie Mennoniten Gemeinde, 2001.

———. *Gesangbuchlein*. Hawley, MN: Spring Prairie, 1998.

Hutterian Educational Committee, ed. *The Hutterian Church Responds to Questions of Faith*. Elie, MB: James Valley Book Centre, 2000.

Hutterite Mennonite Centennial Committee, eds. *A History of the Hutterite-Mennonites*. Freeman, SD: Hutterite Mennonite Centennial Committee, 1974.

———. *Hutterite Roots*. Freeman, SD: Hutterite Mennonite Centennial Committee, 1985.

Idiong, Inno. *How to Live Wisely in the Midst of Acute Poverty*. Rifton, NY: Plough, 1992.

———. *We Failed More than Once, but God's Love Lingers On*. Rifton, NY: Plough, 1994.

Ingoldsby, Bron. "Group Conformity and the Amplification of Deviance: A Comparison of Hutterite and Mormon Dress Codes." *Communal Societies* (2002): 87–98.

Ingoldsby, Bron, and Max Stanton. "The Hutterites and Fertility Control." *Journal of Comparative Family Studies* (Spring 1988): 137–142.

Janke, Dwayne. "They're Here: Bible Stories, Written in Their Mother Tongue, Come to the Hutterites for the First Time." *Word Alive*, Fall 2008, 4–13.

Jansen, Peter. *Memoirs of Peter Jansen: The Record of a Busy Life, an Autobiography.* Beatrice, NB: Self-published, 1921.

Janzen, Peter. "Diary." In Voth, *House of Jacob*, 67.

Janzen, Rod, ed. *God's Salvation Plan.* Hawley, MN: Spring Prairie Colony, 1988.

———. "The Hutterite High School Experience: Boundary Maintenance on the Prairies." *Syzygy* (July 1993): 339–348.

———. "The Hutterites and the Bruderhof: The Relationship between an Old Order Religious Society and a 20th Century Communal Group." *Mennonite Quarterly Review* (October 2005): 505–544.

———. "Jacob D. Hofer, Evangelist, Minister, and Carpenter." *California Mennonite Historical Society Newsletter*, May 1994, 1–8.

———. "Paul Tschetter's Chicago Fire Hymn." *Mennonite Quarterly Review* (April 2007): 261–272.

———. *Paul Tschetter: The Story of a Hutterite Immigrant Leader, Pioneer, and Pastor.* Eugene, OR: Wipf & Stock, 2009.

———. *Perceptions of the South Dakota Hutterites in the 1980s.* Freeman, SD: Freeman, 1984.

———. "The Prairieleut: A Forgotten Hutterite People." *Communal Societies* (1994): 67–89.

———. *The Prairie People: Forgotten Anabaptists.* Hanover, NH: University Press of New England, 1999.

———. *The Rise and Fall of Synanon: A California Utopia.* Baltimore: Johns Hopkins University Press, 2001.

———. *Terry Miller: The Pacifist Politician, from Hutterite Colony to State Capitol.* Freeman, SD: Freeman, 1986.

Janzen, Rod, Stephen Scott, and Hannah Scott. "Communal Aspects of Old Order River Brethren Life." *Communal Societies* (2006), 43–64.

Janzen, William. *Limits on Liberty: The Experience of Mennonite, Hutterite, and Doukhobour Communities in Canada.* Toronto: University of Toronto Press, 1990.

Kalesny, Frantisek. *Habani Na Slovensku.* Slovakia (no city given): Tatran, 1981.

Kaplan, Bert, and Thomas F. A. Plaut. *Personality in a Communal Society.* Lawrence: University of Kansas Press, 1956.

Karolevitz, Robert. *Yankton: A Pioneer Past.* Aberdeen, SD: Northern Dakota State College Press, 1972.

Kienzler, Hanna. *Gender and Communal Longevity among Hutterites.* Aachen, Germany: Shaker Verlag, 2005.

Kimmelman, Michael. *The Accidental Masterpiece: On the Art of Life and Vice-Versa.* New York: Penguin, 2005.

Kingsolver, Barbara. *The Poisonwood Bible.* New York: HarperCollins, 1999.

Kirkby, Mary-Ann. *I Am Hutterite.* Prince Albert, SK: Polka Dot Press, 2007.

Klassen, Peter J. *The Economics of Anabaptism.* London: Mouton, 1964.

Kleinsasser, Amos, ed. *Our Journey of Faith: Hutterthal Mennonite Church, 1879–2004.* Freeman, SD: Hutterthal Mennonite Church, 2004.

Kleinsasser, Jacob. *A Book of Prefaces, Volume 2.* St. Agathe, MB: Crystal Spring Colony, 1996.

———. *Book 6: Hutterian Teachings.* St. Agathe, MB: Crystal Spring Colony, 2001.

———. *Funeral Teachings.* St. Agathe, MB: Crystal Spring Colony, 2003.

———, ed. *A Hutterite Sermon on Luke 23:24–26.* St. Agathe, MB: Crystal Spring Colony, 1982.

———. *Seeking Purity: A Talk to Young People.* St. Agathe, MB: Crystal Spring Colony, 2003.

———. *Teachings for the Celebration of Easter and the Lord's Supper.* St. Agathe, MB: Crystal Spring Colony, 1999.

———. *Teachings on John.* St. Agathe, MB: Crystal Spring Colony, 1999.

Kleinsasser, Jacob, Jacob Hofer, Hardy Arnold, and Daniel Moody. *For the Sake of Divine Truth.* Rifton, NY: Plough, 1974.

Kleinsasser, Samuel. "Community and Ethics," 1993. Provided by Leonard Gross, Goshen, IN.

Klusch, Horst. *Sieben Burgische Topkerkunst aus drei Jahrhunderten.* Bucharest: Kriterion Verlag, 1980.

Kraybill, Donald B., and Carl D. Bowman. *On the Backroad to Heaven: Old Order Hutterites, Mennonites, Amish, and Brethren.* Baltimore: Johns Hopkins University Press, 2001.

Krisztinkovich, Bela. *Haban Pottery.* Budapest: Corvina Press, 1962.

Krisztinkovich, Maria, trans. *An Annotated Hutterite Bibliography.* Kitchener, ON: Pandora Press, 1998.

———. "Some Further Notes on the Hutterites in Transylvania." *Mennonite Quarterly Review* (April 1963): 203–213.

Kuentsche, Hans Friedrich, "The Pentecost Lehren." In Anderson, "Pentecost Preaching of Acts 2."

Kuleshov, Maxim, ed. *History of Raditschewa.* N.p, 1999. Wesley Tschetter Collection, Brookings, SD.

Kulig, Judith C., Cathy J. Meyer, Shirley A. Hill, Cathy E. Handley, et al. "Refusals and Delay of Immunization within Southwest Alberta: Understanding

Alternative Beliefs and Religious Perspectives." *Canadian Journal of Public Health* (March–April 2002): 109–112.

Lambach, Ruth Baer. "Colony Girl." In Chmielewski, Kern, and Klee-Hartzell, *Women in Societies*, 241–255.

Lee, Dallas. *The Cotton Patch Evidence: The Story of Clarence Jordan and the Koinonia Farm.* New York: Harper and Row, 1971.

Lehrerleut Hutterian Brethren, eds. *Lehrerleut Hutterian Brethren Church Family Records, 1771–2006.* Sunburst, MT: Rimrock Colony, 2007.

Looney, Patricia L. "Hutterite Women and Work." Master's thesis, University of Victoria, 1986.

Lorenz-Andreasch, Helga. *Mir Sein Ja Kolla Teitschverderber: Die Sprache der Schmiedeleut-Hutterer in Manitoba, Kanada.* Vienna: Edition Praesens, Verlag für Literatur-und Sprachwissenschaft, 2004.

Macdonald, Sharon. *Reimagining Culture: Histories, Identities, and the Gaelic Renaissance.* Oxford: Berg, 1997.

Mackie, Marlene. "The Defection from the Hutterite Colony." Master's thesis, University of Alberta, 1975.

———. "Ethnic Stereotypes and Prejudice in Alberta: Alberta Indians, Hutterites, and Ukrainians." *Canadian Ethnic Studies* (1974): 39–52.

Maendel, Dora. "Hutterite Christmas Traditions." *Fairholme Focus* (November–December 2002): 7–8.

Maendel, Linda. *Linda's Gluckliche Tag.* MacGregor, MB: Hutterian Brethren Book Centre, 2006.

Maendel, Rachel. *Rachel, a Hutterite Girl.* Scottdale, PA: Herald, 1999.

Maendel, Selma. "Women in Hutterite Culture." *Fairholme Focus* (November–December 1999): 20–21.

Manfred, Frederick. *The Chokecherry Tree.* Albuquerque: University of New Mexico Press, 1975.

———. *Sons of Adam.* New York: Crown, 1980.

Mange, Arthur P. *The Population Structure of a Human Isolate.* Madison: University of Wisconsin Press, 1963.

Mann, George A. "Functional Autonomy among English School Teachers in the Hutterite Colonies of Southern Alberta: A Study of Social Control." Ph.D. diss., University of Colorado, 1974.

Martens, Helen. *Hutterite Songs.* Kitchener, ON: Pandora Press, 2001.

Martens, Larry. "Musical Thought and Practice in the Hutterite Community." Master's thesis, University of Kansas, 1960.

Martin, Alice O. "The Founder Effect in a Human Isolate: Evolutionary Implications." *American Journal of Physical Anthropology* (October 1970): 351–368.

Marty, Martin. *A Short History of Christianity.* Cleveland: World, 1959.

Marx, Karl. *Critique of the Gotha Program.* New York: International, 1938.

Masuk, Lesley. "Patriarchy, Technology, and the Lives of Hutterite Women: A Field Study." Master's thesis, University of Saskatchewan, 1998.

Mendel, Jacob J. *A History of the People of East Freeman, Silver Lake, and West Freeman.* Freeman, SD: Pine Hill Press, 1961.

Michener, James. *Centennial.* New York: Random House, 1974.

Miller, Ann, and Peter H. Stephenson. "Jakob Hutter: An Interpretaion of the Individual Man and His People." *Ethos* (Fall 1980): 229–252.

Morgan, Kenneth T. "Mortality Changes in the Hutterite Brethren of Alberta and Saskatchewan, Canada." *Human Biology* (April 1983): 89–99.

Morgan, Kenneth T., Mary Holmes, Michael Grace, Sam Kemel, and Diane Robson, eds. "Patterns of Cancer in Geographic and Endogamous Subdivisions of the Hutterite Brethren of Canada." *American Journal of Physical Anthropology* (January 1983): 3–10.

Morgan, Kenneth T., Mary Holmes, J. Schlaut, L. Marchuk, T. Kovithavongs, F. Pazderka, and J. B. Dossetor, eds. "Genetic Variability of HLA in the Dariusleut Hutterites: A Comparative Genetic Analysis of the Hutterites, the Amish, and Other Selected Caucasian Populations." *American Journal of Human Genetics* (April 1980): 246–257.

Murphy, Patrick, ed. *2008 Hutterite Directory.* Elie, MB: James Valley Colony, 2008.

———. "Warum ich Hutterer wurde." In Schlacta, *Die Hutterer,* 214–218.

Nachtigall, Gary. "Mennonite Migration and Settlements." Master's thesis, Fresno State University, 1972.

Norris, Kathleen. *Dakota: A Spiritual Geography.* Boston: Houghton Mifflin, 1993

Norton, David L. *Imagination, Understanding, and the Virtue of Liberality.* Lanham, MD: Rowman and Littlefield, 1996.

Ober, Carole. "Complex Trait Mapping in the Hutterites." http://genes.uchicago .edu/hutterite/home.html, 2006.

O'Brien, E., P. A. Kerber, C. B Jorde, and A. A. Rogers, eds. "Founder Effect: An Assessment of Variation in Genetic Contributions among Founders." *Human Biology* (April 1994): 185–204.

Olsen, Caroline Lee. "The Demography of New Colony Formation in a Human Isolate." Ph.D. diss., University of Michigan, 1976.

Oved, Yaacov. *200 Years of American Communes.* Edison, NJ: Transaction, 1987.

———. *The Witness of the Brothers: A History of the Bruderhof.* London: Transaction, 1996.

Packull, Werner C. *Hutterite Beginnings: Communitarian Experiments during the Reformation.* Baltimore: Johns Hopkins University Press, 1995.

———. *Mysticism and the Early South German-Austrian Anabaptist Movement, 1525–1531.* Scottdale, PA: Herald Press, 1977.

———. *Peter Riedemann: Shaper of the Hutterite Tradition.* Kitchener, ON: Pandora Press, 2007.

Peter, Karl A. "The Certainty of Salvation: Ritualization of Religion and Economic Rationality among Hutterites." *Comparative Studies in Society and History* (April 1983): 222–240.

———. "The Decline of Hutterite Population Growth." *Canadian Ethnic Studies* (1980): 97–110.

———. *The Dynamics of Hutterite Society: An Analytical Approach.* Edmonton, AB: University of Alberta Press, 1987.

———. "The Hutterite Economy: Recent Changes and Their Social Correlates." *Anthropos* (October 1983): 535–546.

———. "The Instability of the Community of Goods in the Social History of the Hutterites," 1975. Rod Janzen Collection.

Peter, Karl A., Edward D. Boldt, Ian Whitaker, and Lance W. Roberts, eds. "The Dynamics of Religious Defection among Hutterites." *Journal for the Scientific Study of Religion* (December 1982): 327–337.

Peter, Karl A., and Franziska Peter, eds. *Hutterite C.O.'s and Their Treatment in the U.S. Army during World War I.* Cranford, MB: Lakeside Colony, 1982.

Peter, Karl A., and Ian Whitaker. "The Acquisition of Personal Property among Hutterites and Its Social Dimensions." *Anthropologica* (November 1981): 145–155.

———. "Hutterite Perceptions of Psychophysiological Characteristics." *Journal of Social Biological Structures* (January 1984): 1–8.

Peters, Victor. *All Things Common.* Minneapolis: University of Minnesota Press, 1965.

———. "Pockets of High Fertility in the United States." *Population Bulletin* (November 1968): 26–44.

Pitzer, Donald E. *America's Communal Utopias.* Chapel Hill: University of North Carolina Press, 1997.

Plett, Cornelius F. *The Story of the Krimmer Mennonite Brethren Church.* Winnipeg: Kindred Press, 1985.

Rath, George. *The Black Sea Germans in the Dakotas.* Freeman, SD: Pine Hill Press, 1972.

Redekop, Calvin, and John A. Hostetler. "The Plain People: An Interpretation." *Mennonite Quarterly Review* (October 1977): 266–277.

Redfield, Robert. "The Folk Society." *New American Journal of Sociology* (January 1947): 292–305.

Rhodes, Robert. *Nightwatch: Alone on the Prairie with the Hutterites.* Intercourse, PA: Good Books, 2009.

———. "The Road of No Return." *Communal Societies* (2001): 99–101.

Riedemann, Peter. *An Account of Our Religion, Doctrine, and Faith.* Rifton, NY: Plough, 1970.

Rothkegel, Martin. "The Hutterian Brethren and the Printed Book." *Mennonite Quarterly Review* (January 2000): 51–85.

Ryan, John. *The Agricultural Economy of Manitoba Hutterite Colonies.* Toronto: McClelland and Stewart, 1977.

Sapir, Edward. *Culture, Language, and Personality.* Berkeley: University of California Press, 1958.

Scheer, Herfried. "The Hutterian German Dialect." *Mennonite Quarterly Review* (July 1980): 229–243.

Schell, Herbert S. *History of South Dakota.* Pierre: South Dakota State Historical Society Press, 2004.

Scheuner, Gottfried. *Inspiration Historie, 1867–1876.* Amana, IA: Self-published, 1900. Amana Historical Society Archives, Amana, IA.

Schlabach, Theron, ed. "An Account by Jakob Waldner: Diary of a Conscientious Objector in World War I." *Mennonite Quarterly Review* (January 1974): 73–111.

Schlachta, Astrid von. "'Against Selfishness': Community of Goods as Life Choice." In *Commoners and Community*, edited by C. Arnold Snyder, 257–279. Kitchener, ON: Pandora Press, 2002.

———. *Die Hutterer zwischen Tirol und Nord Amerika: Eine Reise durch die Jahrhunderte.* Innsbruck: Universitätsverlag Wagner, 2006.

———. "'Searching through the Nations': Tasks and Problems of Sixteenth-Century Hutterian Missions." *Mennonite Quarterly Review* (October 2000): 27–49.

Schluderman, Shirin, and Edward Schluderman. "Personality Development in Hutterite Communal Society." In *The Canadian Ethnic Mosaic: A Quest for Identity*, edited by Leo Driedger, 169–198. Toronto: University of Toronto Press, 1998.

Scott, Stephen. *Why Do They Dress That Way?* Intercourse, PA: Good Books, 1997.

Siegel, Bernard. "Deference Structuring and Environmental Stress." *American Journal of Sociology* (July 1970): 11–32.

Small, Meredith F. "Love with the Proper Stranger." *Natural History* (September 1998): 14–19.

Smith, C. Henry. *The Coming of the Russian Mennonites: An Episode in the Settling of the Last Frontier.* Berne, IN: Mennonite Book Concern, 1927.

Smith, Hugh Alan. *When Lightning Strikes.* Scottdale, PA: Herald Press, 2001.

———. *When the River Calls.* Scottdale, PA: Herald Press, 2004.

Smucker, Donovan E. *The Sociology of Canadian Mennonites, Hutterites, and Amish: A Bibliography with Annotations.* Waterloo, ON: Wilfred Laurier University Press, 1977.

Stahl, Lisa Marie. *My Hutterite Life.* Helena, MT: Farcountry Press 2003.

Stahl, Solomon. *The History of Bon Homme Colony, Manitoba.* Elie, MB: Bon Homme Colony, 2001.

Stanton, Max. *All Things Common: A Comparison of Israeli, Hutterite, and Latter Day Saint Communalism.* La'ie, HI: Brigham Young University Press, 1992.

———. "By Their Dots You Shall Know Them," 1990. Max Stanton Collection.

———. "Current Status of Non-Hutterite Teachers in Hutterite Colonies," 1992. Max Stanton Collection.

———. "Getting Lost and Finding Tranquility," 1987. Max Stanton Collection.

———. "Hutterites." In *Encyclopedia of Community, Volume 2,* edited by Karen Christensen and David Levinson, 629–633. Thousand Oaks, CA: Sage, 2003.

———. "The Maintenance of the Hutterite Way." *Family Science Review* (November 1989): 373–388.

———. "Patterns of Kinship and Residence." In *Families in Multicultural Context,* edited by Bron Ingoldsby and Suzanne Smith, 79–98. New York: Guildford Press, 1994.

———. "A Stranger in Their Midst: The 'English' Teacher in the Hutterite Colony School," 2002. Max Stanton Collection.

Stayer, James M. *The German Peasant's War and Anabaptist Community of Goods.* Montreal: McGill/Queens University Press, 1991.

Stephenson, Peter H. "Gender, Aging, and Mortality in Hutterite Society: A Critique of the Doctrine of Specific Etiology." *Medical Anthropology* (Fall 1985): 355–365.

———. "He Died Too Quick! The Process of Dying in a Hutterian Colony." *Omega* (1983): 127–134.

———. *The Hutterian People: Ritual and Rebirth in the Evolution of Communal Life.* Lanham, MD: University Press of America, 1991.

———. "Hutterite Belief in Evil Eye: Beyond Paranoia and towards a General Theory of Invidia." *Culture, Medicine, and Psychiatry* (September 1979): 247–265.

———. "Hutterite Colonies: Stress and Coping in the Context of Communal Life." In *Ethnicity, Immigration, and Psychopathology,* edited by Ihsan al-Issa and Michel Tousignant, 107–118. New York: Plenum Press, 1997.

———. "Pshrien: Hutterite Belief in Evil Eye and Concepts of Child Abuse." In *Canadian Ethnology Service Paper No. 2,* edited by John Ryan. Ottawa: National Museum of Man, 1980.

Theroux, Paul. *The Mosquito Coast.* Boston: Houghton Mifflin, 1984.

Thompson, William P. "Hutterite Community: Archetype Ark: An Historical Study of the Architecture and Planning of a Communal Society." Ph.D. diss., Cornell University, 1977.

Tschetter, Joseph W. "A Brief Biography of Paul Tschetter, 1842–1919." In Hofer, "Diary of Paul Tschetter," 112–113.

Tschetter, Paul G. "Die Auswanderer." In *People of the Old Missoury*, edited by Nancy M. Peterson, 89–98. Frederick, CO: Renaissance House, 1989.

Tschetter, Peter. *Europe 84*. Flandreau, SD: Self-published, 1984. Rod Janzen Collection.

———, trans. "Sermon on Acts 2:43–44," n.d. Rod Janzen Collection.

Ugwu-Oju, Dympna. *What Will My Mother Say? A Tribal Girl Comes of Age in America*. Chicago: Bonus Books, 1995.

Unruh, John D. *A Century of Mennonites in Dakota*. Pierre: South Dakota Historical Collections, 1972.

Urry, James. *None but Saints: The Transformation of Mennonite Life in Russia, 1789–1889*. Winnipeg: Hyperion Press, 1988.

Van Den Berghe, Pierre L., and Karl A. Peter. "Hutterites and Kibbutzniks: A Tale of Nepotistic Communism." *Man* (September 1988): 522–539.

Vonk, Martine. "Schwartz Values and the Hutterites," 2005. Rod Janzen Collection.

Voth, Frances Janzen. *The House of Jacob: The Story of Jacob Janzen, 1822–1885, and His Descendents*. Tucson, AZ: Self-published, 1984.

Wade, Nicholas. *Before the Dawn: Recovering the Lost History of Our Ancestors*. New York: Penguin, 2006.

Waldner, Gary. "Among the Habaner of Czechoslovakia." *Mennonite Life* (April 1966), 84–91.

Waldner, Tony, ed. *Evangelisches Gesangbuch*. Hawley, MN: Spring Prairie Colony, 1984.

———. *History of Forest River Community, 1949–1989*. Hawley, MN: Spring Prairie, 1990.

Walter, Elias, trans. *Preface and Teaching: Acts 2*. Winnipeg, MB: Hutterian Brethren, 1901.

Waltner, Emil, ed. *Banished for Faith*. Freeman, SD: Pine Hill Press, 1968.

Webber, George. *A World Within*. Calgary, AB: Fifth House, 2005.

White, Katherine. "Declining Fertility among North American Hutterites: The Use of Birth Control within a Dariusleut Colony." *Social Biology* (Spring 2002): 58–73.

Whorf, Benjamin. *Language, Thought, and Reality*. Cambridge: MIT Press, 1956.

Wilder, Laura Ingalls. *On the Way Home: The Diary of a Trip from South Dakota to Mansfield, Missouri, in 1894*. New York: Harper and Row, 1962.

Wilson, Laura. *Hutterites of Montana*. New Haven, CT: Yale University Press, 2000.

———. "A World Apart." *Mirabella*, September 1994, 106–117.

Wipf, Butch. *Hutterian Songs: Book 1: A Collection—Songs of Christian Faith*. Brandon, MB: Decker Hutterian Colony, 2003.

———. *Hutterian Songs: Book 2: A Collection—Songs of Christian Faith*. Elkton, SD: Decker Hutterian Colony, 2006.

Wipf, Joseph K., and Dave S. Wipf, eds. *Dariusleut Family Record List*. Cranford, AB: Lakeside Colony, 2006.

Wurz, Edna, and Catherine Masuk. *Rooted and Grounded in Love: The History and Family Records of the Langham Prairie People*. Saskatoon, SK: Edna Wurtz and Catherine Masuk, 2000.

Youmans, Vance Joseph. *The Plough and the Pen: Paul S. Gross and the Establishment of the Spokane Hutterian Brethren*. Boone, NC: Parkway, 1995.

Young, James A. "Tumbleweed." *Scientific American*, March 1991, 82–87.

Zeman, Jerald. *The Anabaptists and the Czech Brethren in Moravia, 1526–1628*. The Hague: Mouton, 1969.

Zempel, Solveig, ed. *When the Wind Is in the South and Other Stories*. Sioux Falls, SD: Center for Western Studies, 1984.

Zieglschmid, A. J. F. *Das Klein-Geschichtsbuch der Hutterischen Bruder*. Philadelphia: Carl Schurz Memorial Foundation, 1947.

———. *Die alteste Chronik der Hutterischen Bruder: Ein Sprachdenkmal aus Fruhneuhochdeutscher Zeit*. Philadelphia: Carl Schurz Memorial Foundation, 1943.

Compact Discs

Acadia Hutterite Choir. *Voices of Victory*. Carberry, MB: Acadia Colony, 2006.

Hofer, Paul, ed. *Die Quelle: A Hutterite Reference Library*. St. Agathe, MB: Crystal Spring Colony, 2005.

Hutterian Eastern Prairie Praise Choir. *The Beginning*. McGregor, MB: Baker Colony, 2005.

Millshof Hutterian Youth Choir. *Rock of Ages*. Glenboro, MB: Millshof Colony, 2004.

Western Manitoba Hutterian Youth Choir. *Oh Lord, Protect and Keep Thy Young Flock*. Decker, MB: Decker Colony, 2000.

———. *O Lord We Praise You*. Decker, MB: Decker Colony, 2004.

Films

Buller, Burton director. *The Hutterites: To Care and Not to Care*. Henderson, NE: Buller Films, 1983.

Hofer, Samuel, director. *Born Hutterite*. Saskatoon, SK: Black Springs Pictures, 1996.

The Hutterites. Ottawa, ON: National Film Board of Canada, 1964.

Nimoy, Leonard, director. *Holy Matrimony*. London: PolyGram, 1996.

Powell, Michael, and Emeric Pressburger, directors. *49th Parallel*. London: Grenada International Media, 1942.

Stanjek, Klaus, director. *Commune of Bliss*. Berlin: Löprich & Schlösser, 2004.

Index

YOUNG CENTER BOOKS IN ANABAPTIST & PIETIST STUDIES
Charles E. Hurst and David L. McConnell, *An Amish Paradox:*
Diversity and Change in the World's Largest Amish Community
Karen M. Johnson-Weiner, *Train Up a Child:*
Old Order Amish and Mennonite Schools
Peter J. Klassen, *Mennonites in Early Modern Poland and Prussia*
James O. Lehman and Steven M. Nolt, *Mennonites, Amish, and*
the American Civil War
Steven M. Nolt and Thomas J. Meyers, *Plain Diversity:*
Amish Cultures and Identities
Richard A. Stevick, *Growing Up Amish: The Teenage Years*
Diane Zimmerman Umble and David L. Weaver-Zercher, eds.,
The Amish and the Media

CENTER BOOKS IN ANABAPTIST STUDIES
Carl F. Bowman, *Brethren Society: The Cultural Transformation of*
a "Peculiar People"
Perry Bush, *Two Kingdoms, Two Loyalties: Mennonite Pacifism in*
Modern America
John A. Hostetler, ed., *Amish Roots: A Treasury of History, Wisdom, and Lore*
Julia Kasdorf, *The Body and the Book: Writing from a Mennonite Life*
Donald B. Kraybill, *The Riddle of Amish Culture*, revised edition
Donald B. Kraybill, ed., *The Amish and the State*, 2nd edition
Donald B. Kraybill and Carl Desportes Bowman, *On the Backroad to Heaven:*
Old Order Hutterites, Mennonites, Amish, and Brethren
Donald B. Kraybill and Steven M. Nolt, *Amish Enterprise:*
From Plows to Profits, 2nd edition
Werner O. Packull, *Hutterite Beginnings: Communitarian Experiments*
during the Reformation
Benjamin W. Redekop and Calvin W. Redekop, eds., *Power, Authority,*
and the Anabaptist Tradition
Calvin Redekop, Stephen C. Ainlay, and Robert Siemens,
Mennonite Entrepreneurs
Calvin Redekop, ed., *Creation and the Environment:*
An Anabaptist Perspective on a Sustainable World
Steven D. Reschly, *The Amish on the Iowa Prairie, 1840 to 1910*
Kimberly D. Schmidt, Diane Zimmerman Umble, and Steven D. Reschly,
Strangers at Home: Amish and Mennonite Women in History
Diane Zimmerman Umble, *Holding the Line:*
The Telephone in Old Order Mennonite and Amish Life
David Weaver-Zercher, *The Amish in the American Imagination*